WALKING
PROUD

The Louis Luyt Autobiography

To my long-suffering wife and beautiful
friend, Adri, and our children

WALKING PROUD

The Louis Luyt Autobiography

DON NELSON
Cape Town

ISBN 1 86806 212 0

First Edition 2003

Second Impression 2003

Third Impression 2004

Publisher: Don Nelson Publishers

PO Box 18600, Wynberg 7824

Cover photograph: Touchline Photo

Cover design: Toby Newsome

Reproduction and typesetting: Virtual Colour

Editor: Sean Fraser

Proofreader: David Denison

Design and typesetting: Lyndall du Toit

Printed and bound by Tandym Print

CONTENTS

PROLOGUE

An autobiography is, for some, an attempt to relive in their twilight days their greater moments in the sun while ignoring the cloudy episodes of their past. For others, it is the occasion to minimise mistakes, claim accomplishments, and to pre-empt the pundits with an obituary of their own making.

I have no such luxury. For most of my adult life I have been praised or pilloried in the press by observers who believed that they knew me better than my friends or family. In newspaper morgues and library databases reside many thousands of stories – some accurate, others almost embarrassing in their praise, and many, especially in recent years, abusive and insulting, even libellous.

I found some solace, however, from Anton Harbor's column in *Business Day* (Friday, 28 March 2003) where he quoted from Janet Malcolm's book, *The Journalist and the Murderer*: '[The journalist] is a kind of confidence man, preying on people's vanity, ignorance, or loneliness, gaining their trust and betraying them without remorse.' I resisted the temptation to respond in print to the untruths and distortions on which my detractors in the press and in so-called apocryphal unauthorised biographies based their stories – often intended to inflame the public mind or further their own gain.

In more than one instance, the creators of these accounts have already received ample reward for their efforts in the form of monetary and other recognition. To repeat their amorphous inaccuracies will merely serve to promote an unworthy cause. They certainly do not deserve any further mention here, and I have no 'death wish' by engaging the Fourth Estate in battle.

Others have described my life as a rags-to-riches story. That it probably was if one wishes to romanticise the saga of a poor country kid relegated to serve the rich and purported to have become a multimillionaire who flits around the world in the luxury of his private jet. But this could hardly tell the full story.

My 'rags-to-riches' story lies not purely in the material. It is the story of someone who also had the good fortune and privilege to meet and build relationships with many interesting people – one who met and married a wonderful woman and raised a close-knit family.

However, in contrast to my lasting relationship with my wife and family and a few true friends, many others were temporary encounters, some soured by circumstance and conflicting interests. That, quite simply, is life and what this book is all about. We are, in a sense, playing on sides all the time, trying to win for our cause, our country or ourselves.

I have always believed that the goal should be victory. Both on and off the sports field, I have played hard to win – but not at any cost. There is honour even among the fiercest of competitors. Those who opposed me in business, sport or politics might have suffered a few bruises in the brawl, but so did I, as part of the game. I have, however, never been guilty – on or off the field – of foul play.

Over the years, I have been described by friend and foe as genial and mean-spirited, democratic and dictatorial, generous and merciless, stubborn and reasonable, and unforgiving and compassionate. Anyone in public life learns to live with whatever adjective or adverb comes his or her way. It comes with the territory, so to speak.

In this autobiography I cover my childhood and adult life, the sports field, and the business and political worlds, but do not dwell on any particular issue too long. In my account of my years as a sportsman, businessman, marketer, industrialist, publisher and politician, I tell the truth as I experienced it, not as I wish it to be. In doing so, I am reminded of the words of the English essayist, William Hazlitt: 'An honest man speaks the truth, though it may give offence; a vain man, in order that it may.'

What's in a name?

That which we call a rose

by any other name would smell as sweet.

William Shakespeare,
Romeo and Juliet, *Act II Sc II*

Chapter 1

WHAT'S IN A NAME?

In the early seventies, I managed to build Triomf, a subsidiary of the Louis Luyt Group (LLG), into South Africa's largest fertiliser company. I was in my late thirties then; I was looking for new challenges and beer was beckoning. Some observers wondered why I would want to challenge – in its own den – the mighty monopolistic South African Breweries (SAB), who were my partners in Triomf Fertilisers and the makers of Lion lager and several other popular beers. These were the same doubting Thomases who questioned my determination in the sixties to take on the big boys in the fertiliser business. But the believers won the day. Despite tight times, LLG Breweries was able to close its lists a month early after its public offering of R4-million ordinary shares was more than 150 per cent oversubscribed.

'One thing is clear about Louis Luyt,' wrote the *Financial Mail*. 'He has no lack of supporters prepared to follow him into the lion's den... The name that attracts the lolly is still Louis Luyt... Just goes to show that, even in these hard times, there's still magic in a name – if it is the right one.'

The *Financial Mail* had, of course, no way of knowing that Luyt was not my original name or that I started out in life as Oswald Louis Petrus Poleÿ. This has remained a closely guarded family secret until this day. I would, of course, like to believe that a Louis Poleÿ Group or LPG might have developed the same 'magic' as the Louis Luyt Group or LLG were I not given Luyt as a last name by my stepfather, or dropped at a later stage two of my three given names – Oswald and Petrus.

I was born in Britstown in the Cape Province on 18 June 1932, the second child of a marriage that never was. After finishing school in Cape Town, Cornelia Petronella Poleÿ returned to this small Karoo town and married a state prosecutor.

9

Two years after the birth of my sister Grace and while she was still pregnant with me, my mother discovered that the man she assumed to be her legally wedded husband was, in fact, a bigamist. Once unmasked, my biological father fled back to Cape Town where he reunited with his first family. My mother's 'marriage' was annulled, we were told, and she sought refuge from sorrow and shame at the modest home of her mother Lodewika. In that little sheep-farming town, where divorce, or annulment of a marriage, was looked upon as the ultimate disgrace, if not a cardinal sin, my mother's anguish can hardly be imagined. The family heaped scorn on her and even reverted to cheap gossip and did not think twice to demean both Grace and me.

Grandma Lodewika provided a secure haven, but life was by no means cushy. It was the time of the Great Depression and everyone felt its effect in one way or another. But while the wealthy in the *Bodorp* (upper town) had to cut down on luxuries, the Poleÿs and others in the *Onderdorp* (downtown) frequently had to go without even the bare essentials.

Four years after my mother's traumatic separation from her bigamist beau, one Charles Lucien Paul Luyt came to the rescue. To those around them – the shortish, plumpish, cultured and quick-witted Cornelia Poleÿ, with her magnificent mastery of mathematics, English and Latin, and the tall, sparsely educated Charles Luyt, with his earthy sense of humour – seemed the perfect mismatch. But, somehow, as it often happens in marriages, opposites attracted and the relationship flourished. But, like many other marriages, heaven had some earthly help when this one was made. Cornelia, no doubt, saw in Charles Luyt the opportunity to give her two children a proper home with a real father. Money could not have been a factor since Charles was an uneducated labourer from the same impoverished side of town.

Even though I was not yet four years old at the time, the formal entry of Charles Luyt in our lives remains sharply etched in my mind. There I was, on her wedding day, holding my mother's hand, standing together with our new father in front of a well-worn Model-T Ford, the scene sharply etched against the harsh Karoo landscape. It was a moment captured on Kodak and pasted into the family album, where I would revisit and savour this sepia-coloured picture time and again for several years until one day it simply disappeared. So did the picture of my sister Grace in the arms of a tall, blonde good-looking man who, according to my mother, happened to have been our real father.

Even though she must have known that the secret of our birth would come out some day soon, Cornelia Poleÿ tried in her own way to exorcise the past by removing and ripping up these reminders. Once we were old enough, she simply told us that our real father was a good man and that he had died. In her early eighties, shortly before she died, my mother would ultimately confess her continued affection for this man and told me his name.

'Did he ask about me?' I enquired.

She shook her head in the absolute negative. I was certain she wasn't being truthful but let it go. Quite recently, the only remaining relative from that time confirmed my father's identity, but I have decided, purely for peace of mind, to let the matter rest. To me, as well as to everybody else, I was a Luyt, although with no real claim to the name. Nothing more, nothing less.

The first home that Charles Luyt provided turned out to be little more than a crude corrugated-iron farm labourer's shack on the huge acreage owned by my mother's wealthy cousin, Stephan Stevens. This shelter was offered to my new-found father as part payment – together with the right to grow vegetables and a monthly wage of £1 10s – in return for endless hours of backbreaking work. Many years later, when I purchased my own farms, first in what was then the Northern Transvaal, and later in the Western Cape, it must have been memories of our discomfort that prompted me to spend lavishly on housing for those who laboured the fields and tended the herds.

Corrugated iron, the preferred material for a roof at the time of my youth, could actually add charm to a privileged existence in a sturdy and spacious brick-walled farmstead, especially when the tapping of a few raindrops multiply into a crescendo and the farmer and his family kneel to bless the Lord for much-needed rains. But a labourer's house built of corrugated iron in the Karoo is nothing more than cold storage in winter and a baking oven in summer. And, instead of kneeling in thankful prayer during the rains, everyone was frantically trying to stop the leaking roof from damaging their few prized possessions. Nonetheless, to us it was home – our first as a real family.

Despite the rather distorted sense of homeliness, however, firmly entrenched in my mind are the evenings when Grace and I were witness to the terrible and angry exchanges between my parents – simply because there wasn't any food in the house. In those days, proper farmsteads were fitted with shiny wooden floors and even carpeting. Our abode had wall-to-wall hardened cattle dung, occasionally replenished and repaired with fresh supplies from the fields. We would never be allowed the taste of beef, but we certainly had no restriction placed upon us by the man in the main house on collecting and using dung in whichever way we saw fit. To this day, I have a scar that serves as a reminder of those days when so much of our existence seemed to focus on the stuff that cattle plop in the kraal or sheds around the farm. As a child, while chopping hardened dung to stoke the fire in our stove, I swung the axe too far back and struck the back of my head. Also, of course, as we grew up, we experimented at least once with the potential of cattle dung rolled in newsprint as a substitute for cigarettes.

In the Karoo, running around barefoot during the summer months was normal even for rich kids. We all periodically went through the pain of having the build-up of dirt and rough skin scrubbed down from *skurwe hakskene* (rough heels), but while the wealthy children stepped into fancy new shoes at a time of their own choosing, we on the wrong side of town were condemned to remain bare-foot much longer – even after the winter frost formed its icy layer on the farm-land. Lucky were those among us whose parents were able to rustle up a pair of second-hand shoes from friends or family when walking barefoot was demeaning at best.

I clearly remember my first pair of shoes. The same kind people in the district who passed along used clothes and footwear from the privileged uptown area to the downtrodden downtowns made possible my right of passage from a barefoot to a shoe-wearing person. But charity, I soon discovered, sometimes came at a heavy cost to self-esteem and dignity.

One day, I was dispatched, soup plate in hand, to collect *kaiings* (cracklings) from one of those fancy weekend town houses owned by wealthy farmers. Like crumbs off the table, these tasty burnt droppings from fatty meat were either passed along to the poor or fed to the dogs, but somehow we found ourselves slightly ahead in the feeding chain. On this, my first collection excursion to one of those fancy abodes, my mother either forgot to give me explicit instructions or I failed to listen properly. I knocked on the front door. A well-dressed woman answered, and looked me up and down as one would something quite unsavoury. 'How dare you knock at my front door?' she snapped. 'Go to the back of the house and wait at the kitchen door.' That day, perhaps subconsciously, I swore revenge – revenge for all the poor people who were then, and still today are, forced to go to the back door.

Even at church, the Luyt family once found themselves ordered out of a pew because it 'belonged' to a rich farmer. The brass plates with names inscribed on them, we were reminded, weren't only there to recognise the givers of gifts but signified ownership. So we came to understand that wealth had its privileges – even in the house of the Lord.

Still, there were areas where the playing field was almost level. Even though the wealthy farm kids whose fathers provided the transport and the playing gear had the edge, whenever the rugby teams were picked, the value of able-bodied boys from the wrong side of the tracks could hardly be denied. In a society where winning was not everything but the only thing and in an ongoing effort to show the neighbouring towns a thing or two, those among the poor who showed exceptional talent and drive were invited, sometimes even instructed, to join the team. Once I managed to make my mark in this sport, there were plenty of opportunities for me to join in with readily available second-hand boots and jerseys.

Rugby in the Karoo in those days was played on bare, stone-hard fields. I sup-pose one might have called it a 'grit-iron' game. With every tackle, scabs on wounded knees and elbows could be reopened and blood and puss would ooze

12

again. These battle scars were worn with pride by boys who saw themselves as men of war in a battle against neighbouring schools. I still remember, many years later, the first time I had the opportunity to play on a field of green grass. There was the constant temptation to dive and slide and fall just for the sheer pleasure of doing so.

Some of our grit arenas came with some scaffolding at centre field that posed as pavilions. On windy days, you might find yourself navigating through clouds of dust and negotiating past tumbleweed blowing across the field. Spectators usually watched from their cars parked along the sidelines, engines running to disperse heat when blankets proved inadequate against the chill. Rugby was a winter sport. I can clearly recall that rush of satisfaction when you scored or showed off one of your best bloodletting dive tackles and the car horns applauded in appreciation. Yes, in those days the cars did the cheering, not the people.

But an 'away' game against opponents from another school had its advantages too. It inevitably meant sitting on the back of an open truck, huddled together under blankets with the girls of the netball team, on dusty corrugated dirt roads. Netball, a game played by girls only, went in tandem with rugby. The top rugby players were entitled to choose where they sat and this was thus an additional incentive to make it to the first team.

My rugby 'career' only took off after we moved from Britstown to nearby Hanover. I was 12 years old then and was soon picked to play not only for the school's first team but, two years later, also for the town's senior team. Even though I had won the hundred-yard dash in Britstown in primary school and had grown into a strapping young giant, the school in the town of my birth never saw fit to give me the break I felt I deserved. Many years later, I would think back on these times. When Doc Danie Craven, then a Springbok selector, saw me run the length of the field in a game against Western Transvaal at Kroonstad, he remarked: 'If a lock forward can run the length of the field, he obviously does not do his job in the tight phases.' Yet, in the testimonial he wrote for me when I was pursuing my doctoral studies in the USA, he wrote on 23 May 1979: 'He is serving or served on several University councils and acts as an advisor to Universities and other prominent organisations. On top of that, he has kept his interest in sport, in which he achieved great heights in several [disciplines], notably rugby, athletics and boxing. Not only did he represent three of our big provinces, but he took part in our Springbok trials where, for some unknown reason, he was overlooked for national honours. He successfully coached at various levels in his spare time.'

Needless to say, even though I was tipped by many as a strong contender, I did not make the Springbok team. But Craven's comment that I was one of the best players never to make the national team hardly softened the disappointment – one that I still harbour today.

I was enrolled at school at the tender age of four and a half years, and although I always managed to make it to the top three in the class, throughout primary school we always seemed to have a girl in first place – something we boys took as an act of prejudice by female teachers. Sharply etched in my memory is Miss Bessie (Elizabeth) Daneel who seemed to have zero tolerance in my case because she appeared to have developed a dislike of my intelligent mother, whom she had taught in the junior grades before she went to Cape Town. Of course, the shame that had befallen her afterwards didn't help matters either.

One day, I suffered the fullness of Miss Daneel's wrath when I lost one of the cardboard pennies that were used to familiarise us with the intricacies of the British monetary system, which then still applied in South Africa. That night, as I undressed, the lost penny that had caused me so much agony and pain dropped unceremoniously from the creases of my clothes and onto the floor. To this day, I believe Bessie Daneel was convinced that this was simply yet another poor kid destined to become a thief, perhaps forgetting that this piece of cardboard was worth nothing.

Memories of my childhood remain cluttered with images of Charles Luyt toiling late into the night around the farm and later in a number of other backbreaking jobs. I can hardly ever imagine him reclining in a chair with me or any of the other children on his knee, as fathers do.

Charles Luyt was a hard man, but hidden at the core were, I believe, the best of intentions. Sometimes he acted mercilessly, to the point of being cruel. As I grew older, an open hand would tighten and close into a fist to punish when he deemed it appropriate, and a slap on the bottom would eventually develop into agonising assaults. As I developed my rugby skills, he became increasingly angry over my waste of time on this idle sport instead of devoting my full energy to honest work.

When as a 14-year-old schoolboy I was pulled aside by a school coach and told that I had been chosen to play for the town's senior rugby team, he looked puzzled by the look of alarm in my eyes. Little did the coach know that I had to break the news to a father who was bound to break out in rage because it would mean extra time away from work. Every other father in town would no doubt have hugged and praised their sons for their great accomplishment.

I look back on all this today, however, not as wilful abuse, but rather as symptomatic of the deep frustration bred by poverty and a sense of hopelessness. I remain convinced that the man who later adopted me and gave me his name had a good heart beating beneath his rough exterior. But Charles Luyt was never able to show any compassion whatsoever. Despite his continued efforts to rise above adversity, he never savoured the sweet taste of real victory or success. He was, to put it mildly, no more than a rolling stone who, at some stage in his life, had to perform some of the most demeaning jobs to keep his family from starving. At one stage, when I was already working in Bloemfontein, he was the driver of the night soil truck in Colesberg. In those days, we lived alongside a coloured family, and that really upset me – not because they were coloured, but because they were so much more sophisticated and financially better off than we were. I felt infinitely inferior to them.

In his twilight years, I urged my father to give up his work as a boilermaker in Welkom. He was already almost sixty and I was then in the fortunate position to give him and my mother a generous living allowance as well as a house and a car, in effect a life without worry. Today, I suspect that this generosity might, in part, have contributed to his death barely a year after he went into retirement. Charles Luyt seemed to have been born to work and without the sense of purpose that that brought, I presume he simply saw no reason to go on living. He just died in his sleep.

His jobs always involved physical input and long hours. I remember the joy around our bare dinner table on the farm when he announced that he had been hired as a drill operator at a company that prospected for water in the district. In this semi-desert area, with its tell-tale windmills, drilling boreholes on farms was important business. The next morning, he knocked on the door of the farmstead and informed my mother's cousin that he would be changing jobs. We were ordered to vacate the corrugated-iron shack immediately.

So we moved back to Britstown and settled into the cramped outer rooms of my grandmother's rented house. For me, this was the nearest thing to heaven I could imagine. Grandma Lodewika oozed all the compassion and care that my father was unable to show and my mother had little time to share. To this day, the mere mention of her name conjures up images of kindness and selfless sacrifice. Like the day when I saw her shimmering outline in the distance, approaching the field where we were watching my father scrubbing away in the midday heat on the farm. The mirage of this kind old lady with a broad-rimmed hat and a basket in her hand grew clearer until I could make out her angelic smile. Then she offered my exhausted father and us food and refreshments. Grandma Lodewika had walked eight miles to perform this act of mercy.

Despite diviners with cleft sticks, supposedly capable of pinpointing water arteries deep below the crusty Karoo surface, the business of drilling boreholes was at best a guessing game and, after one too many dry holes, Charles Luyt was retrenched. He then found employment as a labourer at the South African Railways and we said our sad farewells to Grandma Lodewika's home and settled into our second corrugated-iron home. This three-roomed affair, courtesy of the Railways, was huge in comparison with the shack on the farm. Although it was next to the railway line – and suffered its concomitant noise – the house had real floors and running water and we were entitled to an unlimited supply of free coal. Charles Luyt was now earning an almost respectable £9 a month.

After a short assignment for the Railways in Swakopmund, at the rim of the Namib Desert in what was then South West Africa, where the Luyts languished among German-speaking Hereros and colonials, we returned to the 'Union' – as South Africa was known at the time – and Britstown. It was 1939 and in Europe Hitler's hordes were on the march. We had barely settled in when the instruction came from General Jan Smuts for my father and his co-workers to join the forces in Pretoria or lose their jobs.

In his absence, at the tender age of eight, I assumed the role of head of the household and took a delivery job at the local butcher. The free meat I was given in return for doing the early morning rounds – with a heavily packed basket mounted on the handlebars of the butcher's bike – was more than welcome, but my mother still seemed incapable of making do on the £27 that came from Pretoria every month. In fact, until her dying day, my mother would always spend more than she had. If you gave her a million rand she would spend R100 000 in excess thereof. Soon we were sliding into debt and forced once again to rely on hand-outs and hand-me-downs. During my few idle moments, I found escape from the misery by imagining businesses that would make us all rich and independent.

But I was not the only one in the family who harboured dreams for a better future in business. When Charles Luyt was dismissed as 'unfit for military duties' and returned to the Karoo with an army gratuity in his pocket, he wasted no time. First he started a barbershop, at Hanover this time, and when that failed, a bakery. I was called in to work at the bakery as a jack of all trades, with on-the-job training and no pay. My days started at 4.30 pm, chopping logs to stoke the oven, kneading the dough and preparing the pans. At 2.30 am, I would be woken to stoke the fires in the oven, carefully weighing the dough, filling the pans and shoving them into the oven. Then, after an hour and a half of baking, I would have to remove the 150 loaves of bread before grabbing a light breakfast and rushing off to school. On cold winter mornings, when I was tempted to stay under the warm covers for a few extra minutes, my father would be there to drag me out of bed. Eventually, when this ill-conceived enterprise got the better of him and he overslept, I had to muster my own strength to get up and forge ahead on my own.

To add to my agonising working hours, my father rented one hectare of land with the sole idea of becoming rich by growing vegetables. Twice a week, at 1.30 am, we received water from a fountain flow supplied by the municipality and of course it fell on me to tend to this laborious task. I slaved like a man possessed to grow vegetables that would be acceptable to the local market where we sold our produce to the highest bidder. Mercifully, this venture died along with the bakery.

What had started as a dream to hook every household into buying locally baked steaming fresh bread turned into a nightmare. Even though the war shortages in flour only slightly limited our production, the market never materialised – a fact that never really dawned on my father. His Afrikaans pitch – *Ou Tante Koba is so dom om nie na Luyt se bakkery te kom* (Old Aunt Koba would be stupid not to come to Luyt's bakery) – may have had a nice ring and rhyme to it, but it was lost on folks who had baked their own bread for generations past and present. Nothing, not even the boldest marketing campaign, would change that.

In a few short years, I had the luxury of two lessons on how not to start a business of your own. My father moved on to a job on the national roads as a lorry driver and I could once again focus on my studies and rugby. The latter had come to represent my passport from poverty to privilege – despite continued opposition from my father. One day, I decided, I would have my own business – a successful one that would end all the misery. But for now, rugby would have to do, and, of course, education, which, my mother never failed to remind me, would outlast all the wealth a man could ever make or lose.

Sadly, in 1941, at the age of eleven, my sister Grace succumbed to a heart ailment – the result of scarlet fever that had developed into rheumatic fever during her infancy. I suffered the same fate, but to a lesser degree and, flirting with the possibility of heart failure, trained even harder so that I could participate normally in sport.

I was miraculously healed in 1949 when I attended a faith-healing service at the Bloemfontein Show Grounds, and I firmly believe that God touched me that day. By 1978, I had become the person with the highest life insurance in the world and in the 1950s was judged the 'fittest man ever seen on the Free State Gold Fields'.

In the meantime, the family had grown. In 1937, my half-brother Conrick was born. Next came Lodewika, or Lottie as we called her, then Shirley, Juliana, Elfrieda, Corina and finally Charles Lucien Paul. But then, in 1943, Grandma Lodewika suffered a stroke and we returned to Britstown to be at her deathbed. She was sixty-nine when she died. I was eleven and devastated by the loss.

After a game in the fullback position for Hanover's senior rugby team against Colesberg, I received a letter from the school coach at Colesberg's Collegiate High School, offering me free books and boarding for the following two years. I was 14 years old and ready to finish my final school year at Hanover, where standard eight – or Junior Certificate – was the highest one could reach. This offer from Colesberg would allow me to obtain the Senior Certificate at one of the top schools in the Karoo and, in the process, I would be one of a few in the area – I assumed – to accept what was in effect a sport scholarship.

The wealthy folk of the region sent their children to private schools in Cape Town and I decided that I wanted to go to Rondebosch Boys' High, where one of my classmates was enrolled. But money, or the lack of it, made Colesberg the only viable choice, and although it still lacked the esteem of the posh Cape Town schools, it was nevertheless a school with similarly high standards. In the meanwhile, however, I had to work during the holidays to get some money together before I could leave for Colesberg and, as a result, I cleaned the church and the church hall, wound the big clock on a daily basis, rang the bells on Sundays and pumped the organ during services – all for £1 13s 8p a month. But the worst was that the sexton withheld a portion each month for some arbitrary reason and I had no doubt that this went straight into his own pocket.

My days at Collegiate High School were very taxing. There was simply not enough money to buy even the bare necessities to sustain an almost subsistent lifestyle. I had to slave at the rifle range, manning two targets at a time, just to pay for my laundry and the rare cool drink. Whenever the occasional movie, or 'bioscope' as we called it then, visited the town – with its own generator, projector and screen – I would offer my services to carry and set up the equipment so that I could view the show for free. And some holidays saw me working at the hostel, because there was simply no money for the train fare to Hanover. Apart from the railway ticket, one also had to take a bus to Colesberg station, which was five kilometres out of the town, and another bus from the Hanover Road station, which was 25 kilometres away from Hanover itself. The throwaway shoes of one of the teachers, Mr 'Shorty' Naudé, thus became prized possessions.

It was no surprise, then, that when I left school, it was with a sigh of relief and great expectations for a job. Further education was not even contemplated. I learned that there was a vacancy for a telegrapher at the post office and applied – and was offered the job. Imagine my disappointment, then, when the postmaster, genuinely apologetic, told me after he had read my application form that I was too young. I was 16 and the position called for a minimum age of 18. My world collapsed around me.

I then took a temporary position in the Department of National Roads, and worked during the six-week summer holiday as the surveyor's assistant. Here, I gathered valuable experience working with the theodolite and level in setting out the road between Hanover and Colesberg, but the nomadic lifestyle demanded by the Roads Department was not to my liking so I continued to look for a more stable position.

This, in turn, led me to Mr Naudé, the stationmaster at Arundel, a small railway siding a few miles from Colesberg where my family was now renting a house from the Railways while my father worked as a truck driver on the national roads. This rather helpful neighbour arranged for an interview with the regional offices of the South African Railways at Bloemfontein, stuffed a free second-class rail ticket in my hand and wished me well. So it was that I set out north with my complete inventory of clothes and personal possessions loosely packed in a modest-sized cardboard suitcase.

As far as cities go, Bloemfontein, at that time at least, ranked low both in size and skyline. In fact, regular city slickers might even have looked upon it as little more than a bulging, biggish country town with its bustling main street and few four- and five-storey buildings. But for me, coming from the Karoo where traffic lights would have been objects of great wonder, that first encounter was exceptionally exciting.

I had, however, little time to waste on sightseeing. I went for my interview and, on the second day of February 1949, I was signed up as a labourer on the Railways for a three-month probation period at six shillings a day, after which I was to be appointed as an accounting clerk for £9 13s 8p a month. With this meagre wage, it was obvious that I could not afford to remain in the boarding house where I had spent my first night in town, so – after being turned down by the wife of a local Dutch Reformed minister in charge of a haven for the poor because I was 'too well-dressed' – I moved into a small room about a two and half hours' walking distance from the Mechanical Engineer's Department, where I worked.

But just a few weeks after I started at the Railways, I was summoned to the office of the administrative officer.

'Why did you tell us your name is Luyt?' the fellow behind the desk barked indignantly. 'We just got papers back from Britstown showing that your real name is Oswald Louis Petrus Poleÿ.'

I knew instinctively that no explanation would suffice, and that this little man with his thin moustache and air of self-importance would never understand. I was also angry that, after so many years of slaving under a man called Luyt, I could find myself in this predicament. Why my mother did not officially change our names after she married remains a mystery to this day.

'Must be a mistake,' I said. 'Obviously someone wrote down my mother's last name instead of my father's. Don't' worry. I'll have it corrected.'

And so I did. I contacted my mother, and my father officially adopted me post haste. In 1949, at the age of 16, I formally and legally became Oswald Louis Petrus Luyt.

So, what's in a name? Goethe probably summed it up best when he said that 'a man's name is not like a mantle, which merely hangs about him, and which one perchance may safely twitch and pull, but a perfectly fitting garment, which like the skin, has grown over him, at which one cannot rake and scrape without injuring the man himself'. Over the following half-century, I would come to appreciate the truth of this philosophy.

Stars may be seen from the bottom of a deep well, when

they cannot be discerned from the top of a mountain.

So are many things learned in adversity

which prosperous men dream not of.

Charles Haddon Spurgeon,
English clergyman, 1834–1892

Chapter 2

REACHING FOR THE STARS

There is no doubt that when you stand at the bottom of a well, you see the stars above quite clearly. But for most people down there, the stars remain distant and unreachable. Some of us, however, dare to in fact reach for those stars. And a few even manage to get there. I was fortunate to be among those few. Some measure of talent and lots of hard work, determination and innovation are all required for this journey to the stars, but I was fortunate to have further blessings – the support of a devoted wife, a few loyal friends and guidance from God.

Naturally, once you reach the firmament, others want to know the 'secret' of your success. And when I finally 'arrived', there was no shortage of business, and the writers of society columns all wanted to share with their readers my particular rags-to-riches story. Invariably, the question would arise: 'So, what inspired you?' The answer always seemed quite obvious to me. When you are down there, there is a natural urge to climb upward, as high as circumstances and your own ability will allow you. Of course, we all need that little extra some call luck and others opportunity. But, above all, you need to use the adversity that inevitably crosses your path to help focus the mind rather than allow it to drive you to despair.

When I started my low-paid accountancy job on the Railways in Bloemfontein, I had much time to focus on the future during my two-and-a-half-hour walk to and from the office. My initial priorities were quite basic. Firstly, I needed more convenient accommodation than the remote little room where I holed up at night. Secondly, I needed to prove that I could be the best at my job. Thirdly, I needed to play my way into the Railway's under-19A rugby team. Rugby helped me earn respect and admiration at school and now, I felt, it might help fuel my journey to the stars.

I managed to get a bed in a dormitory at the Railway hostel, which was closer to work – and also to hell. The energy I saved walking was more than expended in regular boxing bouts with a never-ending stream of challengers, some in a drunken stupor, who wished to show this big young boy from the Karoo a thing or two. Drawing on the skills learned at the adjacent gym, where I was a member of the boxing team, I never lost any of the impromptu fights on the lawn in front of the hostel against brawlers from the stockyards and repair shops. Still, I did not altogether escape injury and punishment, and my face and body were often bruised, my hands swollen. Even my promotion to prefect – and the special privilege of a little room to myself – did not compensate enough. Fortunately, a slight wage increase after my first year enabled me to rent a room elsewhere, buy a second-hand bicycle and get on with life.

At the job, however, everything was on track. I managed to make it to first place in the Railways' National Apprenticeship Examination for artisans in which 25,000 across the country participated. To everyone's surprise, I opted to stay in the accounting department. For some reason, I felt that this was more in line with my own talents and might, one day, open the way to a job elsewhere.

The rugby season started with me trying to make it as a flyhalf or fullback, but the coaches had very different ideas for a 178-pound six-foot four-inch 16-year-old newcomer. Soon after my selection as eighth man for the Under-19B team, I asked the senior club coach to move me to one of the senior teams. I was determined to prove that I could mix it up with the big boys, and my aim was to make it to the Free State Under-19s before I turned 17. By that time, I started to play for the club's third team and regularly for the Railways' first team, and later in the season the same coach who did not see fit to include me in his under-19A team, asked me to join them for the final games as Railways was in the running for the championship trophy. And we won, too.

In 1952, when I was still 19, my big opportunity presented itself: I was included in the B-team for the Free State provincial trials at Springbok Park in Bloemfontein. Scarcely six months earlier, a physician had told me that a severely injured right knee signalled the end of rugby for me. At the time, there were dire warnings of amputation unless the swelling subsided. This injury, I was told, would require complete rest. But, instead, I pressed ahead stubbornly and returned to practice, and in the process my knee healed without too much trouble.

Competition at the provincial trials was tough. Six teams fought it out on the field, every player trying to make an impression on his own while at the same time pretending to be a team player. That's the stuff trials were made of in those days – a determined bunch of individuals playing like demons, trying to make that one indelible impression that would make a selector remember them. Doing it in a team with no name jerseys, with 14 equally selfish souls – most of whom had never played together before – was a formidable task indeed, and it certainly did not make for attractive rugby. And our task in the B-team was further complicated by having to face an A-team that included a smorgasbord of rugby stars, some of them Springboks several times over.

Absent from the field was Felix du Plessis, who had led our national team in three tests during the 1949 All Black tour. He had retired in 1951 and was appointed to the Free State selection committee and was now observing play through binoculars from a comfortable seat in the pavilion.

As was customary, the announcement of the team was held over until the reception at the Oranje Hotel, and I was somewhat surprised when Felix du Plessis pulled me aside earlier that evening. I had known this rather heavyset, genial man with close-cropped hair as an opponent in club rugby for one or two seasons. We had had our scraps on the field and on occasion he taunted me: 'You better be careful, young man, or you will get hurt.' He clearly resented this upstart number eight who out-jumped him in the lineouts during his final days on the field. There were those who claimed that Du Plessis had not been in top form in 1949 and that he had been picked by Doc Danie Craven to lead the Springboks largely because of their friendship in the army during the Second World War. But no one ever questioned the character of Felix du Plessis. He was truly a thoroughbred, a class act.

'Louis,' Du Plessis asked, 'how would you feel about playing lock instead of eighth man?'

'Uncle Felix,' I responded, using 'uncle' in the typically South African show of respect for someone older, and trying in vain to contain my over-enthusiasm, 'you can play me in any position – hooker, fullback or flyhalf – as long as I can play for Free State.' In those days, Free State comprised players from the entire province of the Orange Free State as well as Lesotho, and when the names were announced mine was among them. Louis Luyt as lock forward for the Orange Free State! My own name never sounded so good. I could hardly sleep that night. Even before I turned 20, I had made it to one of the country's top provincial teams.

From where I now stood, a few yards up the well, the next star – Springbok colours – certainly looked within reach.

But not everyone shared Uncle Felix's confidence in me. He and the other selectors came under heavy criticism from sport columnist, Dawie Marquard, who found the inclusion of such a lightweight lock in a time when heavier was better, inexplicably dumb. I had only one way to prove them wrong and that was on the field. This thought rested heavily on my mind as our first game – against the formidable Eastern Transvaal team led by Springbok Ben Myburgh – approached. In 1949, they had lost by a single point against a strong All Black side, and the magnificent Myburgh would be only of the many members of the triumphant 1952 Springbok touring team against whom I would be pitted in the coming months. Free State, of course, had two Springboks of its own – forward Piet Wessels and fullback Basie Viviers.

As we trotted out onto the field, I felt somewhat intimidated by the significance of the moment. Here I was, a mere youngster, in the company of seasoned Springboks – some of whom were my boyhood heroes – and trying to prove to the Marquards of the world that my presence was not a mere fluke, a one-time affair. But after I managed to steal away the first ball in the lineout and was able to stand my ground in the scrum and mauls, all my doubts began to dissipate. I knew I belonged. We won comfortably by a 14–8 margin, and I was extremely impressed by the pace, strength and depth of skill of all the players. Some, in fact, were simply awesome. As a former fullback, I was particularly impressed by Jakkals (Jackal) Keevy in the opposing side. Appropriately nicknamed, this Springbok fullback managed to outfox everyone in impossibly tight situations.

Next, we faced the tough Western Transvaal team in Potchefstroom, where a young lock forward, Johan Claassen, was the talk of the town. He proved to be every inch as good as his reputation made him out to be and succeeded in making my fellow lock, Floors Perry – who was given the unenviable task of marking him in the lineouts – look like a flatfooted penguin. As it turned out, Perry had nothing to be ashamed of, having been shown up by a player who could later lay claim to having been the finest lock in rugby history – until, of course, in my view, the great Frik du Preez appeared on the scene to dazzle the rugby world. Despite Claassen's prowess, however, we managed to win that game too. And so did we in the next two provincial encounters.

Marquard, however, remained unconvinced of my abilities even though the more widely read Transvaal rugby pundits such as Dana Niehaus, Hoffie de Beer and Paul Irwin praised my performances and some even called me the 'find of the season'. Marquard kept arguing for a beefier and brawnier man to replace me, 'a mere 175-pounder' (although, in reality, I weighed 212 pounds or 96 kilograms), at lock, and as the local critic he won the day. The selectors summarily dropped me from the team and filled the position with someone heavier. My return to the ranks shortly afterwards could not, however, erase the initial hurt and humiliation. It would, of course, not be the last time I would feel the brunt of what seemed to be irrational action on the part of selectors.

In 1955, when I was at the top of my form, I – together with six other regulars, including our captain, Basie Viviers – was dropped from the Free State team facing the visiting British Lions. We could only speculate that the selectors had either lost their minds or forgot how to spell our names. If they thought that they would surprise the visitors with hidden new talent, they were alarmingly mistaken. The Lions ran gaping holes through Free State, chalking up one of their easiest victories of the tour – and a week later we were all back in the team, with the exception of Viviers. We then went on tour, first defeating Transvaal, then

Eastern Province (who had beaten the Lions 20–0), Border and Boland. But not even my selection as the most outstanding player of the year at the end of the season could quite compensate for my inexplicable axing from the Lions game that would have been my first game against an international side.

In 1957, in one of those odd twists of life, I was selected to lead Free State as captain in its match-up against Eastern Province. In the opposing team was Springbok prop Amos du Plooy, another boy from Colesberg, and in the pavilion sat his father Abel, who had told the press beforehand that he had a hard time deciding who to support because I was like another son to him. By this time, Abel du Plooy certainly had assumed the role of father to me.

I was not the only one who was shocked and surprised, then, when I was excluded from the trials for the selection of the Springbok team to tour New Zealand in April 1956. 'Rugby enthusiasts are surprised at the omission of Louis Luyt from the national trials to be held in Cape Town from April 7 to 14. He was the find of Free State rugby last year...' reported the *Northern Sports Digest*. By this time, the argument that I was a 'lightweight' no longer held, and the *Volksblad* sports editor, Roelf Theunissen, commented: 'At 224 pounds (102 kilograms), one of the heaviest men on the field, Luyt is exceptionally fit and fast.' But I certainly felt the disappointment more acutely than any of the shocked observers or Free State selectors. The Free State Rugby Union then sent an urgent telegram to the selectors to ask that they invite me to the trials, but even their offer to pay my expenses would not move Danie Craven. Instead, he sourced local replacements whenever a player was injured. The remark by Craven the previous year – that a lock forward who can run like that obviously does not do his job in the tight play – was obviously not in jest.

But most surprising to us in the Free State was the inclusion of Basie Viviers as captain of the 1956 touring team at a time when he was not even able to make his own provincial team. Ben Klopper had replaced him both as fullback and captain while I, as leader of the forwards, served as vice captain. So the likeable Basie, no longer at the peak of his performance on the field ,but still very proficient as a singer, was picked to lead South Africa in battle against the mighty All Blacks.

Later we would, however, learn that lock forward Saltie du Rand was originally earmarked for the captaincy until he broke Jan Pickard's nose in an after-match altercation during the trials. Yet Pickard was selected, broken nose and all.

In retrospect, some might argue that I was saved the embarrassment of being part of what turned out to be one of the most ill-fated teams ever to have left our shores. Everyone was wondering how the same country that produced the near-invincible 1951/1952 touring team to the British Isles and France could slide so fast in a matter of just four years. As it turned out, the 1956 tour of New Zealand was a rout and a source of immense humiliation. The problem seemed to have been compounded by a determination on the part of the selection committee to replace every injured player with yet another member of the Stellenbosch team, Craven's alma mater, instead of looking further afield for experienced and hardened talent. All the team's misfortunes, of course, did not soften my own disappointment at being left out in the cold at a time when I was considered to be a rising new star.

There would also be complaints about the partiality on the part of the New Zealand referees who turned a blind eye on foul play by the All Blacks, but we seemed to have picked up on something the All Blacks always continued to practise with great efficiency: If you lose, find an excuse – either bad refereeing or, if you must, claim that you have been poisoned by the home side, a ludicrous excuse that would again surface when they lost against the Springboks in the final of the 1995 World Cup. Perhaps the New Zealanders – and we – take rugby a little too seriously.

Years later, when I got to know Doc Craven not only as a board member of my company but as a friend, we touched on the tender subject of my omission. While he would eventually go as far as saying privately and publicly that I was one of the 'best players never to have made it to the Springbok team', he would never entertain the thought that he might have been responsible for my misfortune. Neither would he admit that some of the many hamstring injuries on the 1965 tour may have been caused by his insistence that the team practise with weights in their boots to help them adjust to wet fields in New Zealand. In postwar rugby, Doc Craven soon became a law onto himself, almost a dictator – a position he thoroughly earned but sometimes, occasionally, in my opinion, abused. He unilaterally suspended the Rugby Board constitution, fired selectors *en masse* and removed Doug Hopwood as captain in favour of the blue-eyed Avril Malan in the early sixties.

Eventually, when as president of the South African Rugby Football Union (SARFU), I seemed to have earned the same reputation, memories of my great disappointment of never having made it to the Springbok team would return every time I saw a deserving player overlooked for no sound reason. I could empathise. Particularly upsetting to me was an unfortunate selection committee episode in 1994. The national selectors had left the brilliant Western Province eighth man Tiaan Strauss out of the Springbok team to play against England in the second test at Newlands. I was completely taken by surprise when they presented me with the team's names and Strauss was not among them, and sent them back to reconsider. But, while it is customary for the president of SARFU to review the names before they are announced, the selectors had the last word, and they remained adamant. Ironically, it was two Western Province representatives, team manager Jannie Engelbrecht and selector Dawie Snyman, who prevailed in their insistence that Strauss be left out. They argued that he had been injured and was unfit and should be saved for the upcoming tour to New Zealand, instead. The aftermath was humiliating. Rumours spread, and the press ran with it, that I was the one who demanded the omission of Strauss. I was portrayed as a provincialistic pariah who had forced the selectors to choose Transvaal's Ian Macdonald instead. The crowd at Cape Town's hallowed Newlands stadium had no way of knowing the real story and when I was introduced before the game the boos echoed far and beyond Table Mountain and spread to other provinces. That booing continued throughout my involvement in rugby.

But back in 1952, in the wake of my selection to the Free State side, came a job offer from the rapidly expanding Free State Gold Fields. Even in those early days, when we still played rugby for reasons other than money, corporations were not averse to throwing out juicy bait to attract talent to their towns. I was flattered by the offer from Free State Gold Fields, but the deciding factor was money. My new job in the accounting office of Western Holdings in Welkom would pay almost three times as much as I earned at the Railways. Even though I initially regretted exchanging orderly and sedate Bloemfontein for this upstart frontier town, with its single paved street and endless rows of houses hugging dirt roads, I soon discovered that the Anglo American Corporation amply compensated by providing its employees with splendid accommodation and an abundance of facilities available for employees' free time – pool rooms, recreation halls, free movies and general entertainment.

When I took up my new post, I discovered that even though my princely monthly salary of £30 was about two and a half times the mere £13 I earned at the Railways, it paled in comparison with the fat cheques paid to the men underground. So I decided to go underground myself and, after passing a rigorous medical examination, I was accepted as an official learner at Union Corporation's St Helena mine. Later I was told that this course was a first for Free State mines. It involved all the phases of underground work, ranging from surveying to sampling, stoping, development and shaft sinking to assaying, ventilation, pipes and tracks, geology, reduction works, compound management, as well as a spell in the Study Department and all other aspects of mining. During the day, we went underground for practical work and in the evenings, we worked on the theory of mining, mathematics, surveying and geology at the Technical College. My first goal was to become a shift boss. I managed to complete the course ahead of the mandatory two years – having received a full credit for my accountancy experience – and, in the process, earned the required credits for the first two years towards a degree in Mining Engineering.

Mr 'Ginger' Gericke of the Union Corporation mining house for which I worked at the time then offered me the opportunity to finish the BSc Mining degree at Wits University where the company would pay all my tuition fees and board and lodging with the undertaking that, during off periods, I would come back to the mines and work as a shift boss at full salary and with all the standard bonuses. It was, however, my parents – with their usual uncanny timing – who decided my fate and future.

My father simply gave up his job in Colesberg and arrived in Welkom without a penny to his name. As a result, I had to pay the £27 the family owed the Railways for removal services and, of course, had to find them accommodation fast... as well as a job for my unskilled father. I also had to fork out £55 a month to keep the family going and my half-brothers and -sisters in school. Likewise, I had to refuse with the utmost regret, a very attractive offer from a Canadian mining company.

Much later, with the experience I had gained on the mines, together with the examinations I had sat at Caltex under the watchful eye of Mr Pat Regan, the resident engineer, I discovered that I met all the requirements for a BSc degree. In the late sixties, I had two invitations from Columbia University and one from North Western University of Chicago to participate in their advanced management courses. Harvard, as well, invited me to enrol in its advance course in business administration.

After successfully completing the official learner's course, I acquired a temporary blasting certificate and was sent underground as a shift boss at St Helena, courtesy of the assistant underground manager, Mr Ted Pavitt. His willingness to go out on a limb on my behalf even before I had completed what was a mandatory two-year period required for a permanent blasting certificate and thus qualifying to be a shift boss, served as further encouragement for me to succeed within the industry.

After a stint as an instructor at the School of Mines at Western Holdings to which I had been seconded, I returned to St Helena to teach mining law, the theory of mining, practical mining as well as *Fanakalo* – the unique mix of languages that developed from a multitude of tribal tongues, including English and Afrikaans, so common on the mines. But at Western Holdings, the student body included types that made the Dirty Dozen look like choirboys in comparison. One particularly obnoxious character with a fearsome pugilistic record was so disruptive and so offensive to some of the other lecturers and learner miners that I had to reprimand him in front of the others during an instructional tour underground. But he saw it only as an opportunity for another conquest and dared me to a fight as soon as we reached the surface. Word, of course, spread fast and by the time we emerged from below ground a crowd had already assembled around the makeshift ring in the recreation hall. Fortunately, I managed to dispose of this big bully rather quickly and soon I found myself riding on the shoulders of German, Italian and Hungarian learner miners, who had suffered most at the hands of the defeated rogue, to the recreation hall, where festivities continued into the night to a chorus of song.

The outcome of my final encounter in the boxing ring would, however, be quite different. It was towards the end of my career at St Helena mines. I was walking through the recreation hall while Johnny Farrell, then Free State welterweight champion and a strong contender for the national title, was going through his paces under the watchful eye of Papa Farrell. Although I hadn't stepped into a boxing ring for quite some time, I allowed myself to be cajoled into an encounter I would rather forget. I was challenged to a sparring session with the champion – a stupid act of bravado from the outset – and knocked Farrell out within the first minute. He hit the canvas with his head first with such a force that he had to undergo emergency brain surgery, and I nearly cost the champion his life.

By that time, however, I had also begun to worry about my own state of health. Despite continuous efforts to improve working conditions underground and the assurance that technology would become much more advanced and safer, the steady line of seasoned workers at the clinic with the dreaded miner's 'phthisis' (Pneumoconiosis) and other serious ailments was beginning to worry me. During my evening runs after an eight-hour shift of which four hours were underground, I tried to clear my lungs of any dust that might have become lodged in my system. It was, I decided, time to move on. I went to Ted Pavitt and, despite the fact that I needed another two years of experience and a further eight subjects to qualify, asked him for a letter of recommendation to be allowed to enrol for the mine captaincy examination. To my great surprise, he conceded and gave me a glowing reference and wished me well. As fate would have it, our paths would cross again many years later after we had both reached the pinnacles of our respective professions. I still have the greatest respect and liking for this extraordinary man, who was by far the greatest and most exceptional boss under whom I ever had the pleasure of working. Unfortunately, however, a man like Ted Pavitt (who was also to be the mentor of top businessman Bernard Swanepoel of Harmony Gold Mines) comes along but once in a lifetime.

In 1957 I had a meeting in Bloemfontein that was to have a lasting and profound impact on my life. I had travelled by car from Welkom to join the other members of the Free State rugby team I captained, before we would embark on a train journey to Cape Town for a game against Western Province. My good friend, Free State fullback Kobus van Noordwyk, invited me to join him and his girlfriend, Magdaleen Berry, for a night on the town. He explained that Magdaleen had a pretty roommate – they were staying at Spes Bona boarding house – and I had a car, and although the idea of a blind date did not appeal to me, I reluctantly tagged along. But once we reached the boarding house, I sent Kobus in alone to first let me know what Magdaleen's friend looked like. But, unbeknown to me, my mystery date had already sent Magdaleen out to do some spying of her own and to make sure that I was not married. Moments later I was introduced to the beautiful Adri. How, I wondered, as we shook hands, could I be that fortunate? That entire evening, I could hardly take my eyes off the demure young beauty from Senekal and before we said goodbye to join the rest of our team at the hotel, I made sure that there would be another date when we returned from Cape Town. When we had met, she had been introduced to me only as Adri, and I thus had to resort to some ingenious means to ascertain her surname so I could ask her out again. Some might call it love at first sight – and, at least as far as I was concerned, I would agree.

In 1958 Adri took up a teaching job at Sasolburg but the four-hour drive to visit her, sometimes right after a strenuous game of rugby, did not deter me in the slightest. I visited her every weekend, and we were finally engaged on 13 June 1958. Adri became my wife six months later, on 13 December 1958, and over the years she was not only my soul mate but my pillar of strength in trying times.

During the second half of 1957, I came across a job advertisement placed by Caltex in the local newspaper and applied. The position was as a sales representative based in Bloemfontein and it was just what I was looking for. I was, in fact, hoping for an opportunity to get away from the mines and a return to Bloemfontein would also allow me to renew my acquaintance with Adri. The marketing manager, Ivan Rose, invited me to come in for an interview. 'But don't make a special trip from Welkom to Bloemfontein,' he said, 'It can wait.' The remark stung. After all, in this province and elsewhere across the country, rugby defined the person. And who, I wondered in my own inflated view of myself, would not want to see the rugby star Louis Luyt and Free State rugby captain? Who would not immediately want to find out why he wished to honour them with his services? But I would soon discover the reason behind Rose's apparent lack of enthusiasm.

I was in Bloemfontein the very next day, and met with Rose in his office. After explaining the duties the job involved, he ushered me through to the general manager, Jimmy Mackie. 'Certainly,' Mackie said, 'we would like to have you on board. You have all the qualifications for the job.' 'But,' he added sheepishly, 'we simply can't match your salary at the mines.' So that, I thought, was the reason for Rose's initial reluctance to have me spend money and time on a special trip to Bloemfontein.

'What can you offer me?' I asked.

Mackie fiddled with the penknife in his hand.

'Well... about half.'

'I'll take it,' I said.

He almost dropped the knife in surprise, but quickly recovered his composure and quite calmly said: 'Then welcome to Caltex.'

Jimmy Mackie had reason to be elated. He was getting someone with a good measure of recognition in his sales office for a mere pittance. But I was also getting what I wanted – an escape from the mines, an opportunity to return to my favourite city and, quite possibly, new girlfriend, as well as the chance to prove myself in the business world.

Somehow, I had a feeling that this would be the start of good things for me. Caltex combined the tasks of three different salesmen – or representatives – to create my new position, and it was my job alone to sell the company products to garages, dealers, industrial consumers and farmers in Bloemfontein and the surrounding district. But this new position also came with a heavy responsibility. They expected me to regain the ground lost by Caltex in the area. After a sales course in Cape Town, I had to become intimately acquainted with the Caltex refineries and oil production process as well as the product range and, towards the end of 1957, I had to write examinations. Fortunately, I excelled, with very nearly full marks.

I hit the ground running, and tackled my new tasks with mercenary zeal. This, I felt, was my one chance to show the world that a Luyt can succeed in business. The memories of the failed ventures started by my stepfather in the Karoo simply served to strengthen my resolve. In 1958 I won first prize for the most significant hike in Caltex sales nationwide by multiplying turnover three and half times over the previous year. My reward was £25, which allowed me to buy the curtains I needed for my apartment. One of my opponents in the field was a certain Gerhard Viviers who, after I took almost 100 per cent of the Dealesville Agricultural Petroleum market, was forced to seek employment elsewhere. In fact, Viviers joined the South African Broadcasting Corporation (SABC) and later became famous as a rugby commentator.

Besides work and rugby, however, I also found time to attend extramural classes at the University of Orange Free State with the aim of obtaining a BA degree. The university did not offer a course in Mining Engineering so I could not pursue this discipline any further, but I was still driven in part by my mother's admonition that while money and fortune come and go, an education is something no one could ever take away. The marketing manager, Ivan Rose, had some difficulty in coming to terms with my desire to pick up a Bachelor of Arts degree in the midst of what seemed to be a promising foray into the world of business. This search for new knowledge and formal education would, however, remain a burning desire throughout my years in the corporate world – only, now knowledge had become the watchword.

In my sales effort on behalf of Caltex, I was greatly assisted by the contacts I made through rugby. Free Staters, in general, liked their rugby and farmers were no exception. Sales in the district soared. But then a terrible drought struck the Karoo and farmers had to turn to the army for help, shipping their livestock out to areas where there was still grazing available. It was obvious that the army was going to need lots of fuel to launch 'Operation Pofadder' – as they called their rescue mission. By this time, I had already switched from the Railways team – which I had rejoined when I returned to Bloemfontein – to Garrison, the army rugby club. In the process, I had also become the first player in Bloemfontein to captain two first-league sides in successive seasons. There I got to know a promising young flyhalf, Jannie Geldenhuys, who many years later became Chief of the Defence Force, and several other young officers. In 1975, Geldenhuys would invite me to accompany him to Angola and afterwards offer me a commission as full – not 'honorary' – colonel in the Engineers Corps in the Civil Defence Force. I had my own unit, the Strategic Protection Unit and, because it involved industrial installations, I was particularly happy there. Not only was I able to put a deal together that would save the army some money, but it would also benefit my employer enormously.

But when I proudly slapped the order for 500,000 44-gallon drums of fuel on the new Caltex manager's desk – Mackie had been transferred – he went ballistic. 'How the hell could you even entertain this order!' he shouted in panic. 'You must be out of your mind! There is no way we can supply that; we don't even have enough drums – not in the entire country!' In the end, of course, we did, enlisting the support of all the competing oil companies. I, however, never received as much as a penny as bonus for the deal.

Next, I pitched for and managed to obtain another massive army contract to supply oil for its tanks, armoured cars and trucks, and again it was met with a similar response. 'What are you up to?' my sales manager complained. 'This is embarrassing. We don't even make this oil.' But the general manager stepped in. 'So what? We'll find a way.' And we did. At the end of the year, my region had once again doubled its turnover – but again my salary remained basically unchanged. As a result, I decided to look around for a company where I might benefit from my own sales efforts and where large orders were welcomed with open arms and not considered problems. I was even beginning to entertain the thought of starting my own company.

As the end of the fifties was approaching, I knew that the stars that once seemed so distant when I stood at the bottom of the well, were now well within reach. In a mere matter of just ten years, I had managed to struggle my way up to where I felt confident about my own future. Exactly where it would lead, I did not know, but I was ready for that one big opportunity I was sure would present itself – my big move closer to those beckoning stars.

No man possesses a genius so commanding

that he can attain eminence, unless a subject

suited to his talents should present itself, and

an opportunity occurs for its development.

Pliny

Chapter 3

OPPORTUNITY KNOCKS

On 26 July 1970, towards the end of a decade that saw my personal fortune rise from scrounging around for pennies at the end of the month to running a large company of my own, the *Sunday Express* carried an interview under a bold heading: 'I am no genius, says fertiliser king Luyt.' I had told the interviewer that my success was due to no more than plain, straightforward hard work coupled with a little common sense and, looking back now on that golden decade in my life, I still believe this to be true.

I had certain talents that were simply waiting for a suitable opportunity to emerge and in 1960 that opportunity presented itself. Nothing dramatic. No fanfare. No thunder and lightning. It started simply with a telephone call from a fertiliser company called Fisons, offering me a position as salesman in the Transvaal. My reputation for moving product at Caltex had spread and Fisons felt that I might be just the man to help them gain market share in the tough fertiliser industry. I agreed to meet in Johannesburg and soon found myself flying to Johannesburg by SAA Viscount, courtesy of Fisons, to meet with its recently appointed regional manager, John Norton, and marketing manager, Nico Mentz.

Everything I heard sounded good. I was offered a region in the Eastern Transvaal, including choice high-production districts such as Delmas and Ogies. Apart from a better salary, I would be entitled to a commission on sales – a prospect I savoured, especially as I realised how much money I could have made had I been working on this basis for Caltex. Adri and I were having a tough time making ends meet and this was the opportunity to turn it all around. I did not hesitate. We shook hands on the deal and I returned to Bloemfontein to prepare for my move north.

Above: The sign on my father's bakery, which was erected in 1946.

Left: This picture was taken in 1939. I am standing behind my sister, Grace, with my stepbrother Conrick and stepsister Lodewieka.

Left: A few of my Standard 9 and 10 pals. We all attended Collegiate High School in Colesberg in 1948.

St Helena Rugby Football Club in 1953. That's me, third from the left in the back row.

The Free State under-19 team in 1951, and again I'm third from the left in the back row.

Then disturbing news reached me. The management at Fisons had changed its mind. It decided to reassign me to the much less productive Nylstroom region. If it wasn't for the fact that I had already given notice at Caltex and was too proud to go back, I might never have made the move north after all. My new region was one of the lowest production areas and offered puny potential for fertiliser compared with the Delmas region. I was thus stuck and just had to make the best of the situation.

It did not take me long after we settled in at Nylstroom to realise just how devastating in terms of sales this last-minute switch in my assignment really was. It was obvious that even a super salesman would not be able to transform a district known for sorghum and cattle farming into a major user of fertiliser. With one door practically closed, I simply had to find another. Striking up a friendship with Maans Rossouw, an outstanding entomologist who also acted as the Fisons agronomist in the area, I spent all my free time learning everything there was to know about insecticides, herbicides and pesticides and the ways in which they might help farmers grow better crops and improve their profitability.

Fisons was only too happy to receive their first pesticide order from me, even though the folk at head office could barely hide their scepticism about this fertiliser salesman who now wanted to move some of their lesser products. In fact, so little did the company care about the pesticide side of the business that it did not even bother to appoint a marketing manager for the products. It wasn't long, however, before pesticides more than made up for the lacklustre market for fertiliser in my area. In 1960 I sold, in addition to fertiliser, a huge chunk of all of Fisons' pesticide production in my region. My salary and commission at the end of the year added up to £25,000, twice the total earnings of the managing director, Peter Nash.

I bought a farm near Nylstroom for £3,500, and Adri and I made a home there with our newborn daughter, Cornelia Johanna. Corlia – as we preferred to call her – was born on 27 July 1960 and, over the years, she would develop into a strong-willed student of law who, some would claim, inherited her mother's good looks and her father's stubborn refusal to compromise principle for the sake of peace.

Like others before me, fatherhood introduced an entirely new dimension to my life and a greater sense of urgency to succeed. My wife and children, I decided, would never have to knock on any back doors or wait in line for hand-me-downs. They would be given every chance in life that I did not have. When you have climbed halfway from the bottom, the terrible thought of slipping back drives you ever upward, despite the rocks others may drop from the top. Afrikaners seemed to be tailor-made for the adage that when you have a bucket filled with crabs not one will reach the top because there will always be another crab pulling it down as it, too, tries to claw itself to the top.

In 1961, I found that success – even at Fisons – was not necessarily welcomed, especially when a salesman not only outsells others in the same firm but also earns more than top management. Without notice, my commission on herbicides and pesticides was lowered from 7.5 per cent to a mere 2 per cent. At the same time, the new sales targets for fertiliser and crop-protection materials were set at unrealistically high levels, making the earning of additional commissions impossible. I seemed to have completed a full circle – back to the Caltex culture where success in sales was rewarded with penalties instead of praise and pay. It was then that I decided to go it alone.

I sold the farm, packed up the family and moved to Pretoria where I established Louis Luyt Enterprises Pty Ltd (LLE), ready to sell anything from fertiliser and real estate to baled Erogrostis grass, which I grew on a farm I acquired in the Delmas district.

Within its first year of operation, LLE bought its first corporate plane – a wing-tipped single-engine Comanche, soon to be exchanged for a larger twin-engine model. Business was growing and my staff increased to five and then to ten, all dedicated salespeople with the opportunity to more than double their income with commissions. I was determined not to make the same mistake my former employers made. It would be my pleasure to see a salesman earn more than me, because in the end it all added up to growth for the enterprise.

I went back to Fisons and asked them to supply LLE with fertiliser under my own brand name, but they responded by offering me a relatively unheard of brand called Bisley, instead. But one farmers' cooperative bought its entire annual requirement in one fell swoop from LLE, so I went back to Fisons and alerted them to my further requirements. This, in turn, led to a memorable encounter with the company secretary Dennis Marchington. The very same man who, when I first approached Fisons for product, cautioned me that I would barely be able to scrape together a living now showed concern for his own company's well-being.

'This is our established business,' he protested at the sight of an order for 46,000 tons that I placed on his desk. 'We will simply not allow you to take away our business!'

'Nobody has established business in this market,' I said. 'You have never sold 46,000 tons to this co-op and you know that. I happened to have taken this business away from your competitors and now you are complaining! All you lose on the deal is the commission you have to pay me on your share. Bisley is your brand and I am establishing a market for it.'

'We have an arrangement with other producers such as AECI and Windmill Fertilisers,' Marchington blundered, inadvertently confirming a cartel arrangement that everyone suspected but no one admitted to. 'That does not allow this maverick type of marketing. We simply will not supply you any longer.'

'Oh, I think you will...' I said confidently and walked out.

Fisons did supply in the end, but not in its regular plastic bags. Instead, the fertiliser came in paper bags, badly stitched at the top and bottom, with the result that, within a few weeks, the packaging began to erode due to the emission of fluorine gasses. At first, I threatened legal action, but in the end simply cancelled the order. Marchington and Fisons won the first round, but I was determined to stick around for the rest of the fight.

I applied for a permit to purchase from suppliers abroad the same fertiliser already being imported by the established 'Big Three' to augment their own production, but word came back promptly from the Under-Secretary of Commerce and Industry, MA du Plessis. He had refused my application. This was the beginning of an uphill battle against a government that seemed intent on setting up roadblocks for years to come. But, then, I was never a member of the Broederbond, that secret band of brothers who seemed to be at the core of every important decision since the National Party had come to power in 1948.

I could only chuckle with amusement in later years when some English-speaking reporters ascribed my success in business as having been able to draw on government favours as an Afrikaner. The truth is, in fact, quite the opposite. The National Party government was, in effect, protecting the three fertiliser companies – AECI, Fisons and Windmill, which were controlled by non-Afrikaner interests – from being challenged by a small trading company called LLE. The government was protecting, if not publicly condoning, the existence of a classic monopoly or cartel in the fertiliser industry. Later, when my company grew into a major supplier, the same Afrikaner government would hasten to try to break my hold on the market so that others, including a state enterprise, could get their 'fair' share.

Fortunately, there were also one or two personalities in government who were willing to buck the system. Commerce and Trade Minister, Jan Haak, was one of them and so was his successor, Lourens Muller, some years later. Haak was genuinely sympathetic and, after listening to my plight, he over-ruled his officials. He instructed Iscor, the state steel enterprise, and Sasol, the government-run oil-from-coal plant, to supply me with their by-products, ammonium sulphate and limestone ammonium nitrate, and allowed a certain quantity of other materials, such as potassium chloride, to be imported. With these important ingredients in abundant supply, we could get to work mixing our own fertiliser.

Senkor (Sentrale Kunsmis Korporasie, or Central Fertiliser Corporation) was born in a shed at Sasolburg. No machinery. No plant. No grand opening. Simply a group of workers with spades, mixing product, and weighing and shoving it into printed bags to be carted off to the market. We had 16 dedicated salesmen in the field, and they were able to move those bags as fast as we could fill them. Senkor, in fact, became the first bulk blender, something that is common today.

Even those fertiliser giants who laughed at us at the outset were beginning to take notice. But we would soon run into the problem that often rears its ugly head not long after market growth begins to outrun capacity - a shortage of capital. Like a plane running out of gas just when it needs that extra thrust during take-off, we would find ourselves on the verge of crashing to the ground.

My rugby days were now winding down and I had still been unable to win Springbok colours – an unfulfilled ambition that would trouble me for many years to come. In 1960, when the All Blacks toured South Africa I found myself in top form, playing, according to the rugby press pundits, some of the best rugby of my career. But, following an unfortunate course of events the previous year, by then it was already clear that I was not even in the running. In the end, I wondered whether I might not have salvaged the situation by swallowing my pride, but then it is my nature not to compromise when I know in my heart that I am not at fault. Perhaps that is a holdover from my youth when I saw my parents and our family humiliated so often.

In 1959, while still working for Caltex, I was sent to the Northern Cape to sell fuel tanks to farmers, and this made it impossible for me to play for Free State against Transvaal. I asked my manager at Caltex, who had made it quite clear that there was no way out of this assignment, to advise the Free State officials accordingly. Whether he failed or forgot to do it despite his assurances, or simply did not reach the right people, I will never know. Fact is, rugby officialdom saw this simply as me being hard-arsed. They left me out in the cold for several of the following games and, with the All Black tour fast approaching and the national selectors scouting around for talent, I shone in my absence. Near the end of the 1959 season, one of the Free State selectors, Japie Jacobz, approached me and suggested that I apologise for my behaviour, which I on principle refused to do. I felt that there was no wrongdoing on my part. Perhaps, if I did, I might still have caught the eye of the selectors in time to make the Springbok team. 'Do you think that I brought this upon myself?' I asked, indignantly. 'How would anyone be so stupid as to forego the opportunity to play in front of Springbok selectors without good reason?' Towards the end of the season, I was in the team once again, but too late to be considered by the national selectors, who had already completed their task. In any event, the charges of my alleged snub certainly must have reached the ears of the national selectors as well.

Even though I moved to Northern Transvaal to work for Fisons in 1960, I was asked to continue playing for Free State, which I did not mind despite the distances involved. In one of our early games, we beat Transvaal by a comfortable margin. Fellow lock and team captain, Frans de Jager, and I were pitted against former Matie captain Avril Malan and Piet Botha and we acquitted ourselves rather well. With his excellent performance here and a good showing during the previous season, I was sure that Frans at least had assured himself a place in the Springbok team to face the All Blacks. But I was proven wrong once again. They chose Avril Malan instead – and made him Springbok captain to boot. Perhaps I was simply mistaken that, since that disastrous 1956 Springbok tour of New Zealand, the Stellenbosch connection would no longer count.

My last game for Free State would also be my first and only against an international side. While the 1960 All Black team crossed the country, steamrollering the provincial teams, Free State fans speculated that our side might just be the one to stop this locomotive. All the speculation, however, placed a heavy responsibility on our shoulders and it was thus with no small measure of nervous tension that my team-mates and I spread across the winter-hardened and bleached Free State Stadium in Bloemfontein.

Wilson Whineray and his seven compatriots in the front gave us their all in the scrums and spared no effort in the loose and the lineouts. But we were a team possessed. I also drew on determination that came with the realisation that this would not only be my last game for Free State, but most probably my only one – ever – against the All Blacks or any other international team.

We won 9–8, but had luck on our side. After several failed attempts by the legendary Don Clarke to convert penalties, All Black Russell Watt was called upon to kick at goal when a last-minute penalty was awarded to the visitors right in front of our posts. That ball never left the ground and shot like a bullet under the crossbar, soccer-style. When I visited New Zealand in 1970, Wilson Whineray told me that when they ran back after this unfortunate attempt by Russell Watt at post, Watt was adamant that he did not want another kick. Whineray had retorted by saying, 'Don't worry, you won't get another kick.' We thus walked off the field, tired winners. Free State became the only provincial team to beat the All Blacks on their celebrated 1960 tour. (Their other narrow defeat was against a Combined Defence Forces team in Pretoria in a game in which the legend of Frik du Preez was born.)

'What a bonny tussle!' exclaimed *The Friend* in a front-page report the day after we defeated the All Blacks. Wrote New Zealand sports editor Terry McLean on 7 July 1960: 'I should specially like to commend Luyt. A bonny forward in a really bonny game.' Some game it was. This was an experience I enjoyed as much in the thick of battle as McLean did from the press box. But, at best, it was a mere consolation prize. Once again, I would see my chance of wearing the green and gold slip past.

While the South African selectors chose to ignore my performance on that day, the All Blacks remembered only too well. In 1970, when I toured New Zealand together with Doc Danie Craven, we were guests at a Sportsman of the Year dinner. This proved to be a welcome relief from a trip that was filled with tension as Doc Craven tried to mend rugby bridges between our two countries in the continuing conflict over apartheid. So intent were the anti-apartheid forces in New Zealand to do us harm that Craven had to be provided with a bodyguard by local rugby administrators. The dinner was thus an occasion for both of us to have a good time away from the pressure. To my surprise, I heard myself being introduced as the captain of the Free State rugby team who beat the almost invincible 1960 All Black team. I turned to Doc Craven and said:

'Doc, they're mistaken. I was not the captain.'

Craven smiled.

'So what, Louis? Stand up and take a bow!'

'But,' I protested, 'what if the press reports this? I will be most embarrassed.'

'They'll never hear about this back home. In any event, you played for the team, didn't you?'

So I stood up, feeling like an impostor, and looked around in vain for someone to whom I could explain.

In the early sixties, after a stint in the Eastern Transvaal and a few games for Adelaars in the Pretoria Carlton Cup competition, my rugby days were coming to an end. Between the pressures of building a new company in the face of heavy opposition from the fertiliser cartel and the government and the desire to spend every free moment with my family, rugby had finally been relegated to a distant third on my priority list. On 12 March 1962, Adri and I had become the proud parents of a son, whom we named Charles Lucien Paul in honour of the man who became my father by default and accepted the responsibility. Our Charles, or rather Lucien, as we call him, would, if I could help it, not ever have any want of opportunity in life.

By 1962 I knew that LLE had the capability to outsell the big boys in the business if only we could lay our hands on more product. We needed proper production facilities instead of the haphazard shovel mix-and-fill operation in a rented shed at Sasolburg. But fertiliser plants cost money – and lots of it. Then Nico Mentz, who left Fisons to join me at LLE, had a brilliant idea. Make the farmers partners in the business. We prepared a prospectus, and went around and sold shares to the farmers, with 10 per cent down and the rest to be paid in two years. The entity in which they put their money was called Triomf (Triumph), a separate company, which we formed expressly for this purpose.

Another talented man who had left the Goliath – Fisons – to join in battle with David – Senkor – was HJS van Zyl, the head of Fisons' phosphate factory. By this time we already discussed the forming of a brand-new fertiliser company that would supplant the rather modest Senkor. We needed a new name and a logo for this new entity and so it was that over lunch one day, this man who knew phosphate production so well, doodled with pen and pencil, and pushed the end product to me across the table. It had 'Triomf' (Triumph) written across an oval.

'There you have it...' he said rather nonchalantly, '... our new logo. The oval is a link in the cartel chain and the name across it, Triomf, breaks it.'

By 1965 after we had sold a quarter of a million rand worth of shares to the farming community, drought struck. By this time I was already scouting around for a location at which to build our factory. But the cartel, as I would soon find out, was not sitting idly by while we were laying plans to launch Triomf as a competitive producer of fertiliser. Their influence showed the moment that I started applying for all the necessary permits and sought potential partners in the new factory.

Naturally, I first focused on the Industrial Development Corporation. After all, this state institution was formed with the explicit mandate to help new start-ups like ours with capital, incentives and professional advice. Instead of seeing Triomf as a start-up, the Industrial Development Corporation (IDC) managing director Sieg Kuschke treated me as an upstart – someone who wanted to make trouble for the establishment and the cartel which he and his colleagues had been cosying up to for so many years and in which they now held a substantial share-holding. In his eyes, I gathered, I was nothing more than a street vendor trying to take up sidewalk space in front of a big store, spoiling both the business and the neighbourhood.

Someone suggested I approach a big municipality, preferably in the so-called Maize Triangle of the Transvaal, which might welcome a brand-new factory such as ours, providing both employment opportunities and tax revenues. Potchefstroom welcomed the idea with open arms and took it upon themselves to obtain government approval. In the meantime, I went to work on obtaining the necessary additional capital.

Properly prepared, I approached Jan Hurter, the head of Volkskas. Having been cautioned by others that Hurter was a banker of the 'belt-en-kruisbande tipe' (the cautious type who wears both a belt and braces), I turned up at his office with written proof of the initial commitment of R250,000 by 3,500 farmers. Apparently, the involvement by the same farming community that helped build his bank moved him to agree to a matching overdraft facility.

Triomf went out on tender and Anglo American's LTA, headed by Dr Wim de Villiers, offered the lowest bid. We accepted. They then moved their equipment onto the site at Potchefstroom, and construction eventually started. Then, suddenly, it stopped.

I received a call from Wim de Villiers. He urgently wanted to see me. This bespectacled, thick-set fellow, who would later become the head of the Gencor mining house and eventually a cabinet minister, arrived with a sombre look on his face. Even though Triomf had paid punctually for work done, he explained, LTA would need a bank guarantee for the remainder of the work. I pointed out that this issue should have been raised when the contract was signed and I reminded him that under current competitive conditions others were quite willing to perform the same work without guarantees. He remained adamant. A bank guarantee in eight days or else...

'Or else?' I asked.

'We move our machinery off the premises,' he replied with the self-assured smile that comes with knowing that you are part of South Africa's biggest conglomerate and talking to the representative of a start-up enterprise. In this case, he obviously felt confident that triumph was on his side.

Before De Villiers was even out the door, I was already on the phone to Hurter's office. It was time to draw on that overdraft facility. Hurter was overseas, his secretary explained. So I made an appointment to see his deputy, Jan van den Bergh. But the trip to his office turned out to be a waste of time.

'I cannot sanction payments on this account,' Van den Bergh explained. 'Mr Hurter did not leave any notation to this effect on your account. So I suggest that we simply wait until he returns so you can take it up with him personally.'

'But you don't understand,' I insisted. 'This is a matter of great urgency. It is a matter of life or death for my company.'

Van den Bergh had the look of a mortician trying to feign pain while handling the family of the deceased: 'I'm really sorry, Mr Luyt, but this will have to wait for Mr Hurter.'

I looked up the chairman of Volkskas, Professor Avril Malan, father of the rugby player by the same name who would eventually join my ranks when I headed the Transvaal Rugby Union. But Malan could offer only tea and sympathy and the promise to speak to Hurter when he returned.

Several days later, when Hurter returned, I was on his doorstep. I would later learn from one of his assistants in the bank that Hurter was quite upset that his secretary had, in fact, made the appointment with me. Our meeting was short and unpleasant. Hurter was a changed man.

'I have decided to withdraw your overdraft facility,' he said abruptly as I settled down in the chair in front of his cleared desk.

'What do you mean?' I enquired, leaning forward but trying hard to hide my disappointment and shock.

'Andreas Wassenaar warned me that you would be bankrupt soon.'

I slowly rose from my chair and gathered my papers together.

'You are dishonest and not worthy of being called a banker,' I said, my voice trembling with anger. 'If I have to go from house to house to sell my company's shares, I'll do so. I despise you and your kind.'

As I turned and walked out, he just smiled. On my way back, I wondered why the South Africa that was supposedly run by Afrikaners should be so hard on its own kind. Was it because I was not one of the chosen few who belonged to the *Broederbond*? Or was it simply a matter of being an outsider who was threatening those privileged few Afrikaners who had 'arrived' and now called themselves part of the establishment? Was it simply a matter of Afrikaner jealousy? We surely had a lot of that going around in our ranks.

My moment of truth with Jan Hurter came many years later when we were both honoured guests at a cocktail party for so-called captains of industry. It was our first real encounter since that unhappy meeting in his office when he reneged on his word. Triomf had by then become the biggest fertiliser company in South Africa and a worldwide contender.

'I could not lend money to a good cause such as Mr Luyt's Triomf many years ago,' Hurter explained to his distinguished audience, still smiling, 'because the Reserve Bank would not allow us to do so at the time.'

Now it was my turn to smile. As Hurter spoke, my company was making larger profits than Volkskas. And Hurter knew it only too well!

When I left Hurter's office on that fateful day, sheer desperation drove me to the offices of the very person who he had claimed cautioned him that my operation was destined for bankruptcy, Andreas Wassenaar of Sanlam. As CEO of one of South Africa's insurance giants – like Volkskas, built on the strength of Afrikaner sentiment – there was, I naively believed, some slight chance that he might want to help us succeed for the sake of the farmers, if nothing else.

'So you really want me to invest in your useless little operation?' Wassenaar asked as he spread his feet across the desk in front of me. 'Yes, I know. All you want me to do is to take over your debt.'

There was little point in continuing the discussion. But Wassenaar and my path would cross later, not once but several times. It is, however, interesting how they all forget the past when they welcome you into the ranks of the establishment in the present. At least Wasseneaar did not make any excuses for not lending me money. But he did approach me when Prime Minister PW Botha called a referendum and needed money to help sell his ill-fated three-chamber concept to the public. During a trip to London, we happened to be seated together on a South African Airways flight when he showed me the handwritten notes for a new book in which he attacked the government and the establishment for waste and ineffectiveness. He was no longer head of Sanlam, but I thought it took some guts to say what he was going to say in public. The book did stir up a lot of controversy and anger among his former peers, but probably not nearly as deep an anger as I felt after that ill-fated meeting with Wassenaar in the early sixties.

Next on my list of potential lenders was Anton Rupert, who, I was reminded by my colleagues at Triomf, had very much the same experience in the forties when his fledgling Voorbrand Tobacco Company suffered from burn-out and needed additional capital to save it from bankruptcy. Voorbrand did indeed go bankrupt. Later, after starting all over again, Rupert would make a bid for the voting shares of Rothmans International. At the time, I recall, it was actually

Wassenaar of Sanlam and Hurter of Volkskas who advanced the money for the acquisition. And later, it was Rupert who in public called Wassenaar 'that small man from Belville' when Wassenaar wanted to fire Wim de Villiers from Sanlam-controlled Gencor, where Rupert was a stakeholder. Their acrimony was so severe that they spent huge sums of money to malign each other in full-page advertisements in mass-circulation newspapers. Such is the way of business, I soon learned, and the way of many an Afrikaner. There seems to be an ever-present element of brotherly envy that makes the story of Cain and Abel look meek in comparison.

I travelled all the way to Stellenbosch to have an audience with Anton Rupert. He received me in his trademark courtly fashion. We talked about the weather and a little about culture. Then came the moment to make my appeal. As I did so, I kept remembering a Rupert who once found himself in the same predicament. All the time, I looked for signs of hope, but his face remained expressionless, his body still. My plea left Rupert unmoved. He lifted his tender fingers in the air like a conductor ready to silence the audience before the start of a symphony.

'My advice to you is simple,' he said. 'Leave it to the big ones and find something else to do. You know, as I sit here, we are subsidising governments with what we have to pay in excise duties just to produce a single cigarette.'

So I returned to Johannesburg, drained and desperate, wondering where we would turn next. It was evident that we had exhausted every possible source in South Africa. Would it be that my business would go the same direction as my father's barbershop and bakery? Will Triomf be just another failure at the hands of a Luyt who tried to break out of the well and reach for the top? The opportunity that had demanded all my talent in order to succeed was now fast receding and threatening to disappear into the dust as LTA started dismantling and removing its equipment.

But there was one last resort – in the person of a well-respected banker who also happened to be an Afrikaner outsider with no special ties to the Broeder-bond or the inner circle of the National Party. In fact, he was a leading member of the opposition United Party, an Afrikaner who managed to make his mark in English-speaking business circles. But what assurance did I have that he was not beholden to the very same fertiliser cartel that seemed to have such a stranglehold on everyone else? None. Still, as chairman of The Netherlands Bank of South Africa - which later became Nedbank – Dr Frans Cronjé was undoubtedly in a position to assist. I simply had to take that chance.

I steeled myself for one more disappointing and humiliating experience as I turned up at Dr Cronjé's office at the imposing midtown offices of Nedbank. While I knew him merely from press reports, Cronjé was probably also relying on pure hearsay to assess this young man who had the gumption to make a cold call to him. I could only hope that Wassenaar's gloom-and-doom assessment of Triomf had not reached his ears. The urbane banker welcomed me into his well-appointed office with a friendly smile and listened attentively to my plight.

'I'll call Gerry Muller, the general manager of our bank,' he said, 'and ask him to see what we can do for you, Mr Luyt.'

Later that day, while I was sharing news of this pleasant encounter with my colleagues in order to bolster their sagging spirits, a call came through from Cronjé's secretary. A meeting was set with Muller the next morning, she informed me. 'Hope you can make it...' I could hardly resist a wry smile. If only she knew how much hinged on this single meeting.

I was on Muller's doorstep well before the assigned time, somewhat sluggish from a lack of sleep and the tension of the past weeks. The night before I had kept Adri awake until the early morning hours, reviewing every aspect and angle of my planned approach. She had become my best counsellor. Not only did she know me better than anyone else, but she had no ulterior motive in giving advice and possessed a refreshing realism and calm logic that was the hallmark of her Kotzé family. Not only on that occasion, but many others since, her input would be crucial. Through the years I would repeatedly come to realise the truth of that old saying: Behind every successful man stands a strong woman.

As I laid out my plans, Muller listened quietly, without interruption. He was obviously weighing every word and thought as he stared intently at me.

'I like what I have heard,' he said as I wound up my monologue. 'So how much do you need?'

Don't be greedy, I cautioned myself. Don't spoil the deal. Ask for the minimum. And I did.

'Oh, that we can do,' Muller observed, 'but it'll only wipe out your current debts. What about working capital?'

He was right. We needed lots more in our war chest if we wanted to win this battle against the big boys. But having Nedbank at least take care of our debts was a start. It was cause for cautious celebration.

I returned to the office to report the good news. Nedbank had thrown us a lifeline. We were still in business. But the problem was far from solved. We needed a big brother in a hurry – otherwise we might well be back begging for money again and again. Under-capitalised ventures tend to wither and die like the crops that disappeared in the wake of the great drought of 1965 and caused so many farmers to pack up and move onto other properties as farmhands and foremen. I had had my fill of that kind of existence and I was ready to break out, whatever it took. Back at Triomf, we all agreed that finding a major investor in South Africa was about as realistic as asking the Reserve Bank for a few free gold bars. In our case, we knew, charity was definitely not going to begin at home. We simply had to look abroad, but where?

43

Success in life is a matter not so much of talent
or opportunity as of concentration and perseverance.

Charles William Wendt,
American clergyman, 1844–1930

Chapter 4

THE SWEET TASTE OF SUCCESS

In July 1970, *The Star* in Johannesburg carried a report by Stanley Hurst under the headline, 'Two tycoons at the top', with a strapline that read 'Louis Luyt – Super salesman 'king' of fertiliser industry'. 'Louis Luyt, ex-Free State rugby forward, former railway clerk at 50 cents a day and one-time frustrated salesman, will set the seal this week on a deal which will make him king of the South African fertiliser industry, estimated to have annual sales worth R100 million,' Hurst reported. "On his side are 8,000 farmers and Mr Harry Oppenheimer whose AE & CI organisation was, until negotiations were completed on Thursday, one of his two major rivals. The amazing rise of Mr Luyt, 38, a genial 6-ft 5-in giant, has been achieved in barely three years – from a time when he hardly had a bag of fertiliser to his name.'

This was the same press that, only a few years earlier, had written Triomf off as the failed attempt of a delusional upstart. They did so, I have to assume, not with malice but in response to rumours and reports about the brush-off I had received from the Afrikaner establishment. Strangely, once I made it to the top, some of the same media speculated that I reached the pinnacle largely as a result of help from the Afrikaner elite. Ultimately, of course, the removal of LTA's construction equipment from our Potchefstroom site served to dramatise our demise in the public eye and led to heavy speculation in the press that I was just about ready to throw in the towel.

But even though the thought never crossed my mind to give up and walk away during those dark days when I was snubbed and humiliated by the likes of Hurter, Rupert and Wassenaar, I did not either – even in my wildest of dreams – anticipate the developments described by Hurst and others in the late sixties. The idea of having Harry Oppenheimer's AE & CI as part of my own operation when another member of his Anglo American conglomerate, LTA, refused to do business with me was simply too far-fetched to contemplate. Such was the aura of gloom painted around my efforts to break the cartel that Gerry Muller of Nedbank, who had agreed to advance a quarter of a million rand to help me buy time, was seen by his peers as a reckless gambler.

In a way, I could not blame them. Anyone else who dared to challenge a seemingly invincible force as I did when I threw down the gauntlet and stepped into battle with the fertiliser cartel – consisting of AECI and Fedmis, which had taken over both Windmill Fertilisers and Fisons Fertilisers – might well have been exposed to the same scepticism. But then I knew that we weren't just anybody. I had little doubt and, in fact, every confidence that my team was capable of accomplishing the unthinkable.

Had we not proven that, with a small, dedicated sales force and by forging a partnership with the farming communities, we could indeed beat the big boys on their own turf? Had we not shown that opportunity combined with talent go a long way toward success in this industry, as in all others?

But now I discovered, as other budding entrepreneurs have done before me, that sheer talent and opportunity on their own do not make for any sort of lasting success. You also need concentration and perseverance. These are not innate qualities. They are cultivated and acquired. My childhood exposure to the humiliation and insults that came with growing up on the wrong side of a class-conscious Karoo town had taught me the need for both concentration and perseverance from a very early age. I was not going to go away quietly. It was simply not in my make-up.

Looking back on those crucial days when I decided to follow up on a brilliant suggestion by Nico Mentz that we embark on a journey to the United States to look for a partner who would be prepared to join us in battle against the titans of the fertiliser industry, the word 'audacity' springs to mind. But then everything I have ever done since leaving Fisons seems to fit that description. I had, in their view, the audacity to sell their own product into their own markets at a profit for myself. I had the audacity to mix my own product and continued challenging them when they cut my supplies. I had the audacity to want to establish a fertiliser factory right on their doorstep. And, just when they must have thought they had seen the last of Luyt, I had the audacity to seek partners abroad to continue the fight.

While some journalists would later have me roaming the streets of New York with Nico Mentz at my side in desperate search for some Samaritan galloping down Park Avenue on a white horse to come to our rescue, the real story is not quite that romantic. Nico started the process when he put forward that we go see Heinz Graetz, who used to work for him at Fisons before relocating to New York to join Esso. He felt that Graetz might be able to open doors for us at this giant oil company, which in turn could provide the money to pull us through when Hurter of Volkskas first pulled the rug from under us. Even after Gerry Muller of Nedbank agreed to an overdraft, it was clear that we still needed a partner. As Muller quite rightly pointed out, the monies that he advanced would merely serve to bind us over and would not eliminate the need for further expansion capital.

So Nico called Graetz to set up a meeting at Esso headquarters in New Jersey, while I went to work on making appointments with a number of other prospects, including Rexall and American Cyanamid – in fact, seven in all. After the long journey via London we checked into New York's Warwick Hotel, tired but ready to get to work the next day with briefcases full of financial projections, market data and the like. We left nothing to chance. The next morning, I did most of the talking. Nico was a valuable ideas man, but preferred to leave the serious negotiations to me. For openers, the Esso representatives tried tough talk and some bluffing, but once they realised that they had a good deal on their hands they became quite accommodating. Their propensity to think big was especially appealing. Nico and I had brought a good deal to the table and it did not take them long to see the potential for themselves in what we put forward.

Before we took a cab to La Guardia airport for the long transcontinental flight to Los Angeles, word had reached us at the hotel that Esso was definitely interested. Apart from the profit potential that Triomf itself presented, Esso obviously saw this as a good opportunity to regain a foothold in South Africa. By the mid-sixties, the horrific memories of Sharpeville were receding and good returns and stability began to lure back companies that had left in the wake of this tragic event and the massive unrest and world opprobrium that followed it. We also had positive feedback from American Cyanamid, which was already well established in South Africa. The $5 million we needed in our war chest to break the stranglehold of the fertiliser cartel seemed secured. So the trip to the West Coast had a relaxed feeling about it. Nico and I could sit back and enjoy the ride, talking confidently about the future, which now seemed as wide open as the endless American landscape slipping by thousands of feet below.

As we flew over the Rocky Mountains into the great state of California I might have remarked to Nico Mentz that these majestic mountains could well signify the heights to which Triomf was destined to rise in future. Maybe I just had the thought and kept it to myself while Nico was trying to catch up on jet lag.

Shortly after our arrival at Los Angeles International and our transfer to the hotel through congested traffic and heavy smog, we called on Rexall Products. The reception at this giant American chemicals company was warm and friendly. The corporate lawyer who sat in on our meeting with the well-known Justin Dart, chairman of Rexall, wanted to know who else might be interested in our deal. I didn't want to divulge all the other parties, but did mention Esso in the passing and he seemed quite impressed.

'Of course,' he remarked, 'they are so big that they could lose $50 million and not even notice it.'

'We only need $5 million of that $50 million,' I said, smiling.

He looked surprised. Even in those days, it was hard for Americans to understand small outlays when it came to capital expenditure. If anything was worth considering, it was worth big bucks. Still, we had set our sights on a modest amount because we knew that that was all that was needed to send our inspired troops into battle. Also, I did not want a big brother bankrolling me to an extent where I would lose control of the company. In the end, however, I decided to sign with Esso, after lengthy negotiations with Cliff Garvin, head of their Chemical Division and later CEO of Esso (now known as Exxon Mobil) – much to the chagrin of American Cyanamid. American Cyanamid, a major contender, was already present in South Africa and – to boot – made me a personal offer for certain shares in my company, but I could not accept. Esso purchased a 50 per cent shareholding in Triomf for $3.5 million and also undertook to underwrite the South African content of the proposed share issue, which was slightly more than a million shares not sold to local investors in one of my private companies, with the control firmly vested in me. We could therefore close the prospectus. I retained control and had the world's biggest oil company on my side. Triomf acquired a 10-ton gorilla as insurance as it entered into serious battle against what was now the Big Two. The press quickly sat up and took notice. And so did the industry and other interested parties.

I received a call from Wim de Villiers. When, he wanted to know, could he move his equipment back onto the Potchefstroom site to complete work on the factory?

'Not so fast,' I replied. 'We need new bids. It's a whole new ball game now...'

'But you should understand,' De Villiers explained almost apologetically, 'the decision to pull out was not mine alone. I have shareholders to answer to and we are part of the bigger Anglo American.'

But I remained unmoved.

'If you are interested in the job,' I insisted, 'a new bid will be required.'

So it was that LTA had to start afresh, spending thousands of rands in additional man-hours and meetings before we accepted the substantially reduced price and allowed them back onto the property. This time I wanted to set the terms. Even though we realised that none of the other contenders would be able to meet LTA's attractive pricing or match their capability and equipment, I needed to have De Villiers sweat a little for all the harm that he and LTA had caused us in the press. LTA completed the job in eleven months and our Potchefstroom factory came on stream in August 1967.

While construction was underway I, in the meantime, enjoyed a welcome break. I had time to relax with Adri and our children. In addition to Corlia and Lucien, we had become the proud parents of another beautiful baby girl on

27 February 1964. We named her Adri, after her mother, but she soon acquired the nickname of Nossie. Looking back today, I treasure those times that we spent together as a family at home and, as my finances improved, the vacations in major cities of the world and exotic resorts. Today I regret not having had the opportunity to have spent more time with my family. Now in semi-retirement, I am no different from millions of other grandfathers who try to make up for lost time with their own children by doting over their grandchildren. But, even if I had to do it all over again, I might well make the same mistakes. I was a man driven by a desire to reach for the stars from the bottom of the pit, who saw the endless hours at work not as an end in itself but as a means to secure a place for my family on the right side of the tracks. Whatever time I spent away from my family, I reasoned, was for their sake because all this work was for their security and well-being. Never, I decided, would I want to see them suffer my deprived childhood.

At the same time, it would be downright dishonest on my part to deny that I enjoyed the excitement of competition and the joy of victory against great odds. Show me an entrepreneur who does not revel in risk-taking and, in my opinion, you have a loser on your hands. Real business comes with calculated risks, often of the kind that causes sleepless nights. When it pays off, it rewards with highs never imagined by the run-of-the-mill salaried soul, and when it does not, it pushes you back into such depths that you might wish you had a regular day job after all. It was simply in my nature to look for new, seemingly impossible challenges and to go for it with all my might.

In 1967, as our factory was taking shape in Potchefstroom, I received an invitation to attend an executive management course at Columbia University. Even though I was not involved in the day-to-day activity on site, I felt I needed to be available at short notice. During this interim period, however, someone talked me into taking up golf for much-needed relaxation away from the pressures at work. But in my case it turned out to be all but relaxation. It was simply another challenge to be mastered at all cost. While others might play golf simply to enjoy the walk and the company and be content with high handicaps, I tackled the game with an almost grim determination. I had to prove to myself that I could bring down my handicap to single digits in a matter of months. So I took lessons and hit balls until my hands hurt. As a result, I managed to reach a very low handicap before other pressing commitments forced me to give up the game altogether. But I never lost my love for the game. Recently, my youngest son Louis dragged me along to a course near my home at Ballito. I managed to play respectably until we reached a long par three with a sizeable pond protecting the green. After dumping several sleeves of balls in the drink before reaching the green, I finally decided to leave my old set of stiff-shaft clubs to rust away happily in storage while I pursue other less frustrating diversions.

48

In December 1967 the factory at Potchefstroom had gone through all its tests and was declared ready to be unveiled and put into full production. Instead of a few shovels and a battered old shed in Sasolburg, we now had a state-of-the-art plant that added industrial skyline to this Western Transvaal city. The grand opening was held only a few days before Christmas, replete with festive flags, mountains of food and rivers of champagne. The mayor and other prominent townspeople turned out in full force to welcome us to their midst – as did the agricultural cooperatives and the farmers who helped make it possible by investing in Triomf. Even Ed Muldoon, a director of Esso Europe, flew in especially for the occasion and his local managing director, Jim Campbell, delivered a speech on behalf of Esso.

The only cabinet minister who turned up and spoke at the event was Carel de Wet, who would later become a good friend. I did not expect him to explain or apologise for the absence of the other ministers who had been invited, but had made lame excuses. We both understood. The Afrikaner government, quite simply, did not favour me. I made the closing speech of the day. I kept it short and light, mentioning our intention to change the fertiliser scene in South Africa, and injecting a little friendly ribbing of the opposition. I guess the members of the cartel were not amused. But the press, who attended in full force, saw it for what it was and the reports were friendly to furiously favourable. In 1995 when, as president of SARFU, I used the same kind of banter in a speech at a dinner after South Africa narrowly beat New Zealand in the World Cup, all hell broke loose in the press. But then much had happened in the interceding thirty years to sour the attitude of the media towards me.

Those who expected to see a fierce fight in the fertiliser field were not disappointed. Bags with the name Triomf emblazoned across a broken oval were turning up in heavy truckloads across the entire Western Transvaal and the Orange Free State. We were selling them as fast as they came off the bagging line. But then, in 1969, the cartel struck back. News came in from the field that the Big Two had pulled their entire sales force from the coastal regions to attack us in our own back yard, and my salespeople were complaining that they were heavily outnumbered. I called an urgent strategy meeting at our offices in Braamfontein, Johannesburg, on a Sunday. Every salesman had a story to tell, and it was obvious that the opposition was eroding our market. After listening carefully to these reports, I turned to Malcolm Moodie, one of our top sales managers, and said: 'Malcolm, you go to the Cape, contact the biggest farmer and offer him a 20 per cent discount on his fertiliser. Only this one farmer. No one else.'

'And you, Gus,' I said to Gus Giradeau, our man from Natal, 'you find the biggest farmer in Natal and make him the same offer. Remember, only one farmer. No more.'

The sales team were horrified and looked at me as if I was deranged, ready to declare me incompetent at the helm and stage a mutiny.

'We will lose our company,' someone said, incredulity clearly showing on his face. 'We don't have enough money to fight the combined strength of the cartel. They're going to kill us.'

'No,' I replied calmly, hoping that a few lingering self-doubts about my master strategy would not surface, 'we're going to kill them.'

'This,' I explained, 'is how I think it is going to work. When they hear about our offer to the two top farmers in the Cape and Natal, you can bet your bottom dollar that they will pull back their salesmen from our area and try to save their business back there by making the same offer or even better to all their clients. And if they don't, you can be sure that we will let the farmers who were left out know that they are paying more for their product than other favoured clients. In the meantime, we can take a loss on just those two farmers we approach.'

It worked. Barely two days after our Sunday meeting, the cartel pulled back its mercenary forces to their home base in the Cape and Natal to respond to our 'challenge'. They were all over the place, making matching offers while we returned to our favoured market in the Western Transvaal and Free State without much opposition.

Next came a call from René du Toit, a director of AE & CI, which would later become known as AECI. Speaking on behalf of the cartel, he requested an urgent meeting to discuss a ceasefire and, hopefully, a truce. I agreed and within a matter of days, a delegation consisting of Du Toit and George Mrkusic turned up at my office. They came with their cards facing up.

'How on earth do you think you can survive with these kind of actions in a price-controlled environment?' they asked. 'We're just killing each other and it will get us nowhere.'

My response, I gather, was no surprise to them either. I held the trump card and did not mind showing it: 'As you can see, gentlemen, Triomf is not afraid to do battle with you. After all, we are no longer just a new upstart you can try to dismiss. We have Esso behind us, remember. So you have a choice. Either come to your senses or this fight will continue.'

'But that is why we're here,' Du Toit ventured, looking across the table at his fellow cartel member for silent approval. 'We want to offer you a share of the market.'

So this is what it had come to. The cartel had decided to stretch and bend the oval link in the chain before it was broken. They had decided to allow the upstart into the club. But at what price?

'And what do you offer?' I asked.

'Well, we were thinking of giving you your present market share with a growth potential twice the actual market growth for five years.'

The numbers raced through my head. The fertiliser market was currently growing at 5 per cent per year. Triomf had a market share of 17.4 per cent. That meant that we could end up with 27 per cent of the total market. Quite a generous offer. But not good enough for someone so seriously courted by the opposition. Up the ante, I decided. Don't show any mercy. After all, this is not an Old Boys' Club. This is a marriage of convenience. Everything had to be done on a prenuptial basis. Later was too late.

I had a quick word outside with Philip Clarke, who sat in on the meeting. 'Let's go for it,' he recommended, 'but insist that the ratio of nitrogen to phosphates to potassium remains the same – in other words, we will stay as mainly phosphate producers and, given our existing sales mix, the other fast-growing plant-food ingredients will, in tandem, pull up our phosphate sales.' This was an excellent suggestion, I immediately agreed.

'Look, gentlemen, Triomf has just over 17 per cent of the market right now. Provided our sales-mix ratio remains the same, we are willing to accept your offer.'

They looked at each other in disbelief. Their opponent, they must have thought, had just shown himself to be a real pushover. One offer and he caves in and accepts.

'Then it is all agreed,' Du Toit said as Mrkusic nodded with a knowing smile.

'Deal,' I confirmed, slightly taken aback by their own gullibility.

The time had come for a celebration over lunch to induct the new member of the somewhat expanded cartel – the fellow who proved to be a much easier pushover than anyone had thought, the toothless tiger called Triomf.

All the while I was wondering how seasoned businessmen could have entered into such an open-ended deal without considering its ramifications. The least they could have done was to review market data before they made such a rash decision. At that time, the market for nitrogen was growing at a whopping 40 per cent per year and potassium at 17 per cent, while phosphate was languishing at a mere 2.5 per cent growth. Phosphate was, however, about three times more profitable than any of the other plant foods and, being a phosphate producer, this deal was like manna from heaven. By agreeing to our terms, the other two had just given Triomf a huge slice of the phosphate market – so much so that they would have to cut back on their own production of this prize product to facilitate Triomf's newly negotiated market share.

But it took the Big Two a few days to figure this all out, but in the end they did, with the help of the Fedmis accounting supremo, Cecil Robinson. This time Alan Milne, the tough managing director of AE & CI, made the call. They had obviously decided to bring in a heavy hitter to try to salvage something from the ruins. Milne was regarded as a shrewd businessman – and deservedly so. Representing the interests of ICI in AE & CI, he was shocked, even angered, by this deal struck on his company's behalf. He came out, guns blazing.

'Mr Luyt, if you think I am going to close some of my phosphate facilities to satisfy Triomf, you've another think coming!'

'No,' I said, 'all I want from you is to adhere to the agreement entered into a few days ago. Nothing more, nothing less. How you manage to rearrange your own affairs to stay within the agreement is for you to decide.'

For several seconds there was dead silence. Then his voice, heavy with quiet determination...

'There will be no agreement unless you relent on your phosphate quota.'

I responded softly with the assurance of someone who knew he had the law on his side.

'I suggest you think again, Mr Milne. Think it over before you act.'

My tone was courteous but firm. There was a definite need to keep the lines of communication open, to keep the peace.

The next call came from George Mrkusic of Fedmis, imploring me to renegotiate. So we got together to redraft the agreement, which in fact suited Triomf quite well in as far as the phosphate content of the sale mix was concerned. Triomf could sell its entire phosphate output, and that suited us 100 per cent. The cartel appreciated my reasonable attitude. But my mind was already racing ahead to the next battle in what I knew was going to be an ongoing war despite our temporary truce. Until this day, of course, it puzzles me that none among the cartel could have figured out that Triomf was in no position at the time to have supplied the huge quantities of phosphates it was entitled to under the initial agreement.

In 1968, after the fiercest price war in the history of the fertiliser industry, Triomf firmly established and entrenched itself in the market place, and in 1969 our profits soared past the R1-million mark. Peter Nash of Fisons would later concede that his company, big as it was thought to be, could never match that kind of profit. In another scoop, during 1968, Triomf acquired the services of a previous boss of mine, John Norton, as its marketing manager. Through the years, he stood loyally at my side as we challenged not only the cartel but foreign competitors in established export markets. John, in fact, became a director soon after he joined me.

In 1968 I received two rather flattering offers. One I declined and the other I accepted with gratitude. The first came from Esso. They offered me the executive chairmanship of all their South African operations. But my future, I felt, was inextricably tied to Triomf, which I truly believed was destined to outgrow the so-called Big Two, so I declined. The second came via a telephone call from Stephen Mulholland, the exceptionally talented editor of the Sunday Times 'Business Times' and later the doyen of the publishing world and, in my book, the man who should be the Minister of Trade and Industry combined with the Finance portfolio. Mulholland told me I had been selected as one of their five Businessmen of the Year.

Even though tough business executives are not supposed to show emotion, I have to admit that this first recognition of my efforts to excel in the tough corporate environment against heavy odds, still stands out as a very special moment. Other similar and even greater awards were to follow, but nothing equals the first time when one is paraded as an achiever at a glittering gala dinner in front of much more accomplished peers.

Despite outward appearances of a happy relationship with Esso, tension began to develop during 1968 as Jim Campbell tried to become increasingly involved in the decision-making process at Triomf. It was, no doubt, a little naïve on my part to believe that Esso would maintain their hands-off approach and be content to simply share in the good profits. No big brother acts that way. More importantly, however, were growing fears on my part that Esso might one day, without prior notice, simply rid itself of its shareholding by selling out to a much less forgiving partner. Big conglomerates tend to have great muscle but no heart. I decided that the time had thus come to pre-empt the possibility of such a sale.

I contacted The Netherlands Bank of Southern Africa (Nedbank) and explained my fears. Gerry Muller and the chief general manager, Kurt de Braal, who had taken a gamble before that paid off rather handsomely, saw no reason why they should not come to my rescue again. They promised to underwrite any buy-out offer to Esso. With my attorney, Laurie Pereira, I flew to Brussels in February 1969 and met with Bob Winslow, chairman of Esso Europe. I held an ace up my sleeve. A fax message meant for Campbell of Esso South Africa had been erroneously despatched to Triomf headquarters. It was damaging in as much as it questioned my ability to purchase their shareholding and came dangerously close to accusing me of using company funds to achieve this - in itself a serious criminal offence.

Of course, this was the first document I presented when I met with Winslow, who subsequently changed colours like a chameleon, finally blushing a bright crimson. 'Overzealous staff work,' he blustered without much effect. But that gave me the high ground and I slaughtered Winslow in the ensuing negotiations. It took us just one day of intensive bargaining to come to an agreement, which – needless to say – was very favourable for me. That same afternoon, all the necessary documents were completed with the help of Pereira and the Esso lawyers and signed by Winslow and me. Esso had sold its 50 per cent shareholding back to me for R3.5 million.

During 1969, Triomf had the rights issue for R3 million to finance its phosphoric acid plant, and this pushed Esso's share – excluding the shares held by me in my private company – to R3.5 million. In effect, I thus bought the Esso shareholding of slightly more than R4.5 million well below the par value, but of course this was not known to anybody else but Esso and myself. This deal would have a marked influence on my personal finances.

Laurie Pereira and I then proceeded to our embassy in Brussels where the ambassador Fritz Steyn countersigned and authenticated the agreement, drawn up in terms of South African law. Steyn was, as we were, pleased with the deal I entered into with Esso because we all decided it was not only good for Luyt, but also for Triomf's other shareholders and the country as a whole.

On our return flight to Johannesburg, Laurie and I had ample time to speculate over what the press would make of this story. There was no doubt on our part that this would be the lead item once the news broke. Our public relations manager, Wollie Wolmarans, who came to us from *Die Vaderland* in 1966, would have to be fully briefed to make sure that we received maximum mileage for this new phase in the existence of Triomf – free from any potential foreign control, thanks once again to Nedbank's backing. But although we had the bank's promise of support, we still had to work out details of how we would structure the financing of the deal. So we threw around ideas and prepared ourselves for the formality of putting the seal on the deal the day after we returned to Johannesburg.

The 'mere formality', however, turned out to be a formidable shock. Gerry Muller and his colleagues at Nedbank stared blankly at me as I showed them the terms of the agreement between Esso and myself and started explaining the payment schedule. I wondered for one moment whether I was at the right bank, talking to the right people. Well, I tried to reassure myself, that must just be the way bankers look when they do serious business too early in the morning. I was wrong.

'But you have a partner, don't you?' asked Muller.

'You are the only partners I have at this stage,' I explained. 'But I will try to sell most of my local holdings as long as I can retain control. In any event, you will have sufficient shares as well as my own security as collateral.'

Muller's face crumpled in pain. He was a good man and a friend, but suddenly he found himself unable to help.

'The bank is too small to finance this deal,' he said.

'But why didn't you tell me this before?' I enquired, anger and disappointment showing in my voice. 'I left here with the clear and full understanding that you could do it.'

Muller was not a man to shirk responsibility, and he realised that they had sent the wrong signal. One man who could help, he felt, was his chairman, Frans Cronjé. Just as Cronjé in his wisdom had sent me to Muller a few years earlier when I was desperate for a loan to tide me over after the Hurter debacle, Muller now passed the buck back to Cronjé. This mild-mannered banker whom I had come to respect and like so much once again proved to be a saviour of sorts.

'Well,' he summed up after listening to both Muller and me. 'Louis left for Europe with the clear understanding that this bank was going to back him. You,

Gerry, seemed to have thought that he would immediately be able to get a new partner. So we have to find one.'

Muller and I stared hopefully at the cherubic figure across the table, rubbing his chin in deep thought.

'South African Breweries are looking for investments,' he mused. 'They're sitting on too much cash, anyway.' Then he stood up to signal the end of our meeting. 'Let me speak to Dick Goss about it.'

As we walked out of his office, both Muller and I knew what 'speaking to Goss' meant. After all, Dr Frans Cronjé was the widely respected chairman of both Nedbank and South African Breweries (SAB).

'Now I think it is going to depend on how well you and Goss can get along,' Muller said as we reached the front foyer of The Netherlands Bank building. 'It's going to be interesting to see how it turns out. You're both headstrong guys...'

Muller did not have to wait long for his answer. True to his word, Frans Cronjé signalled Dick Goss to give me a call, which he did without delay. He was ready to meet me at my earliest convenience. I went across to his offices and we immediately got down to business. That was his style. He impressed me with his straightforward, candid manner and quick grasp – a relaxed man completely at ease in his impressive tall frame and a voice that carried authority. In a way, I guess, I saw Goss as a long-lost brother. This, I soon discovered, would be one case where sameness instead of opposites attracted. Until today, despite the bloody battles we waged against each other in the ensuing years, I respect him immensely and consider him a special friend.

Goss wasted no time. He asked for financial reports and projections, management accounts and the like. I ordered them up and handed him a full set of records, including the impressive market share agreement with the Big Two. I offered Goss the opportunity to have his accountants verify any of the records with my personnel as they saw fit. He then handed the job to his top financial Barsab (Barlow's and SAB's joint venture) man and chartered accountant, Pat Latham. At the time, Latham handled the portfolio for Breweries and I was so impressed by him that I later recruited him to join our ranks at Triomf.

A follow-up meeting was scheduled so that we could discuss the exact extent of South African Breweries' proposed involvement. Goss was happy with what he saw. He wanted in. Representing a company where cash was spilling over like the froth in a hastily poured glass of beer, the cash infusion I needed was , in fact, relatively small fry. I was, however, afraid that he would come with the suggestion to buy a majority share and I would, of course, have to refuse. But Goss, I discovered, knew better. While SAB might insist on full control of everything else they purchased, he seemed to have known that pushing that far with someone who was as intent as he was to keep control in his own domain, would be a sure deal killer.

'I would like to buy into the company,' Goss announced. 'We would like to have 50 per cent and are willing to pay a premium on that.' By the way, he added, Breweries can also be helpful with cheaper finance.

'How much extra are you willing to pay?' I asked nonchalantly, quite relieved that he came with a request I could meet.

'How about 15 per cent?' he suggested.

'We have a deal,' I said. In fact, since I had more than two million Triomf shares tucked away in a private company – a fact known only by Esso and me – my fortunes jumped overnight by almost R6 million.

The new partnership, settled with Breweries in April 1969, meant much more than just money. Triomf, already considered a rising star on the business horizon, had greatly enhanced its public image by entering into a major deal with another frontrunner. The financial press sung the praises of this new partnership in an endless flow of articles and special reports. Both Dick Goss and I had reason to celebrate with champagne instead of beer. It was, as some reporters saw it, a sparkling deal. Profits were soaring and both Goss and my mentor, Frans Cronjé, had good reason to trust their own judgment. Gerry Muller, too, felt vindicated. Nedbank, of course, remained my bankers.

One year after South African Breweries joined us I received a call from Andries Beyers, chairman of one of the country's biggest cooperative societies. He had an urgent and important proposal. The co-ops, he explained, wanted to acquire a substantial stake in Triomf. The idea immediately appealed to me. Here were our major current and potential future clients ready to get a piece of the action. What better way to ensure an almost total hold on the all-important agricultural market?

So it was that I agreed to meet in Pretoria with a delegation led by Beyers – only to discover, to my own dismay, that the same group had already had discussions with Fedmis, the new entity formed by the amalgamation of Fisons and Windmill Fertilisers. This marriage was, no doubt, necessitated by the need to survive as Triomf entered the ranks of the cartel and rapidly taking market share from these two companies in its battle with AE & CI for the top spot.

Now the new entity, Federale Kunsmis (Fedmis), represented 47 per cent of the market against AE & CI's 33 per cent and Triomf's 20 per cent. The use of an Afrikaans name for the new joint holding by two traditionally English-speaking companies was obviously geared towards ingratiating themselves with the largely Afrikaans-speaking farming community. There was no doubt that, in partnership with the cooperatives, Fedmis might well have been able to establish a lasting dominance in the fertiliser industry. Instead, it had overplayed its hand by being too demanding and this had thus prompted Beyers to shop around for a better deal at Triomf. I knew I had to move fast before Fedmis came back to resume negotiations with a more reasonable offer in hand.

56

'Gentlemen,' I said to the cooperative leaders, 'I have to run this by my partners, SAB. So you have to give me an indication today of what you want and how quickly you're willing to move.' After all, the shares had to come from SAB and myself.

'We have the money,' Beyers announced while the others nodded in agreement. 'It is merely question of price and percentage.'

'How much do you want?' I asked.

'Not less than 40 per cent,' came the reply.

'That's one helluva chunk,' I replied, putting on the serious look of a man asked to sell his birthright. 'But I cannot think of a better group of people to be partners with in this business. After all, you are in a way already involved as prime clients. Let's do the deal.'

A quick mental calculation indicated to me that I would have to sell half of my holding and 60 per cent of the SAB holding to satisfy the demands of the co-ops. That meant that the Breweries and I would still have 40 per cent of the company and would be on par with the cooperative shareholding in Triomf.

The cooperatives were willing to pay a premium, and South African Breweries stood to make a handsome profit, but still I walked out a little uneasy. I had just sold 60 per cent of SAB shares in Triomf, without even conferring with Goss. As soon as I left the meeting, I rushed to the nearest phone and tried to reach Goss. He was out of reach down in Cape Town, his office told me, but was scheduled to be returning that evening.

Philip Clarke, my exceptional accounting assistant who was to prove his worth in later take-overs and mergers, drove with me to Johannesburg's Jan Smuts Airport. Goss was surprised to see us and, it seemed, a little concerned.

'What's up?' he asked, with a frown. 'Something wrong?'

'Send your driver home,' I said, smiling reassuringly. 'I'll take you. We have much to talk about.'

'Bad news?'

'No,' I assured him as we got into the car. 'Dick, I have just committed you to selling 60 per cent of your holdings in Triomf.'

'You have done what?' he exclaimed. 'How the hell could you have done that? You're joking, aren't you.'

'No, I'm serious, Dick. And you know what? You got a 100 per cent profit in barely a year and are still part of the action. We remain in control.'

'Why did you not sell the whole damn lot,' Goss chuckled as he broke into a broad smile. 'Come on, this calls for a celebration. Let's stop in at my house and drink all the Amstel I have. And that, gentlemen, is one helluva lot of Amstel!'

That evening we made a small dent in Goss' almost unlimited supply of beer while talking about the implications of this hastily concocted deal with the agricultural cooperatives. How vast its impact would be, we could not quite fathom then. Even with a few beers behind us, we still ended up on the moderate side.

In reality, our partnership with the cooperatives meant that we had acquired an almost total lock on the market. In terms of our market-sharing agreement, Triomf was, of course, still obliged to pass along some orders or to make payouts to the other two. Even if we wanted to, we did not have the capacity to fill all the orders that crossed our desks at Triomf. We urgently needed greater production capacity. I realised that Fedmis would be the last one to talk deals, so my focus shifted to AE & CI. My relations with Fedmis had deteriorated almost beyond repair when I started selling over my quota in response to their unilateral discounting to cut into our markets.

So, one June morning in 1970, during a telephone conversation with Alan Milne of AE & CI, with whom I had developed a warm relationship despite our initial skirmishes, I remarked rather casually: 'Why don't you sell your Modderfontein factory to me?'

'Do you have the R25 million to pay for it?' he shot back at me in typical combative fashion.

'Come on, Alan,' I said, 'I'm just interested in buying Modderfontein. I don't want all of AE & CI's fertiliser interests. But why don't you come over and have tea with me so we can have a serious discussion?'

That same day he turned up at my office. But he was not alone. An entourage of managers followed him and we moved to the boardroom where I was joined by some of my staff in an impromptu preliminary negotiation.

'I was dead serious with my offer,' I informed Milne. I looked at the faces around the table and then turned my attention back to him. 'You and I and all your colleagues know that Modderfontein is not worth that much. But why don't we talk about something more important? How about us getting together, merging our fertiliser interests?'

The usually unflappable and self-assured Milne looked as if he was going to fall off his chair in surprise.

'Are you serious now?' he asked as he collected himself. 'That seems like a great idea.'

'So why don't you sound out Mr Oppenheimer.'

Like Frans Cronjé in his domain, Harry Oppenheimer held a tight control over the multitude of subsidiaries operating under the large Anglo American umbrella. Without his blessing, any talk of such a deal would be a futile and fruitless exercise, a mere pipe dream.

Later that day I received a call from Harry Oppenheimer in person, the dean of South African business and, in his time, arguably one of the world's wealthiest and smartest entrepreneurs. In his trademark soft-spoken, almost modest, manner, he informed me that Milne had spoken to him and that he liked the idea. He had already phoned ICI, the other major shareholder in AE & CI, and they were in full agreement. Negotiations, Oppenheimer suggested, should start immediately.

I then relayed the news to Dick Goss and the cooperatives. They were delighted with the prospect of forming an alliance with this formidable player. Next, in terms of the standing agreement between the cartel, we and AE & CI had to inform Fedmis about our intention to combine forces. Naturally, the idea did not appeal to them but being the product of a recent merger itself, Fedmis had little option but to give its approval, albeit reluctantly and with a great measure of justified reservations.

It wasn't long before the story reached the press and the buzz started. One day it was Luyt's Triomf that was going to call the shots. The next it was AECI that would take control.

Then the deal was off. Then it was all on again. The suspense kept the story going for days. Typical of the kind of speculation at the time was a report in Johannesburg's *The Star* on 18 July 1970. The headline shouted, 'Luyt nears a fertiliser triumph'.

'Mr Louis Luyt, 38-year-old Afrikaans business tycoon of Saxonwold in Johannesburg, is about to gain control of more than half of the country's fertiliser market.

'An announcement that Triomf Fertilisers, of which he is managing director, is about to take over certain fertiliser interests of African Explosives and Chemical Industries (AE & CI) is expected within the next few days. AE & CI is part of the Anglo American Corporation.

'Negotiations have reached an advanced stage. But nobody was available to comment. Mr Luyt flew to Durban early today to meet his sales staff.

'An announcement can only be made when the boards of the big three in the fertiliser world have all ratified any agreement that has been reached.

'It was learnt that negotiations between Mr Luyt and the board of AE & CI have been going on for about a week, with the full knowledge of the third – and so far the biggest – company, Federale Kunsmis (Fedmis).

'If agreement is reached, Mr Luyt will get control of more than 50 per cent of the country's fertiliser market. Last season Federale Kunsmis had between 45 and 47 per cent of the market, AE & CI about one third and Triomf less than 20 per cent.

'The new move can be seen as a direct result of the recent short-lived price war that stemmed from Mr Luyt's efforts to capture a larger slice of the fertiliser market. He was obviously confident that it could be done as four of the five biggest maize cooperatives in the country have taken over 40 per cent of Triomf's capital. As they finance the fertiliser bills of their members, they would naturally prefer to buy from their own company.

'But Triomf's factory at Potchefstroom was unable to produce the huge quantities they would require. AE & CI has several fertiliser factories and provided the obvious answer to Mr Luyt's problems.'

In the meantime, hard bargaining continued behind closed doors. Before the end of July AE & CI agreed to the unthinkable. They accepted an arrangement in which Triomf would hold 51 per cent and AE & CI 49 per cent of a new company to be formed, Triomf Fertiliser (Pty) Ltd.

There is no doubt in my mind that the presence of the cooperatives in my ranks forced my former foes at AE & CI to accept this deal. AE & CI moved from being the biggest in the fertiliser business to seeking a minor partnership with the same Triomf they dismissed as a mere upstart barely three years previously. Not only did it agree to leave control in our hands, it also conceded to have the name Triomf remain and leave me in full charge of operations. It must have been a bitter pill to swallow, having the same man you once wrote off as a passing nuisance as the new boss. But AE & CI knew that without the cooperatives on their side, they were doomed to shrink. Throughout these negotiations I was able to draw on the expert services and advice of Pat Latham who had joined us from South African Breweries, and John Norton, as well as a team of loyal colleagues who were intent on seeing Triomf pull off its ultimate triumph.

The announcement of this landmark deal between the young Afrikaner and the sage Harry Oppenheimer was emblazoned on front-page headlines across the country. The *Rand Daily Mail* carried the bold headline, 'Luyt–AE & CI deal is on', with a strapline that read, 'Triomf will gain bulk of fertiliser trade'.

'Reports of an impending deal between Mr Louis Luyt of the Triomf Group and AE & CI – to give Mr Luyt controlling interest in the marketing of a major portion of fertilisers in South Africa – are confirmed in an announcement on the fertiliser situation, released yesterday,' the *Mail* reported.

This arrangement, the newspaper noted, would place more than 50 per cent of the market under the control of the new Triomf and the remainder in the hands of Fedmis and two small producers. The Big Three had become the Big Two, with Triomf and its new partner, AE & CI, the largest in the country. By the end of 1970, Triomf had captured 56 per cent of the total market.

The year 1970 was, in fact, a very good year, indeed. After having been selected as Businessman of the Year by *Rapport* and Industrialist of the Year by the *Financial Gazette*, of particular importance to me was the latter opportunity to follow in the footsteps of men I admired, such as Harry Oppenheimer and Dr Frans Cronjé. The fact that among those past honourees who joined me on stage were some of my most bitter foes and detractors did not bother me as much as it must have irked them to see me receive the prestigious *Sunday Times* 'Business Times' award.

Early in 1971 a team of reporters from the *Financial Mail* arrived at my office for an in-depth interview. A brief extract from their multi-page account recaps in my own words at the time the strategies and the factors that led to Triomf's ultimate success:

'*Financial Mail*, 16 April 1971 – A Man Called Luyt.

'An FM interviewing team went to see SA's whiz kid, Louis Luyt, and bombarded him with questions about himself, Triomf and his future plans. Louis Luyt faced the FM's interviewing team of Mike Wesfmacoft, Ken Romain, Mike Coulson and Garth Tomkinson.

'Optimistic, foolhardy and heavily reliant on Afrikaner sentiment rather than sound economics. These were some of the observations and comments not only of the national press but also, alas, of the FM on Louis Luyt's brash entry into the fertiliser market in 1965. Less than six years later, Triomf, Louis Luyt's vehicle, has total assets in excess of R17 million, a turnover approaching R60 million per annum and control of more than half SA's fertiliser sales.

'It is little wonder that a mystique surrounds Louis Luyt, for he's something of a phenomenon.

'Q. To what do you attribute Triomf's astonishingly swift rise to predominance in the fertiliser industry?

'A. Complacency on the part of other people. We came into a market where there was an arrangement on market sharing. Now obviously, in this sort of market, there is an element of complacency.

'Q. Did they take you seriously at first?

'A. Of course they didn't.

'Q. And you really got established before they started bothering about you?

'A. I suppose if I had been in their position, I wouldn't have bothered. We came in at the worst time of the year, in the worst drought; but perhaps this helped towards our success.

'Q. What could the big companies have done to defend themselves at the time?

'A. The big boys had the opportunity to do exactly what I did and if they had done it at the time, they would most probably have countered me.

'Q. But within the framework of the quota system, how could one of the big boys have done what you did?

'A. What I did was to issue shares to the farmers; as you know, they could have done exactly the same without affecting the quotas.

'Q. Did you have a broadly conceived take-over strategy from the start or did it just develop?

'A. It was ad hoc; we took advantage of the situations as they developed.

'Q. But you must have had the merger with AE & CI in mind when SA Breweries sold part of its interest in Triomf to the co-ops?

'A. Breweries didn't sell it. I sold it. Breweries didn't even know about it until I went to them and said, "I can give you so much money for your shares."

'Q. Did you go to AE & CI or did they come to you?

'A. I phoned and said I would like to see them as I was interested in Modderfontein, and they came to me. However the price they asked was far too much and we didn't get anywhere.

'Q. They came prepared to sell?

'A. Yes. But they didn't want to give it away. That made me think. I pointed out that there was a situation of price-cutting and deteriorating profits, and I told them that I thought that we could overcome this if they were willing to discuss a merger with me, with Triomf in control. They were quick to grasp the importance of such a move and the same afternoon they went to see Oppenheimer and had a call through to ICI in London. Later that day the financial director of Anglo American, Grey Fletcher, and AE & CI MD Alan Milne came to my offices to discuss the possibilities and we all but finalised it that evening.

'Q. What were your relative shares in the market at that stage?

'A. At that stage we had 23 per cent, which we could not keep up as we didn't have the capacity. Their share was 34 per cent, but they weren't on 34 per cent – they had about 28 per cent.

'Q. How did this discrepancy arise?

'A. Well, we must have taken it somewhere.

'Q. So you were in fact selling more than your quota?

'A. Yes, at that stage a lot more; this was after the co-ops had come in.

'Q. Were you not breaking the agreement?

'A. Perhaps. But when the co-ops were brought in, we had a discussion with Fedmis and they asked us what our aims were. So I said that obviously we were aiming to get a higher percentage of the market. We were still discussing when Fedmis broke out and started to cut prices.

'Q. So you effectively tore up the agreement?

'A. Yes. And so the alternative facing AE & CI was either to merge with us or see profit margins cut to ribbons.

'Q. What would you say is your own specific area of expertise?

'A. That's difficult, I am not really an expert at anything. I am more the guy with a feel for things. And then I get the experts to work it out. Perhaps you could call it marketing.

'Q. Where do you go from here?

'A. We have so many big things that we want to do.'

Already my mind was racing ahead and I was looking for new ventures and other challenges to conquer. Triomf was well on its way now, and was being run by competent people. The time had come for me to climb the next mountain. Little did I anticipate that this new journey would pitch me into a no-holds-barred struggle against a long-time friend and partner and that it would spark a war in some ways so fierce that it made the struggles of the sixties look like a school-hostel pillow fight.

They who drink beer will think beer.

Washington Irving
US author
1783–1859

Chapter 5

SHORT-CHANGING BACCHUS

It was April 1970. At the age of 38, I had had the privilege to join the ranks of Harry Oppenheimer and Frans Cronjé and the satisfaction to be placed at the same table with a long list of other so-called captains of industry – some of whom, I gather, would rather have seen me eat in the kitchen. I was at last considered part of the very establishment that fought so hard to keep me out. For most people of my age, this might have been a time to simply sit back, enjoy the fruits of their labour, concentrate on maintaining the status quo and protect their new-found wealth.

There were the outward spoils of success that I thoroughly enjoyed. Adri and I could at last afford to transform the old house we had acquired in the Saxonwold suburb of Johannesburg in 1966 into a comfortable retreat for our family. We added rooms and a few luxuries and called it Solitaire. Our retreat from the bustle of business needed expansion as our family grew from three to four children with the arrival of another son on 28 September 1968. We named this strong-willed new arrival, Louis Luyt, after his father. He entered the world with the assurance that no one would question his claim to this name and also with the resolve on our part that neither he nor his siblings would ever have to go through the same humiliation their father did. That, after all, is the universal trademark of caring parenthood. We all make it our goal to give our children a better life than our own, only to discover that it is not ours to give. They will find their own way. We can only teach them to walk upright and to stick to set values.

Triomf expanded its offices too. Improved salaries and escalating commissions for salesmen drew additional talent to the company. I have always maintained that growth and profit should not only benefit shareholders and the few at the top but everyone who contributed, from the lowest to the highest. This is how we continued to lure star performers from competitors into our ranks and to beat them at their own game.

We also upgraded our corporate air transport. While some business executives might look at an aircraft as just another perk of high office, I have always viewed it as an important tool in a market where instant mobility and face-to-face meetings with clients counted. We started with a one prop and then progressed to the twin-engine Comanche, then a luxury twin-engine Cessna before I finally purchased a Lear jet in 1968. Two years later, as we set our sights overseas, the need arose for a jet aircraft with a longer range. In September 1970, the *Sunday Express*, describing me as 'one of the country's most air-minded businessmen', carried a story about the Falcon 20D that we were acquiring from French manufacturer Marcel Dassault. Designed to accommodate ten people and a crew of three in complete luxury, this new acquisition would give the Louis Luyt Group longer reach and additional mobility in the crowded overseas market. At the same time, we found other enterprises eager to charter our planes during times when we were not using them. In fact, we happened to be pioneers in this field long before it became popular in South Africa. We again experienced an objection to a charter licence by the ruling government; this time through their national carrier, South African Airways.

The *Sunday Express* quoted me as saying that my wife would be accompanying me and my crew to Paris to fetch the plane. 'My wife says she wants to spend a week in Paris before we come home,' I was reported telling the *Express*. 'But (said the man whose 15 companies have an annual turnover of about R80 million) I told her we couldn't possibly afford it. Mind you, I suppose she will get her way in the end.' Here I was, able to joke about affording things that would have seemed way beyond the furthest constellation when I stared skywards at the stars from the bottom of the pit during my early Bloemfontein days.

These companies ranged from fertiliser to funding, sports equipment to sponsorship, publishing to petroleum, and leasing to real estate. In its Louis Luyt Brewery prospectus in 1971, LLG explained its business range and philosophy as follows:

'The Louis Luyt Group (LLG) is a conglomerate of companies with interests as diverse as petroleum and construction. The unifying factor is that all the companies are strongly marketing-orientated. Underlying all the LLG operations is the technique of establishing where a need exists and then providing a solution; or examining a market which is being indifferently served and then providing an enhanced service.

'The company made a profit of 1.4 million Rands (±US$2 million) for the 12 months to March 31. Then, in August, agreement was reached for the merging of the African Explosives and Chemical Industries' phosphoric fertiliser interests

Left: With OFS team members arriving to play Transvaal (and winning) in 1956.

OFS warm up before a match against Border in 1956 with me, third from the right.

Trials in 1957 and I show my serious intent in the tackle.

Playing against Northern Transvaal in 1957. I'm in the scrumcap with Mof Myburgh behind. Mof made his debut for Northern Transvaal that day.

Our wedding day, 13 December 1958.

Our wedding day in 1958. My parents-in-law Dirk and Cornelia Kotze are on Adri's left and my stepfather Charles Luyt and my mother Petronella on my right.

with those of Triomf and a new company, Triomf Fertiliser (Pty) Ltd, was formed to hold these enhanced interests. The result was a company supplying approximately 55 per cent of the local South African market and turning over R60 million annually.

'Meanwhile, there had been a parallel expansion of Mr Luyt's personal interests – interests that are now formally known as the Louis Luyt Group. Among the more important companies in the LLG stable are:

'Senkor is the cornerstone of the Luyt interests is financing and is a direct sequel to the rather despondent events in 1965 when the nascent Triomf was unable to find a South African financial institution to back its plans. Mr Luyt is convinced that there are many South African ideas in search of financial backing, ideas that are all too often stillborn because of the reluctance of present day financiers to explore any but the obvious roads of investment. In an increasingly tight money market Senkor's favourable liquidity has enabled the group to take advantage of several high yield or fast-growth investment opportunities. While the investment section of LLG is helping others to initiate and carry through useful new enterprises, the Group has also initiated several ventures of its own.

'LLG Petroleum is a wholly-owned subsidiary of LLG (Pty) Ltd, an organisation that purchases and distributes in bulk a complete range of petroleum products. By the end of 1971, two years after its formation, this organisation is expected to be in a profit position. At the moment, the distinctive LLG fuel and oil drums are a familiar sight both in agricultural and industrial markets; as soon as government allocations permit, the intention is to move into the retail distribution field.

'Jet Charters was formed by the Louis Luyt Group as a pioneer in jet charter flights in Southern Africa. In 1969, LLG Jet Charters was formed and acquired a 6-seater Lear jet, which overnight outdated previous charter methods. The concept of a flying boardroom, in which the directors of the company could visit installations as far removed as Johannesburg, Nelspruit, Durban and Cape Town in one day, and without the inconvenience of observing airline schedules, quickly attracted clientele from some of South Africa's major organisations. In 1970 the Lear was replaced by a larger and faster Falcon at a cost of R1.1 million.

'Construction LLG was formed in 1970 to undertake building projects, particularly in the field of medium-cost housing. At present, the company is constructing homes on a 31-stand township at Nigel, Transvaal. Other townships are being acquired and the company intends to increase its rate of production until, early in 1972, it should be completing 12 houses per month. The Louis Luyt Group is also promoting a R1.8 million flats scheme at Ballito Bay, about 30 miles north of Durban.

'LLG Sport is the sponsor of the PGA, by far South Africa's richest golf tournament. This is also the division that holds the franchise for Brunswick sports equipment – and, in particular, for the renowned MacGregor golf clubs. It is also the sponsor of the *Rugby Book of the Year*, the leading annual for South Africa's national game.

'Publishing: The Louis Luyt Group is the publisher of the authoritative annual, *South Africa Today*. This publication is designed as a mirror of the South African way of life and is circulated both domestically and abroad in an attempt to create understanding of South Africa's problems and the manner in which they are being tackled. It is a cardinal principle of the LLG philosophy that business can only continue to expand if South Africa rebuffs the forces that are seeking her isolation.'

With all these companies, one might have thought that I had enough on my plate to keep me busy and happy. Newspapers and magazines, which once pooh-poohed my first attempts to climb the corporate ladder, were now coming to me for opinions about the state of the nation's business. On one such an occasion, early in 1971, I told the *Financial Mail* that there were still too many monopolies in the country waiting to be challenged. Little did they know or anticipate that I would soon be embroiled in yet another David-versus-Goliath battle with one of the country's foremost monopolies.

Unlike others who are content to pitch their tent and enjoy the view after reaching the first peak, I had the urge to move on to the next level. I was young still and full of energy and ideas. Mine was a mission not merely to make money but to help change the South African business scene and to further shake up the very establishment that had now reluctantly accepted me in its ranks.

Early in 1971 rumours circulated that the recently built Whitbread brewery at Alrode, near Johannesburg, was not doing well. Run as a partnership between the British brewer Whitbread, the Rupert Group – with a substantial shareholding – and Jan Pickard's wine group, with a minuscule representation, the undertaking seemed doomed to fizzle out. South African Breweries apparently discounted this new undertaking as just another failed attempt at challenging its absolute mastery of the beer market.

Philip Clarke and I happened to be in London on other business when the topic of Whitbread's struggling brewery cropped up in conversation. What, I wondered, would it take to buy that piece of property? That's what people think about when they have cash on hand – picking up bargains and reselling them, or perhaps renting them out. After all, I had a partner in Triomf by the name of Dick Goss who also happened to be in charge of the massive monopolistic South African Breweries. He might be interested in either renting or purchasing this brewery.

'Why don't we meet with them and see what they want for this operation?' I suggested, sipping ale at our hotel between appointments. Clarke smiled unbelievingly.

'You're serious?'

'Worth a try...' I said.

So we made the call. I explained to the operator who we were and what we proposed to do. Next, Whitbread's chairman, a fellow by the name of Bennett, came on the line. Yes, he purred, it would be a real pleasure to meet. Later that same day we arrived at his 'office'. If Bennett felt he had tried to impress upon us a sense of frugality, he certainly succeeded. The head of his South African operations, a Robin Johnson, who also happened to be in town, crammed with us into Bennett's small threadbare attic workspace. Johnson was very much in favour of selling. Knowing all about the struggling operation at Alrode, it did not take any great insight on our part to know why.

'So how much are you willing to offer?' Bennett asked.

'R7 million,' I said.

The look on Bennett's face conveyed a good mix of both injury and some level of disappointment.

'No, Sir, that is not near enough. It's not even close to what it's worth.'

'Well, Mr Bennett, if you change your mind, please let me know,' I said as Philip Clarke and I stood up from our uncomfortable chairs and made our exit down the creaking stairs. Although I did not anticipate it at the time, barely two years later the same Whitbread would try to sell their Alrode Brewery to me for R4 million. But they would be too late. By that stage, I was already constructing my own brewery. It was SAB that bought Whitbread in the end.

'What a bloody office!' Clarke puffed in his English accent, untainted by years of having lived in South Africa. 'And that bastard had the audacity to ask me from which stable I came when you told him I was an accountant. I nearly said Turffontein racecourse stables!'

Philip Clarke took great pride in his accomplishments as an accountant. And, I suspected, had little tolerance for former fellow Englishmen who questioned his credentials because he had decided to make a new life abroad in one of the 'colonies'. Clarke, who had learned to speak Afrikaans in a remarkably short time – and fluently, albeit with an accent – had also ample reason to regard himself as one of us, not them.

The story about our visit to Whitbread in London spread fast along the rumour mill. We hardly set foot back in Johannesburg when Dick Goss, the beer supremo of South Africa and still a partner in Triomf, called.

'So, Louis, I hear you want to go into beer...'

I explained that, after persistent stories about the failed Whitbread operation at Alrode, I thought it might be a worthwhile buy at the right price. And what would I have done with it if I managed to get it at my price?

'I would have been at your office in a jiffy trying to rent it to you,' I said.

'Good thinking,' Goss perked. 'And I would have rented the damn thing too. SAB is running short of capacity and I can tell you that is one heck of a brewery.'

As I put the phone down, the thought occurred. Why buy a brewery and rent it out? Why not build my own brewery and brew my own beer? I had done that against all odds with fertiliser. Yes, I knew that beer went down people's throats and fertiliser goes into the ground, but here we had the country's largest brewery complaining that it could not supply the need because it was running out of capacity. There was undoubtedly room for others in this lucrative industry, and we had enough cash on hand to establish a foothold and to rake off a few of the millions that frothed around the industry.

I took a few colleagues into my confidence and told them about my plan to enter the beer market. They liked the idea but felt that I might be biting off a little too much for my own good. It was one thing to challenge three complacent fertiliser giants but another to try to tackle the Lion of all lagers and beers. South African Breweries was not an old sleepy giant ready to be mastered. It was a vibrant and vital entity, always on the alert and hungry for prey. It was run by one of the nation's best, a fellow by the name of Dick Goss. He was also a friend, but one who would be destined to become a foe should I make good on my intentions to enter the beer business.

It took me a while to consider all the factors. One that weighed heavily on my mind was the sure possibility of having to do battle with one of my best friends and valuable directors. But then I also knew that it was not in the nature of Dick Goss to take business personally. He would spare no effort to stop me from succeeding in his back yard, but at the end of the day we would remain friends. That much I knew. There was nothing petty about this man. I could hardly anticipate, however, how severe this battle would become.

One of the people at Triomf, who liked the idea – even though he too had reservations – was Pat Latham, our managing director. Pat used to work for South African Breweries and knew the business intimately from the vantage point of someone who had control over its finances. He became my main advisor as we quietly mapped out our strategy.

'We have to get some key people from South African Breweries,' he cautioned, 'if we want to prevent the mistakes of Whitbread at Alrode.'

I agreed. So Pat went to work and recruited Alec Sabbagh of SAB as managing director of the nascent Louis Luyt Breweries. Between the three of us, we drew up a list of further SAB recruits, and eventually brought over Terry Inch to build the brewery; Gordon Den as head brewer; Jannie Bezuidenhout as marketing manager; and Terence Stewart as administrative manager. They all accepted on the basis of matching salaries and the prospect of plenty of excitement and rapid advancement as they helped mount a challenge against the giant they had served so well in the past.

It was our intention, I explained, to use the same formula that worked so well in the case of Triomf. Just as we made partners out of cooperatives and farmers, who were the major consumers of fertiliser, we now intended to bring in the bottle stores and other outlet owners as shareholders in brewery. The idea appealed to the team. This, they agreed, was the only way in which we could be prevented from being shut out from the retail market and be squeezed to death in the same fashion as other would-be SAB competitors in past years.

Goss and his senior staff knew our plans even before we lured over Sabbagh or approached any of the others in their ranks. SAB did not become the formidable force if it was by sleeping at the switch. Ever vigilant and on the watch for the slightest sign of competition, news that the Louis Luyt Group was laying the groundwork for a formal entry into the beer market sent SAB on war alert. Naturally, Dick Goss would be the first to respond. He did so after a Triomf board meeting.

'Louis, I don't think it will work to have us together in Triomf when you enter the beer business,' he announced with a tinge of anger in his voice. 'I would like you to buy SAB's shares.'

I fully appreciated his reaction. My persistence in treading on SAB's turf obviously made our close relationship untenable. But he also understood that my challenge was not on a personal level. After all, Goss was the chief executive officer of the beer giant, not its owner.

'Depending on the price, Dick, I might be interested,' I replied, trying to look disinterested. He then mentioned a price that seemed unbelievably low – no more than half the worth of the Triomf shares held by SAB.

'I'll think about it,' I said casually, trying hard not so show even an element of surprise. 'Give me a week to come back to you.'

This time, in sharp contrast to the early sixties, I had no problem in raising the capital purely on a basis of my reputation. It does help to have the papers swoon over your perceived business acumen and the earnings of your enterprises. Getting all kinds of awards such as Businessman of the Year, Industrialist of the Year and Marketing Man of the Year, also helps. Both Pete van Heyningen of Barclays Bank and Bill Passmore of Standard Bank offered unconditional financing. In the end, I decided to go with Standard Bank's offer of an overseas loan in Swiss francs at the unbelievably low interest rate of 2 per cent.

I thus bought out South African Breweries and now owned 40 per cent of Triomf. The battle lines were drawn and we needed to move fast before South African Breweries had time to regroup and strengthen its flanks. We purchased land at Chamdor near Krugersdorp for our first brewery and started preparing a prospectus. The thought occurred that Anton Rupert might be interested in joining forces with us since he had sold back to Whitbread the stake he held in their brewing venture, and it also occurred to us that his control of more than 180 bottle stores would provide the beginnings of a good distribution network for our product.

So, armed with solid documentation and a detailed business plan, I turned up at Rupert's office in Stellenbosch. This time my reception was somewhat warmer than when I sought financing from him in the early sixties. Instead of a mere upstart, he was now meeting with a fellow member of the establishment. He even listened attentively as I made the case for an alliance between us in this upcoming battle against the big brewer of the land. In the end, however, there was the same standoffish conclusion.

'No, I don't think I would want to be involved,' he said in the soft, measured tones fitting a man who had long regarded himself as the ultimate guardian of the big stick in Afrikaner business circles. 'However, you can leave your papers here and let me look at it and give it some thought.'

I was quietly seething inside as I carefully collected my papers and stuffed them back into my briefcase.

'I don't think I want to do that, Dr Rupert. But thank you for your time, anyway.'

I knew I had no need for his money or financing to build this brewery. This approach was purely an effort to bring into our ranks an established ready-made distribution network. But we could do without it and still be successful. It would simply take more energy and ingenuity, both of which we had in ample supply in our team.

While there was a certain measure of disappointment in the ranks when I reported back the next day on the failed meeting with Rupert, everyone was still chomping at the bit, raring to go. 'Let's get on with the job,' I concluded. 'Forget about Rupert. He seems to think he moves on a different planet than we mortals. In any event, whether he likes it or not, his Western Province Cellars bottle stores will have to buy at least 5 per cent of their beer from us. That is the minimum requirement under our law.'

Louis Luyt Breweries issued its prospectus early in April 1971, and offered to the public four million shares at 50 cents, representing half of the total of eight million issued. Of the remaining four million, I had taken up 3.5 million, while the rest was assigned to other members of my board in parcels of between 30,000 and 200,000. Our estimated capital cost, including the land for our brewery at Chamdor, was R3.9 million. Apart from the R4 million to be raised as equity, we had at our disposal R800,000 in overseas suppliers' credit.

At a conservatively projected market share of 7.5 per cent, we anticipated an after-tax profit of R1.14 million in 1973, rising to R1.3 million and R1.45 in successive years. When we started out, Whitbread – with its lacklustre marketing efforts – held a mere 2.5 per cent of the beer market. The rest was all South African Breweries. While Whitbread began business in South Africa heavily burdened by a brewery that cost in excess of R8 million, our modern facility at Chamdor, with a capacity of 400,000 hectolitres, was being erected for half that price. Chamdor was due to go into full production by March 1973.

Selling shares in any new venture was a tough call at this time. South African investors, badly burned by the 1969 crash, were still reluctant to return to the stock market. Many of the bottle-store owners and other liquor distributors, who we thought would jump at the opportunity to become part of our new venture, sat on the sideline, Rupert-style, watching developments. As expected, South African Breweries had its army out in the field, using both carrot and stick to keep in line those who might be tempted. My men were having a hard time and some seemed ready to capitulate.

Luckily, the press seemed blissfully unaware of the severity of our problems. 'One thing is clear about Louis Luyt,' waxed the *Financial Mail*. 'He has no lack of supporters prepared to follow him into the lion's den...The name that attracts the lolly is still Louis Luyt... Just goes to show that, even in these hard times, there's still magic in a name – if it is the right one.' *Die Vaderland* pictured me as the white knight who was to help restore faith in the stock market. Under the headline, 'Great interest in Luyt beer project', it speculated: 'Louis Luyt might well become known as the person who prompted the South African public to show renewed interest in the share market after the crash of 1969.'

It would be one of the very few instances that the press gave me a pass. Instead of focusing on this wall of apathy that threatened to block our entry into the beer business, they were already speculating over what I might call my beer. Under the light-hearted headline, 'Louis takes to drinking', the *Financial Mail* mentioned 'Protea' and 'Springbok' as likely candidates. But, it told its readers, 'if you can think of a better locally flavoured name for Louis Luyt's planned brew, maybe he'll give you a case or two, some time in 1973'.

Even though I never considered either 'Protea' or 'Springbok' as potential names, both these familiar South African symbols would come back to haunt me 20 years later. In the early 1990s I, as SARFU president, would have my hands full, trying to stop militants within the ANC from replacing the Springbok symbol with a protea in the process of hijacking rugby. Ultimately, I struck a compromise by having a springbok jumping from a bed of proteas. But that was then. In the early seventies, I had not the slightest notion that these two symbols would ever have any special significance in my life. After having been snubbed several times in my attempts to make it to the Springbok rugby team, I had relegated this symbol to my distant past. My focus in April 1971 was not on brand names, but on finding a way to live up to the rosy reports in the press, saving my own name and reputation.

'Luyt is so confident that he hasn't bothered to arrange any underwriting,' wrote one pundit. The truth of the matter was that I knew that, in the event of a shortfall, the Louis Luyt Group would be able to come to the rescue. But that was not the point. I simply could not afford to lose face after all this build-up in the media. There simply had to be a way out. And I chose to do it in one bold stroke

– that was my style. After ample forethought, I moved swiftly. What I intended was a risky move, but then, I thought, so is everything worthwhile in business.

I asked Alec Sabbagh to call the team back from the field and have them assemble in our boardroom. As I looked around the boardroom table, I was shocked to see the toll the setbacks of the previous few weeks had taken on my once energetic sales force. The faces above the sagging shoulders spoke of defeat, almost surrender.

'Gentlemen,' I announced, 'I have decided to shorten your suffering. Instead of making the rounds with our prospectus for a full three months, we will cut it back to two months. We will be closing our offering a month early.'

'You can't do that!' a salesman protested. 'We need all the time we can get to sell these shares. It's not easy, you know.'

The others nodded in agreement, and murmured among themselves. It looked as if I might have a mutiny on my hands. I raised my hand and the room fell silent again.

'Sorry, guys,' I concluded, 'I've made up my mind. We are closing a month early. You will have to make do with less time.'

The tactic worked. The next morning when the news came out that Louis Luyt Breweries had decided to close its offering a month early, the telephones started ringing. The same people who had shown little interest before were now pleading for a piece of the action. Even though I had never said as much, the public perception was that LLB was closing early because it was already fully subscribed. Once the herd instinct took over, that perception became reality, and when we closed our offering a month early, we were indeed one and a half times oversubscribed. Instead of begging for buyers, we had to return R3 million.

Construction could thus start on our brewery at Chamdor, but suddenly we encountered government opposition reminiscent of the days when I dared to tackle the fertiliser cartel. Dr Piet Rautenbach, Director of Planning, refused us permission to proceed with construction at Chamdor. Instead, he ordered us to relocate to a so-called border industry area near the town of Brits. This region, set aside in terms of grand apartheid for industrial activity close to the Tswana homeland of Bophuthatswana, would place us at a distinct disadvantage. It was not only far removed from our market, but would require that we employ twice as many people as we intended.

'In that case,' I told Rautenbach, after I reminded him that SAB had all its operations in and around cities, and in particular, Johannesburg, 'I'll have to return the money of the shares bought in the Brewery to the people who made the investment.'

'Go ahead,' he said. 'It's your call.'

'I will of course have to explain to these disappointed shareholders and the press the reason why I am doing this, you know,' I responded.

72

'Why don't you put that in writing – I will not be blackmailed,' he almost shouted over the phone.

'I shall certainly do so. Can you give me your address? I shall have the letter delivered to you this afternoon.'

Rautenbach promptly obliged and I dictated the letter and sent it across to his office in Pretoria. The next day I received a telex from Rautenbach where he backed off from his rigid stance and issued a permit for Chamdor. But the government, as always, had the last word. When we started marketing our beer, we discovered that a ban had been imposed on all our brands on the state-owned South African Airways and the Railways. And when we applied to the state-run Industrial Development Corporation for a loan to fund our Bloemfontein brewery, we ran into reams of red tape. A loan that would usually be granted on a routine basis became a major issue. In the end, the IDC chairman, Jan Kitshoff, who was a former Secretary of Trade and Industry, authorised R600,000 instead of the million we had requested on condition that we put up the unencumbered Chamdor brewery worth R4 million as collateral. I told him in no uncertain terms what he could do with his loan, and funded the project myself. So much for all the special treatment that Luyt, the Afrikaner, was supposed to have received from the government.

With Chamdor finally under construction, we could turn our attention to marketing strategy and brand names. Security became a particularly important issue as instances of SAB spying at the building site and around our offices came to light. In fairness, it needs to be mentioned that we were not slow either to use whatever means we had at our disposal to gain intelligence on the other side. Neither of us wished to be hit by surprises and both were bent on springing a few of our own.

The work at Chamdor was progressing much faster than projected. We finished the job within a year and were already in production by September 1972, almost a year before the scheduled date. Construction was also underway in Bloemfontein. And although Durban was already in our sights for a third brewery, this was not to come to pass because of an unfortunate set of circumstances.

The well-known Danish brewer, Tuborg, approached us to offer their brand as a foreign supplement to our own local product. The idea appealed. We needed this to counter SAB's Amstel and Carling beers, brewed under licence with the Dutch and Canadian companies. Our negotiations with Tuborg had reached its final stages when the Danish brewers, under apparent pressure from their own government, decided to scuttle the idea. Greg Kukard of the *Sunday Times* noted in a report under the headline, 'Luyt shrugs off Tuborg loss':

'Mr Louis Luyt, the millionaire industrialist, has bluntly refused to try to salvage the beer franchise agreement his LLG Breweries hoped to sign with Denmark's giant Tuborg Breweries. The deal, which had reached an advanced stage of negotiation, was called off this week by Tuborg.

'By cancelling the deal, Tuborg's directors had baffled their fellow country-men in South Africa. The Danish Vice Consul in Johannesburg, Mr Bjorn Andersen, advanced the theory that the Danes called a halt because there was a possibility that LLB would supply to Rhodesia – boycotted by Denmark.

'Mr Luyt laughed this off as economically ridiculous, as Tuborg would have been a low-volume beer catering strictly for South Africa's relatively small premium-beer market. Tuborg would have accounted for about 10 per cent of LLB's sales.

'According to Mr Luyt, the main reason and possibly the only reason for the deal being called off was political, and having seen most of the correspondence that passed between Tuborg and LLG Breweries, I believe he was correct.

'In several letters written to Mr Alec Sabbagh, managing director of LLB, reference was made to political difficulties surrounding the deal. The letters were written by Mr Sven Baltzersen, a director of Tuborg.

'In one letter, Mr Baltzersen wrote: "... [Please] bear in mind our personal observation on the somewhat extraordinary political discussions and feelings among people here." (Written 14 April 1972)

'In another letter, Mr Baltzersen said: "... I had the matter before the board and they did not entertain the offer, which I personally regret, but you know why." This was written in June and referred to the possibility of Tuborg acquiring an interest in LLB. Mr Luyt said Tuborg first raised this possibility.

'It is understood that on all occasions that LLB men visited Tuborg – which approached Mr Luyt for the tie-up in the first place – the political question surrounding the deal was discussed.

'According to observers in Johannesburg, the Danish Government has a large say in the affairs of the Tuborg Breweries, which last year amalgamated with Carlsberg Breweries, Denmark's other big brewery.'

South Africa had become increasingly isolated and the Scandinavians were very much in the forefront, attacking the 'apartheid regime' at every possible opportunity. These Nordic governments were very much in favour of the boy-cotts set by the United Nations, even though they always seemed to be able to turn a blind eye or find an excuse whenever sanctions threatened their estab-lished and most profitable businesses in South Africa. In our case, I gathered, the deal was not quite big enough to warrant such self-induced myopia.

If South African Breweries was having a great time over the Tuborg setback, it was at best a short-lived celebration. I immediately approached the famous German brewer, Becks, who gave us their first-ever overseas franchise to brew its product.

Then, out of the blue, came a call from Anton Rupert. He asked whether he could come and see me in Johannesburg. He wanted to talk about going into partnership with me, he explained. So, I thought with a quiet smile, even Rupert had been caught up in the frenzy and had decided to slide off the fence to join the rush.

'You know that I have already sold all the available shares to the public,' I cautioned him.

'I know,' Rupert insisted, 'but I am thinking of going into partnership with you not only in beer but also in fertiliser.'

When he arrived at my office, Rupert offered to buy half my four million shares in the new beer company, half my shares in Triomf and to take over half ownership of my aircraft. The shares in both LLB and Triomf would be at par, while the payment for 50 per cent in the aircraft would be at its depreciated value. The whole deal would be conducted in hard cash.

'Just think,' he explained, as if this was a novel idea, 'you'll have 180 bottle stores in Western Province Cellars and my sales force will help market the beer. This should give us a solid entry.'

This time it was my turn to think it over. I did and came to the conclusion that having Rupert on my side in this upcoming war would not be a bad idea. I needed extra muscle. Also, he would bring to the table considerable marketing expertise. So I signalled my willingness to talk and Rupert invited Adri and me to join him and his wife, Hubert, for dinner at his Fleur du Cap wine estate, near Somerset West. I took along former Springbok rugby captain Dawie de Villiers, who had become a good friend, and his wife, Suzanne. After a pleasant meal and estate wine in the elegant dining room, we retired to one of the drawing rooms, replete with antique Cape Dutch furniture, for coffee and liqueur. Rupert then took me aside.

'Louis, I'm afraid I just don't have the cash on hand to pay for your shares,' he apologised. 'We are heavily exposed to excise duties before we even earn any income.'

Instead he proposed an exchange of shares. Shares in his liquor company, Oude Meester, for shares in my holding companies for the beer, fertiliser and aircraft companies.

'No,' I replied, hardly able to hide my disappointment. 'I am not interested in becoming a shareholder of Oude Meester.'

'Oude Meester share is the most undervalued on the stock exchange and you will become the second largest shareholder outside of Rembrandt,' Rupert insisted. 'Even bigger than Sanlam.'

At the time, Triomf stood much stronger than his Oude Meester. But Rupert was very insistent and persuasive. Together, he suggested, we would build a strong new conglomerate in fertiliser and liquor. His Rembrandt tobacco sales network might be helpful, too, in the beer marketing effort, he claimed. I started to waiver - Anton Rupert could be quite persistent when he wanted something badly enough. As we drove back to our hotel, I told Dawie de Villiers about my conversation with Rupert. His advice was unambiguous: Walk away! But I, later to my detriment, had already made up my mind to exchange shares with the man who had twice rebuffed me in the past and now eagerly wanted to cobble together a partnership.

Until this day, it is difficult to explain why I made this decision. It might have been vanity, combined with a strong dose of idealism on my part. The idea of two Karoo Afrikaners – Rupert grew up in Graaff-Reinet – forming an alliance against established English interests had a certain appeal. Whatever the reason, it was not a good enough one. This would turn out to be one of my worst business decisions ever.

Others would in future, no doubt, try to figure out exactly how two such divergent entrepreneurs could ever have gone into partnership. In hindsight, I am sure, they might conclude – as I did afterwards – that this was not a marriage of convenience, but a disastrous mix of oil and water in the belief that the larger volume might be beneficial to both. It was an alliance between two entirely incompatible, headstrong personalities set to unravel almost from the very moment it was formed.

Anton Rupert and I thus exchanged shares. The deal made me part owner of Oude Meester, while he acquired a sizeable part of my shareholdings in Triomf, Louis Luyt Breweries and my aircraft company. The press blasted the story across their front pages, causing a ripple that was felt right into the boardroom of South African Breweries. There was a noticeable increase in the number of spies lurking around Chamdor and a frenzy of new activity in SAB's war room. They were obviously thrown into a heightened state of alert by the prospect of having to face a stronger alliance of liquor interests.

'Probably the most significant achievement by Mr Luyt,' wrote *The Star,* 'was his coup in acquiring the formidable backing of the massive Anton Rupert organisation. A vital captive market has been gained through the deal with Dr Anton Rupert in the form of 160 Western Province Cellars bottle stores.'

In another report, the *Financial Mail* noted that LLB would be relying heavily on Rupert's marketing flair. 'He's a fantastic label man as well as the biggest market innovator I've ever met,' I was quoted as saying. 'The first ever king-size and satin-tipped cigarettes.' And I meant every word of it. Anton Rupert was indeed a master of the art. I recall Rupert, during a visit to my office, asking to see the labelling of the products we were about to launch, so I had a few cans and bottles brought in. He took the can, put it on a shelf and retreated a few yards, his eyes fixed on the object. He then put his glasses on and walked closer.

'Do you have a packet of thirty Stuyvesant in your office?' he asked.

'No,' I said, 'but we certainly can send out someone to get one.'

'I want an unopened one,' he said. 'with the cellophane still wrapped around it.'

Within minutes, my secretary was back with the cigarettes. He tore off the gold strip around the cellophane, walked over to the shelf and draped it around the can.

'Now, does that not look better?' he asked, rhetorically.

I had to agree. Anton Rupert's genius when it came to creating product images and appealing to the markets could hardly be questioned. Unfortunately, as it turned out later, my new-found partner was of the firm belief that only he knew about marketing and whatever he said was law. This, of course, was unacceptable to me and slowly the cracks began to show.

In mid-1972, as we were approaching D-Day at Chamdor, the partnership between Rupert and myself was still trying to find a solid foundation. He was still leaving the decision-making and strategic planning to me, as was originally agreed. Before Rupert joined the fray, we had agreed that Luyt Lager would be the first beer we would launch. I, on the other hand, was reluctant to put my hard-earned name on a beer can. Rupert had a point when he cautioned me that lending your name to a commercial product puts it at risk. 'Wait until the pissing contest starts,' he warned. But he also realised and agreed that our first beer needed to be easily identifiable to counter SAB strategy. The big brewer was ready to flood the market with new labels as soon as we launched ours, hoping to confuse the public into thinking that they were buying our product while actually supporting theirs. And six weeks before the actual launch, our suspicion was confirmed. Soon after we ignited the furnaces in a feigned production exercise at Chamdor in full sight of their omnipresent spies, South African Breweries fired its first salvo and launched two new brands into the market. With Luyt Lager, however, we felt there would not be the slightest possibility of brand confusion.

With the help of our public relations department, however, the press put another more interesting spin on the matter. 'The name chosen for the new beer follows in a long international tradition in the brewing industry by carrying the name of its founder – famous names in this category are Tuborg, Carlsberg, Carling, Whitbread and Guinness,' waxed the financial editor of *The Star* – influenced no doubt by the quality of our beer and the lavishness of our launch the night before. 'The eye-catching emblem on the Luyt beer containers is the Luyt family crest dating back centuries in Prussian history.'

In reality, this crest had nothing to do with the Luyt family. The Prussian eagle with an 'LL' emblazoned on its chest was the creation of our advertising agents, De Villiers & Schonfeldt. Tastefully designed, it would eventually also be adopted as the logo of the Louis Luyt Group. In the words of Marshall McLuhan, the media had become the message.

Instead of the modest prediction in our prospectus of 7.5 per cent share of the beer market in the first year, the press was now upping the ante in their forecasts. 'Based on the capacity of the two Louis Luyt breweries at Krugersdorp and Bloemfontein,' wrote *The Star*, 'Luyt Lager, together with Becks Beer (which the company is producing under licence to Becks of Germany), could achieve up to 30 per cent of the total market by the end of 1973.' These beers, it argued, would pose a much stronger challenge than Whitbread to South African Breweries, which still held virtual monopoly of the R140-million market. Luyt Lager was designed to challenge SAB's Lion Lager head-on.

But with prelaunch orders for Luyt Lager totalling more than 2.5 million bottles, we were running the risk of a shortage of bottles. So, to supplement our supply of new bottles, Alec Sabbagh sent out the troops to buy up all the used bottles they could find. In the end, this would not only prevent us from running short of supplies but also result in a considerable saving. New bottles cost substantially more than the 'almost-new' bottles that were collected and resold by the so-called bottle bag merchants. This was a practice followed routinely by SAB and the other smaller breweries in the past. We regarded this as normal practice in the beer industry and did not give it as much as a second thought.

It was on this note that Adri and I boarded the Falcon jet on a trip to Europe. After dropping us off at Munich for the 1972 Olympics, pilots Graham Woodhouse and Pete du Plessis, accompanied by engineer Terry Green, continued on to Paris where the aircraft was to undergo its compulsory annual check and be serviced by Marcel Dassault. Adri and I then set about enjoying our first vacation away from the family and work, watching the world's super athletes compete, while we waited to be picked up by our crew on their way back home.

We enjoyed the time by ourselves, eating at good restaurants and shuttling from one exciting event to another. But it was difficult for me to immerse myself completely and forget about the looming battle back home. I recall drawing strength from the performance of Lasse Viren in the 10,000 metres. He was brought down when the reigning 5000-metre champion, Mohamed Gammoudi, tripped and fell in front of him. But, instead of giving up, Viren got up and, incredibly, not only caught up with the fast-disappearing pack, but won in record-breaking time. This spectacular performance reaffirmed my belief that nothing is impossible where there is the will and the belief in yourself and God. Finnish ex-policeman Viren went on to win the 5000-metre event as well and repeated the double win four years later in Montreal.

The Munich Olympics will, however, not be remembered for the performance of superstars like runner Viren, swimmer Mark Spitz – with a record number of gold medals – or gymnast Olga Korbut, who mesmerised the world. On 5 September, with only six days of the Games left, eight members of the Black September terrorist group slipped into the Olympic Village, killed two Israeli team members, and seized nine others as hostages. Early the next morning, all nine were killed during a shoot-out with the West German police. After suspending competition for 24 hours and holding a memorial service at the main stadium, IOC president Avery Brundage ordered, 'The Games must go on'. But it did so under a shroud of sorrow. Many left early, including Mark Spitz, because the Americans feared that, as a Jew, he might be targeted next.

Adri and I decided to return to Johannesburg. Kobus Becker, one of my brewery directors, met us at the airport and from the moment I saw him I had an ominous feeling of pending disaster. This was not normal.

In an urgent application, South African Breweries had applied to the Rand Supreme Court to order Louis Luyt Breweries to return two million bottles, which, they claimed, belonged to them. SAB also asked that the court prohibit any further purchases of their bottles by us or any other outsider. They claimed that they were in danger of running short of bottles on the eve of the launch of LLB's product. While we were preparing to counter this action, we noted with some satisfaction that Rupert's Oude Meester cellars, in which I was a partner, had brought a court action of its own against SAB, claiming that the latter had violated their registered brand name with the recent launch of a beer called Master Brew. This beer was a clear attempt to pre-empt LLB's new products. By naming its beer Master Brew, Oude Meester insisted, SAB was infringing its rights as Oude Meester had already registered the term 'Master' as part of several names to be used for current and future liquor products.

The press seemed quite relieved to move away from the sad events in Munich to a less lethal battle for bottles in a high court. As we arrived at the courthouse, a troop of journalists and cameramen waited to greet us on the steps. Dick Goss was there with his counsel and gave me a friendly wink as we stepped into court. I wondered what his take on events would be when we would have a chance to sit down one day and review this – and other battles that were sure to follow – over a glass of beer, preferably one of mine. At Goss' side were his general manager, Colin Hall, and counsel, Sidney Kentridge, who would in future years not only represent me in several landmark cases but also become a good friend. As was to be expected, Dick Goss and I had had little direct communication since we parted company and prepared for combat. It would not be good for morale on either side and might even have been interpreted by some as weakness and treason to have opposing commanders-in-chief meet during a war. Despite the customary courtesies and Dick's genial demeanour, we all knew this was only the first of many more battles in and out of court in the imminent war. South African Breweries was not about to give up its lucrative hold on a captive market to an unwelcome intruder because two CEOs liked and respected each other.

'Luyt Lager will be sold in bottles, which to a substantial extent will be SAB bottles,' Kentridge argued. South African Breweries, he claimed, would suffer 'irreparable harm' unless there was an immediate remedy. The big brewer could not resist complaining about the knowledge of SAB's business acquired by LLB through former top employees such as Sabbagh, Bezuidenhout, Den, Inch and others. It was a strange sight, seeing the lion crawl on the floor in front of presiding judge Oscar Galgut, whining instead of growling. In the end, Mr Justice Galgut took a Solomon's decision with the following ruling: Luyt Breweries could keep the two million bottles it had acquired from the bottle bag merchants, but was barred from buying any further bottles with an SAB label. Likewise, he ruled that SAB was also barred from buying any bottles from bottle bag merchants with a Luyt label. I knew that both Goss and I were in some trouble, more so Goss because of the huge volumes SAB handled. The sorting, washing and removing of labels to circumvent the court order were just beyond human capacity. So, within one week, Goss and I got together and resolved the bottle conundrum fairly smartly, and I was more than satisfied with the outcome.

Our Becks beer was ready to be released in November 1972. But even more controversial was a product called Madison, released in March 1973. We were already brewing this beer with a 7 per cent alcohol content to compete with SAB's Carling Black Label when Alec Sabbagh found himself in New York crossing its famous Madison Avenue. How about it, he thought. The name 'Madison' had a nice American flavour to it. James Madison was one of the nation's favourite presidents, and the name had a wholesome foreign ring to it. We all liked the idea and our own 'American' brand was thus born. Barely weeks after Madison made its splash, we received a letter from the advertising control board informing us that SAB had complained about our use of the term 'American' as the beer was a domestic brand. We agreed to change our advertising, but insisted that SAB should desist from calling Castle Lager 'South Africa's favourite beer' as it had no cause to that claim. Castle Lager had a mere 8 per cent of the total market in comparison with its flagship Lion Lager, which had a whopping 65 per cent of the market. So the same advertising board that pounced on us now found itself unable to enforce a ruling on SAB.

The battle over bottles hardly stopped after the court episode. Both sides continued to buy each other's empties, as mutually agreed, from bottle bag merchants. We had a special bottle designed for Madison, identical to the one used for Carling Black Label, but with a slightly longer neck. Quite naturally, bottle bag merchants would sort these into the Carling lots and it would end up in SAB's hands, The thing is that the Madison bottles could only be identified with great difficulty and, much to our delight, they jammed SAB's bottling plants, causing costly stoppages.

The beer war soon expanded to the townships where so-called shebeens were only too willing to bootleg SAB and LLB beers in spite of the antiquated Liquor Act prohibiting black people from selling alcoholic beverages. One side would immediately snitch on the other when it got wind of a new delivery, usually with the help of well-planted spies. Reminiscent of the prohibition era in America, police raids would follow reports of new contraband supplies of 'white' liquor in Soweto. But instead of destroying supplies as they did in the United States during the prohibition, the South African police would confiscate it and take it to their own canteens. I suppose we might have written these raids off as involuntary charitable contributions to the police benevolent association.

One of my greatest supporters was shebeen owner Godfrey Moloi. Such was his notoriety that upon his death in August 1998 at the age of 64 after a long battle with cancer, the *Sunday Times* carried a lengthy report on the Al Capone of Soweto. 'He became a walking billboard for Louis Luyt in the '70s,' the *Sunday Times* noted, '[when] he bought beer for his shebeens from Luyt's brewery, and proudly called himself Godfrey "Louis Luyt" Moloi.' Moloi was known as a tough man who scared off his competition. But he was also generous. Despite this carefully nurtured toughness and gangster image, Moloi had a kind heart. The *Sunday Times* quoted a contemporary who knew Moloi from his childhood as the son of a priest, saying: 'You cannot take the Christian out of a Zulu.' It was indeed my honour to have had this man as my namesake and friend.

By the end of our first year, we managed to capture 14 per cent of the total beer market and were already very profitable. In the slow winter months our market penetration remained the same, and although our financial results were less impressive, we were still well within budget projections. South African Breweries had thrown all its might into the fight and we were reciprocating in kind. To this day, I feel that we might have fared even better had Rupert and I presented a unified, cohesive alliance. Instead, our strength was sapped by internal squabbles and lack of cooperation at the top.

After a trip to Germany, Anton Rupert nonchalantly told me that we were now the proud owners of Highlands Brewery in Swaziland, purchased on our behalf for R1.5 million from the Holsten family. He had met the Holstens during interval at a symphony concert featuring Herbert von Karajan in Berlin and discovered that they wished to part with their Highlands Brewery in the small African kingdom. The reason was obvious. The brewery was losing money, hand over fist. Not only did I feel Rupert had paid too much for this insolvent company, but in fact that he should not have bought it at all – particularly not on his own, without consulting me. So, after we conducted a due diligence audit where we found only non-performing assets, I suggested to Rupert he cancel the deal. Rupert refused, because, he protested, he had given his word to the Holstens. In the meantime, labour problems – which had plagued the previous owners of Highlands Brewery – escalated. Our manager, Fred Roach, a former British police and intelligence commissioner, was banned from the country. I demanded that he be allowed back in, which the authorities refused. I then simply closed the operation. Rupert was furious and insisted that I re-open, but I told him curtly that selling beer was not like selling cigarettes. It is a different kind of operation. I refused point blank. But, in the end, I still had to foot the bill for this acquisition, and my plans for the proposed brewery in Durban had to be scrapped.

During another trip to Germany, Rupert bought the Kronenbraü trademark, which was purported to date as far back as 1308. It was a mere house brand and very few people knew of it, but Rupert made quite an event out of it. He purchased Clydesdale horses and a wagon equipped with old oak casks. This wagon was paraded through towns during special events across the country to promote Kronenbrau 1308, which was purportedly brewed in oak casks. There is no way, I told Rupert, that we can brew beer in wooden casks. He seemed entirely unperturbed. The horse-drawn carriage with the kegs was merely a promotional ploy, he insisted. The beer can be brewed in anything. In the meantime, I had a battle on my hands pacifying Becks, who were not happy with the Rupert association. I later discovered that it was because of a cigarette deal in Germany that had soured and saw Rupert lose the Peter Stuyvesant trademark in Germany.

In the meanwhile, my LLB sales force continued to complain that instead of helping them, as originally intended, Rupert's tobacco salesmen had become 'spies'. They were reporting to Stellenbosch and this became both irksome and annoying. To cap it all, we discovered that bottle stores in the Western Province Cellars chain were treating our beers as just another product instead of giving it preferential treatment – as envisaged in our initial understanding.

Ours was thus indeed a house divided, so I flew down to Cape Town for a showdown with Rupert at his Stellenbosch offices. I told him straight to his face: 'We are partners, you are not my boss and I want out of this partnership – either I buy you or you buy me out.' It came as no surprise to him. The only matter that concerned him was on what terms we would part. Like someone who knows that his or her spouse is anxious to escape an unhappy marriage, Rupert now upped the ante as far as it would go, nit-picking at everything as he went along.

Here we were, two grown men, having to argue over whether I was responsible for the fuel cost involved in the trip to Paris during the Olympic Gamess in 1972. It was a pleasure trip, Rupert insisted. No, I explained, it was a necessary trip to service the aircraft and my wife and I did not even return with it but paid our own way back on South African Airways. Then came the matter of my buying back his share in the Falcon jet. It had appreciated in value, he insisted. You owe me an additional R200,000, plus the cost for the Paris trip. I threw up my hands in despair.

I offered to buy Rupert's shareholding in Louis Luyt Breweries. No, he insisted, I am in liquor already. I will buy you out, he said. He offered me a mere 75 cents, which reflected the par value of the shares. We agreed that I would return the Oude Meester shares and that he would return the shares in Triomf. Gys Steyn, an attorney and CEO of Oude Meester, drew up a hand-written agreement that very evening. There was no celebration – just a cold handshake and a sense of relief on both sides that this unhappy partnership had come to an end.

I could not but remember the words of warning uttered by both the late Jan Pickard and the late Dr Albert Wessels at the dinner where I received the Marketing Man of the Year Award: 'Stay away from Rupert – he is not a good partner,' Pickard had said. Wessels, too, warned me as a father would, but I ignored their wise counsel.

But one more unpleasant task awaited. John Norton, who had replaced Alec Sabbagh as managing director of LLB, was waiting for me back at our plane at Cape Town airport to hear the outcome of my discussions with Rupert. His deep disappointment was predictable. Still, he had the assurance that I would make room for him at Triomf.

Next, I received a call from Dirk de Wet, head of the Eastern Transvaal Cooperative, who also served on Triomf's board. He urgently wished to see me. When he turned up at my office the look on his face prepared me for bad tidings, but not quite the shocking news he would convey. Together with leaders of the five cooperative shareholders in Triomf, he had attended a meeting at the Carlton Hotel that afternoon, arranged by Hendrik Smit, chairman of Fedmis, our main opposition. Anton Rupert had been there too, telling them that he had had a fallout with me and that he wanted them to join him in ousting me from the fertiliser business. Dirk said that he and the other five bluntly refused to be part of it. I simply could not understand the underhanded duplicity of Anton Rupert.

Rupert offered and succeeded to buy out the minority shareholders in Louis Luyt Breweries by telling them what a bleak future lay ahead and hastily changed its name to Intercontinental Breweries. For the next five years, he ran up reported losses well in excess of R65 million before he decided that he had had enough and exchanged his beer shares for some of South African Breweries' wine interests. In hindsight, I know without a shadow of doubt that I would have succeeded in the beer industry, because my companies were still able to market to the man in the street – we were not above him and that is what beer marketing is all about. I sometimes wonder what the state of affairs would have been had I not been so weak as to team up with a man who had so disappointed me in the past.

In 1991, I was approached by Dr Dawie Botha, a former professor at law at the University of Pretoria and a promoter for my doctorate in law at the same university. He had joined Bateman's Engineering as a legal advisor. Bateman's had been approached by an overseas investor who wanted to start a brewery in South Africa, but the law prescribed South African ownership as peremptory for a brewing licence. Naturally, I was interested and we identified a brewery in the UK. The brewery had been standing idle and we were negotiating to purchase it and ship it across to South Africa. Bateman's initial partner had not materialised, so I began looking for a new partner – and found one in Interbrew, the Belgian brewer. Our association, however, came to naught and, although they were compelled to pay me US$3 million for not honouring our agreement, they did not do so, but I had little stomach to fight them in a Belgian court and decided to call it a day. I therefore called off the plans, and the subsequent loss of quite a few million rand taught me another expensive lesson. But a glutton for punishment I seemingly remained.

A man's reputation is not in his own keeping,

but lies at the mercy of the profligacy of others

— calumny requires no proof.

William Hazlitt,
English critic and author,
1778–1830

Chapter 6

A REPUTATION LOST

On 30 April 1974, the *Rand Daily Mail* carried a banner headline spanning its front page, 'R1 300 million Luyt deal massive boost to economy'. 'Mr Louis Luyt, head of the giant Triomf fertiliser group, has pulled off the biggest export marketing coup for South Africa by securing orders worth R1 346 million (US$ 2000 million) that will more than double the size of the industry in this country,' wrote the *Mail*. 'The orders, to be spread over a 20-year period [sic] (10 years) will give further impetus to the country's economic growth. A R66-million plant, to be built at Richards Bay, will make South Africa one of the world's largest fertiliser producers.'

'The deal,' the report went on, 'will give a major boost in the years ahead to the profits of the two listed partners in Triomf – AECI and Triomf Fertiliser Investments. It also entrenches the pivotal role of Mr Louis Luyt in the fertiliser world and opens the way for large export earnings for Mr Luyt's partners in TFI, the agricultural cooperatives.'

On 3 November 1978, the same *Rand Daily Mail* carried another banner headline: 'It's all true!' The accompanying report stated: 'South Africa's biggest political bombshell burst yesterday when Mr Justice Anton Mostert made public startling evidence which has confirmed reports in the *Rand Daily Mail* and *Sunday Express* of massive misuse of public money through Department of Information secret funds. Judge Mostert released evidence that shows beyond any doubt that *The Citizen* newspaper was financed out of State funds.'

'And in evidence under oath,' wrote the *Mail*, 'Luyt named former Prime Minister John Vorster, the Minister of Plural Relations, Connie Mulder, and Hendrik van den Bergh, former head of the Bureau of State Security, as key figures in the secret project to finance the newspaper.'

Side by side, these two reports – a little more than four years apart – demonstrate the extent to which my good reputation was destroyed by my involvement in what came to be known as the Information Scandal. It did not matter that a multitude of other notable South Africans such as super golfer Gary Player, banker Piet Liebenberg and heart transplant pioneer Christian Barnard were also enmeshed in this web of deceit. Even less did it matter that we all became involved for, what we thought at the time, the good of the country. None of us were diehard nationalists. In fact, we were all recruited precisely because we were not party-political lackeys but independents who never hesitated to criticise the government when needed.

No one who followed my dealings with the government in the period immediately preceding my fateful decision in 1975 to become part of this grandiose state-funded scheme to promote South Africa abroad could have had any doubts about my independence. In fact, for the best part of the early seventies, I found myself embroiled in a running battle with Afrikaner officialdom over price controls and the establishment of the phosphoric acid plant at Richards Bay. Instead of viewing the growth of Triomf in the export markets as a boon for South Africa – as the *Rand Daily Mail* had – these officials were hellbent on preventing Triomf gaining any further advantage over its main competitor, Fedmis.

The idea to build my own phosphoric acid plant had started to take shape during a tour of South America. At the time, Triomf was already aggressively marketing its fertiliser and crop-protection products abroad to make up for the curtailment of opportunities at home. In 1975, for example, the foreign sales accounted for 77 per cent of our total profits. We were, however, beginning to run into opposition as countries turned to manufacturing their own product instead of buying from foreign suppliers. Triomf thus needed to find alternative markets to make up for this diminishing demand in finished products. Why not phosphoric acid instead? Countries that had opted for local manufacturing would continue to rely on foreign sources for their supplies of phosphoric acid used in the manufacture of high-grade fertiliser, we argued. Foremost among these markets was Brazil, but there were several others as well.

On my return, I called on Lourens Muller, then Minister of Trade and Industry, to sound him out. He was one of the few high-level government officials with whom I had developed a good working relationship. I found him to be a helpful, genuine man with no hidden agendas and the guts to stand up and be counted when he saw an injustice. Due to political considerations, he was overlooked when the position of State President became vacant in 1978 and Free Stater Alwyn Schlebusch was appointed instead.

In 1971, when Muller was Minister of Police, I turned to him for help during a flap over Sunday sport that could easily have developed into an international incident without his timely intervention. He did not disappoint. I was getting ready for church one Sunday when I received an urgent call from Brian Henning, who headed the South African Professional Golfers' Association (PGA). The PGA – of which I became the sponsor at the urgent request of Gary Player and Brian Henning when the sponsor bowed out – now found itself in a real bind. The final round of the PGA championship at Huddle Park on Saturday had been washed out during a heavy rainstorm and the organisers had to settle for Sunday play, as several foreign participants were unable to stay until Monday. To conform to the old Transvaal law that prohibited professional sport on a Sunday, Henning allowed the fans to attend free of charge. This gesture failed, however, to mollify a certain police major who stepped in and prevented the contestants from teeing off. Henning was thus in a quandary.

I volunteered to call Muller and explained our dilemma. He immediately understood the potential ramifications and told me to convey to Henning his permission to go ahead. I did so by telephone, jumped into my car and drove to Huddle Park. On my arrival, I found the players waiting around while Henning was still locked in argument with the major.

'No one,' the major repeated for my edification, 'has any say in this matter under my jurisdiction. No, not even the Minister.'

So I picked up the telephone, called Muller again and updated him on the major's intransigence. He asked to have him come to the phone. Whatever Muller told the major turned him from a pit bull into a lap dog. The game thus resumed. But there was nevertheless an aftermath. The PGA, as organisers, and the Louis Luyt Group, as sponsors, were taken to the magistrate's court and fined R20 under the Sunday Observance Act. The PGA wanted to pay the fine, but I told them not to do so. The case then went to the Appellate Court in Bloemfontein, and was ruled in our favour. It was indeed a heavy price to pay for principle, but it was worth it.

This was, of course, not the first time that I would find myself in conflict with a government whose actions seemed to play squarely into the hands of those who wished to see South Africa banned from all international sport competition. My support as a sponsor of the PGA to have the African-American golfer, Lee Elder, participate on the South African tour irritated some in government as much as it pleased those who wished to see us keep – and indeed expand – our contact with the outside world. Muller, as I recall, was among those who supported us in breaking the racial barrier in golf.

On the basis of these past experiences, I thus had reason to expect a sympathetic ear when I stepped into Lourens Muller's office to share my plans for a phosphoric acid plant after my return from South America. I informed him that Triomf had plans to establish a plant either in South Africa or Brazil. While we would naturally prefer South Africa, the final decision would very much depend on the availability and price of phosphate rock. The only supplier in South Africa happened to be Foskor, a state-run operation owned by the state's own Industrial Development Corporation.

Equally proactive as Minister of Trade and Industry as he was in the post of Minister of Police, Muller gave me his unqualified blessing. I therefore approached Foskor to find out whether it would be able to supply enough phosphate rock, used in the manufacture of phosphoric acid, at a competitive price. They offered to supply the 1,200,000 tons needed by Triomf on an annual basis, at R7 per ton, free on rail at their Phalaborwa plant. This was at a time when they were delivering rock to Iran at between $11 (R8) and $13 (R10), so this price seemed reasonable to both Foskor and us.

In the meantime, we had been scouting around Richards Bay on the northern Natal coast for a suitable site. This location appealed because it not only presented a convenient natural harbour for bulk carriers, but fell within a so-called border industry region where attractive government tax and other incentives applied. The Town Council of Richards Bay offered thirty hectares at R25,000 per hectare and undertook to supply all the infrastructure needed for the project.

When I saw Lourens Muller again, I could report not only on favourable discussions with Foskor, but positive developments at Richards Bay, too. A firm overseas contract, Philip Brothers – later Salomon Brothers and now Salomon Smith Barney – had also entered into an agreement to buy all our phosphoric acid at a minimum price based on current world market prices. This contract would enable me to raise financing without much of a problem. Muller was delighted – and so was the *Rand Daily Mail* once the story became public.

As always, however, whenever officialdom was involved in my business plans, initial elation soon made way for deflation. A fax arrived from Foskor. An apology. They would no longer be able to supply all Triomf's needs, we were told, because there was another South African company interested in manufacturing phosphoric acid for export. Also, Foskor continued, it needed to renegotiate the price. It did not take much intelligence to figure out whom the 'other company' was. It had to be Fedmis, which – as the only other major player – also happened to be closely associated with Foskor through cross directorships. All this after I had already concluded contracts that relied on Foskor's undertakings.

At my request, a meeting was called at Lourens Muller's ministerial residence in Pretoria. In attendance were Etienne Rousseau, chairman of both Foskor and Federale Volksbeleggings, a major shareholder in Fedmis; Jack Kearney, the managing director of Foskor; Jan Kitshoff, the secretary for Trade and Industry; and Hendrik Smit, the chairman of Fedmis. Accompanying me was my managing director, René du Toit. If ever the word 'incestuous' was amply illustrated, this was the occasion, I thought, as Muller opened the meeting with a few words of welcome. Here I was, facing a tripartite of state and semi-state entities ganging up on me as the outsider because I had the temerity to beat them to the punch with what seemed to be a good money-making prospect. And I felt sorry for Muller who had to preside over this gathering.

Rousseau 'respectfully' requested the opportunity to make a few introductory remarks of his own.

'You had the audacity, Mr Luyt, to go over my head to the Minister to resolve a purely commercial issue,' he said, eyes flashing from behind his spectacles. 'And then you went into discussions with Foskor without consulting me as the chairman.'

'I equally respectfully beg to differ, Dr Rousseau. I'll tell you why I did not want to see you. I don't trust you. How can you be the chairman of both Foskor and the holding company of Fedmis without finding yourself in a serious conflict of interest?'

I had clearly touched on a raw nerve.

'You will not insult me,' he shot back, 'and I will make sure that you are not the only man in this country that makes money out of fertiliser...'

'No, Dr Rousseau,' I interjected, 'you are not going to dictate my future. I am my own boss and master of my own destiny. Not you or anyone else in your companies for that matter.'

Muller then stepped in.

'Please, gentlemen, let's calm down,' he said in measured tone, and then turned to Rousseau. 'Louis was the one who created this opportunity to market phosphoric acid abroad. Now you want to piggyback on his ideas to make money for your company. I have seen the contract between Triomf, Philip Brothers and Foskor and, in my view, it is binding. I suggest that you keep to it. If you want to get Fedmis into this business as well, you'd better find a way to have Foskor produce more phosphate rock, unless, of course, Louis is willing to share with you.'

Foskor was thus obligated to supply our needs, but used a loophole in the contract to increase its price to R13 per ton instead of the initial R7. In 1977, there was a further escalation to R21 per ton. Ultimately these increases, coupled with prohibitive rail transport costs – despite subsidies approved by the Minister of Finance, Chris Heunis – would begin to price us out of lucrative contracts abroad.

Once again officialdom had the last word. Shortly after this tempestuous meeting at Muller's house, I received another call from Dr Piet Rautenbach, the Secretary of Planning. Our land purchase at Richards Bay, he claimed, was null and void. The municipality did not have the power to sell us the land at a reduced price. 'We have already moved onto the site', I explained, 'and construction has started.' But Rautenbach was unmoved.

'You will pay us R80,000 per hectare,' he insisted. 'And what's more, you will have to provide your own infrastructure – roads, electricity, the lot.'

I asked Dawie de Villiers, who had stayed on as a member of Triomf's board after he won election to Parliament, to seek relief from the Minister of Planning,

Jannie Loots. But this, too, was to no avail. We were told to comply with Rautenbach's ruling or remove ourselves. We were thus left with no choice. The cost of the land escalated, and the construction of roads and electricity added yet additional cost.

Next came a call from the Department of Water Affairs, informing us that we were not allowed to dump the by-product gypsum in the ocean as was customary with major producers of phosphoric acid in the United States and Morocco. We argued that if gypsum had a harmful impact on small fish, as our officials insisted, the United States – with its stringent environmental laws – would long have passed the necessary legislation to control such dumping. The government remained intractable. Build a 25-kilometre pipeline into the sea or stop operations, we were told. So we went back to the negotiating table to try to find an alternative. In the end, we – at considerable cost – had to build a shorter pipeline to lead the gypsum into a swamp area where the state wished to reclaim land.

But there was more to come...

The tax concessions routinely extended to all new industries in so-called border areas such as Richards Bay were removed with the stroke of a pen. Triomf, the Decentralisation Board argued, suffered no disadvantage by establishing a factory at this outpost. They made no allowance for the fact that we had to train unskilled rural people and set ourselves up in an area far removed from our raw materials. We, in fact, were denied the tax allowances extended in terms of Section 15A of the Income Tax Act to any beneficiation of raw materials for export. This added up to a further cost of more than R8 million in the first year of operation.

'The whole history of our relationships with the Decentralisation Board and other agencies involved in luring industries to the border areas persuaded us that the ideal and actuality of decentralisation are poles apart,' I noted in Triomf's 1976 annual report.

We were completely at the mercy of the state-run South African Railways to ship phosphate rock over a distance of several hundred kilometres from Foskor's Phalaborwa operation to our plant in Richards Bay. We negotiated special rates based on the use of tippler equipment to be installed by the Railways at our plant, and were told that the tippler would be ready by October 1976, in good time for the commissioning of our plant. Instead, we were nonchalantly informed that the installations might not be ready until April 1977. Even though it was solely responsible for the delay, the Railways saw fit to revert to normal rates instead of the much lower rate negotiated based on the tippler facilities.

'We feel that we are being unreasonably penalised for the South African Railways and Harbour's inability to complete the task,' I told my shareholders. 'The South African Railways and Harbours, however, has a book of rules, a book of tariffs and it has no ability or apparent desire to move outside them; neither has it shown any willingness whatsoever to do justice to the situation. It is rather frustrating that one is powerless against mistakes of another party and that their mistakes are for one's own account.'

The government also introduced price controls that prevented us from passing escalating labour, power, coal, petroleum and rail costs on to the consumer. It was only through aggressive sales abroad that Triomf managed to compensate for shrinking profits at home. In the process, however, I could not resist voicing my disgust with the way in which the National Party government and its officials were suffocating private enterprise. I expressed fears that if costs continued to escalate we might find ourselves unable to compete abroad.

It was early in 1975 that Wollie Wolmarans arrived at my office with an interesting request. Formerly our press liaison and public relations manager at Triomf, Wollie had moved on to establish the public relations firm of Wolmarans, Deans & Ferreira, with us as their main account. Wollie explained that he had, with the help of sponsors, established an organisation called the Committee for Fairness in Sport, and needed me as its chairman. 'After all,' he continued, 'you are known as someone who has sponsored all kinds of sportsmen and events to help South Africa regain ground lost as a result of the anti-apartheid pressures.'

It was indeed true that I had been actively involved in all facets of sport. Apart from my sponsorship of the PGA, I assisted the promising black tennis player, Peter Lamb, to go abroad. Track athletes Fanie van Zyl, Ewald Bonzet and Danie Malan had also come to me for financial help. In addition, my private jet made sure that the 'One Hour' athletics meeting at Stellenbosch remained the most prestigious event for a number of years. In 1970, when the All Blacks visited South Africa, I had also made myself available to host receptions and to provide facilities for sightseeing tours. In fact, a barbeque for the whole team at my home would become a regular event whenever the New Zealand rugby team toured South Africa.

When Wollie came to me with his request, New Zealand's newly elected Labour Government under Prime Minister Norman Kirk had just instructed the All Blacks to cancel the upcoming Springbok visit. They had done so under severe pressure from groups such as HART (Halt All Racist Tours) and CARE (Citizens Association for Racial Equality), which threatened violent disruption at stadiums if the tour went ahead. At the same time, Black Africa's Supreme Council of Sport had threatened to boycott the Commonwealth Games in Christchurch if the Springbok tour was not called off. In England, the South African expatriate, Peter Hain, was gaining ground in severing rugby links. The International Olympic Committee followed suit. Soon South Africa would be completely isolated. Something had to be done.

'So, what do you want me to do as chairman of this...?' I asked Wollie.

'... Committee for Fairness in Sport, or CFFS for short. Nothing, really,' he said. 'We just want you to lend your name to this effort. You are known as a sports personality and possibly its greatest benefactor without any ties to the government. To have any effect, it has to be a totally private effort.'

'Who else do you have on the board?' I asked.

'People like Gary Player and Wilf Isaacs.'

No one could question Player's credentials as one of the world's best golfers, a patriot and a non-politician, and Wilf Isaacs was also highly respected in cricket circles around the world. So I saw no problem in accepting the invitation to join these two men on the board of an organisation that came highly recommended by my PR advisor.

Unbeknown to me, however, I had just been successfully recruited as a front for a government-funded propaganda operation, hatched behind closed doors at the Department of Information and determined to turn around a losing battle by going underground with a wide-ranging covert campaign. The CFFS was, I would later learn, the brainchild of Les de Villiers, who – as Eschel Rhoodie's deputy – masterminded many, but not all, of the Department's covert programmes.

I liked what the CFFS proposed doing. Wollie recruited Leslie Sehume, a combative and well-respected black journalist, as the chief executive and – like me and the other directors of this group – Sehume was also, I am sure, blissfully unaware of the government's involvement. The CFFS' first advertisement, 'Who is discriminating now?', was an effective indictment of the world's double standards. Appearing in the *New York Times*, the *London Daily Telegraph* and other major newspapers, this full-page advertisement accused the International Olympic Committee and other international sport organisations of double standards by blackballing South Africa while turning a blind eye to gross human-rights transgressions in bloody dictatorships elsewhere. It caused quite a stir but, as is always the case with advertising, one would never know what its real impact was. More transparent was the success that the CFFS had in projects such as sponsoring the outstanding black South African middle-distance runner, Sydney Maree, to attend Rutgers in the United States and later compete internationally in the Olympics for the USA.

One day, Wollie arrived at my office with R20,000 in cash and asked me whether I would mind if this contribution from an anonymous donor might be handled through my personal account. Having myself been an anonymous contributor to scholarship and travel funds for athletes in the past, the idea of donors wishing not to be identified did not raise any alarm bells. It protected one from being flooded with other less deserving requests. Also, it occurred to me that, given the controversial nature of some of the CFFS' actions and messages, some well-meaning donors might have preferred not to be openly associated even though as patriotic South Africans they sympathised with its cause. What did bother me was the cash. Wollie assured me that the money was clean and that all he needed was a personal cheque from me to facilitate payments and keep the books legitimate.

But after the Erasmus Commission submitted its report, I received a call from the office of the Receiver of Revenue. They had to talk to me urgently about R20,000 I had received from Eschel Rhoodie. Why did I not declare the amount and what was it for? Again, I went to the Receiver's office along with my auditor Fourie du Preez. The fellow who interviewed us was rather embarrassed, he told us, but he had to ask me straight out about the R20,000. Then it dawned on me: the cash in Wollie Wolmarans' briefcase. In no time, we furnished the Receiver's official with proof of the cash deposit into my bank account and the contra-payment cheque to CFFS. This time, the official's embarrassment was very real. Apologies came fast and furious.

I had, however, opened a Pandora's box by openly associating my name with the CFFS. Not long afterwards, I received a call from Cas de Villiers in Pretoria, requesting an appointment to discuss plans for a new think-tank called the Foreign Affairs Association. While I did not know De Villiers, I was certainly familiar with the names of other people he mentioned as having agreed to serve on his board. They were Gerry Muller of Nedbank, and prominent entrepreneurs such as Raymond Ackerman and Aaron Searle. When he arrived at my office a few days later, De Villiers produced papers to prove the organisation's *bona fides* as an independent, privately funded body set on promoting open non-partisan debate and top-level contact with the outside world. The idea of lending my name to such a laudable effort together with men of substance interested in promoting their country appealed to me and I agreed to come on board. But once again, I had, like several other independent-minded business executives, become an unwitting front for the government.

In the years that followed, the FAA hosted a number of influential academic, political and media personalities from abroad and arranged conferences in Europe and the United States. It proved to be a useful catalyst for top-level debate over a wide range of topics relating to South Africa and its worsening international standing. Even the most strident members of the South African opposition participated fully in events, operating – I presume – under the same mistaken impression that the FAA was a purely private non-partisan effort to foster open and frank international exchanges.

One morning in September 1975, about a week before the Currie Cup rugby final between Northern Transvaal and the Free State at the Free State stadium in Bloemfontein, I received a call from the Minister of Sport, Dr Piet Koornhof. Through my extensive involvement with sport, I had come to know Koornhof reasonably well. In his effort to accommodate interracial contact in sport, he would at times bend the rules. That morning, however, he had a request of his own. Would it be possible, he asked, to arrange for him and a few friends to fly down with me to Bloemfontein for the Currie Cup final on my BAC 111 and to squeeze out a few tickets?

There was nothing particularly unusual about this request. With a corporate aircraft that seated more than 20 passengers in great comfort and my special connections with the rugby adminsitrators of the Free State, it was certainly within the realm of reasonability. His group, Koornhof explained, included General Hendrik van den Bergh, Van Zyl Alberts, and a fellow by the name of Dr Eschel Rhoodie.

Only a Martian who had just landed on Earth would have asked who Van den Bergh was. Everyone knew this lanky, jovial former top cop as the celebrated 'mastermind' behind the capture of Nelson Mandela, Walter Sisulu and others at Lilliesleaf Farm in Rivonia where they were reported to be plotting the violent overthrow of the South African government. Van den Bergh's new position as head of the Bureau of State Security might have precluded him from talking much about the present but not from regaling his colourful past. Few were unaware of his influence on Prime Minister John Vorster, his fellow inmate at Koffiefontein, where the Smuts government had interned them as alleged Nazi sympathisers during the Second World War. I assumed, therefore, that Koornhof, as a junior minister in the Vorster cabinet, could benefit greatly by doing favours for this man who was generally seen as the grey eminence at the Union Buildings. Then there was Van Zyl Alberts, a tall, slight man with a modest moustache. I had met him in the early sixties when the newly established Louis Luyt Enterprises rented office space from Rentmeester, an insurance firm where Alberts was a director. Alberts, I would learn later, also happened to be a member of the Koffiefontein old boys club. But what about Rhoodie? I refrained from asking, but Koornhof volunteered:

'As Secretary of Information, Eschel Rhoodie is bent on helping where he can to break barriers in sport. He has been very helpful to me. By the way, he tells me that he once played at centre for Transvaal against you in a game against Free State in the fifties when you were captaining Free State.' I could not recall it, but pretended I remembered.

I told Koornhof that I had space on my plane and, after contacting Steve Strydom of the Free State Rugby Union, confirmed through my secretary that they would all be seated in the presidential box. The trip to Bloemfontein and back was rather uneventful. The rest of my party included former Springboks Piet Greyling and Piet Uys, both of whom worked for me, and a number of other regulars. During a private moment, Van den Bergh enquired whether my plane might be available for special government excursions into Africa. Yes, I said, we were available on charter to everyone willing to pay. Soon not only Van den Bergh, but many of the movers and shakers at the Department of Foreign Affairs would become clients. These were, however, business transactions. Pure and simple.

Strangely enough, however, another entirely separate event threatened to overshadow the trip. Actors Richard Burton and Elizabeth Taylor were visiting South Africa at the time and, out of the blue, I received a rather impertinent request from a public relations firm to fly Burton and Taylor – free of charge – first to Zimbabwe and then to Botswana. And, the caller added, for this honour, the guests were inviting me to join them. My response was, needless to say, unpublishable. Later, of course, I found out that Welshman Burton was an ardent rugby supporter and wanted to be in Bloemfontein for the Currie Cup final. This time, I invited him to join me on the flight. Rumour had it that he was hellbent on going, but it was Liz who prevailed after what appears to have been a rather heated debate between two of Hollywood's temperamental stars.

On Saturday, 27 September 1975, Free State lost narrowly in controversial fashion during the dying minutes of the game against Northern Transvaal when the latter's Pierre Spies fumbled the ball forward, caught it again and scored a try. It was also the day I would lose my innocence and independence from the government without realising it. At the time, I was blissfully unaware of the scheming behind the rather motley group of men. It was solicitation by stealth, the extent of which I would only hear about much later from Les de Villiers. As the person who originally, with the help of Wolmarans, involved me as an unwitting front for the CFFS, he was at that very point fighting hard against any further entanglement of my name and person. He felt that having me serve on the board of the FAA as well was risky because the press might become suspicious when the same name popped up in several supposedly independent pro-South African pressure organisations. But Eschel Rhoodie went ahead regardless, instructing Cas de Villiers (no relation to Les de Villiers) to approach me.

As it turned out, Koornhof's companions had other things on their mind besides rugby when they made their request . It was an opportunity for Van Zyl Alberts to renew old acquaintances and for Rhoodie and Van den Bergh to scout prey. Eventually, I would learn that shortly before that fateful trip to Bloemfontein the three, together with Information Minister Connie Mulder and Les de Villiers, had decided to buy South African Associated Newspapers (SAAN) and its failing flagship, the *Rand Daily Mail*, with secret government funds. Despite vehement protest on the part of De Villiers, who felt that the risk was too high for both me and the project, the others had decided that I was the ideal person to lead the assault. Van Zyl Alberts, then serving as managing director of the magazine *To the Point*, was considered too lightweight. What was needed was someone with the means and the influence to launch a friendly take-over bid. *To the Point* was later revealed as yet another creation of the Department of Information.

Van Zyl Alberts did not take long to make the next move. Barely days after the trip to Bloemfontein, he came to see me, armed with a sheath of papers. SAAN, he noted, was losing money. Its shares were sinking fast and it might be ripe for the plucking. Already 'involved in publishing', he was certainly interested in acquiring control of SAAN with the help of a trust and formidable overseas partners such as Germany's Axel Springer and US publisher John McGoff. What he needed, however, was someone like myself with name recognition and no particular party affiliation, who could lend credibility to this nonpartisan coalition. He felt that by establishing moderate ownership and control at SAAN, the *Rand Daily Mail* could be turned around. Advertisers who had deserted in protest over the paper's 'left-wing' leanings would thus return. All that was needed to obtain control was a few hundred thousand shares.

I told him I might be interested, but that I first wanted to conduct my own research. The SAAN annual report I obtained from my broker showed an operation in dire straits. My own calculation revealed that one would be able to buy control for probably less than R4 million at current share prices and recoup double that amount through asset stripping. It was too good an opportunity to pass up. But there was a catch. One thing the SAAN report did not tell us was the identity of the major shareholders. It was obvious that as soon as we started buying large blocks of SAAN shares on the Johannesburg Stock Exchange, the alarm bells would go off and the door would slam shut.

When I told Alberts about my interest, he indicated that he had already managed to purchase a few thousand shares, and suggested that we continue to use the merchant bank Hill Samuel, which had concluded these purchases on his behalf, to act on behalf of our consortium.

Given the high profile and general respect I enjoyed in the business community at the time, I was rather surprised and somewhat taken aback by the response at Hill Samuel when Alberts and I told them of our plans. They wanted assurances and guarantees from me. I told them to call Dr Frans Cronjé, chairman of Nedbank, who would tell them that I most certainly had sufficient resources of my own to make the bid. The fellow at Hill Samuel smiled apologetically as he handed the telephone over to me.

'Dr Cronjé wants to speak to you, Mr Luyt.'

Cronjé invited me to meet him at his office as soon as I had concluded my discussions at Hill Samuel. He was, as always, courteous and friendly when I arrived, but I detected a hint of concern too.

'Louis,' said Cronjé, after a brief exchange of pleasantries and the customary South African offer of a cup of tea, 'you know that I also serve on the board of SAAN. I am therefore obliged to inform our chairman, Ian McPherson, about your plans.'

'But...' I protested.

Photographed at the Triomf factory in 1967.
photo: Sunday Times.

Believe it or not I was a 4-handicap golfer in 1967. Here I am practising at Zoo Lake.

Our happy family, taken in 1969. Louis Junior sits on my lap, with Corlia, Lucien, my wife Adri and Adri Junior.

In 1970, at the age of 38, playing for Adelaar against Tukkies and tangling with Springbok lock Johan Spies in the lineout.

Relaxing in the change room after the Tukkies game.

'No, Louis, I have no choice.'

'But you should know we are not planning a hostile take-over,' I informed him.

'Yes,' he said, nodding, 'I gathered that much. And you should know that I am not against such a take-over at all. In fact, I would strongly suggest that you go and see De Villiers Graaff. He might be interested as well.'

Although he did not say so at the time, I gathered that as a member of the United Party once ably led by his good friend Sir De Villiers Graaff, the idea of leading SAAN back to its original roots must have appealed to Cronjé. After all, Cronjé as a prominent UP member, must have felt considerable pain seeing the old party of Smuts being dismantled and torn apart by the same radicalism that was now alienating the business community from the *Rand Daily Mail*.

'Yes, I would certainly welcome Sir Div as a participant,' I answered.

Cronjé immediately picked up the phone and called Cape Town. Before I walked out of his office, I had an appointment to see De Villiers Graaff. Cronjé was true to style. The man who helped me enter business when others tried to shut me out was now once again opening doors, even though he ran the risk of being ostracised by other board members for doing so.

Two days later, I flew down with a fellow from Hill Samuel at my side to meet with De Villiers Graaff at his offices on Church Square, near the Houses of Parliament in Cape Town. In my view, this intelligent man with his sonorous voice and charming manners might have gone much further in politics had he had a tougher and more ruthless demeanour. Instead, he will be remembered as the ultimate gentleman who could have been a truly remarkable leader, but never realised his potential. De Villiers Graaff came from an old family with traditional Cape values and was, no doubt, well suited to make the introductions to the members of the Bailey Trust who held a substantial chunk of SAAN shares. Older men with old money, they were obviously highly suspicious of outsiders such as myself. Before we went to see them, Graaff and I sat down to compare notes. He was willing to put R1 million into the partnership and I readily agreed to match his investment. With R2 million out of the four required, we would be in control.

During our short walk across the square to the offices of the Bailey Trust, De Villiers Graaff cautioned me not to expect a warm reception. They had shown little enthusiasm, he informed me, when he called to set up the appointment. It was even worse than expected. Clive Corder and his stone-faced colleagues around the room had obviously received word from Johannesburg to stand firm against this intrusion from outside.

De Villiers Graaff did all the talking. In eloquent fashion, he gave assurances that there was no intention to change the political direction of the newspaper. The purpose was simply to bring it back to old values. It would be pro-country, but definitely not pro-Nationalist.

But, despite his best efforts, Sir De Villiers Graaff failed to burn off the chill in the room. Afterwards, in Johannesburg, I met with Lathan Slater, the chairman of the Argus Group, which also held a substantial share in SAAN. From what I had heard, the Argus might well have been interested in getting rid of this drain on their profits and had simply been waiting for the Bailey Trust to take the lead. The Argus chairman listened attentively, but I went away with the impression that he would rather rot in hell than sell to an Afrikaner – even if he brought along Harry Oppenheimer himself to plead his case. Oppenheimer, incidentally, was reputed to have been one of the major players in both Argus and the Bailey Trust. No one, however, knew exactly to what extent he or others were involved. It was a secret, we were told.

At Cape Town airport, I passed Ian McPherson, chairman of SAAN, who had just flown in from Johannesburg, and I was left with very little doubt that he was on his way to meet with the same crowd at the Bailey Trust offices. Only in his case, I thought as he glanced furtively in my direction, the meeting would, instead, be a rallying of the troops. Who knows, he might even be invited to stay for sherry and a few old boy jokes about this fellow Luyt who had had the nerve to drag poor old Div into his despicable scheme to grab SAAN. On the way back, the representative of Hill Samuel respectfully requested to be relieved of his assignment. I readily agreed. He was never enthusiastic about the take-over bid and I suspected that he might even, deep down, have wished to see us fail.

The decision soon afterwards by both the Bailey Trust and the Argus Group to hold onto their shares in the steadily deteriorating SAAN came as no surprise. By this time, we were sitting with about R200,000 worth of SAAN shares and a heap of publicity, much of it vitriolic. It was only natural that the *Rand Daily Mail* and its sister publications would pull all the stops to vilify me for launching an 'unfriendly' take-over bid. The editorial staffs were obviously afraid that their days might well be numbered and they were pulling no punches in their counter-offensive. Gone were the halcyon days when the English-language press sang my praises as one of South Africa's most innovative businessmen. I had been transformed into public enemy number one – a power-hungry politico bent on destroying the 'opposition' press.

At the same time, however, praise and encouragement came from English-speaking South Africans who believed that there was indeed a need for a newspaper in their own language that would be both balanced and fair, one that would promote the country instead of breaking it down with a daily barrage of negative reporting. I got the clear impression that this 'silent majority' was yearning for a pro-South African paper that would inform the outside world instead of feeding it with ammunition to attack us at world forums – a newspaper that would rather assist in forging change in the minds of people instead of forcing it.

These were the considerations that came into play when General Van den Bergh approached me, shortly after the take-over failure, with the request that I make myself available to head up a new newspaper. I also then learned that both the CFFS and the FAA were government-sponsored organisations and the abortive take-over bid from Alberts' side had been funded with government money. Now the Prime Minister, General Van den Bergh assured me, had given the go ahead for the establishment of a brand-new English-language newspaper with government funds. The idea was to provide seed money and then to withdraw once the paper was able to function on its own.

'We were thinking of having Van Zyl Alberts, who is already the managing director of another government-funded publication, *To the Point*, head up this new paper,' he explained. 'But that won't work. What we need here is someone with both the necessary status and credibility, someone who is not affiliated with the National Party and has acted independently. In fact, Prime Minister Vorster personally suggested that you be the one to take on this task on behalf of your country.'

As someone who has always believed in straight dealing and brutal honesty, even when it hurts, I was deeply troubled by the mere thought of having to live a double life. Furthermore, if the public attacks on my person by the *Rand Daily Mail* and others during the take-over bid were any indication, it was clear that an avalanche of abuse was bound to follow my debut as a publisher of a competing daily newspaper. At the same time, I was quite flattered to have been singled out by the leader of my country to take on this gargantuan task. It posed an exciting challenge. Instead of merely making more money for myself, I would be doing something worthwhile for my country. After discussion with various 'experts' in the field, I came to the conclusion that this new paper might well turn a profit and stand on its own after a matter of a year or two.

As to the government's involvement in its creation, it had been pointed out that, in their day, other prime ministers, such as Generals Smuts and Hertzog, had sanctioned the use of state funds to buy shares in newspapers such as *Die Volkstem*, *Land en Volk* and *The Friend*. This had been done to ensure that the Afrikaner got a fair shake in these important newspapers. Vorster and his functionaries thus had a precedent in making this approach.

In the end, however, all the rationalisation does not help to soften the traumatic impact my decision to go along with this scheme would have on my life and the lives of my family. When Rhoodie told him that I would be heading up the new paper, Les de Villiers came to see me at my home in Saxonwold, Johannesburg. While he was in favour of the idea of such an 'independent' newspaper, he advised me as a friend to steer well clear. It was far too risky, he said. A few years later, he wrote as follows about this meeting in his book *Secret Information*:

'I heard about this decision very much later and when I was told, I supported the grand idea but did not feel much enthusiasm for Luyt as the publisher. I even went to the trouble this time of trying to dissuade him at his home in Saxonwold, but he persisted. The Prime Minister, he maintained, had asked him through others to undertake this task so he had no choice in the matter.

'Secretly, I knew that although this may have been his best argument for accepting, there were other reasons as well. Louis Luyt had always liked new challenges and he had reached a stage in his business career where everything was going just too smoothly and routinely after the stormy years when he challenged and beat all the greats in the fertiliser business.

'Now Luyt had suddenly seen a new peak and it was not in his nature to refuse the challenge. His adept public performance as a prospective publisher during the abortive SAAN take-over attempt had whetted his appetite and nothing was going to deter him from going ahead at Vorster's request.'

I had indeed signalled my willingness to play ball and around the end of November 1975 I met with Van den Bergh, Rhoodie, Alberts and De Villiers in a private suite at the Burgerspark Hotel in Pretoria. Accompanying me was my auditor, Fourie du Preez, who I had to take into my confidence. We talked budgets and business plans. According to our calculation, the R12 million the government was willing to make available would be sufficient. As long as we could count on a monthly interest calculated at a rate of 12.5 per cent per annum, we felt that we might be able to operate on that income alone and leave the principal amount untouched. I indicated that Triomf would be able to hold the funds and pay 12.5 per cent – the going overdraft rate – in interest. This was readily accepted as the going bank rate at the time was well below this and the presence of these funds on my books would help remove suspicion of outside funding.

At a follow-up meeting on 5 December 1975, the matter of where the money was to be held was not even raised. This second meeting, scheduled to be held at Van den Bergh's offices and then at Rhoodie's home, eventually took place at the home of Les de Villiers. Such was the media interest in my movements after my take-over attempt of SAAN that I could not afford the risk of being seen near either Van den Bergh or Rhoodie. The gathering in De Villiers' thatched upstairs lounge was attended by the same group who gathered at the Burgerspark Hotel, but this time they were joined by Information Minister Connie Mulder. Du Preez brought along our revised budget and Alberts, at Rhoodie's suggestion, pulled out his own set of financials. According to him, our figures were unrealistically high.

'Well, if you want to do it, go ahead,' I said to Alberts, signalling that I was about ready to leave. From the corner of my eye, I thought I saw a flicker of hope in De Villiers' eyes. Similarly, Fourie du Preez, who had earnestly advised me against this move and to walk away, looked relieved. They might have their wish after all. But Van den Bergh would have nothing of the kind.

'Louis, the Prime Minister wants you personally in this role. No one else,' he insisted. Then, turning his bespectacled gaze away from me to the rest of the room, he added: 'The Prime Minister also asked me not to become too involved myself. But he wants me to keep my ear on the ground and report back to him on a regular basis.'

Mulder stepped in to reassure me that the government would make up any shortfall, as it would be unfair to have me lose money on this deal. The interest on the R12-million loan to Triomf was intended to cover running expenses but one never knows, he said. Everyone agreed.

All these issues of who asked whom to do what, where the money was supposed to be going and how it was to be spent seemed crystal clear at the time. At a later stage, however, they would all grow into major issues of contention as some tried to add their own spin in order to save their own skins. Before we adjourned, however, there was one other little matter that needed to be settled. The name of the paper. Bandied about were names such as *The Guardian*, *The Republican* and the *The Tribune*. My personal choice, *The Citizen*, won the day, but not without a few wisecracks around the room. 'At least you know what kind of watch to give to those with long service,' Les de Villiers joked. 'We should be happy that you did not pick Omega or Piaget as a name. That would have inflated your budget even more.'

The Citizen project, originally code-named Sun King by Eschel Rhoodie, was promptly renamed Annemarie after his daughter. I had little time for pseudonyms. The beginning of 1976 found me spending long hours away from Triomf in preparing to launch the newspaper. As we progressed with our plans, appointing staff, acquiring equipment and renting offices, we kept revising budgets. Our supposedly lavish budget eventually turned out to be way too conservative. But while ours missed the mark by about a 100 per cent, Alberts' figures were a few thousand per cent off.

On 7 September 1976, the first issue of *The Citizen*, South Africa's new morning daily with the conservative approach, appeared on the streets of Johannesburg, Pretoria, Cape Town, Durban and Bloemfontein. Our first-day sales topped 140,000 but slipped back to 60,000 and eventually 40,000 before starting a steady climb upwards. There was nothing unusual about the initial circulation figures. New publications always enjoy substantial short-term sales before falling back, reaching it lower base and building long-term support. What did come as an unpleasant surprise, however, was the slow growth in advertising revenues, in part due to a slowing economy.

While I did not expect the *Rand Daily Mail* to take this challenge lightly, the lengths to which it went in digging into my past came as something of a shock. In April 1976, several months before our launch, a confidential memorandum from their development manager, John Fairbairn, to 'friends' at the *New York*

Times, Washington Post and various other American newspapers was leaked and appeared in the Afrikaans afternoon paper, *Die Vaderland.*

Some 25 per cent of the readers of the *Rand Daily Mail*, Fairbairn lamented, had a loose association with the paper. 'They see it as prejudiced in political reporting, inaccurate in its news reporting, that it does not wish to promote racial harmony, that it is irresponsible, untruthful and dangerous, and that it is against South Africa,' he wrote. This new newspaper to be launched by Luyt, said Fairbairn, will be directed at these disgruntled readers. Suggestions, he said, as to how one could counter this would be most welcome. According to Fairbairn, the *Mail* was already gearing up for an all-out war against me personally. One contact at the *Houston Chronicle* was asked to urgently check out a rumour that I had purchased a farm in Texas in violation of strict exchange-control regulations.

But what I learned from Rhoodie barely a week after *The Citizen's* appearance on the streets was much more disconcerting than the *Mail's* efforts to dig for dirt. Apparently, Dr Bruno Saager, head of the Union Bank of Switzerland, who provided the channel for the R12-million loan transferred to me, let it slip in conversation with his friend Anton Rupert that the government had a role in *The Citizen.* Immediately on his return from Zurich, Rupert called on Prime Minister Vorster to express his concern over this 'government interference' in the press. In characteristic poker-face fashion, Vorster feigned ignorance. After Rupert left, Vorster instructed Eschel Rhoodie through Van den Bergh to fix the problem. In great haste, Rhoodie and Les de Villiers travelled to Italy where Saager was relaxing at a spa, pulled him out of a steam bath and leaned on him to correct 'the misunderstanding'. From what I could gather, Rupert was satisfied with Saager's explanation that he was mistaken in his assumption.

I then approached Rhoodie and suggested that we change the relationship into a proper business transaction. We would sign an agreement whereby the state would simply lend me the money. This would make it possible for us to deny any government involvement in the project. Rhoodie thus agreed to a loan for 10 years at a nominal interest rate of 3 per cent, but interest free for the first two years.

Soon, however, I was beginning to have serious second thoughts about the project. The constant threat of exposure and the increasing attacks on my person by the *Rand Daily Mail* were only part of the problem. Right from the outset, Rhoodie and I found ourselves at loggerheads. We would jointly decide to have the government – through *The Citizen* – sponsor the Grand Prix at Killarney, only to have Rhoodie turn around and deny any such discussion afterwards. It wasn't long before I also became aware of his direct interference with my staff in an effort to manipulate editorial content. This, I felt, would raise suspicion and I warned him to lay off. Under no circumstances did I want editor

Johnnie Johnson, or in fact any of the staff, to draw any connection between the newspaper and the government. But Rhoodie persisted in planting unsubstantiated stories favourable to the government through 'privileged leaks', including false information about the death of black activist Steve Biko in jail.

In the meanwhile, costs escalated to the point where I had to start spending my own capital to keep the paper running. Even though Standard Bank sat with R40 million of my shares, it demanded due diligence before extending my long-standing low-interest $3-million Swiss loan. But with the government's involvement I no longer had the luxury of total transparency. I had to forego the facility and pay back the loan. Deep down, I suspected that there might have been an ulterior motive on the part of Standard Bank, which had close ties to SAAN. I, in fact, voiced this at the Erasmus Commission inquiry who, in typical fashion, incorrectly - and stupidly – reported that I said Standard Bank raised the interest rate they charged me. I had to pay for equipment out of my own pocket and sign a personal guarantee for the printing plant installed at Perskor on behalf of *The Citizen*. On one occasion, I was asked to secure a personal loan from Volkskas Bank as secret funds were drying up. Within a matter of months, my personal exposure topped R3 million.

By March 1977, barely six months after *The Citizen* made its first appearance, Rhoodie and I were no longer on speaking terms. We were riding a tiger, sitting at opposite ends. Only, I found myself at the front end, having to feed it. I decided that the time had come to stop the madness.

During April 1977, a meeting was arranged in a room at the Johannesburg Airport Holiday Inn. Fourie du Preez accompanied me. On the other side of the table sat Information Minister Mulder, Rhoodie and Alberts. The initial niceties soon gave way to recrimination and accusation. Tired of having to cope for months with duplicity, double-talk and double-dealing on the other side, I could no longer contain myself.

'You are a James Bond,' I told Rhoodie. 'You don't talk to me like that. I hire guys like you. I don't work for them. I don't work for Dr Mulder either. I am doing these things for nothing.'

Rhoodie turned out to be most probably the most dishonest man I have ever met. But I also quickly figured out his *modus operandi*: He would plan a crime and then, before committing the deed, he would consider every possible scenario and step from the end result backwards to cover every eventuality. He had an answer for everything.

We had reached the end of the line. I wanted out. It was decided that Alberts would 'buy' the paper and continue running it. In a subsequent meeting with Mulder in Cape Town, financial matters were discussed further. In accordance with the government's original undertaking to compensate me for any personal losses, the principal sum due for repayment was reduced to R10,118,000.

Back in Johannesburg there was much to do. Triomf had entered a critical stage in its development of overseas markets as Richards Bay started shipping phosphoric acid to overseas markets. During the day, this heavy workload would keep me completely occupied, but in the evenings and during free moments my thoughts would keep returning to *The Citizen*. I knew that it was only a matter of time before this episode would be revealed. I looked at my children across the dinner table and wondered how this would affect their lives. Will they have to suffer insult and taunts at school? Will they understand, as Adri certainly did, that I was driven not by self-interest but by a sense of duty? Would they end up equating patriotism with stupidity after seeing where it had taken me?

Towards the end of 1977, reporters were openly gossiping among themselves about the state funding of *The Citizen* and a number of other secret projects launched by Eschel Rhoodie and his team. Les de Villiers, who had by then left the government to take up a position at a private firm in New York, told me shortly before his departure that he had had a visit from Hugh Murray of the *Sunday Express*, who informed him that his paper had the whole story but was unable to publish it. It was all still a matter of hearsay. 'One of these days,' I said, 'they will have their proof. Someone will give it to them before long.'

That someone turned out to be Retief van Rooyen, a lawyer friend and confidant of both Rhoodie and Prime Minister Vorster. Apparently overburdened by what he regarded as gross mismanagement of state funds by Rhoodie, Van Rooyen started sharing his concern with acquaintances and before long found himself as a star witness in front of a secret enquiry into exchange-control violations under Justice Anton Mostert. On 27 September 1978, I met with Mostert who informed me about the developments. There was nothing intrinsically wrong with *The Citizen*, he told me. His only concern was that there might not have been any authorisation for the use of these funds. This amount, he told me, was, in any event, a small drop in the ocean. Much larger sums were at stake.

On 4 October, I thus agreed to testify under oath before Mostert, and was assured that it would all be on a strictly confidential basis.

Mostert indicated that he was aware of both Vorster's and Mulder's involvement in *The Citizen* but that Defence Minister PW Botha, who had assumed the premiership, denied any responsibility. Although he knew about the project, Botha claimed he had a certificate that would exonerate him from any complicity whatsoever. Mostert indicated, too, that it was his intention to 'clear' my name with Botha when he next interviewed him. He left with a full set of documents relating to my relationship with the government.

Then, on Saturday, 28 October 1978, *Sunday Express* reporter Kit Katzin turned up at my front gate and requested to see me. I refused. He left a note indicating that his newspaper had the whole story and was going to splash it across its front page the next day. I immediately phoned Mostert. He fell silent and then said, 'You have nothing to fear. You are clean. There are other people who should worry'. The *Sunday Express* story – under the banner headline, '*The Citizen* secret revealed' – contained full disclosure plus a large measure of conjecture. In the months that followed, I would be subjected to a barrage of vitriol in both the English-language and Afrikaans press. Somehow, it seemed as if the press was trying to elicit a response to libellous statements so that they could have the opportunity to question me in court. I was not about to give them that satisfaction.

I had become a recluse at Saxonwold, licking my wounds and wondering how I could have been so naive as to become involved with such a losing proposition. As false charges mounted in the press, individuals whom I had considered friends started avoiding me. Among those whom I least expected to abandon ship was Dawie de Villiers. This likeable former Springbok rugby captain, whom I had provided with a free office, back-up staff and funding to get elected to Parliament, swiftly resigned his directorship at Triomf and jumped ship. Many 'friends' who had begged for invitations and favours in the past now lost my unlisted telephone number and shunned me in public. My partners at what was now AECI, on the other hand, wanted to know how much of Triomf's money I had sunk into *The Citizen*. I invited them to undertake a full audit and the matter was put to rest.

I did, however, receive a call from Sidney Kentridge, that outstanding senior counsel who had represented Triomf in previous court actions. In fact, I found it rather odd that he would want to contact me, as he was perceived to be openly on the side of SAAN.

'Louis,' he started, 'I have a strange feeling that you are avoiding me. Why?'

'Sidney,' I admitted, 'I am too ashamed to look you in the eye.'

'Yes, I do think what has happened is absolutely wrong. But, Louis, I know one thing. You would never have done anything dishonest. I suggest you come see me. If you don't want to see me in chambers, we can meet at my home.'

'Thanks,' I replied, 'but I don't think that's necessary. If it were, I'd be on your doorstep in a hurry.'

'What about the loan?' Kentridge asked. 'Have you repaid it?'

'Not yet,' I informed him, 'but I have the cheque ready.'

'Don't,' Kentridge advised. 'They will only say this is a rich man buying himself out of a prosecution. Wait until all this is 100 per cent completed.'

I followed his advice – and it turned out to be sound indeed. Eventually, the state sent a functionary, Mr Decker, to my office to pick up the cheque for R10,118,000 after due calculation of the monies still owed to me in the aborted running of *The Citizen*. Later that same day, Decker was back with the cheque. He needed it certified. Also, the state wanted me to sign an undertaking that I would not sue for damages and that this transaction represented a full and final settlement between us.

It was difficult not to laugh. The mere thought of coming back all the way from Pretoria for a certified cheque seemed ludicrous. And here was the state begging me to lay off. Did they not realise how anxious I was to put this episode behind me and to move forward without any skeletons in my closet? I thus gladly signed the agreement and sent Decker off with his certified cheque.

In 1978, I put up for sale my BAC-111 – I owned a Lear jet too – and received word that the film producer Francis Ford Coppola was interested in buying it. He hired the plane for a visit to the East and decided that this 'baby' was for him. Pete du Plessis and Mel Colyn, my pilots at the time, had to actually restrain Coppola from knocking nails into the beautiful wood panelling – so that he could hang his own paintings – until he had paid over the asking price. He then offered me a vineyard in California in exchange, but I insisted that I wanted cash. In the end, then, Coppola's paintings weren't even hung and the deal was never consummated.

In 1979, Triomf showed a taxed profit of R25 million, and Rob Abrahamse of Nedbank hosted a lunch for me in their boardroom. 'Welcome back, Louis,' he said as he raised his glass. 'You are now one of us again. Back in business.'

Within a year, Triomf recorded an even greater profit of R50 million – more than Nedbank – but being back in business and making good profits was not everything. I needed my reputation restored. But, as others discovered long before me, a man's reputation is not in his own keeping. It lies entirely at the mercy of others. Calumny would continue long after *The Citizen* episode faded in the public memory. This scarecrow would be dragged out and paraded in public whenever my opposition in business, politics and sport found themselves at a loss. I am reminded of the expression used by General Jan Smuts, one of my all-time heroes in South African politics: 'Let the dogs bark – the caravan will move on.'

We all make our mistakes. I had made my most significant one in the mid-seventies when I relied entirely on emotions instead of good business sense. In retrospect, I can certainly say that entering into this grandiose project with the government bordered on recklessness. But at the time it certainly had its appeal. We were a nation under siege and I could not resist the call to play a role after the Luyt/Graaff/Springer/McGoff bid for SAAN failed the Bailey Trust test.

This experience was, however, not without benefits of its own. It gave me the opportunity to sort out good-weather friends from the real ones. More importantly, it brought Adri, the children and me closer together as a family. While I had become only too accustomed to the strength and resoluteness Adri brought to our partnership in marriage, I now discovered that my children were made of the same stuff. Despite the animosity and venom they encountered at school where children of either misinformed or mischievous parents bandied about false stories about me, they stood strong and remained supportive.

As we approached the eighties, however, I was gearing up for another battle with the government. This time I was accused of monopolistic practices by the same authorities that once tried to stop me from challenging the fertiliser cartel. As I primed myself for this new challenge, I felt reinvigorated. This was my opportunity to battle in the open with the same government that had given me so much grief in secret.

In all human activities,

particularly in matters of business,

times of stress and difficulty are seasons of opportunity

when the seeds of progress are sown.

Thomas Woodlock

Chapter 7

SEASON OF OPPORTUNITY

The year 1975 was a particularly successful one for Triomf. We more than made up for the declining markets at home that resulted from government price fixing by developing alternative markets for both our fertiliser and crop-protection chemicals overseas. At the end of that year domestic sales accounted for only 23 per cent of our overall profits. The government responded by further lowering domestic prices by 8 per cent and in 1976 introduced a formula limiting us to a 16 per cent return on depreciated capital.

We approached the government for relief from spiralling labour, power and railage costs and not only were our representations summarily dismissed, but a 20 per cent deposit was levied on imports of raw materials and in 1977 more stringent price fixing followed. Suddenly we found ourselves facing a new formula that pegged our returns to 15 per cent of our depreciated capital instead of 16 per cent, while facing further rail increases.

'At times, the impression is created that private enterprise profits are a sin,' I informed my shareholders in my 1976 annual report.

The same opposition press that supported me in the past was now highly critical. On 6 May 1977, the SAAN-owned *Financial Mail* described my attack on government interference in private enterprise in my annual report as a 'smoke screen'. They saw the interest on a loan of R15 million towards the completion of the Richards Bay plant as a negative and concluded 'Triomf is not a share to hold'.

By grossly understating Triomf Fertiliser's cash flow and disregarding the fact that the major shareholders, including not only myself but also AECI and the agricultural cooperatives, were indeed there to back it up, the *Financial Mail* painted a dismal picture. Other members of the SAAN stable – the *Sunday Times, Sunday Express* and *Rand Daily Mail* – followed suit. The headlines at the time spoke for themselves. They ranged from 'Luyt's acid test' to 'Triumph or disaster? Can Luyt sit it out?' and 'Triomf deeper in debt?' But *The Diamond Fields Advertiser*, apparently, did not check with SAAN's 'war room' before it went to press with a report under the headline 'Triumph or Triomf', in which it indicated that 'Triomf had already sold most of the first year's production from its R95-million Richards Bay phosphoric acid plant' and that orders were waiting from Japan and Brazil.

Any reasonable or knowledgeable analysis of the annual accounts of Triomf Fertiliser for the year ending December 1976 proved that we were not only capable of coping with problems caused by market fluctuation and government inter-ference, but showing the ability to rebound. Some readers, I had hoped, would have taken the time to do their own analysis and realise that, with assets of close to R200 million, Triomf could hardly have been over-extended, with loans totalling about one quarter (most of which were contractual shareholder loans that could have been converted into fixed capital at anytime) and the prospects of massive phosphoric acid sales abroad.

At our annual general meeting, I assured shareholders that Triomf Fertiliser Investments had sufficient financing facilities to meet maturing repayments on our Richards Bay phosphoric acid plant until the cash flow improved. Not only did we have R4 million available immediately, but also the contractual undertaking of AECI to match this amount. Triomf, I explained, had been offered overseas loan facilities but we preferred to borrow locally. I have always shied away from foreign exposure because of the dangers inherent in exchange-rate fluctuations.

What most readers did not realise was that behind these growing attacks on my company and my person was the fierce resentment aroused in the media after my take-over bid of SAAN and the subsequent establishment of *The Citizen*. I was no longer the Businessman of the Year. Instead, I was painted as the ogre that was to be feared. Even some Afrikaans-language newspapers were joining the fray in sympathy with their comrades in the English press. I was experiencing a foretaste of what the so-called Fourth Estate can do when they set themselves the goal of ruining a reputation and pulverizing an opponent.

This flood of negative reporting was also showing its effect on our share price, which spiralled sharply from 420 cents in 1975, where it stood before I became involved in the SAAN take-over bid and the establishment of *The Citizen*, to a mere 120 cents in mid-1977. It was painful for me to see this decline in a com-pany that had taken the Johannesburg Stock Exchange by storm in its initial public offering in 1972. Starting at 400 cents, it rapidly climbed to 450 cents before settling at 420 cents in a scene that, in the words of one journalist, resembled a free-for-all loose scrum on the floor of the exchange. Consensus at the time was that Triomf was the share to have and hold. Now, barely five years later, the same company with the same fundamentals and much more to offer in potential profits, found itself battling to stay above 100 cents, largely as the result of deliberate poor and distorted publicity.

At first, the *Financial Mail* tried to dismiss *The Citizen* as a publication intended 'more for the naartjie (tangerine) throwers than decision-makers'. Then it tried to question the circulation audits of *The Citizen*. When that did not manage to blow this intruder away, the attacks were directed at me personally and Triomf. The SAAN 'war room' had clear instructions to use whatever it took. And they did – and I found myself unable to respond even to libellous statements as legal action on my part would have given them the opportunity to seek discovery in open court. For the first time ever, my hands were tied – and this because of a secret newspaper deal with the government.

I have since come to realise the power of the press the hard way. Pitted against me was the SAAN group, incensed at being challenged in their own lair by an upstart newspaper, but I also faced a group controlled by secret and clandestine shareholders that had a near monopoly on viewpoints expressed in English. I was boxed in from both sides. On the left, I had to fight off the press and, on the right, the same government with which I had gone into a 'secret' partnership in establishing *The Citizen*. The officials who saw it as their duty to prevent Triomf from making good profits obviously had no knowledge of my 'secret' link to officialdom, but I doubt whether it would have made any difference if they did.

The often-repeated claims of South Africa as the last beacon of capitalism in Africa seemed far from the truth indeed. It turned out to be – at best – a useful slogan to lure investors. If South Africa was a beacon, it was a crumbling one. Ironically, in the nineties the new African National Congress (ANC) government, which was expected to nationalise everything and destroy our much-heralded capitalist world, dismantled much of the socialist creations and controls of the seventies. Unfortunately, they then proceeded to introduce their own set of restrictive rules relating to employment and investment. Even though it was done in the name of black empowerment – a very laudable cause indeed – government once again served to inhibit local business as well as foreign investment.

But back in the seventies there certainly was no question of free market practices at home and we in the fertiliser industry had thus been forced to look abroad for markets. Despite all the negative reporting, I knew that our phosphoric acid plant nearing completion at Richard's Bay was bound to provide a major boost to our exports and make us less dependent on the strictly controlled domestic market.

But at home, the government had another big surprise in store. In May 1977, one month before the first tanker bound for Japan loaded phosphoric acid from our Richards Bay plant, it announced the appointment of a commission of inquiry into what it claimed to be monopolistic practices in the fertiliser industry.

The irony apparently escaped most observers. Triomf, on one hand, was being portrayed as a failing enterprise, ready for the dump heap, and on the other, as a giant that made it impossible for competitors to exist and survive.

On 9 May 1977, Economic Affairs Minister Chris Heunis announced that, following an investigation by the Board of Trade and Industry, an inquiry would be launched into the multimillion-rand fertiliser industry under the Monopolies Act. On one hand, the Board of Trade and Industry found that the market-sharing agreement between Triomf and Fedmis, which gave us 90 per cent of the market, 'was not in the best interests of all parties, particularly the fertiliser users. On the other hand, it recommended that the government deny its termination, as requested by me. Underlying this anomaly were ongoing efforts by the government to reduce our competitive advantage over its favourite godson, Fedmis. The government obviously found itself in a dilemma. They were determined to derail Triomf, but Fedmis happened to be a passenger and hanger-on.

It had come to light, the Board said, that the marketing structure in the fertiliser industry had reached a situation in which Triomf had attained 'such a decisive competitive share above Fedmis and other competitors that the summary ending of the agreement in the present circumstances could have far-reaching and possibly extremely detrimental consequences for the fertiliser industry and its consumers'.

Behind all this gobbledygook was the desire to give Fedmis more of a competitive edge in a campaign that started at that acrimonious encounter at Lourens Muller's residence between me, Rousseau and the others from the Industrial Development Corporation, Federale Volksbeleggings and Fedmis. While the government was prepared to live with the monopolistic agreement between Triomf and Fedmis because it benefited the latter, our partnership with AECI and the agricultural cooperatives was squarely denounced.

Triomf enjoyed an unfair advantage over Fedmis, the Board claimed, because of its partnership with AECI, a major provider of nitrogen-bearing minerals necessary for fertiliser. It also questioned the considerable shareholding of the country's largest agricultural cooperatives, through Sentrale Landboubevorderings-maatskappy (Edms) Bpk, in Triomf, which placed it in a 'privileged position over other competitors in distribution'. No mention was made of the special treatment accorded Fedmis by the state-owned Foskor in the supply of phosphate rock after they seized on our idea to export acid.

In the meantime, Foskor, the ultimate government monopoly in the supply of phosphoric rock, continued to fix prices at will. In a matter of three years, from 1974 to 1977, when we went into full production, the price of rock spiralled from R11.50 to R21 a ton. As we required 2.9 tons of rock to produce 1 ton of acid, our cost per ton of product had risen by about R24 per ton when we started shipping in June 1977. With the South African rand trading well above US$1.50 to the rand, it made exports both difficult and expensive.

In contrast to the flags and festivity that heralded our entry into the manu-facture of fertiliser at Potchefstroom in 1967, there was thus no fanfare when Richards Bay started pumping phosphoric acid into the hold of the first giant tanker. The only photo opportunity was of John Norton, marketing director at the time, and a Japanese delegation being shown around while the cargo destined for Tokyo was being loaded. Looking back, I wonder whether it would not have made sense to have arranged a proper baptism for this impressive structure, which is still generating massive foreign-exchange earnings for the very country whose government once seemed set on its annihilation.

A few months after we started production, I had the opportunity to show State President Nico Diederichs around the plant. As the man who held the post of Finance Minister for many years, he was duly impressed with its huge foreign earnings potential. Fairly recently, Khaya Ngcula, chief executive of the IDC, which now owns the plant at Richards Bay, referred to it in passing as a cash cow that makes so much money that the government is embarrassed by it.

'Yes,' I responded, 'that is the factory the government "stole" from me.'

In the period leading up to the commissioning of our Richards Bay plant, the Philip Brothers contract had been cancelled due to fluctuating rock prices. Afterwards, I happened to receive an intensive but rather expensive education in international arbitration law. We found ourselves in a drawn-out legal battle when Gazocean, a French company, reneged on its obligations as our appointed exclusive agent abroad. The French company had approached us after we started negotiations with the Mexican firm of FFM and offered a much higher floor price, so we decided to switch. On 15 December 1975, Triomf and Gazocean signed a long-term exclusive marketing agreement and established a joint Bermuda company, Phosocean, to act as a conduit for export sales from Richards Bay. Gazocean, already active in the shipment of oil and natural gas, promptly ordered two new tankers to transport phosphoric acid, and already under construction was yet another large natural gas tanker, named the *Benjamin Franklin*. Just a few months before the *Benjamin Franklin* was completed, the bottom fell out of the gas market and Gazocean sat with a white elephant and heavy financial commitments. Rumours had it that the company was ready to go into liquidation.

In March 1977, Gazocean asked us to cancel our deal or change the terms, so we tried to salvage what we could in an alternative agreement. The new deal required them to pay a $35-million penalty, transfer all its shares in Phosocean to Triomf for the nominal sum of $1 and have all their directors resign from its board. In terms of our settlement, they also had to reorganise themselves into a shipping company according to the laws of France. Gazocean would not be entitled to more than 35 per cent of these shares until the full $35-million penalty had been paid to us. The other shareholders were to be nine French banks and investment companies. Gazocean undertook to put up 30 per cent of the value of the new company and obtain financing for the balance. Without consulting us, it went ahead and used our marketing agreement as collateral to obtain this 70 per cent in additional financing. It then turned around and offered us a third mortgage over the ships if we undertook not to call it up for a stipulated period. We refused to be suckered in by all this fancy footwork and insisted that the original agreement be reinstated.

Gazocean responded by seeking – and, in fact, obtaining – the French government's assistance in their plans for an early liquidation. They applied for arbitration to the International Chamber of Commerce (ICC) in Paris. We concurred. Next, they withdrew their application and sought a ruling against us in Johannesburg. This ploy failed because they could not prove *locus standi* in South Africa. We thus found ourselves back in Paris at the ICC, where QC Mark Littman of London, former Chief Justice Ogilvy Thompson and former Appeal Judge Oscar Galgut were appointed as arbitrators. But before the tribunal could convene, it first had to hear an urgent application in Johannesburg from Gazocean, questioning the validity and powers of this tribunal. Sidney Kentridge, the late John Coetzee and Tom Cloete, who later became judges of the Supreme Court, represented Triomf while Gazocean's legal team consisted of Issie Maisels, Arthur Chaskalson and Dr Piet Henning.

Even though it irritated me enormously to have to go through this litigation with a French concern that, in my view, had showed gross disregard – if at all – for binding agreements, the experience was not without its benefits. I had the opportunity to get an insider's view of foreign arbitration laws in action. Instead of sitting on the sidelines, I was actively engaged. I devoured all the relevant case law I could lay my hands on. In a way, this incident served to satisfy a long-held passion I have always felt for the law. I had the opportunity to discuss strategy with Sidney Kentridge and to observe this truly outstanding legal mind in action against an equally outstanding Issie Maisels. I could not, of course, contemplate at the time that Arthur Chaskalson, who assisted Maisels, would – in the 1990s – be the presiding judge of the Constitutional Court that had to rule on Nelson Mandela's appeal against a ruling in my favour in the Supreme Court. This first encounter was civil and superficial in comparison with what would follow in the years to some.

The outcome of the Gazocean litigation reminded me of an expression accredited to the American jurist Oliver Wendell Holmes. 'Lawyers,' he noted, 'spend a great deal of time shovelling smoke.' When the smoke cleared, all the litigation in Johannesburg and eventually in Paris, came to nothing. The case was settled and we walked away with a measly $500,000, most of it going towards paying our lawyers.

While we were engaged in this futile French minuet with Gazocean, we looked around for another more suitable partner to join us once the music stopped. Soon we focused on Interore, an affiliate of Occidental Petroleum. In 1977, I travelled to New York to strike a deal with Occidental's chief executive, Armand Hammer. This diminutive man with the looks of evangelist Norman Vincent Peale and the self-promotional zeal of a Dale Carnegie, seemed so taken with my story that he welcomed me as if I was a long-lost son. Strange father-son pair we would have made, with all of my six-feet four-inches towering over his five-feet few inches.

Even though Hammer liked to embellish a little – as, I suppose, we all are prone to do at times – the short version of his life story was impressive in itself. As a 22-year-old Columbia University medical school graduate, Armand Hammer went to Russia to help the Lenin government cope with its post-war plagues and to collect $150,000 owed to his father's company for drugs shipped during the Allied blockade of Russia's ports. Dr Hammer, whose Russian-American father was serving time in Sing Sing prison on an abortion conviction, travelled to Russia and bartered a million tons of US wheat for a fortune in furs, caviar and precious stones. He also met with Lenin, who persuaded him to take a concession to operate an asbestos mine in the Urals. The mine failed, but the export-import business opened by Armand and his younger brother Victor in Moscow, prospered. Soon the Hammers were acting on behalf of Ford, Parker Pen, US Rubber, Underwood Typewriters and dozens of other foreign companies. Armand Hammer came out of retirement at the age of 60 to head the failing Occidental Petroleum Company in which he had invested $60,000 as a tax shelter. And, from a net worth of $34,000, he built Occidental into a billion-dollar enterprise, the twentieth largest in the United States. Through Interore, Occidental had a 10-year contract in hand for the supply of 1.5 million tons of super phosphoric acid to the Soviets every year. In trying to supply the rising demand at home, Interore was looking for additional sources to honour its obligations in the Soviet Union and elsewhere.

Now sitting opposite me behind his big desk and against the backdrop of photographs of him in the company of celebrities and leaders, the little man sipped quietly at his tea while he listened to me and members of my team and cast furtive glances at his own set of advisers. I have always found it odd that he would have tea brought in only for himself without offering any to his guests. After all the back and forth, it came to a handshake and a good deal of trust between the two of us – both reputed to have come from nothing to something and now intent on making more together. But the deal was never finalised. Even though Interore, with its extensive reach into Russia and other large users of super phosphoric acid, could have been useful to us, it was clear that there might have been a conflict of interest in other markets.

The press in America liked to use the word 'eccentric' whenever they wrote about the little doctor's lifestyle. While I have been criticised in the press for supposedly having a television set in every room before it became customary for many South African households to have more than one, I must admit that I never contemplated having eight in my bedroom like Hammer did. When he proudly showed off this feature in his opulent bedroom during one of my visits to his home in a posh Los Angeles suburb, Hammer explained that by keeping eight sets going on different channels he made sure that he did not miss out on anything important happening around the world. His minute indoor swimming pool was another feature I hardly needed to copy in either my home in Saxonwold or in my vacation residence at Ballito. Instead, I built the swimming pools outside and made them bigger so more people could enjoy them with me.

I guess this was the big difference between Hammer and me. Instead of planning for my own pleasure alone, I would buy, build and install for the enjoyment of my family and friends. My plane, my homes, overseas apartments, the pool-rooms, the reception rooms and the Olympic-size swimming pools were all acquired with the family, business contacts and friends in mind. As president of the Transvaal Rugby Football Union in the nineties and later as president of the South African Rugby Football Union, post-game dinners and celebration parties for the teams became regular events at my house in Saxonwold.

With the exception of the squash courts at both homes – basically intended for Lucien, Louis and me – everything else was for the guests. Never would anyone sit in my office and watch me sip tea on my own. Instead, important guests were offered à la carte luncheons in my executive dining room from a kitchen run by Hubert Jarlet, or Froggy, as he preferred to be known. This outstanding chef-restaurateur, who managed one of my favourite restaurants in town before I lured him over to Triomf House in Auckland Park, made a lasting impression as he recited the choices of the day in his charming French accent. So lasting an impression did he make, in fact, that he eventually became a director of the fertiliser company, and put on a great façade as the overseas investors' representative, using a rare show of deception to eventually manipulate the 'transfer' of Triomf's assets.

In 1981, when South Africa started to feel the brunt of ever-increasing sanctions, Hammer approached me with an offer to buy 50 per cent of my stake in Triomf for R100 million (US$140 million). He was confident that, with his influence in Russia, he could convince them to import phosphoric acid from Richards Bay. We also talked about the possibility of an exchange of shares – Occidental shares for Triomf shares. But the South African Reserve Bank vetoed the proposed deals and this wonderful deal came to naught. As the Cold War intensified during the early Reagan years, Hammer found himself under increasing criticism for his cosy relationship with the Soviet Union and when he died in 1990, he was a lonely figure, but one who nevertheless left quite a legacy.

Within the first few months after our Richards Bay plant went on stream, we shipped four loads of phosphoric acid to Brazil and landed a firm 10-year contract with the Japanese. Together with our partners, AECI, we also struck a deal with Kynoch Feeds and Polyfos. Sales to these two local companies represented some 25 per cent of the capital expenditure on the Richards Bay project.

Led by the SAAN group, the press, however, continued to cry wolf in their concerted effort to topple *The Citizen* by destroying me at my home base. They raised fears among investors by suggesting that Nedbank, a major lender and respected bank in our Richards Bay project, might itself be in deep trouble because of us and other 'high-risk exposures'. Some suggested that I was just about ready to throw in the towel and sell out to Fedmis. Others implied that liquidation was around the corner. Suggestion succeeded suggestion, rumour raced after rumour. All of it was geared to hit me in what they regarded, mistakenly, as my soft underbelly – to make me let go of the dreaded competitor in the news world.

The strange thing about it all, though, was that Triomf, in 1975, was able to lend no less than R14 million to *inter alia* SAB (R3 million) and AECI (R5 million), and deposited R3 million at both Standard Bank and Trust Bank. Triomf was clearly sitting on too much cash and could hardly have been classified as a company in dire straits!

Flipping through the reports several decades after this relentless campaign of calumny, I am reminded of the many times Adri and I found ourselves sitting across the dinner table after the kids had retired to do their homework, exchanging words of encouragement and plotting the next defence. In the end, of course, there would be no way in which I could or even would wish to continue with *The Citizen*. It was clearly a terrible, egotistical and misguided decision to have allowed myself to be drawn into that ill-fated project. At the same time, there was no question in my mind that Triomf would rise above the rancour and silence the hecklers. At times, when I would show even the slightest sign of wavering, Adri was there to encourage me in her own calm and reassuring manner.

On 19 August 1977, through much deliberation and thorough consultation with AECI and the cooperatives as my major partners, I decided to seek a delisting of Triomf's shares from the Johannesburg Stock Exchange. The response in the SAAN stable was predictable. They were noticeably angered by the prospect of having their target slip away. But we were on firm ground. Even the *Rand Daily Mail* had to agree that there was nothing in the law that prevented us from taking this step. 'Say what you like about the motives or morality of Triomf Fertiliser's intention to delist its shares – there is nothing in the existing law to stop it,' its financial editor wrote on 20 August 1977. 'Unless Triomf's directors can be persuaded to change their minds, the company will disappear from the lists in the next two months.'

Five days later, a delegation headed by JSE President Chris Freemantle came to see me at Triomf House, begging that we remain on the Exchange board. I agreed to do so on the condition that we be allowed to issue new shares at market value without a prospectus, if needed. Initially, they had insisted that we could only do so by means of a rights issue accompanied by a prospectus. But this would have required full disclosure at a time when I was least prepared to do so for fear that the government's 'loan' for *The Citizen* might become public in the process.

On 28 August 1977, after the dust had settled, Willem Laubscher of *Rapport* explained as follows in an article headlined 'Bigger say for Luyt': 'This week's drama around the delisting of Triomf boils down to one thing. That is that Mr Louis Luyt is no longer willing to push personal money into the company without having larger control. In reality, what he requested from the Johannesburg Stock Exchange was permission to issue shares without a prospectus. Initially the exchange said no, it must be a rights issue. This Mr Luyt and his directors found unacceptable. Instead, with 76 per cent of the shareholding behind them, they requested to have Triomf delisted. In terms of the law, only 51 per cent of the shareholders are required to be in favour of delisting so the JSE had no other choice but to accede to Mr Luyt's original request.'

This proposal was not, however, a novel one as other companies listed on the JSE did exactly the same thing with full JSE approval, and without as much as a murmur from the governing board.

I came to discover – as others did – that in all human activity, but especially in business, times of stress and difficulty are in fact seasons of opportunity when the seeds of progress are sown. I expected the seeds sown at Richards Bay to grow into healthy and sturdy fruit-bearing plants. I was not disappointed.

Keeping steady at the helm at a time when the so-called experts told others to abandon ship was not easy. But it paid off. In 1979, there was a major and sustained recovery in the price and the demand for fertiliser in general and phosphoric acid in particular. We had sold our entire output not only from Richards Bay but from all our other dry-fertiliser plants as well.

'As was foreseen in my last chairman's statement,' I could tell our shareholders in Triomf's 1979 annual report, 'the fortunes of your company showed a radical improvement during the past financial year. With consolidated trading profit in excess of R25 million (US$35 million), profitability exceeded the best ever previously recorded profit in 1975 by more than two and a half times and showed an improvement of 7.8 times on that of the previous year.'

In 1979, the company's gross assets increased by approximately R23 million to a total of R231 million (US$325 million). The improved cash flow, therefore, enabled it to repay all its outstanding foreign loans, which totalled R22 million (US$31 million).

By early 1980, after two years of deliberation over alleged monopolistic practices in the fertiliser industry, yet another commission, the Mouton Commission, was just about ready to bring out its long-awaited report. I made my move. On 23 May of that year, I bought out the 40 per cent shareholding of the agricultural cooperatives in Triomf for a total sum of slightly more than R51 million (R714 million in today's terms). For me it was a very good deal indeed. The share price had soared from a low of 90 cents in 1977 to 630 cents, with the share having been split earlier in 50-cent units.

Dawie de Villiers, who had hastened to distance himself from Triomf and me two years earlier when *The Citizen* saga came to its climactic conclusion, now wished to speak to me urgently in his new capacity as Minister of Trade and Industry. Having appointed him as a director of my company and funded his entry into politics, it was no doubt not an easy assignment to confront me on behalf of his new employer.

'Louis,' he complained, 'we are on the verge of bringing out the Mouton Report that was supposed to force the cooperatives to sell their shareholding in Triomf. Now you have gone ahead and bought them out before we could act. It makes us look like fools.'

'Dawie,' I said, 'you are fools. You could have gotten what you wanted without a commission of inquiry. But you obviously had to impress the people at Federale Volksbeleggings and Fedmis with your actions.'

The long-awaited Mouton Report fell on Parliament with a faint thud, like a damp squib. There was nothing to act upon. The urgent recommendations were thus tabled, but I had already pre-empted them. Their recommendation that the cooperatives sell their shares in Triomf looked as stupid as it sounded.

Richards Bay had, in the meanwhile, not only fulfilled my own expectations. It had become a convenient outlet for Fedmis, which followed suit with its own phosphoric acid plant and we had paid Foskor, in terms of a government-enforced agreement, a hefty premium on all our sales above a certain floor price. In 1980 alone, this additional payment added R2.7 million to the tens of millions in revenue Foskor earned from the sale of phosphate rock to Triomf.

In October 1980, *Finance Week* featured a story about the recovery at Triomf and my enlarged interest. 'Where did you get the money to buy out the cooperatives?', their reporter asked me.

'A couple of years ago, when Triomf shares were 90 cents, it was unsettling, but I am in a very healthy state now,' I was happy to respond.

How much do you owe the bank? The audacity of the press never ceases to amaze me. Why would I share my dealings with them? I owed nobody a damn cent. In fact, I had a R16-million (US$ 22.5 million) loan to Triomf on the books reflected as a 'shareholder loan'.

'Nothing. I'm unencumbered.'

At the end of that year, my income in dividends topped R7 million, and my salary was R60,000 a month. In 1980, Triomf ranked among the top 20 companies in the country, its gross assets totalling almost R380 million (US$532 million) and its long-term loans standing at R36 million (US$50 million). A 10-year review showed that Triomf averaged an annual dividend of 23.6 cents (47.2 per cent) that was way ahead of other companies in the chemical business. Average earnings per share topped 51 cents per year (101 per cent) since Triomf was first listed in 1972. In every analyst's book, all this added up to the profile of a company in extremely solid financial shape – the leading player in the South African fertiliser industry.

With the dawning of the 1980s, I found myself with time on my hands and tried to make up for time lost time during the stressful seventies when almost every hour was occupied with emergency planning and damage control. As a result, the family began to spend more time together – between obligatory business appointments – at my apartments in London and New York and we went on vacations to the Seychelles, Mauritius and other exotic islands. I had time to reflect on the importance of family above anything else and learned to relax with a good wine and my favourite light classical music. Listen to any high-powered business-person and you will invariably hear that what they resent most is the fact that they could not spend more time with their family.

Corlia, our hard-working little daughter who always insisted driving with me wherever I went, was 20 at the time and achieving good grades at Stellenbosch University where she was studying law. At 17, Lucien was getting ready to leave school and go to university. He was already a very good athlete and rugby wing three quarter, playing for Helpmekaar High School. Here he would upstage his father by scoring a record 23 tries in a single season. Adri, our headstrong third child, turned 16 and was excelling at English and Business Economics at Damelin College. Louis Jr was only 12 but he was already beating me on the squash court. In fact, a few years later, he scored a remarkable victory against Ian Holding, then the South African champion. Even though Ian was a guest at our home and almost certainly gave Louis a few points on a platter, I know that this was a hard-earned win. It was not in the nature of Ian Holding to throw any game. Even at this early age, my namesake showed the desire to follow in my footsteps in business.

At the turn of the eighties we were living what would be considered by most as a rather privileged life. We had stepped out of the nightmarish seventies into the light of day. Once again, there was laughter around the house and good times with new friends and the old ones who had stuck with us through it all. We came out of the ordeal stronger and wiser, and felt comfortable in the knowledge that we were able – with faith, family and friends – to survive the storm.

I shared some of my wealth with schools and universities and, in those early 1980s, donated close to R2 million; with further contributions over the years, the amount was quite possibly closer to R10 million by the time I retired. I also donated my extensive Law Library, worth at least R2 million, to the Free State University. This was apart from the many students I helped with bursaries through the years. In 1980, I received my PhD from Columbia Pacific University with my thesis 'A Critical Analysis of Arbitration Through the Court of Reconciliation and Arbitration of the International Chamber Of Commerce', and Free State University bestowed on me an honorary DCom degree in 1983. In 1986, I was made an honorary professor of law at the University of Pretoria, and lectured widely on arbitration at different universities, as well as acting as arbitration advisor for a number of attorneys.

But it would not be long before we were tested once again. In the mid-eighties, this comfortable cruise at high altitude would yet again run into severe turbulence. I would discover how easily a suggestion to change a modest overdraft facility could develop into a monstrous debt when left, unsupervised, at the sole discretion and mercy of the bankers alone.

I sincerely believe... that banking establishments are more dangerous than standing armies, and that the principle of spending money to be paid by posterity, under the name of funding, is but swindling futurity on a large scale.

Thomas Jefferson,
US president,
1743–1826

Chapter 8

TRUST MISPLACED

It was the best of times, it was the worst of times...' These oft-repeated opening lines from Charles Dickens' *A Tale of Two Cities* aptly summarise my experiences during the early eighties. After the disastrous outfall of my ill-advised foray into newspapers, there was full recovery and my company's and my personal fortunes reached new heights. I was voted by the *Sunday Times* as the third wealthiest person in South Africa, where my listed share portfolio alone exceeded US$69 million and Triomf had its best ever year in 1980. I was able to enjoy the fruits of my labour and spend more time with friends and family. But even then the dark, threatening clouds were gathering on the horizon.

The year 1982 saw South Africa face its worst recession since the Second World War. This economic uncertainty, coupled with extremely high interest rates, relatively weak agricultural prices and a countrywide drought, resulted in a 9.63 per cent drop in the demand for fertiliser. It was the worst year for the industry in a quarter-century. The export market, which had long been the mainstay of Triomf, showed similar shrinkage. But we were not only hampered in our competitiveness by South Africa's high rate of inflation compared with other nations. Instead of being able to take advantage of the long overdue rapidly sinking rand, we found a slackened demand worldwide as major users of our product cut back in their own agricultural production. Due to government price controls in South Africa, we were unable to react efficiently and expeditiously to these negative developments on the free market. We had to absorb increases in interest rates, railage and raw material costs instead of being able to pass them along to our consumers – largely because of the tremendous power organised agriculture wielded with government. This power was all too prevalent when, in 1980, Triomf was on the verge of merging with Fedmis and, despite having received the green light from the Competitions Board, the government thwarted the move. Not surprisingly, Triomf and other fertiliser companies all showed greatly diminished profits in 1982.

Reforms introduced by Prime Minister PW Botha, when he narrowly defeated the beleaguered Connie Mulder for the premiership, had come to naught. The establishment of a so-called tricameral parliament with separate 'own-affairs' chambers for whites, coloureds and Indians merely served to further anger the disenfranchised masses. I still recall my own surprise when, oddly enough, I was asked by Andreas Wassenaar, head of the massive Sanlam insurance giant, to make a contribution towards party-political advertisements to propagate the plan during the referendum. Instead of providing a solution, this grandiose scheme – which required a massive extension of the parliamentary buildings in Cape Town – created a new set of problems of its own. Botha, who was elected President – to signify his 'nonpartisan' overseeing role in the central multiracial cabinet – found himself fighting on two fronts. On the South West African (Namibian) border, our troops were trying to contain Cuban and Russian-assisted SWAPO insurgents, and within South Africa the newly formed United Democratic Front (UDF) was posing additional challenges through violent protest. Led by Archbishop Desmond Tutu and Reverend Allan Boesak, the UDF was a loosely knit broad-based organisation representing more than 600 different member groups. It was formed to challenge the Botha government on the 'fraud' it had committed against the people by excluding the large mass of black South Africans from the decision-making process. In reality, even though it only later openly admitted to these links, the UDF served as a front for the banned African National Congress.

When we look back at the mid-eighties in South Africa, we see images of burning buildings and the masses marching in protest. The outside world saw a country that was running amok and a government seemingly out of control, and the Reagan and Thatcher governments found themselves under increasing pressure from anti-apartheid forces clamouring for total sanctions. More importantly, overseas financial markets were beginning to respond negatively and finally, in 1985, the rand began to show the strain and went into free-fall.

In a frantic last-ditch effort to save the situation, the Botha government promised drastic reforms to provide friends abroad with much-needed arguments against sanctions. In 1985, Foreign Minister Pik Botha journeyed to Europe to meet with US Assistant Secretary for Africa, Chester Crocker, and brought him up to snuff on the upcoming 'dramatic announcements' to be made by President Botha at a National Party convention in Durban, Natal. We are all now only too familiar with President Botha's disappointing performance on 15 August 1985. The press subsequently pictured the South African leader as having stumbled on the banks of the Rubicon, where he had turned around rather than crossing it as he had promised. In fact, to this day the debate rages on as to whether Botha's foreign minister was guilty of making too much of the president's intentions or whether Botha – under severe pressure from FW de Klerk, Magnus Malan and other conservatives – was forced to toe the line. To me, this debate matters much less than the ultimate effect the actual event had on Triomf and me personally.

Within a year after the disappointment of the Rubicon speech in Durban, South Africa found itself almost completely isolated. The US Congress had passed the Comprehensive Anti-Apartheid Act in 1986 and, when Reagan vetoed the bill, easily mustered the required two-thirds majority to override him. Even diehard conservatives from the Deep South - the kind we despised as the 'real racists' – deserted our cause and voted for the sanctions bill in order to hold onto their seats. With the US officially in the fold, other countries had no choice but to join in the action.

Even more devastating, however, was when the American Ambassador to Pretoria, Herman Nickel, called for sanctions of the markets. Even before the blanket official sanctions were introduced, the chaos in South Africa's streets had frightened away foreign capital. The same foreign companies that were once willing to face criticism and protests for the sake of good profits found the hassle factor too burdensome as revenues dwindled in our recession-hit, unstable country. As early as March 1985, Willard Butcher of Chase Manhattan Bank, one of South Africa's biggest lenders, decided to pull in US$700-million loaned to Nedbank after this institution failed to roll over US$13 million, which became due and the Reserve Bank did not have the dollars to redeem this amount. As word got out, others started to panic and followed suit. Then, after the Rubicon speech, the run turned into a rout. First, the Reserve Bank Governor Gerhard de Kock made a hasty trip abroad to try to stop the massive bleeding and when this failed, Finance Minister Barend du Plessis imposed a four-month freeze on all overseas loan repayments. Du Plessis also froze foreign investment, but indicated that interest would still be paid during the moratorium.

The onerous and unenviable task of negotiating a standstill agreement with the overseas banks was left to the Director-General of Finance, Dr Chris Stals. This brilliant banker, who later succeeded De Kock as governor of the South African Reserve Bank, was successful through hard bargaining in the so-called Standstill Coordinating Committee – under the chairmanship of Swiss banker Fritz Leutweiler – in the Butcher Hall (nothing to do with Willard) to reschedule repayments. At the time, South Africa owed $23.7 billion of which $14 billion was on immediate demand by US and other foreign banks. While the government debt concerned the country at large, the billions owed by private banks affected not only them but also us, their clients. Triomf, as a major client of Nedbank, was about to realise the full meaning of the adage that a banker is someone who lends you an umbrella on a sunny day and wants it back when it rains.

We certainly had no problems with our bank when we made record profits in 1978, 1979, 1980 and 1981 and even in 1982. We were in a favourable position, where we could borrow virtually any amount from any of the country's major banks. But our fortunes soon began to tumble as the South African economy deteriorated. The country's growth in gross domestic product (GDP) fell from 8 per cent in 1980 to zero in 1982. All of a sudden, we found ourselves indeed in need of bridging finance. Nedbank obliged. At the end of 1982 our overdraft stood at R52 million despite a drastic decline in agricultural activity both at home and abroad. This amount represented about 10 pr cent of the previous year's turnover and most of our financing was funded through shareholders' loans.

While our debt exposure was clearly within limits and we had good reason to believe that, with the expected upturn in the next few years, we could easily ride it out, interest rates were reaching alarming new heights. Quite understandably, Triomf's financial staff were eager listeners when Nedbank's forex managers, led by Ed Vosloo, came to them with a proposal that Triomf take its overdraft overseas where interest rates were approximately one-third of the going rate in South Africa. It was explained to our managing director, the late Kobus Becker, and financial director Nic van Rensburg that we would be joining several other valued customers who took advantage of Nedbank's foreign borrowing facility – in terms of new powers granted to commercial banks by the South African Reserve Bank. In reality, Nedbank – like other banking institutions – would simply borrow large sums on short-term in Eurodollars and other currencies abroad and pass along the more favourable interest rates to their clients on a long-term basis, while rolling it over constantly on a short-term basis. And, what was more, in Nedbank's case, they went further and borrowed directly from clients and depositors in foreign countries where they took deposits on short term and lent out on long term. This, of course, had to be very well hidden in off balance sheet transactions. But, as I only discovered relatively recently, most of Nedbank's borrowings were for the purposes of state funding, as the government of the day found it impossible to raise any loans on its own accord because of its apartheid policies.

What looked like a splendid deal to us at the receiving end, later turned into a disaster. With political and economic conditions worsening, the rand took a battering from abroad. World Bank figures showed South African foreign borrowing rising from about $13 billion in 1982 to $19.6 billion at the end of 1984. With the depreciation of the rand, external borrowings had soared during this period from R14 billion to R38.5 billion. Two-thirds of this borrowing were short term and had to be repaid or rolled over within a year.

Starting at an exchange rate of $1.40 per rand in 1980, our currency fell to 50 US cents over the next five years. Within 24 hours of the Rubicon speech in August 1985, the rand plummeted to 35 cents and then further to 26 cents.

The 'Rubicon rand' might have become the butt of many jokes, but we at Triomf were hardly in a laughing mood. Both Triomf and Nedbank were guilty of not providing forward cover on our foreign loans, but – given the facts that emerged later – forward cover could certainly not have been available for the massive amounts borrowed overseas. Indeed, if that were the case, why could the Reserve Bank not have paid over the dollars when the loans fell due? Triomf was, however, saddled with the total exposure.

Gone was the umbrella. Triomf's loan with Nedbank, which started at R52 million (or US$59 million), had now ballooned to unmanageable proportions after the bank moved it overseas in three instalments. Instead of bringing the loans back when the rand dropped to 82.5 US cents, which would have been the point of parity, lower interest off-shore and devaluation considered, Nedbank hung unto these and other overseas loans without any forward cover being sought or Triomf timeously advised to take out. In fact, they firmly believed that the rand would recover. And so did we. Ed Vosloo unstintingly believed that the rand would recover to its earlier value and was strongly against forward cover being taken out.

Next, the bank suggested we issue them with preferential shares in Richards Bay in order 'to lighten our loan burden' and before long we were liable to pay additional interest at a time when the phosphoric acid market had fallen into a severe slump. In the meantime, the price of imported sulphur skyrocketed as a result of the rand's devaluation. This, in turn, meant further borrowing and greater debt exposure.

Eventually, Nedbank made a desperate attempt to keep us going for a little longer while it tried to disentangle itself from the mess it had created. The lengths to which it would go to buy time is illustrated by documents that surfaced during a Supreme Court case brought against them by Standard Chartered Bank of Canada, representing Cansulex, from which Triomf purchased sulphur. On 20 November 1985, when Triomf was already completely illiquid and heavily over-borrowed given the devaluation of the rand, Standard Chartered sent the following telex to Nedbank: 'Please supply extremely urgent full general report on Triomf. Reply extremely urgently.Tlx at very latest today. Urgent.'

Nedbank immediately answered: 'Triomf Fertiliser Richards Bay Co Pty Ltd is one of the largest manuf in the country. Experiences manages [sic] holding company is quoted and figures are available as in the rest of the fertiliser industry. The company has suffered setbacks but they are trading normally and would in those circumstances be regarded as good to their normal commitments in the course of business.'

The extent of Nedbank's problems and openly debated practices at the time became public as foreign banks joined the rush to reclaim their money after the Rubicon speech of August 1985. When senior South African officials travelled abroad to plead for patience during the standstill negotiations that followed, Nedbank featured as a major talking point. 'Before the debt moratorium was imposed,' reported *The Star* on 10 September 1985, 'Nedbank, South Africa's third largest bank, had been an active player in the markets, trading not only in rand but also several third currencies. Its branches in New York, London and Hong Kong were ordered to close and authority was transferred back to Johannesburg 'to enable the Reserve Bank to maintain close control over Nedbank's foreign-exchange operations'.

Four days earlier, Nedbank had got the government to bail it out. An official announcement, issued on 6 September, revealed that 'the South African Reserve Bank (SARB), with the approval of the minister of Finance, Mr Barend du Plessis, [stood] fully behind Nedbank, including all its branches and subsidiaries overseas.' The government undertook to 'assist Nedbank in bringing about the orderly disposition of its foreign exchange obligations and meeting the liquidity needs of its overseas operations'. In hindsight, this was nothing more than an arrangement by which to repay the government's loans – via Nedbank – to overseas lenders.

So, Nedbank got its parachute. But what about Triomf and the other unfortunate passengers on this kamikaze journey? Were they also going to be bailed out before the crash? Quite definitely not. But other victims had 'Big Brothers' to take the pain on their behalf.

Much earlier in 1985, at the first sign of trouble, I had called on Dawie de Villiers in his capacity as Minister of Trade and Industry. As a former director of Triomf, who was familiar with our operations and the problems that beset us, I felt that he might be able to intervene on our behalf to save a vital industry and in particular the Richards Bay plant. Dawie then passed the buck to the Industrial Development Corporation (IDC). On the basis of my past experiences with this state-owned entity, I saw my chances of getting a fair hearing from them about as slim as the possibility of PW Botha releasing Nelson Mandela from jail and including him in his cabinet. I proved to be justifiably pessimistic. The IDC insisted on a thorough investigation of Triomf's affairs and books before they turned us down, citing 'far too optimistic' long-term projected benefits. (Today, of course, they are basking in the sun of those over-optimistic figures.) A memorandum sent to Nedbank by the IDC confirmed my suspicion that this was merely a continuation of an ongoing vendetta against me. In this document, they made it clear that they would only consider a partnership arrangement with Triomf if I was forced to leave the company. As always, the government had the last say in this matter too. In the end, I did indeed leave, and the IDC rather disingenuously acquired our factory at Richards Bay – albeit through a front known as Indian Ocean Fertilisers (Pty) Ltd. The shareholders were purported to be inter alia the government of Togo. Togo, in itself, is a rock exporter and it made little sense to invest in a facility so far away from source and utilising another country's product. Today, the Richards Bay plant is one of South Africa's major foreign-currency earners, making profits of hundreds of millions of rands annually and firmly in the control of the IDC.

By the time I applied for government intervention, AECI was no longer a partner. In February 1984, I had approached this Anglo American subsidiary and urged it to step up to the table as a 49 per cent shareholder. Their lack of support – despite contractual obligations to that end on the one hand, and the exorbitant profits they made out of selling spent sulphuric acid to Triomf at Somerset West and Modderfontein, on the other – was in my view unconscionable. I made no progress and decided to obtain legal advice from gurus Sidney Kentridge and Fanie Cilliers. After one quick glance at the contract that had governed our purchases of acid from AECI since 1969, both had no hesitation in expressing their considered opinions that the contract was void for vagueness. Armed with this discovery, I approached AECI's managing director Dennis Marvin with the following ultimatum: Either discuss new pricing terms for the sulphuric acid and your continued contractual involvement to make 49 per cent of the funding requirements available or we will nullify the contract. Marvin went to Gavin Relly, chief executive of Anglo American, who instructed him to unbundle the merger. AECI thus took back the Chloorkop and Somerset West factories and another dry-fertiliser facility in Natal, while I retained Richards Bay and the Potchefstroom plants.

Chris von Solms, an AECI director at the time, struck a deal with me to purchase the Potchefstroom factory for R85 million cash. He assured me that the deal was agreed upon by both ICI and Anglo American Corporation, the major shareholders, and we in fact had already exchanged letters of intent. Then, at the very last minute, Von Solms walked away, defying legal action. I was too proud to even go further. I would kill them once again in the marketplace, I thought. But this was not the only questionable act from this reputable company. After the break-up, they would lure away my entire sales force in Natal without as much as a phone call. For that, I made them pay dearly.

When the unbungling became reality, Von Solms insisted on a R5-million 'settlement' as we had retained the only profit-producing factories. I then issued AECI five million Preference Shares in a private company that had no assets, and liquidated the company a year later.

Might Triomf have received a more sympathetic ear from the government if it still had AECI on board when I approached De Villiers and the IDC? I would never know for sure. However, on the basis of another experience two years later, I have good reason to suspect that it might have thrown us a lifeline if I still had Anglo American and its subsidiary at my side. In late 1986, I would discover just how rapidly the Afrikaner government would close ranks behind AECI and Anglo American when challenged. I was on my own at the time and had arranged a barter deal between Romania and the agricultural cooperatives at the request of Dr Hennie Davel of the Maize Board. In terms of this deal, Romania would exchange urea for maize at a time when farmers were sitting with a glut in production.

My son Lucien, Rian Oberholzer and I were in the process of taking the previously agreed orders from the cooperatives when the Maize Board reneged on its initial approval, siting legal requirements that dictated that we pay cash for the maize. I thus paid R1 million out of my own pocket for the first shipment. In the meantime, AECI rushed to the authorities, objecting to my importation of urea, even though it regularly supplemented its far-from-adequate local production with duty-free purchases of its own from abroad. The Board of Trade and Industry thus slammed a duty of 1000 per cent on the Romanian product, arguing that it needed to protect local industry against dumping. All my representations and arguments were to no avail, even though I had the very able Dr Piet Gouws of Nampo, the maize growers' association, fighting with me like a man possessed to have the restrictions lifted. I was never paid for the maize and thus lost a cool million. AECI was, in the meanwhile, allowed to import the urea shortfall without any duty imposed upon it. One might say, I became one of the world's top private foreign-aid donors. This episode showed just how strong an alliance between big business and the government can be when threatened by a loner from outside the laager.

Two state-owned enterprises to which we appealed for some relief were equally uncooperative. Both Foskor (the company through which the IDC eventually acquired my Richards Bay factory), which had it within its power to assist with more reasonable pricing of its phosphate rock, and the South African Railways, whose inflated transport rates placed a heavy burden on us, remained inflexible. Instead of making concessions that would help our plant at Richards Bay survive, they opted for its demise and a loss of business. The government, it seemed, was set on seeing both Triomf and me, personally, destroyed. 'Could it be that Foskor will make a bid for the plant?' *Finance Week* asked. Eventually, of course, it was the Industrial Development Corporation (through Foskor) – and purportedly done by a foreign-owned entity – that ultimately moved in to secretly acquire, in a round about way, the Richards Bay plant at a bargain-basement price from Nedbank. The deal was eventually consummated in financial rands, which made the transaction even more distasteful, and the buyers were permitted, for two years, to bring back proceeds from exports in financial rands, with the only condition that they capitalise the additional income. But I was indeed extremely hurt that the senior partner of our attorneys of record, Billy van der Merwe, oversaw my company's demise after his partner, Laurie Pereira – who was also Triomf's deputy chairman – proposed him as one of the liquidators 'to look after our affairs'.

When I later dumped Pereira, one of his former partners, Connie Myburgh, told me that Pereira was very upset because he purportedly lost millions when we liquidated Triomf. The truth of the matter was that Pereira did not invest one

As Patron of the Johannesburg Junior City Council in 1971, I congratulate the Junior Mayor and Mayoress.

I receive the Marketing Man of the Year award in 1972. Behind me from left to right are P.M. Plastow, Albert Wessels and Anton Rupert.

Tienie Britz after he won the South African PGA at Huddle Park, a tournament I sponsored in 1973. Announcer Rufus Papenfus is in the middle.

Welcoming the Lions captain Martin Johnson, with Steve Tshwete in 1997.

Sitting in my Falcon 10-seater in 1970.

Celebrating the launch of Luyt Lager in the appropriate manner.

cent of his own money in Triomf. He borrowed R277,000 (or the equivalent of US$380 000 at that time), from me to buy the original shares he held in Triomf. These were indeed worth millions later, but the loan and interest were never redeemed and I eventually wrote them off.

So, in September 1985, Nedbank was handed its parachute and we were about to go down in the wreckage I believed was not of my making. At the time, Professor Dawie Botha and I had the opportunity to discuss the Nedbank situation with the then deputy president of the South African Reserve Bank, Dr Japie Jacobs. What he told us was, of course, nothing new. It simply officially confirmed what we already knew.

'Nedbank,' Jacobs told us, 'should be forced to go under for what they have done on the overseas markets. There is no excuse. Instead, I had to go around and reassure its foreign creditors and depositors that they would get all their money back because we, the Reserve Bank, would pick up the pieces and back Nedbank.' Later, he would confess to me that he discovered that other banks also merrily used the rather lax Reserve Bank rules at the time and, in the end, the country's total exposure by way of these transactions amounted to about US$ 10 billion.

'So, what about Triomf?' I asked, rather facetiously, 'Aren't we supposed to be the cause of all Nedbank's problems?'

'You,' Jacobs added grudgingly, 'are but a drop in the ocean – a minor part of their problem.'

What he did not raise – but we all knew – was that Nedbank apparently had the ear of the press, and a PR machine ostensibly worked ceaselessly to shift the blame onto us. It served the bank well that we were made the scapegoat by the press instead of admitting that it had got itself into deep waters through rather optimistic transactions on behalf of us and some of their other trusting and unsuspecting clients. Even though the US$59 million owed by Triomf only constituted a small portion of Nedbank's purported $900-million foreign exposure, the press continued to ascribe the bank's liquidity problems to us.

On 4 July 1986, I instructed my attorney, Laurie Pereira – who was then still acting for me – to start legal proceedings. After consultation with my regular legal adviser, Fanie Cilliers, we sent a letter to the management of Nedbank, informing them of our intention to press claims against them. Following, in part, is how we formulated our two main grievances against Nedbank:

'First Claim: There was at all material times a banker-customer relationship between Triomf and yourself. As you are aware, Triomf at all times relied upon your advice and guidance in the transactions referred to hereinafter. In 1982 Triomf had substantial overdraft facilities with you.

'You then urged upon Triomf to convert some of these facilities to an off-shore Eurodollar loan. You offered to arrange the conversion through your London office. You explained that the advantage of the conversion lay in the fact that the Eurodollar loan was available at rates of interest considerably lower than the overdraft rates prevailing locally.

'Triomf accepted your advice. You thereupon effected the conversion by arranging three Eurodollar loans through your London office. The first was arranged in about March 1982 for US$25,000,000, the second in about November 1982 for US$20,600,000 and the third in about May 1983 for US$13,400,000. The loans were arranged and have since then from time to time been rolled over upon maturity, for periods ranging from about two to six months at a time.

'As a result of the conversion from a SA Rand liability to a Eurodollar liability, Triomf became exposed to adverse movements in the rates of exchange. You did not advise Triomf to take cover against that exposure.

'As a result of the subsequent very substantial weakening of the SA Rand as against the US Dollar, Triomf's Rand liability increased dramatically. Despite the benefit of the lower rates of interest charged on the Eurodollar facility, Triomf consequently suffered a massive loss. The amount of that loss to date amounts to some R83,800,000.

'Triomf holds you responsible for that loss. It does so because it believes that you acted unlawfully in urging it to take its liability off-shore and in failing to advise it to repatriate the loan when you should have done so.

'When you urged Triomf to convert the facility, you no doubt realised that it would thereby expose itself to the risk of a volatile rate of exchange. You were well aware that it was a risk Triomf could ill afford. You failed to alert it to the imprudence in the circumstances, of exposing itself to that risk. You failed in that regard to discharge your responsibility to Triomf properly and to inform and advise it on the risks inherent in the conversion which you urged upon it.

'Even if you could be excused for inducing Triomf to convert the facility, you clearly failed in your duty to it by failing to advise it to repatriate the facility when the rates of exchange moved against it. When the Rand value dropped to US$0,825, the effect was to neutralise whatever benefit Triomf might have derived from the lower interest payable on the Eurodollar facility. The justification for the conversion accordingly disappeared. You should at least at that stage have advised Triomf to return the facility on-shore. Your failure to do so was imprudent in the circumstances.

'As a result of information which has recently come to its knowledge, Triomf has reason to believe that in urging the conversion and in failing to advise Triomf to repatriate it, you were motivated by your own self-interest in the following respects:

'You were apparently embarrassed by your continued exposure locally, to the facility granted to Triomf, in that it adversely affected you in the asset ratios you were required to maintain under the provisions of Chapter IV of the Banks Act,

23 of 1965. The conversion allowed you to structure the facility as a loan to which you purported not to be a party, but a mere conduit. In that way you were able to remove the facility "off-balance sheet" and so avoid the aforementioned embarrassment.

'In fact, you were apparently a principal in the transaction and not a mere conduit. You took deposits and on-lent as principal and not as agent. You took a position in the transaction in that you borrowed at rates of interest lower than those at which you on-lent to Triomf. In this way you earned very considerable profits.

'Triomf has been informed that your London office acted improperly in the manner in which it raised and structured the Eurodollar loans. This aspect is still being investigated and we accordingly do not wish to elaborate at this stage.

'What is apparent however, is that, whilst advising Triomf and purporting to do so only in its best interest, you were in fact motivated by self-interest, or, at least, laboured under a very considerable conflict of interest. Your conduct in the circumstances, was unlawful and in breach of your duties under the Financial Institutions (Investment) of Funds Act, 39 of 1984 and its predecessor, and in breach of your fiduciary duties owed to Triomf in the circumstances.

'Triomf accordingly holds you responsible for its aforementioned loss.

'Second Claim: In May 1985 you insisted that Triomf make forward sales to you of certain anticipated foreign exchange earnings of US\$48,000,000. Triomf protested but acceded to your insistence, only because it was at your mercy at the time.

'Triomf accordingly made the forward sales to you. They were affected at the prevailing forward rates of exchange of SAR1:US\$0.52.

'Upon maturity of the forward sales, the rate of exchange had deteriorated to about SAR1:US\$0.38.

'Most of the anticipated foreign exchange earnings did not materialise. Triomf was accordingly obliged, or so it thought, to allow you to buy in the US Dollars acquired, at the adverse rate of exchange prevailing at the time. As a result, Triomf suffered a loss of R10,200,000. Even on the foreign exchange earnings that did materialise, Triomf was considerably worse off as a result of its forward sales of those earnings.

'Unbeknown to Triomf, the forward sales to you were apparently illegal. The anticipated foreign exchange earnings were, to your knowledge, no more than just that. With the exception of a firm sale of US\$9,000,000, the balance of US\$39,000,000 constituted no more than Triomf's budgeted sales for the year. No contracts had been concluded and no firm orders received. In those circumstances, the forward sales offended the Exchange Control Regulations read with your authority as authorised foreign exchange dealer circumscribed by the Reserve Bank in its "Blue Book".

'Triomf was in any event induced to make the forward sales, against its will and only because it was compelled to do so by the very considerable pressure you exerted on it at the time. In the circumstances and within the fiduciary relationship between yourself and Triomf, that pressure constituted undue influence that rebounded to Triomf's material prejudice. The forward sales were accordingly avoidable at Triomf's instance. Insofar as it might be necessary to do so, Triomf hereby cancels those sales.

'Triomf accordingly denies that you were entitled to debit its account with the aforementioned loss. It regards the loss as having been one for your account.'

We also made it very clear that these claims were not exhaustive and that other claims would be pursued at a future date. To us it was a clear-cut matter where forgiveness and understanding had no roles to play. If we were the patient and Nedbank the doctor, the situation would have been almost tantamount to malpractice and culpable homicide. Instead of seeking to redress their own failure to implement the necessary safeguards, it now sought to have us take the fall all on our own.

Shortly after Pereira's letter was hand delivered by Willie Kruger and Philip Clarke, I received a call from Nedbank's boss, Gerry Muller who, at first, refused to accept the letter from Kruger and Clarke. The letter was thus left on his desk. By this time, his sidekick, Rob Abrahamse, who spearheaded Nedbank's ill-conceived sortie into foreign financial markets and who had to shoulder all the blame for the catastrophic consequences – with the board of the bank ostensibly completely ignorant of what had happened, had left for the Netherlands to start a new life. 'Louis,' he had told me before his departure, 'do you really think that Nedbank would borrow hundreds of millions from abroad without having to seek the approval of its board?' He urged me to talk to the chairman of Nedbank's board and former Finance Minister, Owen Horwood. 'He's the one who should make the decision,' Abrahamse had said. 'They owe you at least a five-year moratorium.' The meeting with Horwood never materialised. Horwood, strangely enough, retired from active politics as Minister of Finance 'because of ill health' but shortly afterwards rejoined Nedbank as its chairman. The former position, in my opinion, no doubt, came into good stead when the Reserve Bank had to bail out the bank.

Both Gerry and Rob were good friends, but when friends make mistakes and try to shift the burden onto you, it hurts even more than when your enemy screws you.

'Louis,' Gerry said, referring to my letter, 'I don't think we want to respond to this. Let's negotiate, instead.'

'Gerry,' I replied, 'as a result of what has been done by your bank, my company is about to go under. What is there to negotiate?'

'Why don't you put Richards Bay under provisional liquidation,' he suggested.

'After you have agreed to do that we can sit down and negotiate. That would take the heat off the bank and it would be a lot simpler to come to an agreement.'

An almost billion-dollar loan at 2 per cent interest of course helped a lot.

On a Sunday, 13 July 1986, I proceeded to Nedbank's offices in Johannesburg to sit down and discuss my separation from a company that had become so much part of my life with a bank that had, in effect, put me on the map. It was like giving up a child for adoption, knowing full well that the new parents intended to sell it to the next best bidder, whole or in parts. Accompanying me was Dr Dawie Botha and on Nedbank's side were Gerry Muller, Anton van der Merwe-Vance, Chris Liebenberg – one of the general managers, who would later become Minister of Finance in President Mandela's cabinet – a few other bank officials and Phil Pencharzs of the legal firm Edward Nathan & Friedland, which represented Nedbank.

For Triomf to have any chance of survival and for me to salvage part of my own interests, I had no other choice but to accept a settlement whereby Nedbank would take over control of Triomf. For me to have gone for Nedbank would have been suicidal. I would have lost everything – with Nedbank in the same boat – especially as I had signed, in my personal capacity, for all the public company's financial commitments. Born out by the stresses and strains of past months and mindful of the toll it was taking on my family, I thus agreed to bow out and hand over control to the bank. The final settlement, I was told, would have to be approved by Jan van der Horst, chairman of Old Mutual, Nedbank's major shareholder. As we waited for the call to be made, I wondered why Nedbank could not have had the same controls and oversight when they toyed with Triomf's and other companies' futures on foreign financial markets. At that stage, Dawie Botha returned to the boardroom after a trip to the men's room. He had a disturbed look on his face.

'Louis,' he whispered, 'can we talk outside for a moment?'

I made our excuses and followed him into an empty office across the hall.

'Louis,' he urged, 'don't accept their deal. Just now, when I walked past Phillip Pencharzs' office' I heard him tell Van der Horst to accept the deal. You know what he said to Van der Horst? "If we don't, in the words of a former Prime Minister, the alternative would be too ghastly to contemplate." They are clearly afraid of what might happen as a result of what they have done to you.'

Dawie and I both knew what these words – made famous by John Vorster when he urged the country into reforms – meant in this instance. Nedbank was obviously petrified about what might happen if I decided to press charges and they had to defend their actions in open court. But, I felt, winning the battle with an already deeply troubled Nedbank in court would be nothing more than a pyrrhic victory. It would leave us both with nothing. So I decided to go ahead and close the deal, bad as it was.

We both sat silent as I pulled out of Nedbank's cavernous parking garage and headed towards the suburbs. It was early evening on a Sunday. Barring a few night-watchmen in heavy coats warming their hands around coal-burning drums, the streets were deserted. As we reached Jan Smuts Avenue, Dawie urged me to stop. He hurriedly climbed out and bent over on the sidewalk, vomiting violently. After a while, he stepped back in, looking slightly embarrassed.

'Couldn't help it,' he explained. 'What happened out there made me sick to the stomach. You have just signed away a lifetime's work. For what? To cover up their mistakes. These people really make me sick.'

On 14 July 1986, Richards Bay went into voluntary provisional liquidation. Nedbank announced that it had acquired a 75.1 per cent interest in Triomf, with my group retaining no more than a 5 per cent interest. Gerry Muller's explanation afterwards that Nedbank did not intend to remain in the fertiliser business and was looking for prospective buyers simply served to fuel further speculation. I relinquished my position as chairman. Phil Clarke, who was appointed after I had fired Becker for leading the company into this mess and then going on a fishing holiday with two other senior officials during the toughest days in Triomf's history, remained as managing director for a while before also bowing out.

While Nedbank conceded in our agreement that certain liabilities laid at my door as a major shareholder of Triomf were not justified and therefore written off, this was cold comfort indeed. I walked out of the company, which I had built over almost 20 years into one of South Africa's major foreign-exchange earners, practically naked. Were it not for the substantial diversified investments I had made in other operations over the years, the Louis Luyt Group would have suffered the same fate. Fortunately, my family was well taken care of through the trusts I had established in the seventies. But, as someone who lost a couple of hundred million in the process, I could certainly sympathise with the many small investors who had put their faith in Triomf and were now short-changed by its untimely and unnecessary demise. But it was the workers at Triomf's Richards Bay plant who suffered the most when it was put under provisional liquidation. I took little comfort from the fact that I had, over the years, paid back my investors a few times through a generous dividend policy.

If there was any hope that Nedbank might try to reinvigorate Triomf, its appointee as chairman, Frans Davin, soon put any such speculation to rest. By antagonising Nampo, which had acquired a stake in Lanchem and hence in the listed Triomf and which represented most of the country's maize farmers, he lost their undertakings to buy exclusively from Triomf. I cancelled and reversed the Nampo share deal. In the process, Davin severed Triomf's final lifeline and allowed it to drift out into the ocean – rudderless and hopeless, ready to be picked bare by bargain hunters.

The restructuring and asset-stripping that followed Nedbank's foreclosure of

Triomf was painful to watch from the sidelines – but revealing nevertheless. Nedbank literally gave away the Potchefstroom facility at a mere R58 million to AECI – a long shot from the R85 million Von Solms had negotiated with me (and accepted) when we unbundled the 'merger agreement' with AECI.

Suddenly, however, an 'overseas company' showed interest in buying the phosphoric acid plant at Richards Bay and, at the giveaway price of US$20 million, Indian Ocean Fertilisers (Pty) Ltd officially became the new owners. Later, an anonymous informer sent me a set of Indian Ocean Fertilisers minutes, revealing that the real 'owner' was, in fact, Foskor. Letters to Barend du Plessis, then Minister of Finance, and to the Reserve Bank to ask for an explanation was not even responded to. The minutes were included for their scrutiny and must have been rather embarrassing.

Later, in the words of John Skeen, a former Triomf employee who also deserted me for AECI and later became managing director of AECI's fertilisers, the government became both the major supplier of rock and producer of acid, with rock a subsidiary product – a monopoly to top all monopolies, but one that would not raise even a single eyebrow in the same circles that hurried to appoint the Mouton Commission to investigate Triomf's alleged domination of the fertiliser market. While we were forced to sever our links with the agricultural cooperatives as major consumers, the government now allowed itself to become dominant both as a supplier of raw materials and producer of the finished product. So much for free enterprise and anti-monopolistic practices...

'Trust not any man with thy life, credit or estate.' I should have heeded these words of Burleigh instead of allowing my financial staff at Triomf to place blind trust in the expertise of our bank of choice, which, let it be said, served us very well up to a certain point. In fact, it was largely on the basis of our past experience and absolute trust and confidence in Nedbank that Triomf allowed them to take it along uncharted waters, trusting them to do what was right and proper. Instead, we – and others – fell prey to the ill-conceived scheme of a bank we trusted implicitly. To us, it was in short a matter of trust misplaced.

I sometimes wonder what might have been if I had become one of the select few in the Broederbond. Would I have received better, or even preferential treatment from the national government? Would there have been a willingness to make certain concessions or to hand me a parachute? Or might I have been better off by not being an Afrikaner at all? After all, I had seen Oppenheimer and other English-speaking South Africans receive special treatment as well. Perhaps it was my stubborn refusal to kowtow and my impudence in challenging officialdom that caused the backlash. Who knows?

Today, Nedbank is South Africa's largest bank and highly respected. I no longer bank with them, but cannot forget that they were the people who believed in me when everybody else doubted me. But, in the end, they – through reckless forex dealings of their London operation headed by Joel Fisher – were also the people who destroyed the Triomf they had helped me to establish so successfully.

Before the end of the eighties, I would once again, however, find myself at loggerheads with the government. But this time it would have nothing to do with business. It concerned the ever-thorny issue of sport and politics.

Serious sport has nothing to do with fair play.

It is bound up with hatred, jealousy, boastfulness,

disregard of all rules and sadistic pleasure in witnessing violence:

in other words, it is war minus the shooting.

George Orwell

Chapter 9

SERIOUS SPORT

I would imagine that followers of pop psychology might have a field day probing my on-off relationship with the sport of rugby, the British sport that has so permeated the Afrikaner psyche for the past century that it seems he might have invented it himself. Some may argue that rugby has, since my early childhood, provided me with a convenient escape from poverty and hardship. And they may have a point. Others may contend that my inexplicable exclusion from the Springbok rugby team made me obsessively compulsive about proving to myself and others that I really did deserve to wear the green and gold. Perhaps they, too, have a point. There will also be those who would simply dismiss me as a masochist or a glutton for punishment, a bruised and battered soul going back on the field time and again to be beaten up just one more time for the sheer pleasure of doing battle.

Rugby certainly gave me a chance in my early years to compete with the rich boys on equal terms, even though my borrowed boots were somewhat worn and torn. I did find a diversion from the stresses and strains of my youth by participating in the give and take on the field, fighting a war minus the shooting. And I never quite managed to get over the deep disappointment of being passed over several times by the Springbok selectors during my prime years.

I would, however, explain my lifelong, sometimes tumultuous and tempestuous relationship with rugby in much simpler terms. From my boyhood years, I have had a deep love for the game and a respect for most, if not all, of the people who played it. Like all other endeavours in life, there were – and, indeed, still are – those who see this grand game as an opportunity to score petty personal and political victories instead of playing it for its own sake and allowing it to promote sportsmanship and camaraderie among men.

While I can certainly see the value of rugby in building a man's character, I am not blind to its uglier flipside either. The description of rugby as a hooligan's game played by gentlemen and soccer as a gentlemen's game played by hooligans, does not always hold true. In this day and age, where professionalism has turned the game into a profession, greed quite often takes the front seat while team spirit rides somewhere in the back, along with chivalry and chauvinism. Rugby can indeed be a hooligan's game played by hooligans – a war minus the shooting.

Far be it from me to blame others for the current state of affairs. I happened to be the one who was partly responsible for letting the genie out of the bottle by making it financially feasible for talent from elsewhere to move to the Transvaal years ago. In the process of team-building, I found it necessary to lure good players by assisting them with jobs, cars and home loans – but often at my own expense, however.

At the same time, I spared no effort in fighting against all forms of state interference and control of the game. An Afrikaner government prohibiting the All Blacks from including Maoris in their team was as unacceptable as an ANC government forcing quotas on the modern game. Let everyone play and succeed on merit, regardless of colour or creed. We have all seen how the black minority in the United States has become a dominant force in American football, baseball, basketball, boxing and athletics. Instead of the mere 10 per cent they would be entitled to under a quota system, they have accomplished a 90 per cent representation in some teams – and purely on merit.

Eventually, of course, I would lose this war against government interference as those who egged me on developed cold feet and threw up their hands in surrender. Today, thanks to these *hensoppers* [surrenderers], South African rugby is just about completely at the mercy of the government. It is merely a matter of time before it takes total charge of the game.

During the seventies and eighties, I appointed several former team-mates and opponents on the rugby field to positions in my own businesses. While I was certainly mindful of the value to my firm of personalities with name recognition, this was certainly not the main consideration. There was a variety of other reasons.

'Louis Luyt (pronounced "Late"), the young fertiliser millionaire who locked the Orange Free State scrum when they beat Wilson Whineray's All Blacks in 1960, is turning into a fairy godfather for Springbok footballers, as he was a benefactor to a great extent of the 1970 All Blacks,' wrote former All Black Graham Thorne in the 1970s. 'Luyt has given jobs to Frik du Preez and Piet Greyling, two of the great South African players of the 1960s, in his new LLG Brewery.' In fact, in later years, it was Piet Uys, the brilliant Springbok scrumhalf, who joined me and served with great distinction.

Thorne had been a member of the 1970 All Black team I had taken under my wing at my own expense. I had shown them around South Africa, trying to promote good relations and better understanding at a time when pressures for an all-out sports boycott were building. I must have done something right because Thorne, when his guest editorial appeared in the *Sunday Express*, was living in South Africa, happily married – out of my home – to a local beauty. After my involvement with the 1970 team, there were several other occasions where I put my own money and time into trying to facilitate rugby contact with the outside world, even as the doors were shutting around us.

Piet Greyling was not only a rugby star, but also an accomplished salesman when I appointed him, and Frik du Preez was experiencing some financial difficulty with his sport centre when I offered him a position. But even if Frik had no sales or business skills - of which he had plenty, incidentally, plus charm – I would still have considered it a real privilege having this magnificent all-time great among my ranks.

Former Springbok scrumhalf and captain, Doc Danie Craven, whom I appointed as a director of Triomf, was a living legend long before I stepped out on the concrete-hard rugby grounds of Hanover and Colesberg as a youth. Even though he was largely to blame for my exclusion from the Springbok team in the sixties, I could not help but like the man and, as it turned out, put myself in the line of fire for him on several occasions. I did not, however, know that while leaving me out of our international rugby side, he had merely saved me for top billing in another much more challenging game of secret sport diplomacy.

Another scrumhalf and Springbok captain, Dawie de Villiers, whom I appointed as director of the Louis Luyt Group, played only after I had retired. When this agile theologian, with his sharp sense of humour and likeable manner, decided to exchange the pulpit for politics and came to me for assistance, I was more than happy to oblige. It was my opportunity, I felt, to help a young man with new ideas and a fresh political outlook to enter the ranks of the National Party. I provided him with offices and a motorcar and funded his campaign. Dawie easily won the parliamentary seat vacated by Dr Carel de Wet, who had left for London to take up the position as ambassador.

Like so many others, however, my friendship with Dawie would be put to the test in the late seventies when the truth about *The Citizen* surfaced and the press had a field day, tearing away at my family and me. Even though I could understand Dawie de Villiers' desire as an aspiring young politician to distance himself from the Vorster and Mulder past and position himself in the present with PW Botha, the unseemly haste and finality of his separation from my family and me troubled me. His public denials and denouncements then stood in sharp contrast with his reaction in the early seventies when *Rapport* ran an article criticising our relationship.

'Dawie de Villiers, one of South Africa's most popular rugby captains, has been pushed out of rugby by sport politics,' the Afrikaans Sunday newspaper wrote. 'Because he mixes with "the wrong people" in Transvaal rugby, he did not make it as a national selector. As the result of caucusing, with the Transvaal Rugby Union playing a crucial role, Dawie is now lost for rugby for at least three years... Transvaal's sudden change of heart in opposing Dawie is rumoured to have been in response to his directorships in the Louis Luyt Group and his friendship with the dynamic millionaire. Mr Luyt is not very popular with certain people in the Transvaal Rugby Union. Recently, for example, the Transvaal Union, under the chairmanship of Mr Jannie le Roux, threatened to cancel its donation of R50,000 to the Rand Afrikaans University, earmarked for an international sport stadium. Mr Luyt had given R200,000 for the stadium and it was to be named after him. According to rumours, Transvaal rugby bosses were afraid that if Dawie became a national selector, it would further Mr Luyt's chances in the South African rugby world.'

At the time, Dawie shrugged off the inaccurate speculation of the article, assuring me that nothing would come between us as friends. Some seven years later, however, I found myself alone, drowning in a sea of smears as the media fed off the so-called Information Scandal. Dawie had moved on and was amply rewarded with a cabinet post. All private contact ceased and in 1985, when I really needed him, as Minister of Trade and Industry, to broker the same state assistance for Richards Bay that others were receiving at a time of unusual national economic stress, he simply passed me along to unsympathetic colleagues at the IDC who openly desired my demise.

Back in the early seventies, when *Rapport* wrote their piece about my supposed ambition to control Transvaal and South African rugby, I was thoroughly and totally occupied with business and had no design on Le Roux's post as the president of the Transvaal Rugby Football Union. While it is true that I donated R200,000 for a new stadium at Rand Afrikaans University, I actually did so with the stipulation that it not be named after me and that it had to be open to all race groups. The only kernel of truth in the article was its reference to Jannie le Roux's resentment of me as a result of the rumours.

Contrary to the widely held belief that I summarily decided that I was destined to be the new ruler of rugby in South Africa, my initial entry was mostly a matter of circumstance. After a five-year lay-off I had a brief return to rugby in 1970, playing for the Pretoria club, Adelaars, at the age of 38. Even though I was beyond my peak, I still gave it my all. After a gruelling game against Police on a Tuesday in the Carlton Cup competition, the opposing front row, Springbok Mof Myburgh, remarked that he doubted whether the All Blacks in the upcoming test the following Saturday could match our ferocity. But I knew it was time to finally call it a day.

In 1970, I was not only buying the boys at Adelaars a few rounds after the match, I was also in a position to offer the visiting All Black team hospitality and sponsored a side-tour for the team so they would have an opportunity to fully appreciate our great country. My largesse was certainly inspired by the desire to see us win out against the anti-apartheid forces bent on isolating South Africa from world rugby.

Only a few months earlier, I had been an eye-witness to the unruly, violent behaviour of Peter Hain's protestors who tried to disrupt the Springbok tour of Britain in every way possible – both on and off the field. Bands of demonstrators carried banners, formed picket lines and strew tacks on the playing grounds. Under these circumstances, it was not surprising that the Springbok team lost against both Scotland and England and barely managed to draw against Ireland and Wales.

It was clear, too, that the same type of opposition was already building up in New Zealand and I felt that everything possible should be done to counter the campaign. One way was to show the visiting All Blacks that overseas propaganda had little relation to reality in South Africa. I did so at my own expense because I could afford it. And I thoroughly enjoyed doing it.

During the 1970 All Black visit, I had the privilege to befriend All Black coach Ivan Vodanovich. Later described by one of his peers in New Zealand as an 'honest toiler instead of a shiner,' Ivan had played three tests for New Zealand in the fifties and served the game in many other ways before being appointed coach of the touring team.

It was Ivan's bad luck to be put in charge of the remnants of a once great team badly in need of reconstruction. Even his best efforts were not enough to prevent the All Blacks from losing the 1970 series in South Africa and a year later against the British Lions on home ground. He will, however, always be remembered for his kindness and compassion. Until shortly before his untimely death in 1995 at the age of 65, Ivan Vodanovich was a familiar sight at hospital wards where he would call on injured and sick players armed with a gift and words of encouragement. From 1970, our paths would cross several times as we exchanged favours and hospitality.

During the 1970 tour, I also had the opportunity to renew my acquaintance and friendship with Colin Meads, whom I had first encountered 10 years previously when we were opposing forwards in the celebrated Free State win against Whineray's All Blacks. From his debut for the All Blacks against Australia in 1957 until his final appearance against the British Lions in 1971, 'Pinetree' Meads starred in 55 test matches. Having played against him, I readily agree with Willie John McBride's description of Meads as being as 'hard as the hobs of hell'. In 1970, however, he was left to warm the benches for most of the tour after having broken his arm in an early encounter. Meads and I were also destined to have quite a few memorable encounters in the years that lay ahead.

Quite fittingly, like Frik du Preez in South Africa, Colin Meads was named Player of the Century in New Zealand. While these two lock forwards showed similarities in their toughness, lineout play and excellent ball sense, I think Frik had the edge in having been the most complete all-round player the game has ever seen. He could run like a wing, kick like a fullback and sidestep like the best in the back line.

Starting his career against England in 1960 and finishing in Australia in 1971, when captain Hannes Marais had him lead the team on the field for the final test, Frik represented South Africa 38 times. This test record has been and will be surpassed many times in future, especially in this modern day and age where internationals are about as regular as interprovincial games. His prowess as a player, however, will not be equalled for quite some time.

My first formal link with the Transvaal Rugby Football Union (TRFU) came in 1976 when I was asked by Kevin de Klerk and Anton Oberholzer to make myself available as president of Diggers. Until then, my involvement in Transvaal rugby was limited to occasional attendances at big games as a guest of TRFU president Jannie le Roux and his colleagues. I represented Diggers at the TRFU for one rather uneventful year. When I decided not to make myself available for re-election, Le Roux insisted that I stay on as honorary vice president. The emphasis was indeed on 'honorary'. As such, I played no role in the TRFU's grand plans to transform the ageing Ellis Park into a state-of-the-art stadium.

Built in 1928 on a landfill and garbage dump granted to the TRFU on a long-term lease, the original Ellis Park was named after Councilman JD Ellis, who helped to clinch the deal. A loan of £5,000 enabled the rugby bosses not only to level and seed the field, but also to build the stadium. From its opening in June 1928, when the All Blacks narrowly defeated the Springboks 7–6, until 1980, when it was finally closed to be rebuilt, Ellis Park had hosted a total of 18 tests – 10 of them wins, and two draws, against six losses – and had, over the years, seen many exciting clashes at provincial and club level. With some adjustments and additions, Ellis Park managed to accommodate a record crowd of 105,000 for the 1955 test against the British Lions. This record crowd unfortunately suffered the same let-down as those who attended the first test in 1928, when the British walked off the field with a narrow 23–22 victory over the Boks.

The new concept in 1980 called for corporate entertainment as a means to boost revenues and to provide more comfortable seating for the general public. The new stadium would be able to accommodate a maximum of 80,000 people. The TRFU started out with R1 million of its own and intended to raise another R12 million through the sale of suites and life memberships, ranging from 10 to 25 years.

From the very outset, the financially strapped Transvaal union had a hard time paying its bills. With the lacklustre performance of its team, the TRFU could hardly expect 10-year commitments from hard-nosed businesspeople. Winning teams fill stadiums and make money, while losers play for their own recreation. The problem was further compounded by the usual cost overruns.

So it was that, in 1981, Jannie le Roux called on me. He was in desperate need, he explained, of someone who could help the TRFU obtain a bank loan. I prepared a new financial plan and made a few calls. First, we went to see Volkskas with Corrie Borman and Wouter du Toit in Pretoria. I told them that I would be willing to advance R500,000 in the interim on condition that my exposure would rate *parri passu* with their loan in the event of foreclosure. They rejected my offer and instead committed themselves to a R6-million loan at a fixed interest rate of 14 per cent.

In a meeting with Francois Oberholzer, chairman of the Johannesburg municipality's management committee, my plea on behalf of the TRFU and Ellis Park fell on sympathetic ears. The city clearly saw the value of a world-class stadium for future events and undertook to extend a R6-million loan at no interest. There was, however, a caveat to both these offers. They stipulated that a new company should be formed to oversee the finances at Ellis Park. The bank, the city and the TRU would have equal representation on its board, and I was asked to serve as chairman.

I did not expect Jannie le Roux to be very happy with the arrangement. Eating crow is no fun, but having it fed to you by a man whom you had accused of eyeing your post, is even worse. Still, I thought rather naively, Jannie might – as I would have done under similar circumstances – accept the arrangement for the sake of survival and seeing a dream come true. After all, his own position as president of the TRU remained unassailable and the TRFU would have full use of the new stadium. But instead of calling me, Le Roux delivered his response on the public airwaves. I was on my way to work when my car phone rang. It was a fellow from the South African Broadcasting Corporation.

'Mr Le Roux,' he said, 'has just told you and everyone else in a radio interview to go to hell. What's your response?'

I shrugged it off – there were many other more important things on my mind – and, in any event, slugging it out on the airwaves was hardly my idea of conducting an argument. Jannie le Roux felt that I was muscling in on his territory and he had obviously over-reacted. He was a man under severe pressure. At the same time, I believed that my continued presence on his committee – even as honorary vice president – would create continued dissension and stress. Once I reached the office, I dictated a note to the TRFU, resigning from my position, and returned my member's badge.

In 1981, the squabble over who should be in charge of Ellis Park soon faded as much more momentous happenings in New Zealand took over the front pages and the newscasts. Led by Wynand Claassen, who was given the unenviable task after Morné du Plessis pulled out without warning, the South African team encountered anti-apartheid shock troops wherever they moved. These protestors, marching under acronyms such as HART and CORE, were indeed a hardcore version of Hain's hordes who had tormented the South Africans in England some 10 years previously.

Before the Waikato game at Rugby Park in Hamilton, 400 protesters stormed through a fence and occupied the field with their arms linked. While the police attempted to clear the grounds, rumours of a stolen light plane on its way to crash into the grandstand, reached the organisers and the game was cancelled.

Even though all the other games were completed under heavy guard, there was constant series of disruptions. A few days after the Rugby Park incident, hundreds of demonstrators were forcefully removed from the South African Consulate. Amazingly, under all this pressure, the Springboks managed to enter the third and final test with the series even. In this deciding match, three magnificent tries by Springbok winger Ray Mordt were overshadowed by interruptions around the field and in the sky. Flower bombs were dropped from a light plane, some of them hitting the players. And, finally, a questionable penalty awarded by the Welsh referee, Clive Norling, deep in injury time, robbed the Springboks of a draw.

At the start of this messy tour I found myself in New York – where I had some business after I had received my doctorate in Business Administration at Columbia Pacific University (CPU) for my Thesis on International Arbitration – with promoters Drs John Bear (Berkeley) and Marc Kennedy (University of Michigan.) After me, famous best-selling author John Gray and International lawyer John Walsh also chose this university to obtain their doctorates.

During 1997, Columbia Pacific University (CPU) fell foul of the Department of Consumer Affairs, the watchdog after consumers' rights, and was told to close its doors – just as they did with hundreds of similar institutions. The Department, through a letter dispatched to every single graduate, assured all who received their degrees before 1997, that their degrees, if obtained before 1997, were authentic, legal and valid. I was, to say the least, a very relieved man indeed when I received this comforting assurance.

Tom Selfridge had, in the meanwhile, approached Les de Villiers, who had moved to New York, with the request that the Springboks stop over in the United States on their way back from New Zealand. De Villiers thus turned up at my New York apartment with the angular Selfridge at his side. Might I be of help, Selfridge – speaking from the vantage point of both player and national administrator – wanted to know, in having Dr Craven sanction this detour, as it would be of great value in promoting this great game in the land of football and heavy padding. I called Doc Craven and offered to fund the American leg of the tour and he agreed.

144

Soon after the announcement, all hell broke loose as anti-apartheid pressure groups threatened the US Olympic Committee with a general boycott and disruption of the 1984 Los Angeles Olympics if the Springboks were allowed to set foot in America. When a series of national television encounters between US Olympic chairman Peter Uberroth and Selfridge ended in a stand-off, anonymous death threats followed. The Springboks nevertheless did stop over in the US and played three games under strict security.

The test took place in inclement weather at a secret venue near Albany and was attended by all of 39 spectators, most of them state troopers. Not even the non-playing Springboks were present. As a decoy to confuse the demonstrators, the remaining Springboks were carted off in a bus to the Baseball Hall of Fame in Cooperstown.

While no one cares to remember the precise score of this runaway victory for the Boks, it will no doubt go down in history as the worst-attended international game ever. For the record, the score at the final whistle was 38–7, with Ray Mordt recording his second hat-trick of the tour and the first ever in an international rugby encounter on American soil. The disastrous 1981 tour of New Zealand and the United States turned out to be the last opportunity for a South African team to play abroad until 1992.

The 1984 Olympic Games in Los Angeles was boycotted by the Soviet Union and several other Communist nations for reasons entirely unrelated to South Africa. We only featured in an indirect way when Zola Budd, running in the 3,000-metre final under British colours, tripped in a collision, taking local favourite, American Mary Decker, down with her. It gave the Americans the opportunity to blame Decker's defeat by Maricica Puica of Romania on the South African.

Peter Uberroth, however, emerged with a whopping profit for the first time in the history of the Games. He did so through the clever use of sponsorships. While I had no sympathy with his politics, I had to admire his business acumen, so it gave me great pleasure indeed when South Africa could more than double his financial results with the 1995 Rugby World Cup.

That same year, 1984, I was given the opportunity to apply myself to the task of trying to stop the bleeding at Ellis Park and salvage the TRFU. Relying heavily on infusions from Volkskas and a R3-million loan from the city of Johannesburg, the TRFU had managed to complete the stadium in 1981. For the next three years, however, it found itself unable to meet its mounting obligations. Interest had escalated to R20,000 per day, and Volkskas was in effect the owner and administrator of Ellis Park, with the TRFU as a tenant in constant arrears. The TRFU was thus in serious danger of being sequestrated. Within the TRFU, pressure was also building for Jannie le Roux to resign. He was facing charges of ineptitude and mismanagement. One issue that came up in discussions – and began to leak to the press – was the allegation that suite holders had been forced to buy their liquor from Le Roux's store. His management style was thus seen as dictatorial and undemocratic. At least one of these charges was blatantly false – as one of the suite holders at Ellis Park, I certainly had no problems buying liquor from wherever I wished.

Early in 1984, Le Roux once again approached me for help. This time we drew up a document and had him sign it in his capacity as president of the TRFU. The plan called for wide powers to enable me to restructure the relationship between Volkskas, the Johannesburg municipality and the TRFU. Following, in part, is the way it was worded:

'Proposed scheme for Ellis Park as submitted by Louis Luyt. Strictly confidential. Memorandum: In order to avoid the sequestration of the TRFU and to minimise the financial losses of all concerned with the stadium, I propose that a new company, "Ellis Park Stadium Incorporated" be established, preferably under Section 21 of the Companies Act of 1973 as amended.

'Purpose of proposed scheme: The very survival of Ellis Park depends on the urgent implementation of a new financial structure for the stadium. It is quite clear that the current annual interest burden of around R7 million (i.e. even before administration costs) cannot possibly be redeemed through income from current activities at Ellis Park.

'Ellis Park is a rugby venue par excellence but also extremely suited to soccer. The site is important and should be retained. If the debt crisis can be resolved, Ellis Park will no doubt be financially just as healthy as other stadiums such as Loftus Versfeld and Newlands where sufficient earnings are generated from, primarily, rugby and advertisements to cover costs. Ellis Park will have the added advantage of an income from soccer.

'The Transvaal Rugby Football Union (TRFU) obviously lacks the funds to ensure the survival of Ellis Park. It is also clear that the TRFU should now relinquish the administration of the stadium. I have been given wide powers by the TRFU to act on its behalf and to negotiate a new deal in order to find a solution.

'Certain sacrifices necessarily need to be made to put Ellis Park in a position to cover its administration and maintenance costs and I contend that the only workable solution is embodied in the following proposals.

'Right of ownership: It is essential that the right of ownership of Ellis Park be vested in the new company, Ellis Park Stadium Incorporated, hereinafter referred to as EPSI. To that end, the City Council loan of R3 million should be redeemed in the way as hereinafter discussed and the property should be bought from the Council.

'Proposal: Johannesburg City Council – The City Council undertakes to write off its R3 million loan to the TRFU and transfer the whole of Ellis Park to the new company in return for which they will receive Springfield that is currently mortgaged to Volkskas. The TRFU will agree to both transfers.

146

'Proposal: Volkskas Limited – Volkskas undertakes to write off its entire debt against the TRFU and reinstate an interest-bearing loan of R17.5 million, which amount will include the electronic scoreboard, against the new company.

'Proposal: Redemption of Volkskas debt – The debt will be repaid to Volkskas as follows:

'By converting Ellis Park to sectional title; and/or selling or leasing over 99 years the private suites in the stadium.

- EPSI will own and manage Ellis Park, initially from offices at Triomf House, Milpark.
- A Board of Directors of 12 members will be appointed.
- Volkskas will initially have 6 nominees, to be reduced to 3 after the loan has been repaid. Volkskas will retain 3 nominees in recognition of its contribution to the success of the new venture.
- The Johannesburg City Council may nominate 3 members if it so desires.
- As an interim measure, the Louis Luyt Group will have 3 nominees, representing future suite holders/owners. Representation of suite holders/owners will not be linked indefinitely to the Louis Luyt Group and holders/owners will be entitled to elect their own representatives.
- Ultimately the suite holders/owners will nominate 6 members of their choice, after the Volkskas nominees have been reduced to 3.
- A Director will be appointed as executive in charge of the running of EPSI. The Director will report to the Board or a committee of the Board.
- I will be available as Chairman until another Chairman is nominated by the parties concerned.
- The TRFU will have no representation in EPSI.

'Suite holders: General – A random test of 10 suite holders evoked a 100 per cent positive response to the proposed purchase or 99-year lease plan.

'EPSI will endeavour to remove points of irritation such as inter alia the following:
1. Suite holders will be allowed to provide individually, but orderly, for their own liquor and catering.
2. Suite holders will buy the right to use their suites, with no additional costs, at all times and for all events at Ellis Park. (Clients of EPSI will therefore know that there will always be 7 500 seats on which no income would be received for an event.)

'In regard to the proposed purchase or 99-year lease plan the following salient points can be mentioned:
1. The rights of current lessees of suites as well as the rights of other lessees will be protected.

2. Whether leased or sold the new lessee/owner will be allowed to sell, alienate or dispose of his facility as he sees fit.
3. Volkskas will offer a financing package to accommodate those who cannot afford to buy or lease their suites outright for cash.

The TRFU
1. The TRFU will be contractually obliged to play all future international and provincial rugby games at Ellis Park.
2. The TRFU will have first rights over the use of Ellis Park for international and provincial games.
3. TRFU will have to clear with EPSI the dates for all other games.
4. The TRFU will retain their current offices.
5. The TFRU will retain their current suite facilities.
6. The TRFU will pay 20 per cent of all gate takings to EPSI.
7. The TRFU will cede all its rights to EPSI in respect of liquor and catering, the restaurant, advertising and other sources of income pertaining to the property.

'The need for an urgent decision: An interest burden of approximately R20 000 a day makes the need for an urgent decision imperative. A test match, other games, advertisement and tenders have to be catered for and arrangements in regard to other sports, particularly soccer, have to be carried out timeously.

'My proposals are conditional on all parties, Volkskas, the City Council and the TRFU accepting them. The immediate implementation of my proposed scheme therefore warrants the highest priority from all parties.

'Signed L Luyt, Johannesburg, 8 March 1984.'

Jannie le Roux accepted the plan in his capacity as president of the Transvaal Rugby Football Union and sent it back to me with a signed attachment giving me a 'mandate' to act on behalf of the union. In writing, he 'delegated to Louis Luyt powers to negotiate, make arrangements, sign contracts and take all other necessary steps in an endeavour to solve and overcome the problems of the union as he deems necessary at his own discretion.' The only condition was that I protect the TRFU's continued use of the stadium.

This time Volkskas played hard ball. It was evident that relations between the TRFU and Volkskas had reached a point where the bank would not negotiate with anyone, least of all with someone who had the sanction and support of Jannie le Roux.

In the meantime, the bank had a stadium with little income as the Transvaal team hobbled along from one defeat to another and attendance dwindled. Opposition against Le Roux's 'management style' also reached the point where there was plenty of talk about revolt, breakaways and take-overs. The TRFU was a ship lost at sea, and ready for mutiny.

After eight on a Sunday evening in October 1984, I received an urgent call from Gerhard de Haas, an official at the TRFU. He was at the home of Trens Erasmus across the street and asked whether they could come over to see me. He apologised for the late hour and the short notice, but he added, it was a matter of great importance and urgency. I could guess that it had something to do with the ongoing controversy at Ellis Park and wondered while I waited for the gate guard to announce their arrival, whether I would once again be asked to draw up contingency plans for the rescue of Ellis Park.

Gerhard De Haas, who had worked for me at Triomf before he accepted the post at the TRFU, knew me well enough to get straight to the point once we settled into my home office. I did not know Trens Erasmus all that well, but I was well aware of his close relationship with Jannie le Roux. Some, in fact, described him as the 'grey eminence' behind the throne and others, rather less kindly, as Jannie's henchman.

'Jannie le Roux will be asked at the next union meeting to resign,' De Haas said in a matter-of-fact way. Erasmus nodded in agreement. 'We know that this campaign is driven by Professor Jannie Ferreira of Rand Afrikaans University. Nobody knows who will be the next president, but we have ample evidence that it might be someone that will not measure up to the job at hand.'

I did not know Jannie Ferreira at all. But, as it turned out, I would soon get to know him.

'Louis,' Trens said, clearing his throat, 'we would like you to make yourself available as the new president. You are someone we can trust. You have the skills.'

Both men felt that, at this difficult juncture, someone with business skills was needed to bring Volkskas back in line. The bank, they told me, was just about ready to pull the plug on the TRFU. A hard-nosed man would be needed at the top to lift the TRFU out of this morass.

'Gentlemen,' I said, 'what makes you think I would be acceptable to the member clubs of the TRFU? And who says that I even qualify to be elected as president? I am no longer a member of the committee.'

'We have already checked,' De Haas said. 'As a former president of Diggers and a former honorary vice president of the TRFU, you are certainly entitled and qualified to be a candidate.'

Again, Erasmus nodded in agreement.

'Wait, gentlemen,' I interjected, 'not so fast. Does Jannie le Roux know what we are discussing right know. What would his reaction be?'

Erasmus now took charge.

'No, he does not know, but let's go and see him right now.'

Erasmus thus made the call, despite the late hour. Jannie le Roux was still up and about – sleep did not come easily at times like these – and, yes, he was ready to talk.

We got into my car and made the trip to Jannie's home in Westcliffe. I allowed the other two to make their pitch. On one hand, I liked the challenge. On the other, I dreaded the additional burden that this rescue mission would place on me at a time when I had my hands full with pressing issues in my own business. In any event, I craved for more time with my family, not more headaches and commitments outside. I was thus ambivalent about the entire proposition and happy to leave the outcome in their hands.

Jannie's face lit up as De Haas and Erasmus laid out their plans to have me step in and prevent a take-over by Ferreira and his friends. He turned to me and said: 'Louis, I think this is a bloody good plan. I hope you will agree to go along. We'll certainly do our best to muster all our supporters on your side.'

He then picked up the phone and started calling honorary vice presidents and life members, as well as the chairmen of the three clubs that still supported him. He urged them to support me as his successor and prevent the 'rebel clubs' from taking over the TRFU. The groundwork was laid for the crucial election the following evening.

The one person who did not take kindly to this turn of events was my wife. 'Stay away from this mess!' Adri urged me. 'We can do without these people. Let us live our lives.' I should have listened to her. Indeed I should have listened and run...

That Monday evening, I would discover first-hand just how low the morale was at the TRFU. As agreed the previous evening, Jannie le Roux announced his resignation and so did his vice president, Corrie Borman. When he sat down, one of the vice presidents stood up and proposed my candidacy. The vice presidents and life members voted unanimously in my favour. That all went according to plan, but what followed was not in the script. Thirteen club representatives abstained and when my election was announced, they stood up and followed Avril Malan and Mickey Gerber out of the hall. They were obviously aware that they would have been outvoted and through this dramatic walk-out they were at least able to dramatise their displeasure.

That Tuesday I had several important decisions to make. I told Jannie le Roux to keep using his office for a little while. I had no desire to move in behind his desk. 'After all,' I said, 'you've built this stadium and you are still a life member of the union.' By then, he had already fired his general manager, Robert Denton, for his collusion with the breakaway clubs. He had saved me the trouble of doing so myself, but this would not be the last word on Denton. He would soon return as Volkskas' gofer at Ellis Park.

My first concern was the rebelling member clubs whom, I felt, had some valid grounds for complaint but were overreacting. For the TRFU to be rebuilt, I needed their cooperation and I was willing to go a long way towards meeting their needs. So one of the leading Transvaal players, Okkie Oosthuizen, assisted in arranging a meeting with the leaders of these dissenting clubs.

Instead of coming to see me in my capacity as the new president of the TRFU, Jannie Ferreira insisted that we meet at his offices, so – for the sake of compromise – I swallowed my pride and proceeded to his cramped quarters at Rand Afrikaans University. He had me cool my heels for a while in the small reception area before inviting me into his office. Apart from the one-upmanship, I realised that there had been another reason for having me wait when I squeezed my way past Avril Malan and Mickey Gerber to the empty seat in Ferreira's office. The three had apparently needed time for last-minute caucusing.

Malan took the lead in setting out a list of demands. As long as I agreed to these conditions, he said, they were prepared to negotiate with me. I bristled but managed to contain myself. Peace-making is a difficult process and it was apparent that matters had been allowed to slide close to the edge after years of infighting and backbiting at the TRFU.

'Avril,' I cautioned, 'issuing ultimatums is not a good beginning for sound negotiations. Negotiations mean you have a point of view and I have a point of view. Negotiation is to see how close we can move to each other in order to reach common ground.'

We then settled down to serious discussion and agreed to continue at a full follow-up meeting of all the clubs. It was evident that Malan and Gerber wanted to change the constitution to give the clubs a greater say and reduce the powers of the president, his deputies and the life members. I sympathised with their viewpoint, but reminded them that this would require a change of the constitution and not merely a presidential proclamation.

A few days later, when we gathered at Ellis Park with representatives of the clubs, Jannie Ferreira stood up to tell me that they would support me as long as I did all I had promised to do. It seemed as if we were on our way to building new and better relationships within the union. I could, however, not let the evening end without expressing my surprise at their silence in the past.

'Why,' I asked, 'have you never spoken out and recorded your grievances?'

Malan then told me that they had never been allowed to do so. I found this difficult to accept, especially as this was coming from grown men representing the interests of their respective clubs. But I let it pass. We needed to restore trust and cooperation and tranquillity within the TRFU, and I was determined to see that goal accomplished.

The next day, 30 November 1984, *The Star* reported favourably on the meeting. 'Dr Louis Luyt was a popular figure at last night's meeting with a laid-back style of leadership,' the newspaper reported. 'Instead of shouting down members in the style of his predecessor, Jannie le Roux, Dr Luyt gave all a chance to air their views.' We seemed to be off to a good start.

Next on the agenda was the matter of Ellis Park and Volkskas. The bank, through Johan Claassen (not to be confused with the Springbok lock forward of the same name), signalled its intention to take charge of the stadium and to place it under control of a new company called Ellis Park Stadium Pty Ltd.

Deeply in debt and running into arrears at the time, the TRFU had little bargaining power and simply had to sign over the lease to the bank. In return, we were allowed to rent the stadium. Volkskas would let us keep 25 per cent of our gate earnings, plus R100,000 of the advertising revenue. I also managed to squeeze in a clause stipulating that in the event Volkskas wished to sell the lease, the TRFU had the first right of refusal. This stipulation, which slipped through without any objection from the other side, would serve us splendidly at a later date.

Robert Denton returned as the bank's choice to manage Ellis Park Stadium, and Volkskas asked me to make myself available as chairman of the management company, a position I accepted. Soon, however, it became apparent that this post was nothing more than a title. The real decisions were taken by a triumvirate at Volkskas consisting of Claassen, Hennie Diederichs and Piet Morkel and put into practice by their chosen surrogate, Robert Denton. My resignation as chairman hardly came as a surprise to the men at Volkskas and was no doubt welcomed by Denton. The two of us were just about as mismatched as he had been with Le Roux. But while Le Roux had the power to fire him, I had no authority in the matter as Denton was now in the employ of Volkskas.

But Volkskas had not only offered me a post without substance. When I moved into the offices at Ellis Park, I found it stripped bare and I had to dip into my own pockets to buy furniture and pay the staff. The TRFU was, in reality, a bankrupt concern and, as such, at the mercy of the bank.

It was evident that until Transvaal started a winning streak it would not be able to fill seats. Even the most ardent fans were beginning to defect. In desperation, I started using my own funds to 'buy' good players. Men like Jannie Breedt, André Skinner and Piet Kruger, and later the brothers Michael and Carel du Plessis, joined our ranks. Remuneration came in many forms. Cars, allowances and match fees. I tried to do it as discreetly as possible, staying within the rules. But the newspapers picked up on criticism from other unions, who accused me of conducting a chequebook war. In the meantime, my old foe and friend Jan Pickard was engaging in the same technique, having paid a reported R30,000 to lure former Free Stater, Theuns Stofberg, away from Northern Transvaal.

It was common knowledge that Northern Transvaal's flashy flyhalf, Naas Botha, commanded considerable favours from his union that they, quite understandably, paid without question. Botha was pivotal to their success and, no doubt, worth every penny they might have paid. All the criticism rolled off my back. What the Transvaal fans wanted to see was a winning team and they got one.

There was, however, a fine but very distinct line between using your own private funds and dishing out largesse from the coffers of the rugby union. When

I took over the TRFU, I was confronted with several cases in which the union had paid monies to sweeten the package for office holders. It was my unpleasant task to ask the coach, Apies du Toit, to refund the TRFU for monies advanced to him to purchase a house. I felt sorry for him, as I am certain that he rather naively believed that the 'loan' had been perfectly above board. But, in the process he lost his job as coach. Okkie Oosthuizen found himself charged with accepting money from Rand Afrikaans University (paid by the union) for playing in the Transvaal team. I helped him with legal advice – through Fanie Cilliers – and he was finally exonerated.

Looking back today, this fuss over payment and perks for players and coaches may seem rather petty. Nowadays, millions exchange hands to purchase players and coaches. Rugby has become big business and some players look upon the green and gold as a mere work uniform rather than the mantle of honour it once was. But, as I discovered as early as 1984, we had to pay the piper if we wanted to make music and bring in the crowds. In the process, I might well have been guilty of helping to light a small flame that would eventually turn into a runaway veld fire in the mid-nineties, threatening to consume the traditional structures.

As we started playing better rugby and winning games, the seats at Ellis Park began to fill. Advertising increased rapidly. Sponsors who had avoided the TRFU like the plague now knocked down our doors. At the end of 1985, Volkskas proudly announced their first 'profit' of R500,000. While I was quite happy to see the bank satisfied, I privately questioned the validity of this figure as it did not take into account the salaries paid by the bank for Ellis Park staff involved in the running of the stadium.

Rugby historians pointed out that sponsorship of players actually started as early as 1891 when the first touring team from Britain came to South Africa to teach the local yokels a thing or two. At the time, Cecil John Rhodes gave the British team, led by Scotsman WE Maclagan, certain financial guarantees. The visitors brought with them a trophy donated by the chairman of the Union Castle Line, Sir Donald Currie, to present to the best local team. The British had played 20 games, won them all, and racked up 228 points against 1. Griqualand West received the Currie Cup, which was destined to become the ultimate symbol of provincial rugby supremacy.

From the day I took control of the TRFU, I kept the image of this famous trophy foremost in my mind. Since 1974, when it lost in a final against Northern Transvaal, Transvaal had gone through a decade of decay. It had last won the cup in 1972 when it beat Eastern Transvaal 25–19. Starting in 1977, Northern Transvaal won the Currie Cup four times in a row and when its dominance ended, Western Province followed with a record five consecutive cup wins. This run ended in 1986 with a 22–9 victory over Transvaal in the final at Newlands – the first time we had been able to get that far in 12 years. I felt that we were more than a match for the Capetonians but had paid dearly for our mistakes. Nonetheless, in that same year we won the Lion Cup during a season that saw Ellis Park filling the seats and even hard-nosed sport writers getting excited over Transvaal's resurgence.

In 1987, with a game against Transvaal at Ellis Park, Northern Transvaal once again racked up three Currie Cup wins in a row. This clash in front of a capacity home crowd ended in a particularly painful defeat. We were the dominant team, having scored the only two tries of the game, but Northern Transvaal's Naas Botha – as he has done so many times before – demolished the opposition with his boot, man alone. His team's 24 points against our 18 included four drop goals and four penalty goals.

Then came Natal in 1990. In 1991, Transvaal reached the final against Northern Transvaal, but again lost with Botha once more dominant. In 1992, we once again reached the Currie Cup final and ended up with a heart-wrenching 14–13 loss against Natal, which had emerged as a formidable force after being readmitted to the A Division in 1986. Ironically, I was one of those who insisted that the South African Rugby Board pull Natal out of the B Division so that it could pay its way and lighten the burden of the other major rugby unions.

Transvaal's magnificent 21–15 victory in the 1993 Currie Cup final against Natal at Kings Park in Durban was the crowning moment. I have to admit that I was crying with joy inside while trying my utmost not to show any tears on television as the trophy was handed to the Transvaal captain and passed around by the players. We had gone into the game as the underdogs. Critics had begun to see Transvaal as the 'after-12' team – we looked like Cinderella during the season but turned into a pumpkin when the clock struck 12 and the final began. Transvaal had won the trophy for the first time since 1972 and broken a 21-year dry spell. In 1994, we retained the cup with a comfortable 56–33 win over Free State, but this time with super coach Ray Mordt in charge.

Equally significant and satisfying was our repossession of Ellis Park Stadium. In 1987, Johan Claassen of Volkskas came to me with the news that the bank had agreed to sell the stadium to him for a mere R26.5 million – just about half its total exposure.

In his personal capacity, Claassen had made quite a name for himself as a businessman. Starting with the purchase of stocking company Arwa, based in the Free State town of Parys, he – with the help of Volkskas – quickly rose to fame by completing a series of other impressive take-overs in a matter of months. At the time of the Arwa take-over bid, he had actually wanted to borrow US$1 million from me, but I had not seen my way open to provide these funds in foreign currency. I smelled a rat. I suspected round-tripping could be lurking in the wings – although, of course, I could well have been wrong.

Now Claassen had smelled a great new deal and he was as excited as a fox seeing a helpless chicken fluttering before his very eyes. He offered the TRFU 10 per cent of the shares and invited me to join him and his associates at Tollgate's head office in Cape Town for further talks. I agreed, wondering quietly what the reaction would be if I pulled out the agreement between the TRFU and Volkskas and highlighted the clause that gave us first right of refusal.

Before I left for Cape Town, I went to see Chris Ball, managing director of First National Bank. Ellis Park Stadium is up for sale, I told him, and we might be interested in buying it. Would his bank be interested in becoming our partner in this bargain hunt? I would never know to what degree Ball's enthusiastic agreement was driven by the deal or by the opportunity to stick it to a competing bank. I left assured, however, that he was not about to share our conversation with anyone on the other side.

With attorney Manie Rhoode at my side, I joined Claassen, Mervyn Key and Robert Denton for discussions at the plush Cape Town headquarters of Tollgate, an undertaking that would later dominate the headlines for its questionable business practices. Denton was present in his capacity as managing director of Ellis Park Stadium, aware no doubt that the outcome of these talks might well determine his own future too.

I laid out three possibilities. Firstly, we could accept Claassen's offer of a 10 per cent shareholding. Secondly, we could simply remain with the status quo by having TRFU continue to use the stadium under existing conditions.

'And thirdly,' I suggested after a long pause, 'we could actually purchase the right from you to buy the stadium from Volkskas.'

The last statement elicited quite a bit of laughter and banter on the other side of the table. I sat patiently, waiting until the jolliness subsided.

'So, what's the price?' I asked.

It was clear that Johan Claassen and his colleagues had come prepared for every eventuality.

'How about R34 million over the asking price of R26.5 million?'

I barely batted an eyelid.

'First, of course, I have to see written proof of your option.'

Claassen shoved the document across the table.

'You can keep it,' he said. 'It's a copy,' and added with a smile, 'What's more, we already have all the financing in place through the bank.'

'So what would you do for income after you have sold all the suites and the seats and paid off the bank as you have planned? After all, the TRFU might decide to move to another venue.'

Claassen looked unfazed.

'Thank you, gentlemen,' I said as I stood up and gathered my briefcase. 'I'll get back to you.'

As we stepped out into the street, Rhoode turned to me.

'Louis, are your serious? Are we really going to pay R34 million for the right to purchase the stadium?'

This time it was my turn to chuckle.

'Never. You don't pay for something you already have.'

On the flight back to Johannesburg I mapped out the next step. It called for Rhoode to pay a visit to the legal adviser of Volkskas, a certain Jacobus Wepener, and advise him that we were now exercising our pre-emptive right to purchase the stadium at the asking price of R26.5 million.

What followed was very much in accordance with our own script. Wepener took our offer to the management and came back with a firm 'No deal'. I then had Rhoode write a letter to the bank, informing them that we had written proof that they were willing sellers and we, as legitimate first-option holders, were now merely exercising our right to purchase the stadium at the asking price of R26.5 million.

Next, Robert Denton asked me to join him for lunch. While he had no say in the matter, Volkskas was obviously using him as a convenient channel to test my resolve.

'The bank,' Denton told me, 'will never sell to you. They like Claassen and his special deal.'

'I am not concerned,' I assured him, mindful that whatever I said would be passed along to the folks at Volkskas. 'Why? Because we hold the first option. They have no other choice but to sell to us.'

Wepener made the next move. Volkskas, he informed us, was not selling the lease but only the sublease. So the head lease did not enter the equation. This time I went to see Wepener together with Manie Rhoode and informed him in person that we would not accept a 'simulated agreement'. If need be, we were prepared to take the matter to court. We left a firm offer in writing and left.

It was on a Friday after lunch when a call came through from Hennie Diederichs. Volkskas, he informed me, would sell Ellis Park to us but on one important condition. 'We need the check for R26.5 million in our hands in exactly one week from tomorrow, otherwise the deal falls through.'

I immediately went to work, making calls and setting up meetings with Chris Ball and his staff at First National Bank (FNB). This, however, was also the rather unfortunate time when Ball took his annual vacation – somewhere in the Kruger National Park. The folks at FNB took full advantage of the time limitation by pressing for concessions on our part. At one stage, it looked as if the whole deal was off when they insisted on having Ellis Park's name changed to First National Stadium. Understandably, the City Council remained adamant that the name of its former councilman should remain. Next, Volkskas stepped in to make it a condition of the sale, but we managed to cross this hurdle too. We did, however, find ourselves tripping up at several others. FNB waited until the early morning hours of the due day to slip in a few more encumbering clauses, courtesy of Johan Meiring.

On that crucial Saturday, at three in the morning, the agreements were eventually signed and sealed and, by midday, after a nap and a quick shower, I met with Hennie Diederichs of Volkskas at my Ellis Park office. Minutes later, Phillip Canton, an officer from First National Bank entered with a cheque for R26.5 million in hand. Diederichs and I exchanged pleasantries and payment, and proceeded to the presidential suite at the stadium where a curtain raiser was already in progress.

I was indeed proud of this achievement, but the match spirit was marred when Jan Pickard insisted on having at least R40,000 prepaid as his (Western Province) share of the gate money. I thought it was a dastardly act towards a fellow union in despair.

Just before the main match between Transvaal and Western Province started, the announcement was made: Ellis Park once again belonged to the Transvaal Rugby Union. Understandably, the cheering that greeted this momentous news seemed quite subdued compared with the wild applause and merriment that followed our impressive win over Western Province. But then few outside our inner circle knew exactly how much it meant to have the stadium back where it belonged.

Monday house cleaning at Ellis Park started with the firing of Robert Denton as manager. I don't think this was any surprise to him, given the many times we had crossed swords over what I regarded as unnecessary foul-ups and a failure to stick to the task on his part – and his apparent resentment of my 'brisk' management style. I was particularly concerned about his tendency to strike deals with advertisers on the fly instead of following a strict standard procedure with fixed rates. Also, his absurd approach to grasp control of Ellis Park with Riaan Eksteen of the SABC and Abdul Bahmjee of the Premier Soccer League (PSL) affected me even more. Sieg Fraenkel, who worked for Denton at the time but did not like him, had disclosed these backdoor dealings to me. I received a fully documented concept, which Denton had negligently thrown into the waste-paper bin in his office, and I confronted Eksteen, who in turn made a quick exit with apologies all round.

Faan Venter thus became the general manager of both Ellis Park and the TRFU, and I appointed my son-in-law, Rian Oberholzer – who was working as marketing manager in the Louis Luyt Group – as marketing manager for Ellis Park.

The first order of business was to utilise 'dead stadium space' behind the posts. Experience elsewhere has shown that while seats at both ends of the field were the last to sell, corporations found it quite acceptable to pay hefty rentals for luxury entertainment space in these locations. We called in the architects and engineers and received back plans for a total of 88 suites behind the two goal posts. I made a few calls myself and had Rian go around to offer these suites for sale. Even before we started construction, the seats were all fully subscribed. Some were sold for cash and others on a 10-year lease basis at an annual increase of 15 per cent. Our cost was R4 million and the revenues from these sales brought in a hefty R25 million. We had reduced the total seating at Ellis Park from 80,000 to slightly less than 60,000, but ended up with considerable cash and more productive quality space for everyone.

In terms of our agreement, First National Bank received a lot of free advertising around the field and above the large-format television screen. It also took owner-ship of several suites. We were paying an interest of 1 per cent above prime on their loan, and the bank thus had reason to be happy. It was getting more than its proverbial pound of flesh out of the deal. At the same time, it indicated that there would be no objection should we decide to take Ellis Park public as long, of course, as they had their merchant arm act as the lead bank in such an offering. Little did I anticipate the eruptions that were to follow our joint decision to list the stadium on the Johannesburg Stock Exchange.

The question remains:

Are we prepared to tread a road without apartheid?

Danie Craven

Chapter 10

A ROAD WITHOUT APARTHEID

The fax from Doc Craven sounded desperate. Under the heading 'Perhaps my swan song', he lashed out at those in rugby circles and within the government who were tormenting him over the so-called ANC incident. He told me that he intended to hand this emotionally worded document to members of the South African Rugby Board, but in the end decided against it. It wasn't necessary. His description of the forces against change as men with 'petty empty barrels' turned out to be quite accurate. Their bark was much more aggressive than their bite.

Nonetheless, their insults, the name-calling and accusations and back-stabbing did hurt. I can attest to that as Doc Craven requested me to act and do battle on his behalf. As such, I found myself directly in the line of fire, often acting as a shield. To be referred to by your own government as a 'traitor' and a 'supporter of terrorists' was a new and humiliating experience for us both.

The flavour and intensity of this struggle between us – Craven and I – and the rest, including government, over reforms is amply illustrated by an extract from the three-page fax received from Craven on 14 September 1988, which has remained hidden in my files until now.

'The so-called ANC incident, which received widespread local and overseas publicity, made me think, for it seems that the same forces with their petty empty barrels and the same methods are still operating, which accompanied the D'Oliviera crisis with its devastating harm to our country and nation,' Craven noted.

'The "thunderous applause" that welcomed Prime Minister Hendrik Verwoerd's ban on Maoris in All Black visiting teams in the sixties', Craven pointed out, also accompanied the announcement at a recent National Party rally in the Pretoria City Hall 'when I was called an undesirable and detestable *interloper*' for trying to correct this wrong.

'I could continue ad nauseam [on] such incidents and what I had to endure and suffer,' he wrote. 'I was even chased out of the office of a senior cabinet minister with the words: "I detest you for the despicable man you are." Today I can perceive and analyse the situation in which my country and nation find itself, and the abyss to which we are heading looming on the horizon and coming closer to us, or rather we to it.

'Perhaps I should have brought my own battle into the open before,' Craven observed, 'but now that I am again called all kinds of names and accused of all kinds of sinister motives, and not being trusted after all I have tried to do for my country, and in the process worked myself day and night to the bone, I refuse to take it. Unfortunately, too, I have to do so in public, as was done with the accusations against me, and I will primarily do so through my own world, the rugby world and politically only when that world also suffers and comes to a dead end. Yet I do so with some hesitancy because I love the members of the [South African Rugby] Board and the many people I have worked with, upon whom I now place the choice of for or against, even against me.

'This noble struggle for the sake of my country and nation now faces a crisis which brings it to the crossroads, for what we have tried over years, and in many respects made a success, has been destroyed and leaves the Board, not only the choice between the present political majority's attitude and myself and others, but between the old and the new road past the abyss. The cardinal question, however, is whether the old Board which did not accomplish much over nine or ten years will be able to achieve anything on the old road?

'The Board is now publicly asked in so many words whether it intends to integrate or rectify its matters, to choose between persons who support the ANC incident and those opposed to it, those who support the government in its present stand or not. Everything now revolves around the ANC and not the motives behind the visits in which they were involved or whether something was achieved, or what our road stood for. The propaganda is so ANC involved that nothing else matters. We have as a result turned back to square one and have taken the abyss with us. Our first choice remains, however, a new road or not and only then can we decide whether a new Board is necessary or not. The question, still remains: Are we prepared to tread a road without apartheid, for such are the heads we must count, not others.'

What had brought Craven to this point where anguish seemed to have affected his usually impeccable syntax? And why did I find myself, together with Danie Craven, right in the middle of an incident that threatened to split the South African Rugby Board apart and turn the wrath of the government against us? Why indeed me? Having been elected to the executive of the SARB in 1986, two years after I took over as president of the Transvaal Rugby Football Union, I was a relative newcomer – considerably more junior to the likes of Fritz Eloff of

Northern Transvaal and Jan Pickard of Western Province or even Steve Strydom of Free State. (In 1984, Jannie le Roux had willingly vacated the post of TRFU president to make way for my election, but then – oddly enough – had decided to hang onto his position in the SARB and opposed my election to the national body. He called all the smaller unions in the Board and urged them to vote against me. In 1985, I did not make myself available, but in 1986 I was elected unanimously to the SARB executive.)

My opposition to certain aspects of apartheid and my willingness to stand up and be counted when it came to reforms had been well publicised in several newspaper accounts and press interviews. I was probably among the first few who openly suggested, in the mid-eighties, that Nelson Mandela be released from prison. I made no bones about my utter disappointment with the Botha government's lack of imagination in trying to meet the challenges of the time in an intelligent and imaginative manner. I was one of those who took the brunt of the Rubicon debacle, losing tens of millions as a result of government ineptitude coupled with speculative forex dealings on my behalf by Nedbank.

'As in the past, Dr Luyt proves that he is not one for sitting on the fence,' reported Peter Farley of *The Star* on 19 September 1985. 'He believes that for too long businessmen have not said what they have felt because they have feared reprisals from Government. Now he is prepared to stand up and be counted. "The black vote must come," he says.'

Farley quoted me as saying that 'there is no point in exchanging a bad white government for a bad black government'. 'However', Farley continued, '[Luyt] firmly believes that power must be shared among all people of South Africa... He says the Government should institute a referendum of all the black people in the country to find out exactly who they want to lead them. Although he would not be drawn into a discussion of Nelson Mandela, he accepts that "if the results of that referendum mean certain people be released from jail – so be it".'

As a director of Triomf, Craven had become quite familiar with my ongoing battle against unfair state intervention and discrimination in my business. He figured me, I gathered, as someone who might well rush in where angels feared to tread when the issue was important enough. And he assumed correctly. I have never been good at keeping my mouth shut and sitting back when I felt strongly about anything. Looking back, I sometimes wonder whether my life might not have been simpler and smoother had I been able to go with the flow and stick with the status quo. Smoother and duller, no doubt, and less satisfying, certainly – it is simply not my nature to be a spectator.

Following the troubled 1981 Springbok tour of New Zealand and the United States, the anti-apartheid forces had doubled their efforts to stop all international sport contact with South Africa. Rugby was a favoured target, as they believed –

quite correctly – that this was the soft underbelly in a country obsessed with this sport. Apart from minor visits in 1982 by the South American Jaguars and the English team in 1984, South Africans had been effectively limited to playing among themselves.

Even the selection of coloured Western Province flyhalf Errol Tobias in 1984 – as a replacement for Naas Botha who had left for the United States to try out as a kicker in the Dallas Cowboys football team – failed to soften overseas attitudes. Despite a magnificent performance by Tobias both on and off the field – he was selected on merit and not merely as token to impress our critics – the pressure continued. Tobias had set a standard I had supported right from the outset – that the only colour that matters is that of our jerseys. Unfortunately, this has now changed. Nowadays, we want to count players in terms of their skin colour rather than the skill they bring to the game.

In 1985, we were anxiously awaiting the arrival of the All Blacks and the opportunity to prove to them, the world and ourselves, that we were still world champions. Our back line – including Johan Heunis, Ray Mordt, Danie Gerber, and those brilliant Du Plessis brothers, Carel and Michael, who would eventually join Transvaal to lift it to new heights – was arguably one of the best ever fielded by the Springboks. The South African talent that emerged from the Springbok trials, we felt, was more than a match for the impressive squad picked by the All Blacks. We were preparing ourselves for an exciting tour.

Then came the disappointing news. Two New Zealand lawyers, Phil Recordan and Pat Finnegan, had gone to court to argue that the tour was in violation of the Gleneagles decision by the Commonwealth that prohibited any team sport contact between its members and South Africa. Judge Casey ruled in their favour. The players appealed to the chairman of the New Zealand Rugby Football Union (NZRFU), Ces Blazey, who had stood firm in 1981 under similar pressure when anti-apartheid forces tried to prevent the Springboks from touring New Zealand. This time, however, Blazey refused to play ball.

As to be expected, there was great disappointment among both the All Blacks and the Springboks. The anti-apartheid forces had it right – this was one area where you could really hurt many privileged white South Africans who were still reasonably comfortable despite economic sanctions. The Springboks thus embarked on a consolation tour of their own country and, at the conclusion, players such as Ray Mordt and Rob Louw left for Britain to play – for money – in rugby league.

Many of the players in the All Black starting line-up were invited to play for world invitation teams during the International Rugby Board's centenary celebrations at Twickenham in London. I saw an opportunity and lured several of the promising players who were not selected for Twickenham to play for the Transvaal Invitation side against Transvaal at Ellis Park. We packed the stadium and a new star was born. His name was Grant Fox, and he would soon become a household name not only in All Black country but abroad, too, and one of New Zealand's most prolific points-scorers. Both Doc Danie Craven and his deputy, Professor Fritz Eloff, were quick to condemn me for embarrassing Ces Blazey by including some of his players in my invitation team although I knew that the same two men were co-conspirators in schemes of much greater dimension and impact.

Contrary to general belief, largely fed by erroneous press reports, I was not the mastermind behind the controversial Cavalier tour of 1986. In fact, I was as surprised as everybody else when I read in the papers that the Barbarians, a member club of the Transvaal Rugby Football Union, was scheduled to play against an All Black team at Ellis Park.

My surprise soon turned to anger, however. Who were the people, I wondered, behind this event? While the announcement was made by Barbarians president Chick Henderson, it was obvious that a visit of this nature could only be arranged and sanctioned by the South African Rugby Board. First, I talked to Chick and let him have a piece of my mind for having been left out of arrangements concerning the home venue of the TRFU. He told me that nothing was final and everything still depended on arrangements by the real organisers. Next, I called Doc Craven who declined to talk about it on the telephone.

'Louis,' he said, quite atypically apologetic, 'please come see me so we can discuss this.'

Before I left for Cape Town, I consulted with counsel, Wim Trengove. Some might accuse me of being overly litigious, but I had learned through past experience that even though you are not always assured of getting a fair shake in court, it is still the last resort in most civilised societies. In any event, it helps to switch on the light before you enter the room. My consultation with Wim was not aimed at starting a court case over the matter, but merely to be reassured of the TRFU's rights to Ellis Park. Wim did not hesitate. In terms of the SARB constitution, Trengove advised, any rugby game played at Ellis Park fell under the control of the TRFU, even though Volkskas still owned and managed the stadium.

When Craven and I met in Cape Town, he was ready to release some of the details, but not all. I detected considerable embarrassment. After all, here he was, facing the same man who he had only a short while ago accused of jeopardising South African rugby by including a few All Blacks in an exhibition match. Now he had to admit that he himself sanctioned a full rebel tour.

'A private company is in charge of the arrangements,' Craven explained. "Robert Denton and Volkskas have been negotiating with Andy Haden on the All Black side to bring out a New Zealand team as individuals.'

'Doc,' I said, not able to resist the temptation to rub salt in the wound in the same way he and Eloff had when I was sitting on the other side of the table, 'you are now putting our rugby in jeopardy. What's more, there is no way in which this game will take place at Ellis Park without my consent.'

Doc Craven looked a little shaken. But there was more. I insisted that, in terms of the SARB constitution, I – as an ordinary member – was entitled to all the minutes of the executive meeting at which the decision was taken to sanction this rebel tour. I discovered that there were indeed two sets of minutes.

The minutes circulated on pink paper to all the members of the SARB stated clearly that the executive had decided to call off the tour. Another set of minutes on white paper, which had been withheld from the rest of us, said exactly the opposite. It set out detailed plans by the Board to circumvent its own ruling and lend full support to an alternative tour arranged privately by Ellis Park Stadium, without my knowledge.

Following are the translated versions of the conflicting minutes, written in Afrikaans by SARB secretary Stephen Roos and signed by Doc Craven in his capacity as president. They were all dated Thursday, 18 July 1985:

'Minutes of the meeting of the Executive of the SARB [the 'pink' minutes for general distribution]: Thursday, 18 July 1985. SA Rugby Board Hall, Boundary Road, Newlands, Cape. 11h15 until 13h00: 14h00 until 16h00.

'Present: Dr DH Craven (Chairman), Prof FC Eloff, Prof JT Claassen, Messrs LOJ Fourie, BW Irvine, CCA Loriston, SW Malan, DGH Nolte, S Strydom, the Manager and the Secretary. Absent: Mr CG Mdyesha and JAJ Pickard.

'Welcome: The Chairman welcomed everyone and thanked them for attending the urgent meeting at short notice.

'New Zealand to South Africa: The Chairman gave a full report on the reasons for the cancellation of the tour; that the action against the New Zealand rugby union has been withdrawn but that the judge had decided that the case should proceed right up to the Privy Council in England. The top players in South Africa have been denied the opportunity to play at an international level.

'Press release: That after extensive discussions, the following press statement be issued: "At an urgent meeting in Cape Town today the executive of the South African Rugby Board placed the cancelled tour of the New Zealand team to South Africa under a magnifying glass. In the process the President of the Board, Dr DH Craven, consulted with the chairman of the New Zealand Rugby Football Union, Mr Ces Blazey, in regard to possible alternative plans, among others an invitation by the South African Barbarians to the All Blacks as individuals. The executive decided against any such alternative plans. [Instead] it has been decided that the Santambank Currie Cup series in the A and B divisions will be decided in a double round."

'Matters receiving attention: None.

'Matters proposed by the Council: None

'Signed on behalf of the Board: DH Craven President'

The 'white' minutes, restricted to members of the executive, read as follows:

'Confidential minutes of the Executive of SARB:Thursday, 18 July 1985. SA Rugby Board Hall, Boundary Road, Newlands, Cape. 11h15 until 13h00: 14h00 until 16h00.

'New Zealand tour to South Africa: Even though the tour has been cancelled, 29 of the 30 players, including Mr B Lochore, are still interested in touring South Africa. That while the Board is not in a position to invite the players, a private institution is interested in bringing the All Black team to South Africa; That the tour will be delayed by a week and the itinerary will therefore have to be revised.

'Court case: That in order to take the court case to the Council the Board has promised the New Zealand Rugby Football Union NZ$1 million to cover legal costs and to compensate for the loss of sponsorships etc.

'Private tour (arranged by a private institution): That the tour takes place under the following conditions:
- That the tour is approved in principle;
- That when the team arrive in South Africa, the Board assumes authority over the tour;
- That the amateur status of the New Zealand players is not placed in jeopardy;
- In the event the tour caused any problems for the Board and its member unions, it will be taken over completely by the private institution with the help of a Board representative on its working committee.

The unions are required to give the following undertaking:
- That every union pay 60 percent of the gross gate money into the private institution's bank account. In the event of any credit at the conclusion of the tour, a pro rata share will be refunded to the Board.
- The first two games would be considered as Board games and the gross income be paid to the private institution to help cover the cost of the tour;
- That the existing tour arrangements with New Zealand regarding referees, tickets etc. will remain in force;
- That all [previously] scheduled tour games against provincial teams and the Springboks be played;
- That the South African teams be selected by the South African Selection Committee;
- That overseas guests be invited by the Board for its own account;
- That a percentage of the gate money (10%) of each game be paid to the Board to help cover its cost;
- That the existing TV fees be retained by the Board;
- That the Board and the private institution renegotiate with SATV in regard to games that will be televised;
- That the first two games be presented by the Board and not the union;

- That the following Action Committee be appointed: Dr DH Craven, Prof FC Eloff, Mr JAJ Pickard and a member of the private institution.

'Signed on behalf of the Board: Dr DH Craven. President.'

An addendum to the minutes went on to stipulate the following:

'Addendum: 18 July 1985
'The South African Rugby Board (the Board) herewith undertakes in terms of a decision taken on 18 July 1985 concerning Ellis Park Stadium (ES) or its assigned representative:
'That it will see to it that every rugby union to which it assigns a game against Mr Denton's proposed invitational team from New Zealand: Present and administer the game in the customary fashion; Pay [to ES] 60% of the gross income from spectators (including season ticket holders and suites) within 14 days after the game.
'In addition, a written undertaking to this effect will be delivered to ES within seven days, together with a guarantee from the Board.
'ES will be granted for its own account at least two games controlled by the Board, preferably at the beginning of the tour, to be staged at Ellis Park.
'Signed on behalf of the Board: DH Craven. President.'

Hardly had I managed to get over the sheer audacity of Volkskas and its appointed point man at Ellis Park, Robert Denton, to concoct this plan without my knowledge or authorisation, when Craven came back and asked me to assist. My first impulse was to say no, but on second thoughts, I felt that it would be silly to kill the project simply because I resented the way it was hatched. It certainly had some merit.

South Africa needed to break out of the straightjacket in which it found itself. According to Craven, the All Black players had become worried about the plan and needed reassurance that Denton and Volkskas would not fold once the heat had been turned on. He felt that I was the right person to take charge and that the TRFU, rather than the stadium or a bank, should act as the host. There was simply no way in which the SARB could openly extend an invitation after promising its counterparts in New Zealand that it would honour the cancellation of the tour.

I therefore flew to Hong Kong, accompanied by Denton, attorney Mervyn Key, and Johan Claassen of Volkskas, and we met with Ian Kirkpatrick, Andy Haden and Andy Dalton. We agreed on the details. At that stage, Denton had already secured sponsorship from Yellow Pages. I also undertook to extend an official invitation on TRFU letterheads to every player. This removed the final obstacle and the tour was on – despite plenty of noise and objections from the

NZRFU management and their government. All but two members of the original All Black side arrived in South Africa as the Cavaliers, willing and able to undertake the full tour. The only two who failed to show up were David Kirk, who accepted a Cambridge scholarship instead, and John Kirwan, who had to decline to rush to the bedside of his ailing father.

The team arrived under the able leadership of manager Ian Kirkpatrick and coach Colin Meads, both legends in their own time. While Kirkpatrick did not quite match Meads in fame, the former All Black flanker and captain played in almost 40 tests for his country. Captain of the Cavaliers was Andy Dalton, who had the distinction of being the first All Black hooker to throw the ball into the lineout. He did so with great skill.

Shortly after their arrival, I entertained the entire team at my home at Saxonwold. They were all in great spirits and I was left with no doubt that they were playing for their country. That is exactly how everyone else, including our players and management, would perceive the tour. Any doubts about their status were removed when the 'Cavaliers' insisted on performing the haka before the final test.

The South African Rugby Board capped the South African players who played in the four tests, which were completed on successive Saturdays with the same referee, Ken Rowlands of Wales, in charge of the games. It was a very exciting series and a hard-fought one, marred at times by dirty play. In the second match of the tour, the Northern Transvaal flanker Burger Geldenhuys hit Andy Dalton from behind, breaking his jaw and forcing him onto the bench for the remainder of the tour. At Doc Craven's instruction, Geldenhuys was excluded from all four tests.

After wasting several good chances in the second test, in which they went down 19–18 to the visitors, the Boks won the series 3–1. On the team's return to New Zealand, Colin Meads was obliged to apologise to the New Zealand Rugby Football Union, and the players were suspended for one game. Rowlands, however, paid a much heavier price. He was blackballed from international refereeing for the rest of his career.

Not only Ellis Park and the TRFU, but also several other unions as well as the South African Rugby Board, made good profits. Of course, rumours did the rounds that the New Zealand players received millions through Swiss, Hawaiian and other bank accounts. While I could testify with certainty that the SARB did not make any payments, I could well believe rumours that US$120,000 may have passed from the sponsors to each player. Most in South Africa felt that the exercise was worthwhile, but there were some exceptions.

At the conclusion of the second test in Durban, which we narrowly lost after an unusual dropkick miss in front of the posts by the usually invincible Naas Botha, I was approached by Fritz Eloff. He had the look of a man in deep distress and severe pain. At first, I thought that the narrow miss by Botha, his own Northern Transvaal superstar, might be the reason behind for the furrow on his forehead. But I stood to be corrected.

'Louis,' he said in a sombre tone, 'I'm dead against this tour. It will certainly further spoil our relations with the international rugby world.'

I did not know whether to laugh out loud or to cry. Did he not even suspect, I wondered, that I might have had access to that secret executive memo in which he not only recorded his full support for the rebel tour but was also named to the SARB's action committee to oversee arrangements. Instead of belabouring the issue, I decided to let it pass. In retrospect, perhaps I should not have done so.

In any event, I had a foretaste of what I would be facing in the coming months and years – not only on the part of Fritz Eloff, but many others who managed to switch colours like chameleons. I would ultimately fall prey to this game of manipulation in 1998 when the very people who had urged me to take all necessary action to resist a commission of inquiry to protect rugby against political interference forced me out.

Unfortunately, President Nelson Mandela was required to testify and this created a huge public outcry. The result was a dramatic change of loyalties by the very same people who voted for the action in the first place. They were like seaweed shifting back and forth in the current of public opinion.

I was deputised by Craven to go to London to explain the Cavalier tour to a specially formed emergency committee of the International Rugby Board. Accompanying me on this trip were Jan Pickard of Western Province and Steve Strydom of the Free State. Jan came with a prepared speech and drew a few yawns. The committee was simply not interested in arguments. Instead, it focused on the audited financial reports I spread out to prove that the SARB had no part in any payments to the players.

Frenchman Marcel Martin was one familiar face on the committee. I had occasion to meet him at a luncheon hosted by Carel de Wet, the South African Ambassador in London at the time. Martin, who was then working for Mobil, had little real rugby experience beyond refereeing in second-league games, but this had not deterred him from speaking with great confidence and authority on all matters relating to the sport. He proved to be something of a thorn in our side that day and would return in the mid-nineties to become a veritable bed of nails. We left the meeting with a stern warning to the SARB to desist from sanctioning further rebel tours.

In 1987, I had yet another chance to lead the way with a second rebel tour. This time the TRFU hosted the South Pacific Barbarians with sponsorship from First National Bank. FNB had replaced Volkskas as our main lender when the TRFU took over ownership of Ellis Park. The players were mainly from Fiji, with a few Tongans and Western Samoans thrown in for good measure – precisely the type of team a Verwoerd could not have imagined in his worst nightmare. Although Ellis Park gained handsomely in the process, my main purpose was to show the hypocrites who kept punishing us for imagined discrimination that there was no colour bar in rugby. Even though the SARB was not involved, the International Rugby Board felt obliged to warn the SARB that it ran the risk of expulsion should it allow any further rebel tours. I thus gave Doc Craven my solemn undertaking to refrain.

Even before the Cavalier tour took place, the IRB had rewarded the South African Rugby Board for its adherence to the rules by excluding our national team from the first World Cup in Australia in 1987 – and the second in the United Kingdom in 1991. But few realise that if it were not for South Africa, the World Cup would, in fact, not have become a reality. In 1985, when this competition was proposed, New Zealand, Australia and France voted for its adoption, while the British and Irish Unions came out in opposition. South Africa cast the deciding vote in favour, making it a reality even though it already knew it was to be excluded.

In 1987, I felt obliged to announce a formal break with the National Party. I had reached a point where I could no longer watch in silence while the country was slipping towards the abyss. It was my hope that President PW Botha had more in mind than simply a tri-chamber arrangement that gave coloured and Indian people a say together with whites. It was, I insisted, time for a fourth chamber, even if it meant that the still-banned ANC might be elected.

The *Cape Times* was one of the newspapers to pick up on this statement in their editorial. This move, the paper said, brought a fresh air to South African politics. 'Mr Luyt's move will not be greeted with enthusiasm by an ageing, grim, played-out Nationalist leadership, which is looking more Russian by the day,' it concluded.

Fresh from the so-called Dakar Safari as a member of a delegation – led by the former leader of the Opposition, Frederik van Zyl Slabbert – that met with Thabo Mbeki and other exiled ANC leaders, Tommy Bedford approached Danie Craven. In the Senegalese capital, Bedford told him there were discussions about possible ways in which liberalisation in sport could break the deadlock. As a former Springbok, Bedford thought that rugby might well be the best avenue for such an exercise. Craven, in turn, had his thoughts wander my way. Not only had I shown a willingness to stand up and be counted politically, but I had also proved that I would be willing to take the less popular route when necessary.

Although Craven called me from Tygerberg Hospital – where he had undergone heart bypass surgery – to ask me to take his place in a delegation of sport administrators set for talks with the ANC leadership in London, I had the impression he would not have gone even if he had been in mint condition.

The crafty Craven obviously had no inclination to rush onto the battlefield without the proper reconnaissance, so he promptly assigned me and a Broederbonder on the executive, Johan Claassen, the former Springbok rugby captain, to the task. Among the other sport officials mentioned were another two Broederbonders, Hugo Olivier, representing gymnastics, and Duimpie Opperman, president of the South African National Olympic Committee. Joe Pamensky, I was told, would represent cricket.

First, Duimpie Opperman discovered conflict in his schedule, then Joe Pamensky let it be known that 'the timing' was not right for cricket as they first wanted to be 'able to demonstrate a reliable track record'. Next, Olivier, too, made his excuses. Finally, Johan Claassen let me know that he would have to provide reasons for his absence to Potchefstroom University where he was employed, which, of course, he could not do in view of the sensitivity of the mission. Then there was one. Me.

Should I still go? All Craven's grand ideas of showing the ANC the human side of the Broederbond were thrown overboard. The ANC would face one man with no ties to this inner circle of Afrikaner politics. Only someone who came with the full endorsement of Mr Rugby and would not be afraid to speak out either way – in London and in Pretoria. In the end, I gathered, they liked this idea.

I went with little expectations. Having been fed as much propaganda about the ANC 'terrorists' as they had had to swallow about the evil Afrikaners, I think we were equally suspicious of each other as we gathered at the Grosvenor House Hotel with Tommy Bedford as the facilitator. I bought the drinks and the food and did not mind at all. After all, I had had to pay my own way to London, as this was one charge that would look rather suspicious on the books of the SARB. So, what was a little hospitality on top of all that?

I sat down with the two Pahad brothers, Essop and Aziz, and a few others. Neither side had much of an agenda. It was simply a get-to-know-each-other gathering, but it was interrupted on the second day when news came through of Dulcie September's assassination in Paris, presumably by South African Special Forces. When parting company, the members of the ANC delegation indicated that they would like to arrange a follow-up meeting with the rest of their leadership. Tommy Bedford would continue to serve as the line of communication.

On my return to South Africa, I immediately proceeded to Cape Town to report back to Doc Craven. My suggestion was that we should continue the discussions. While not much had been accomplished, I felt that we were at least chipping away at the sharp edges on both sides. In the end, there might even be some grounds for cooperation, I said. Craven seemed satisfied and anxious to pursue talks.

Barely two months later, word came through from Craven that a second meeting had been arranged. This time in Frankfurt. Once again Doc Craven asked to be excused, as he was still quite frail after his surgery. Bedford and I thus proceeded to Frankfurt at my expense, where I had booked accommodation for us both in the Frankfurter Hoff – a room for Bedford and a suite for myself, which could serve as a safe meeting place.

This time, Thabo Mbeki turned up with several top advisers. He struck me as a very personable, intelligent and, above all, shrewd person. Nothing escaped his notice. I could see why others had reported back so favourably on this dapper, pipe-puffing rising star in the ranks of the ANC. I couldn't know at that stage that the man across the room, lounging back in an easy chair and sipping away at a glass of scotch, would be in control of our country before the millennium was out. Our conversation ranged far and wide, but I made it clear from the very outset that I was not there to represent the government or even a faction of it. My interest was rugby. Every time Mbeki would make demands for reforms in the government, I would remind him of that. He pressed on nonetheless. Mbeki knew how things worked.

Eventually, I suggested that I might well go back and see whether I could convince the South African government to 'release your leader, Nelson Mandela'.

His eyebrows rose and he straightened up in his chair.

'Nelson Mandela is not our leader,' he – quite rightly – corrected me. 'He is on the executive, [but] our leader is Oliver Tambo.'

Our talk also turned to the current plight of the exiled leadership. He told me that they were all suffering hardships abroad, but he needn't have said so – I could gather as much that from his own well-worn appearance, as well as that of his delegation. This was one leadership that was obviously not spending monies for their own comfort but rather on the cause, I thought. It would only be much later, after they had taken control of the South African government, that they would be charged by Archbishop Desmond Tutu of having taken over the seats vacated by whites on the gravy train.

From my side, I emphasised the need to stop the violence. Serious talks, I argued, can never start unless there is a moratorium of sorts. Whether I wanted to or not, I was being drawn into the political arena. But then sport and politics have always been joined at the hip in South Africa. The South African government made it so by imposing its own apartheid rules on sport and now the ANC and its supporters were using it as a lever to try to pry open the gates to power. Unfortunately, once it succeeded to power in 1994, the ANC would be equally intent on using sport to further its own policies.

On my return, I called Craven to tell him that these talks had entered a stage at which I felt compelled to inform the government. Craven agreed. So I called Foreign Minister Pik Botha's office and requested an urgent meeting. He was on his way from Cape Town and suggested that we meet in the VIP suite at what was then Jan Smuts Airport. With my son-in-law, Rian Oberholzer, at my side, we rushed to the airport in the early afternoon, where we were welcomed by Botha lounging behind a coffee table with a bottle of Grünberger Stein on ice. He had his Director-General, Rusty Evans, at his side.

I wasted no time. While Evans was pouring the wine, I briefly explained the purpose of my visit and handed Botha a copy of a written memorandum I had prepared in haste that same morning. Translated from the original Afrikaans, it read as follows:

'Secret Memorandum handed to Pik Botha. 9 June 1988.

'The chairmen of the various sport organisations agreed to have discussions with members of the ANC in an effort to soften the boycott against South Africa. The persons who were assigned to have talks with the ANC were Dr Danie Craven (rugby), Mr Joe Pamensky (cricket), Mr Hugo Olivier (gymnastics) and Mr Rudolf Opperman (SA Olympic Committee).

'Shortly before the scheduled meeting at the end of March 1988, Dr Craven had an operation and the other three gentlemen indicated that they were no longer willing to attend. Dr Craven asked me and Prof Johan Claassen of Potchefstroom University to attend the meeting in London with members of the Executive Committee of the ANC. Prof Claassen encountered a problem as he first had to obtain permission from the Rector (of his university) and was obliged to give a reason for the visit.

'I had two days of discussions with four members of the ANC, including three members of their Executive Committee. At the time, these talks were somewhat complicated by our actions against the ANC bases in Botswana and the assassination of Mrs September in Paris – considered by the ANC as having South African involvement.

'It was, however, decided that these talks were sufficiently positive to have it referred to the ANC executive with a recommendation that further talks be held.

'At very short notice, another meeting was scheduled for 28 May 1988 [in Frankfurt]. Once again, Dr Craven was unable to attend due to ill health and I had to attend these discussions with three members of the ANC executive under leadership of Mr Thabo Mbeki.

'Although our discussion initially concerned sport the focus shifted to political problems as the primary issue. I expressed myself strongly against violence in my encounter with Mr Mbeki. On the first day very little was accomplished, especially after the apparent failed negotiations between Mr Wynand Malan and Mr Mbeki and other members of the ANC [in Lagos]. I decided, however, to continue for another day in an effort to break the impasse. On Sunday we continued the discussions at my hotel in Frankfurt.

'It became clear that it would be extremely difficult to convince Mr Mbeki and the members of his delegation that unless violence ceased there would be no chance of success in negotiations.

'Mr Mbeki was adamant that before any negotiations could take place their political leaders, and especially Mr Nelson Mandela, should be released so that they can take part as well. Exiles living abroad should also be allowed to return.

'I pointed out to Mr Mbeki that I am participating in discussions simply because I would like to see peace in South Africa and that in the final count the government of the day would have to decide whether it could accept his proposals and continue with negotiations.

'I also indicated that the government would never release political leaders unless it receives the assurance that there will not be protest marches. Mr Mbeki said that if its leaders were released, the ANC would guarantee, as long as it receives a few weeks notice, that there would be no protests.

'Once again I raised the subject of violence and Mr Mbeki replied that as soon as negotiations started violence could cease on both sides. I told Mr Mbeki that I was not certain that the South African government would accept these terms and suggested that instead the ANC should give an undertaking to stop the violence. Once violence ceased, I told him, the government would withdraw its troops from the black townships.

'Mr Mbeki insisted that negotiations should start immediately with black leaders for a new dispensation in South Africa. I told him that I did not see this as a problem as there was the desire on both sides to establish peace in the country. If the desire is great enough, we will succeed, I said.

'I made it clear, however, that in my view neither a timetable nor a fixed agenda should be set for negotiations. Mr Mbeki agreed that these negotiations might be lengthy.

'It became clear that the ANC has strong support; they have 98 embassies around the world.

'Mr Mbeki said that the hierarchy of the ANC is available for a meeting that can be arranged at short notice as long as top officials such as yourself are included – otherwise it would have to be conducted on a lower level.

'I am aware that I find myself on a terrain where I am not an expert but as a concerned Afrikaner I believe that this development presents us with an opportunity to enter into discussions without loss of face in an effort to establish peace in South Africa.

'I am also quite willing to make my private aircraft available to you for a meeting in Botswana or Zimbabwe or any other venue, but preferably as soon as possible.

'I might just add that I do not believe that the ANC feels that it has been weakened in any way or is losing the battle; on the contrary, our setbacks in Angola served to strengthen their stance against South Africa.

'If South Africa and the ANC can come to an agreement, it should be outlined in a joint document that would prove the good intentions of both parties.'

Botha finished reading the document, handed it to Evans and stroked pensively over the thin moustache on his upper lip.

'Are you serious about this?' he asked in a voice that might have been the envy of many an actor.

I nodded.

'As serious as anyone can be.'

'Well, this is so important that I am going right back to Cape Town to hand this to the president and discuss it with him,' Pik Botha announced.

We finished our wine in a hurry as I assumed that Pik Botha was on his way back to Tuynhuys in Cape Town to confer with his namesake, President PW Botha. For the next few days, I anticipated at least some kind of response. Nothing. A week went by. Still nothing. Another week. In the meantime, details about the meeting were beginning to circulate among members of the SARB executive. I heard that Jan Pickard was insisting that the Board should get rid of me because I had talked to the ANC. Steve Strydom from the Free State then went to the press with the story.

While in Cape Town for a Currie Cup game between Free State and Western Province, I called Dr Jannie Roux, Director-General in PW Botha's office, to find out what had happened to the memorandum I had handed to Pik Botha. JR, as Roux was generally known, also happened to be the father of that splendid scrumhalf, Johan Roux, who played for both Transvaal and the Springboks. No, he said, he had never seen it. But he was interested in receiving a copy so he could investigate the unnecessary procrastination. Not long after our conversation, two high-ranking police officers turned up at the SARB offices at Newlands to collect the document. That Saturday, Roux was Pickard's guest at the rugby.

Shortly afterwards, Rodney Hartman of the *Sunday Star* reached me by telephone at my apartment in New York. The embattled Doc Craven had given him my number. I told Hartman that I had handed a memorandum to Pik Botha. And Pik's response? He did not hand it to President Botha, he had told Hartman, because it did not add up to too much. It wasn't that important. I wondered what had happened to deflate the Foreign Minister's distinct enthusiasm on the way to Cape Town after our meeting at Jan Smuts Airport. Did he, in fact, fly straight back to Cape Town or had he simply climbed in his limousine and proceeded to Pretoria?

'So, what are you going to do?' Hartman asked me. 'The government will be onto this.'

'Mr Hartman,' I said, 'the country does not belong to Mr PW Botha alone. It belongs to us ordinary folk as well.'

But by now my phone was ringing off the hook. Back in South Africa, I was told, all hell had broken lose. There was even talk of taking steps against me; suggestions that I might have to surrender my passport. The Afrikaans newspapers in the Nasionale Pers Group were quite hysterical about my and Craven's nerve to talk to 'terrorists' without the permission of the government. Little did we know exactly how hypocritical this entire outburst was. Later, we would learn that the government was already engaged in efforts of its own to arrange the release of Mandela and to buy peace from the same 'terrorists'.

Throughout all this uproar, Craven somehow managed to stay in the background. It was the wily old man at his very best – keeping others focused on the moving pieces on the chessboard instead of his hands. But the dust had hardly settled when Craven called again. This time, he told me, the ANC wanted to meet us in Harare in Zimbabwe.

'No way, Doc, I protested. 'I have had quite enough of this back-stabbing and brotherly brawl.'

But Doc Craven would simply not take no for an answer. This time, he himself would be accompanying me, he said. The whole ANC executive would be there, including Mbeki.

'You started the process and it is crucial that you be there to provide continuity,' Craven insisted.

Once again, Dr Craven prevailed. And, once again, Tommy Bedford was the designated facilitator. From his office in Durban came a faxed copy of a letter written by Christopher Laidlaw, the New Zealand High Commissioner, dated 17 September 1988. The latter turned out to be the mailbox for messages between Bedford and the ANC: 'Dear Tom, A note to let you know that the other invitees to the birthday party here on 15/16 October have accepted the invitation. They and I await with great interest the outcome of the prefects' meeting in South Africa to investigate the errant behaviour of the Head Prefect and to see whether he either just gets 100 lines or has his badge taken away. Yours in obscurantism, Christopher R Laidlaw – High Commissioner.'

This letter from Laidlaw was indeed an exercise in obscurantism and designed to confuse even the brightest of interceptors. Before passing it along to me, Bedford felt obliged to scribble little notes such as 'SARB' behind 'prefects' meeting' and after 'Head Prefect' the explanation 'Doc/you'.

Christopher Laidlaw had been a member of the 1970 All Black touring team that enjoyed my hospitality as I tried to make their visit a memorable one. He was singled out for special treatment when he had to undergo an appendix operation in Aliwal North and returned to Johannesburg on board my private jet. Bedford's friendship with Laidlaw dated back to the days when they both attended Oxford University.

On 14 October 1988, Doc Craven slept over at my house at Saxonwold before we proceeded to Harare in my plane. I had arranged a small party and Doc was in a relaxed mood, telling a string of jokes – some of which seemed to shock the other guests, who included Avril Malan. Doc had clearly regained at least some

175

of his strength and his spirit had improved considerably. The morbid 'Swan Song' memorandum, which he had sent to me a month earlier, seemed long forgotten and filed away.

At the crack of dawn, we left for the airport, where my jet was waiting, primed and ready to fly us to the crucial talks in Harare. I was taking my 20-year-old son, Louis, along to witness history in the making. Tommy Bedford joined us at the airport. During the journey to the Zimbabwean capital, we were updated on the latest news by Bedford who had had further exchanges with the ANC since the obscure fax from Laidlaw. But nothing he told us properly prepared us for what happened when we stepped into the meeting room with the ANC leadership.

On our arrival at the Sheraton Monomotapa Hotel, we were informed that the ANC had reserved a conference room for the meeting. They, it seemed, would not need the suite I had booked for this purpose. I recall having cautioned Doc Craven not to go in until we had set out the ground rules for the discussion. He proceeded downstairs with me in tow. Next, we found ourselves in a spacious room bathed in bright lights and entangled in electrical cords. The TV cameras were rolling and flashlights popped all over the place. Thabo Mbeki grabbed me in a Soviet-style bear hug like a long-lost comrade, while Doc Danie was welcomed as if he was a visiting head of state.

Once the media had had their fill of this unique photo opportunity, they were ordered to pack up their stuff so the talks could begin. From his position as chairman, the ANC's Alfred Nzo acted like an elder statesman. Deliberate and calm. Mbeki respectfully deferred to him, but was obviously very much in charge. As the only female member of the delegation, Barbara Masekela acquitted herself exceptionally well. Having studied both in Britain and the United States, this sibling of famous musician Hugh Masekela had an urbane, organised demeanour. As Cultural Minister in the government-in-exile, she would eventually take charge of fund-raising and social events in the Mandela government. But for now her focus was on Danie Craven, with whom she seemed to have developed a special chemistry.

The Pahad brothers were familiar faces, but I met for the first time a man by the name of Steve Tshwete with whom I would develop a love-hate relationship over the next few years. As we shook hands, I could not help but notice the icy, piercing look in the eyes behind his thick lenses. As the talks developed and we got to know a little more about each other, I began to understand what I can only describe as his hatred. I could fully appreciate that a man who had suffered the indignity at Robben Island of being buried up to his head and then used as urinal by white guards would harbour an intense resentment against white people.

My son, Louis, remarked as we returned to our room after that meeting, 'Dad, we will never fully grasp what some of these people had to go through in the name of our safety and comfort.'

176

As the talks progressed, however, Steve began to relax, even to the point of enjoying our company and the little hospitality we could offer by way of second-rate Zimbabwean wines. I could kick myself for not having brought along a few bottles of South Africa's best.

As president of the South African Rugby Union (SARU), Ebrahim Patel was a key member of this meeting, aimed in part at helping to merge black and white interests in rugby under a single banner. Craven had started negotiations with SARU as early as 1977. Initially run by Abdul Abas from Kimberley, SARU claimed to represent black and coloured interests in South African rugby. After Abas died, Patel took over as president of SARU and intensified the pressure. A soccer player who had never kicked anything on the field that was not round, Patel was evidently a member of the ANC, even though he later insisted otherwise. During the Harare gathering, he would often turn to Mbeki and Tshwete for advice. 'You are my boss,' he would say to them, 'and you've got to tell me what to do.'

Bedford sat in on discussions only as a silent spectator. Not so silent was a white fellow by the name of McGregor who apparently fled from Germiston to Botswana to join the ranks of the ANC-in-exile and now felt obliged to keep interrupting us. Either he shuts up, I informed the meeting, or we leave. I had my plane ready and it would have taken us no time to pack up and depart. The next morning McGregor was gone.

Doc Craven was not at his best. He tended to ramble a little. He might have been thrown off balance by the professional preparedness of the other side, or perhaps by the unexpected respect and warmth that came across the table from Mbeki, who insisted on calling him Oom [Uncle] Danie.

It was clear that the ANC wished to see something concrete come out of this gathering. Outside, the press was eagerly waiting to lay their hands on some kind of joint statement. But, after two full days of talks, it became apparent that there was little agreement on key issues. I was ready to collect my papers and go home.

Mr Mbeki suggested that I prepare a document, which he and Patel could then look over.

'No,' I replied, 'you do that so that Dr Craven and I can review it and make changes where necessary.'

The document eventually materialised, and Doc Craven and I made our changes, which were then incorporated into the 'joint statement' released to the media. Afterwards, I called Mbeki in London when the ANC denied any concessions to South African sport made at the Harare meeting. He made all kinds of excuses. I began to get some measure of what FW de Klerk and his cohorts would face in the seemingly endless talks that followed his famous speech in parliament in February 1990. Following is the text of the document that was compiled and issued by the ANC:

'Joint statement of the South African Rugby Board, the South African Rugby Union and the African National Congress: Harare, Zimbabwe – 16 October 1988.

'A meeting attended by representatives of the South African Rugby Board (SARB), the South African Rugby Union (SARU) and the African National Congress (ANC) was held in Harare on the 15th and 16th October 1988. The meeting came about because of the common desire on the part of all the participating organisations to ensure that rugby in South Africa is organised according to non-racial principles.

'The meeting confirmed this position and agreed that South African rugby should come under one non-racial controlling body. They agreed to work together to achieve these goals and called on all people of goodwill inside and outside South Africa to support this process. They also agreed that the accomplishment of the goals stated here is a necessity for South African rugby to take its rightful place in world rugby.

'The leaders of the South African Rugby Board and the South African Rugby Union met with the ANC solely because of their belief that it can play a positive role to achieve the common objectives shared by the SARB and the SARU. These leaders are ready to meet at all times and shall meet any other parties or groups that may also play such a role.

'The ANC accepted the good faith and sincerity of the rugby administrators at the meeting and undertook to use its good offices to ensure that non-racial South African rugby takes its rightful place in African and world rugby to which we have referred.'

Hardly had the meeting broken up when I received a call from Adri. There was a firestorm raging in South Africa. In response to television footage and newspaper photographs showing Craven and me walking into the open arms of the 'terrorists', Fritz Eloff, Steve Strydom and Ronnie Bauser had felt obliged to condemn the meeting in the strongest terms. Jan Pickard refused to comment before his departure for an IRB meeting in Europe. We braced ourselves for another barrage from within our ranks and censure from government circles as we headed back towards Johannesburg.

A report in *The Star* on Monday, 19 October 1988, claimed that the SARB might split over the issue. 'There is considerable confusion over whether South Africa's rugby bosses are about to split,' reported *The Star* under the headline 'Split or unity? Utter confusion in SA rugby'.

The SARB deputy president Fritz Eloff was quoted as saying: 'Dr Craven had informed me fully of the Zimbabwean talks, and I was satisfied, but then I read that the SARB and ANC had issued a joint statement. I felt obliged to issue a statement to express my personal feelings. While I have nothing against talks with recognised black political and sports leaders, I am not prepared to negotiate with terrorist organisations committed to violence.'

National Education Minister FW de Klerk responded even while the talks in Harare were still in progress. On 17 October, during a public meeting in Lichtenburg, he described it as 'shocking' that 'the president of one of South Africa's national sports bypasses the government and turns to a terrorist organisation that is engaged in terror attacks on innocent civilians every day'. He issued a warning to 'sports people' not to allow themselves 'to be used by the ANC to further the ANC's aims'. Implicit was the threat that we might find ourselves without travelling privileges in future. He said the state would have to re-evaluate its relationship with and support of the South African Rugby Board – 'financial and otherwise'.

Craven, ignoring both Tommy Bedford's and my advice on the way back from Harare to refrain from becoming involved in a political debate, could not resist the temptation. He called the De Klerk speech 'irresponsible' and accused him of wanting to see the SARB split. 'If a split has to happen, let it happen,' Craven said.

Next, President Botha told a National Party gathering in Benoni that he had 'impeccable proof' that this 'gang of terrorists' saw sports as an 'important terrain where they could perpetrate their subtle subversion'. The ANC, he claimed, had clearly indicated that they would use rugby 'to sow divisions in the ranks of responsible South Africans'. And he issued a warning to both Doc Craven and me: 'Don't allow the revolutionaries to make cheap propaganda out of sport.'

All the while, unbeknown to us, of course, Botha's own surrogates had been as busy as termites, working underground to try to establish secret channels of communication with the ANC. While I might concede that both De Klerk and Botha had it right as far as the ANC using sport to accomplish political goals, I felt at the same time that we needed to start somewhere. We simply had to find some way to break the log jam caused by government policies.

Only a few voices in the wilderness expressed their support for our efforts. Flip Olivier, an administrator and referee from the Southern Cape, insisted that 'Dr Craven and Dr Luyt should rather be supported when they want to do something for our sports people'. The South-Eastern Transvaal Rugby Union also sent a message to the SARB in favour of the talks. In contrast to the Afrikaans press, which had had a field day picturing Craven and me as 'traitors', most English-language papers praised the effort and condemned the government for its ham-handed reaction.

An editorial published in *The Transvaler* on 21 October under the headline, 'Dragging politics through rugby', took De Klerk to task for 'intercepting the ball from the offside position'. It condemned him for issuing threats and praised us for our efforts. 'Dr Craven and Dr Luyt had at least shifted the log jam when, up to now, there had been only intensified sports sanctions,' it commented. 'It will be a disgrace if their bold efforts are nullified in the cause of short-term political expediency.'

As we approached the annual general meeting of the South African Rugby Board, Craven decided that the time had come to face the issue once and for all. The attacks seemed to have reinvigorated him. He was no longer the defeatist who agonised over his future in the 'Swan Song' memorandum of 18 September. On the Thursday evening before the annual general meeting scheduled for the next afternoon, he appeared at the Ambassador Hotel in Sea Point before the guests of Northern Transvaal who had won the Currie Cup, ready to do battle.

Doc was brilliant. In no time, he had everyone hanging onto his every word, eating out of his hand. Everyone, except two, that is. When he concluded with an ultimatum, challenging those who were not ready to ditch racism in rugby and walk along the path of reform to leave, Boetie Malan of North-Eastern Districts and Daan Nolte of Eastern Transvaal walked out. The next day, at the annual general meeting, the SARB formally declared itself against racism. Malan and Nolte were replaced. The matter, so it seems, had been put to rest.

But Pretoria was not ready to rest. From De Klerk's office came a summons. Danie Craven called with the news and informed me that he would not be able to make this meeting, as he was due to be in Chile on rugby business. I was thus assigned to face De Klerk with the rest of the executive in tow.

Before I left Johannesburg for this encounter I called my good friend, Wynand Malan, who had defected from the National Party to become an independent. He knew De Klerk well. Watch out, he cautioned, he is one of those 'velvet-glove, iron-fist' types. Soft exterior, but hard as steel on the inside.

So, while Craven was eating steak and meeting rugby friends in Chile, we gathered in De Klerk's spacious office on Church Square in Pretoria. I soon got the impression that the other members of the SARB executive were merely meant to serve as spectators while De Klerk reprimanded me over my and Craven's alleged wrongdoings.

De Klerk started gently but became increasingly agitated. Holding up a photograph of Alfred Nzo, he elaborated on the 'evil' ways of the man. Belabouring the obvious, he informed us that the South African security forces were watching Nzo closely. Next, he produced pictures of the ANC's victims, including black South Africans tortured by Nzo's cadres. His manner was pedantic.

The message, however, was clear. Craven and Luyt had stepped out of line and needed to repent. Consider that two years later, as state president, De Klerk embraced the very people whom he now portrayed as the evil ones. He was clearly not as tough as I was led to believe by Wynand Malan.

Then it was my turn.

'When you made the speech at Lichtenburg, you threatened that you would put us under house arrest and take our passports away.'

'I was speaking *ad hominem*,' De Klerk replied, smiling.

As we walked out of the meeting, he grabbed my sleeve.

'I had you worried there for one moment, didn't I?' he said. 'Why?'

'You talked about us selling out the country,' I remarked. 'You gave us a lot of sensitive information. How do you know that there was not someone here who is pro-ANC?'

When we walked out, a journalist asked me whether I was going to resign. I told him that I would abide by the decision of the TRFU. If they wished to see me go, I would. 'No man is my master, and I'll bow to no one – only God,' I said.

At two in the morning, Craven called from Chile. He seemed agitated and very upset.

'Why the hell did you resign?'

'No, I didn't,' I assured him.

News travels fast. But it is not always accurate. I would certainly learn to live with this fact through the following decade, until eventually it led to my real resignation from rugby.

Later, in May 1994, at Nelson Mandela's presidential inaugural lunch in Pretoria, my thoughts wandered back to the day when FW de Klerk lectured me over my and Craven's 'traitorous' behaviour. There he was, as an honoured guest witnessing the installation of a new president by the very same 'terrorists' he had first denounced and then, in fact, helped bring to power. Did that make him a traitor too? In fact, he had gone to lengths I would not have approved of in even my most generous of moods. During his speech, President Mandela praised Craven and me for our initiative in the eighties. De Klerk stared straight ahead of him, I was told.

Following De Klerk's dramatic lifting of the ban on the ANC and the Pan African Congress and the start of serious political negotiations early in 1990, there were renewed efforts to implement the Harare declaration. The SARU and SARB seemed, however, unable to get beyond talks about talks about talks. There were simply too many in the SARB who were opposed and the demands from SARU were hardly reasonable.

Early in 1991 Ebrahim Patel called me with a suggestion. Why, he suggested, don't you have the TRFU show the way by accepting the black-run Transvaal Independent Rugby Football Union (TIRFU) as an affiliate on provincial level? We thus brought the parties together and agreed to amalgamate and incorporate into the executive of the expanded TRFU, Patel, Brian van Rooyen, Bill Jardine and Khaya Ngcula (who would later become chairman of the Industrial Development Corporation). With our newly formed non-racial structure as a concrete example, we could now proceed on a national level.

I invited to my office in Milpark, Steve Strydom of the Free State, Nic Labuschagne of Natal, Koos Vermaak of Eastern Province and Hentie Serfontein of Northern Transvaal Rugby Football Union. With Patel at my side in his newly appointed position as deputy president of the TRFU, we started twisting arms. Why, we asked, don't we apply the TRFU model and make the SARB truly representative of all rugby in South Africa? Patel was at his best.

'Why did you keep me away from this man for so long,' Serfontein asked me, pointing at the broadly smiling Patel. 'He's great!'

Nic Labuschagne was mandated to inform the SARB in Cape Town that unless it acted within two weeks, we – as an action group – would go ahead on our own. The next day I was having lunch at Ellis Park's Touch Down restaurant when Nic called from Cape Town.

'They want to see us all,' he said. "We have a meeting set with Craven and the executive at 10 tomorrow morning.'

The next morning, we all punctually assembled at the offices of the South African Rugby Board in Newlands. Craven and the executive had us cool our heels for almost an hour, so when one of his staff members came through to inform us that they were ready to see us, we informed him that we were not ready. In fact, we held our own discussions for another half-hour before we entered the boardroom.

A fellow in a pink shirt introduced an expert trade-union negotiator. I wondered aloud why we needed his services, as this was not about trade unions but rugby administration. He knows how to deal with the ANC, it was explained. But we are not negotiating with the ANC, I insisted. Unless, of course, we were trying to take over the negotiations between De Klerk and Mandela, I saw this as a discussion between rugby people, not politicians. Craven argued that the people with whom we were dealing were in fact ANC supporters. I agreed but stood firm. We should not start off with preconceived ideas, I argued. Let's assume we are talking to rugby people.

'Doc,' I insisted, mindful of the bad chemistry between him and Patel during the Harare talks, 'I think you should recuse yourself from these talks. You and Patel will never get along. It might be counter-productive to have you at the same table.'

'I never wanted to be there anyway,' Craven fumed.

He then asked us to leave so that the executive could take matters under review. A half-hour later we were called back.

'Louis,' Doc Craven announced, 'you have been selected as the chief negotiator. Hentie Serfontein and Hennie Erasmus will be your back-up. Another executive member who will assist you is Nic Labuschagne. Arrie Oberholzer will take the minutes.'

Then he announced Steve Tshwete as his choice to chair the discussions. I strongly objected. He was, in my view, too political. Even though he played rugby in his youth, there was no doubt in my mind about his intentions to use the game as a pretext for other power plays.

'Tshwete is very familiar with our goals,' Craven explained. 'He's a good guy.'

I grudgingly agreed. This, I felt, was one of the dumbest moves ever made by the wily Danie Craven. I would, however, soon change my mind. Tshwete acquitted himself exceptionally well as he steered discussions along, taking care of every detail and keeping everyone focused and calm. Craven's move was a master-stroke. Tshwete was simply outstanding.

Negotiations started two weeks later. After just one day at my Millpark offices, we had reached agreement on most points. There were still a few loose strings that needed to be tied, but there was enough to let the outside world know that we were merging black and white rugby interests in one central body. SARU and the SARB were to join on a 50/50 basis under a new name, the South Africa Rugby Football Union or SARFU.

One issue that would cause great concern to Craven was a resolution that Patel would serve as a joint president of SARFU. This came in response to an unsolicited suggestion by Arrie Oberholzer, who was, in fact, supposed to be there to take only the minutes and nothing else. That left me with Hobson's choice – to insist that there be a sunset clause and that the presidency should revert to one person after an interval of one year and then to an open election. As it stood, Craven would serve as president until March 1993 before stepping down in favour of Patel who would then serve for one year before a new president was elected. SARU received eight seats on the executive and SARFU retained its 11 seats. Decisions, however, were to be on a consensus basis.

But, at the last minute, Patel refused to sign.

'I first have to go back to my people,' he objected.

'You have no choice,' I insisted. 'You came here with a mandate like everyone else. What the fuck have we been doing here all the time!' Steve Tshwete supported me vehemently and used much the same language before he virtually instructed Patel to sign.

Patel finally put pen to paper and then made a joint appearance with Nic Labuschagne at a press conference. But the individual provinces still had to endorse the agreement. Weeks later, at a meeting of the SARB, several were still agonising over the issue.

'Gentlemen,' I said, 'you'd better make up your minds. The train is leaving. You either step on board or get left behind.'

Eventually, they all signed on. Western Province, reputed to be among the most liberal of unions, was the last one to accede. SARFU could start functioning on the consensus guidelines spelled out in the merger agreement. It was the best under the circumstances, but by no means perfect. Patel, who looked very much like the good cop in the beginning, was now turning into the bad cop – no doubt under considerable pressure from the National Sports Council (NSC), which served as the ANC's Trojan horse in South African sport.

While we had our hands full on the finance committee to accommodate this marriage and its new demands, the NSC had set its sights on that innocuous antelope that had graced the jerseys and blazers of South Africa's national rugby teams for almost a century. The springbok, they charged, had become a symbol of race and had to be wiped out. There was talk of replacing it with the protea, our national flower.

I found the entire argument ridiculous. When Paul Roos and his team picked the springbok as their emblem in 1906 for the first overseas tour to Europe, there was no policy of apartheid. At the time, South Africa was still ruled by Britain. In any event, I was not about to allow the politically inspired NSC to dictate to South African rugby what it might or might not wear or display on their garb. Patel assured Craven that he, as a former member of the executive of the NSC, was taking care of things. He came back and assured us all that it was quite in order to keep the springbok.

But then, on the eve of South Africa's re-entry into the world of international rugby, Patel dropped a bombshell. The NSC had decided against 'allowing' the springbok emblem, he announced. Deep into the early morning hours, Patel, Craven and I huddled with several representatives of SARFU at an office at Loftus Versfeld in Pretoria to try to break the impasse. Even though we had the support of Nelson Mandela, the NSC remained adamant. Craven reminded Patel that he had told us all that the matter had been settled.

'Doc, you misunderstood me,' Patel protested.

'Listen,' Craven answered, 'I've told you already – I'm not deaf or stupid. You told me it was all okay.'

Tempers flared and we made little progress. At 2.30 in the morning, Craven finally stood up and gathered his stuff.

'You can take the springbok and do with it whatever you want,' he said as he walked out. 'I'll never sit next to that false man again,' Cravan fumed.

We were thus left on our own. Eventually, we agreed on an interim crest showing a springbok jumping out of a bed of five proteas. This, we were told, would remain unchallenged until after the World Rugby Cup in 1995. Then it would have to be reconsidered once again.

We were having a taste of political interference by instalment from the would-be new rulers of South Africa. Little did I know at the time how onerous future instalments would become. But at the time we were only too happy to return to world rugby. A little pain and aggravation with the joy of being back in the international arena seemed a small price to pay.

I cannot give you the formula for success,
but I can give you the formula for failure – which is:
Try to please everybody.

Herbert B Swope,
US journalist

Chapter 11

IN NEED OF PRAYER

When I took over the reigns at the Transvaal Rugby Football Union (TRFU) and managed to win back control of Ellis Park stadium for the union, I had no illusions about the potholes and bumps on the road ahead. The TRFU owned the stadium in name alone. It was heavily indebted to First National Bank, which had advanced the money to us to buy out Volkskas. FNB was quite happy with our sizeable and timely interest payments, as well as the free entertainment space in the form of the many suites and ample advertising that came with the deal. It was also quite amenable to the idea of a public offering as long as it could make extra money on the deal. It was thus agreed that I would give the signal as soon as the turnaround at the stadium warranted a listing on the Johannesburg Stock Exchange. Naturally, FNB stipulated that a bank of its choice should handle the matter.

With the leasing of 88 suites behind the goal posts – coupled with increased gate and advertising revenues – Ellis Park soon reached a stage where the bright red ink turned crimson and then to black. In 1988, I went to FNB on behalf of my board with the proposal that we list Ellis Park on the Johannesburg Stock Exchange. The bank agreed and instructed its merchant arm, Firstcorp, to get to work. Tom de Beer, Financial Director of Gencor, Michael Katz and Ed Hern, who as CEO of Ed Hern Rudolph acted as the leading broker, were all nominated as outside directors to the board of EPS. Nominated to represent the TRFU were Avril Malan, Gustaf Pansegrouw, Chris van Coller and me.

After a private placement of major blocks of shares with a few favoured Firstcorp clients such as Southern Life and Gencor, we made our public offering from 3 June until 24 June 1988. We were all anticipating a mad rush for a piece of this valuable property. Instead, we met with a deathly silence. In the blame game that followed, Ed Hern and others who sought excuses, suggested that investor resistance might be because Triomf's demise was still too fresh in the public mind. Considering the way in which Nedbank succeeded to portray me as the culprit instead of taking responsibility for its own unwise dealings in foreign exchange, I could see how this might have affected the market negatively. Still, when we had first issued our prospectus, none of the major participants, including Hern, had had any misgivings about the timing. They, in fact, were bullish to a man.

What followed was not the finest moment in JSE history. In the last week of our offering I received a frantic visit from the folks at Firstcorp to inform me that the expected demand had not materialised. They felt that the form of our offering might well have had something to do with the disappointing market. It was a hybrid listing, the first of its kind, linking 1-cent shares to 99-cent debentures. Would I, then, be willing to underwrite the remaining shares if FNB took 10 million and Firstcorp 2.5 million? Entirely aware of the soundness of the product, I had no hesitation in agreeing and ended up with slightly in excess of 10 million shares.

The prospectus of Ellis Park Stadium Limited included a severe encumbering clause that read: 'Dr Louis Luyt (55), Executive Chairman. Dr Luyt is a prominent South African businessman and, although a director of companies, has no executive responsibilities other than his commitments to EPS and the TRFU.'

I received no salary and the directors did not offer one. All that was on offer was a car, contribution to my pension and sick funds, and accident insurance.

Despite its continuing good profits at the gate and from sponsorships, Ellis Park's shares dropped to around 80 cents in the following six months. I went to FNB to express my concern. We should take the shares off the market, I suggested. This could be done, I felt, by the TRFU with a straight loan from the bank. There was indeed sufficient cash flow at Ellis Park to underpin such a transaction, but FNB insisted on personal guarantees from me. Instead, I approached Trust Bank on behalf of the TRFU executive committee. We asked for a R30-million loan to enable us to mop up the shares and regain control over Ellis Park. Anticipating an escalation in price as the TRFU offer became public, Trust Bank settled on a loan of R35 million instead. This would enable the rugby union to settle on a price of R1.05 per share, if needed, and also cover legal and other costs.

When I announced this development at the next meeting of the TRFU executive there was some banter around the boardroom table about the monies that were to be made in the process. I quickly and very firmly put a stop to this: 'Gentlemen, this would be tantamount to insider trading. I don't want anyone involved in buying and selling shares. Anyone who does might end up paying more in fines and legal fees than he makes and, what's more, he will be short-changing his own union.'

Next, I called an Ellis Park board meeting and asked Ed Hern to mop up shares at 80 cents. He assured me that he could deliver two million, almost immediately. In the meantime, I lent R6 million to the TRU out of my own pocket to start the process going. Firstcorp made an offer on behalf of Southern Life at R1.05 per unit, and we accepted. When I asked for delivery, however, I was informed that Southern Life had changed its mind and now wanted R1.075. I objected but Firstcorp told me that they were unable – or, rather, unwilling – to act against a valued shareholder with an FNB board member. When I informed Trust Bank about this development, they suggested that we go ahead. In their view, it was still a worthwhile transaction.

The other shoe dropped when First National Bank informed me that they would only sell at R1.10. They had us over a barrel, so I accepted and urged Firstcorp to conclude the deal without any delay. In terms of the debenture deed administered by FNB, we were committed to pay interest to the holders at the end of June each year. The first interest payment was due at the end of June 1989 and we were fast approaching this deadline. Firstcorp procrastinated for more than a month, despite repeated warnings from my side. The last day of June thus came and went and we had to pay debenture holders 10 cents per unit, or a total of R3 million, in interest. I will never know with certainty whether this delay was intentional or due to sheer inefficiency. I do know that it caused severe problems in the ranks of the TRFU and for me personally.

At Trust Bank, incidentally, one senior employee, Gerbie Srydom, had purchased 100,000 shares at 80 cents and sold it to the TRFU at R1, making a quick profit of R20,000. Piet Badenhorst later fired the gentleman when he took over the reins at the bank, but until then he remained happily in his post. At the time, of course, there was no legal restriction to insider trading among bankers.

When I, on behalf of the TRFU, approached Tom de Beer of Gencor with an offer of R1.05 per unit, he told me that his company had already sold its one million shares.

'I hope you are happy with the sale, Tom,' I ventured, puzzled by the deal. As a director of Ellis Park, he had never let on to anyone that he was about to get rid of Gencor's holding in the stadium.

'Yes,' he replied, 'we're quite happy with what we got.'

To my surprise, I discovered that Gencor's one million was part of the two million shares Ed Hern had promised to mop up in a hurry at 80 cents per unit. This only came to my notice when Hern had the nerve to demand a refund for the extra 30 cents per share to be paid to Gencor on behalf of TRFU. Needless to say, the acrimonious correspondence and other exchanges that ensued finally severed links between Hern and myself. Personally, I felt that both De Beer and Hern, as directors of Ellis Park, should have informed the board – or me, at least – of Gencor's desire to sell.

When the dust settled, TRFU sat with all the shares, a heavy loan at Trust Bank and enough finger-pointing to fill two boardrooms and a good part of the stadium. Not surprisingly, most of the fingers were directed at me. The same people who questioned my contribution to the recovery of the TRFU and Ellis Park were now insisting that everything that had gone wrong had been my fault. Despite assurances by our merchant bankers that nobody on the boards of either Ellis Park or the TRFU gained personally by the announcement of the delisting offer, the JSE referred 'evidence' to the Registrar of Companies.

I issued a vehement denial of any wrongdoing on our part and placed on record my intention to sue for defamation. Even though Ellis Park shares had been bought on behalf of the TRFU before the bid was announced, it was done merely to build the rugby union's stake before the price escalated – it had not been for resale purposes. Even the *Financial Mail* had to concede, albeit reluctantly, that there was no case here. In the meantime, its competitor, *Finance Week*, attacked me for allegedly being ready to leave the TRFU in a bankrupt state.

When I originally accepted the assignment as president of the truly bankrupt TRFU left behind by Jannie le Roux in 1984, I had made it clear that mine would be a five-year assignment. The minutes of my acceptance speech at the time clearly reflect that intention. In fact, Mickey Gerber, who was elected deputy president, was earmarked to take over from me in 1989. Unfortunately, he relocated to Cape Town in 1987 for business reasons and a replacement had to be found. In my view, Gustaf Pansegrouw, a wealthy man with a solid demeanour who once opposed Gerber but was subsequently brought onto the executive of the TRFU, would have been a wise choice. Instead, however, the Executive Committee nominated as the three best candidates for his post, Jannie Ferreira, Chris van Coller and Gert Augustyn. Van Coller was elected as my deputy.

We assigned Van Coller to oversee the TRFU's centenary celebrations in 1989 as chairman of the organising committee. To my surprise, given Van Coller's position as an accountant at a firm that was later taken over by PriceWaterhouse, the books were in a shambles when the rather disappointing centenary celebrations ended. Sponsorship support fizzled and arrangements soured – especially when Derick Minnie, who promised the world in sponsorship but was overruled by his chairman at the paper company for which he worked, could not deliver. Although I did not express my reservations openly, I was beginning to have doubts about Van Coller's suitability to head the TRFU.

After the difficult delisting, coupled with the knock we had had to take in terms of the interest we had had to pay due to Firstcorp's procrastination, the TRFU had bounced back rather well. A renewed clamour on the part of the member clubs for a bigger share of the profits showed that the situation had at last normalised. Once again the TRFU and Ellis Park were on their way to profitability and I felt that the time was ripe for me to step down. But there was still one obstacle that had to be overcome. Trust Bank insisted that I stay on to look after their loan, as they did not wish to repeat the experience Volkskas had had with the TRFU under Jannie le Roux.

At a meeting of the executive, Avril Malan said that in his view Chris van Coller was not yet ready to take over. With the support of the other executive members, he pleaded with me to stay on as president. I thus agreed to continue in the position for a while longer, but made it clear that a successor would have to be found. We all, however, underestimated Van Coller's burning desire for the post.

Early in February 1989, Van Coller turned up at my office with Gustaf Pansegrouw at his side. After the customary exchange of greetings, we sat down over a cup of coffee. Van Coller had a dark look in his eyes. He looked like a Mexican desperado with his drooping moustache and sullen complexion. This little man with the penchant – like Faan Venter – for betting on horses, seeemd to be accusing me of utilising TRFU funds for personal use. I learnt that he had gathered the executive at the Sunnyside Park Hotel where he freely bandied about charges of dishonesty on my part – all based on a dossier compiled by TRFU manager Faan Venter, ably assisted by my former personal assistant at Triomf, André Both, who had come across to the TRFU at my behest. Somehow, the word 'dossier' seemed to pop up whenever trumped-up charges and unfounded rumours were collected and collated to execute a palace revolution.

Shifting away from the petty personal allegations that were evidently compiled to build a case but, in effect, had very little substance, Van Coller began to zero in on bigger things.

'You've misled us,' he said. 'Instead of making profits, both the TRFU and Ellis Park are making a loss.'

'No,' I said, 'we made a profit, but a lot less than we would have as a result of Firstcorp's bungling and procrastination. But you knew about that, as I have kept you informed all along.'

Pansegrouw looked perturbed.

'Chris,' he said, 'it is you who has misinformed us. I don't want to be part of your scheme any longer. I have better things to do.'

And, with that, Pansegrouw got up and left.

I could not help but marvel at the fact that a certified accountant with so little knowledge could practise in this generally highly respected field. But, undeterred, Van Coller proceeded to lay the groundwork for what he and his supporters perceived to be a certain victory over me and the establishment at the TRFU. On 18 February 1990, he repeated his charges in an interview with *Rapport*. But these, according to him, were not the only reasons for his intention to be elected as president. He wanted stricter control of financial matters and see the clubs benefit more from the union. He wished to see a 'more democratic' management. Reading this, I wondered how he intended to divide the profits among the clubs he had accused me of having manufactured. Was this a case of sharing a dream?

Undeterred, *Die Vaderland* ran a story on 25 February 1990, the day of the election, confidently predicting that I would be ousted as president. The story appeared under the byline of André Bester. When I saw Bester a few days later, he looked terribly embarrassed.

'Dr Luyt,' he explained, 'I did not write that story. It was written by my editor, Gerhard Burger.'

I shrugged it off as merely another instance where advocacy had got the better of journalistic ethics. However, for a man to allow his name to be used so indiscriminately left me perturbed. It had not been the first time and it would certainly not be the last in which the press would be used to try to determine the outcome of a battle involving me. My only problem was that I always found myself on the 'wrong' side. But, then, a yearning of popularity had never been part of my make-up.

Much has since been written about the outcome of the meeting chaired by Avril Malan. Some reports even had me leave the room, which was, like many other stories, a total fabrication. I remained in the room after I made a short statement, looking Van Coller straight in the eye, cautioning that I would not allow anyone to impugn my integrity and get away with it. I was sitting right next to Van Coller when the result was announced. In fact, I could not have cared less if I did not make it.

Apparently, many of the votes he had assumed to be on his side evaporated. I came out the winner. Van Coller was ousted from the executive and Gert Augustyn was elected vice president. Venter and Both left the employ of the TRFU under somewhat of a cloud immediately thereafter.

But this was not the last word from Van Coller and his supporters. At a meeting of three member clubs at the Carlton Hotel, one of Van Coller's supporters, an attorney, the late Alan Levin, was reported to have boasted that he would deliver 'Luyt's head on a platter' in a sure vote of no confidence at a special TRFU meeting. Attendance at this downtown gathering was sparse. Ludie Toerien of Roodepoort Club, who was there, was later forced by his club, led by Nic Smith, to withdraw in writing from these proceedings and apologise.

A year later, Van Coller called me and arranged for an interview. 'I was misled and I am sorry,' he said unashamedly. (When I later told George Rautenbach, who had supported Van Coller at the time, he laughed out loud. 'And,' he said, 'we thought he was the numbers man. He's a bloody fool and a liar!') Van Coller then begged me to help him get back into rugby.

'Rugby is my life,' he pleaded. 'I can't live without it.'

I promised to do my best, and a few weeks later I sent him an invitation to join me in the presidential box at Ellis Park for a provincial game. I tried my best to make him feel welcome, but could not help but notice the furtive glances of disapproval from members of my executive.

That Monday, I received a visit from them. While it was my right to invite whomever I wished, they explained, Van Coller was certainly not welcome in their midst after what he had done. But my dilemma was solved when he left for Cape Town for what was euphemistically referred to as a 'promotion'. His charges, however, remained fodder for others intent on perpetuating the battle by any means.

We were making good profits at Ellis Park as advertising soared and the fans filled the seats. In fact, we had a waiting list of over 130 corporations clamouring for private suites. The demand for season tickets soared. We also rented out the stadium for soccer matches and concerts. By 1993, the TRFU had wiped out its entire debt with Trust Bank.

We had managed to earn up to 35 per cent on our investments and were able to fund the entire union, as well as transfer cash into our capital reserve fund. The TRFU would soon have more money in the bank than all the other unions combined – as well as SARFU.

Our turnaround should, in part, be credited to the timely assistance from the Johannesburg City Council in 1991. That year, we had come very close to our overdraft limit with Trust Bank and had been in danger of having to pay penalty interest of 4 per cent above prime. While trying to find a way out, I advanced Ellis Park an unsecured loan of R8 million before I turned to the city for assistance.

Having redeemed our R3-million loan from the Council in 1988 through the transfer of Southdowns Golf Club, which belonged to the TRFU, I now felt at liberty to make a new approach. Why not grant rugby the same R10-million loan facility granted to cricket at an attractive 10 per cent? The Johannesburg City Council responded favourably. Even though I had to sweeten the deal by granting the city 250 season tickets and two suites, it was a small favour in return for a timely bail-out.

When you have a winning side on the field, everything else falls in place. Transvaal had reached the finals in 1991 and 1992, and in 1993 won the Currie Cup for the first time in many years. Ellis Park managed to pay back my loan and soon settled its outstanding exposure with Trust Bank. In 1993, I suggested to the TRFU executive that we set up a trust to manage Ellis Park, thus ensuring proper oversight and sound fiscal management of this valuable property. The proposal was endorsed and twice unanimously approved by the TRFU at annual general meetings.

In terms of the trust set up by a tax expert, Professor Henry Vorster of Vorster Pereira, TRFU executives and prominent outsiders were elected as A and B trustees. Apart from me, others who agreed to serve included Avril Malan, Willie Kruger, Jomo King, Hugh Bladen, Rian Oberholzer and Gert Augustyn. The trust deed was duly registered and available for public inspection at the Master of the Supreme Court. It was clearly stipulated that the trust was merely a custodian of funds generated and to be utilised for the sole benefit of the TRFU.

Later, the A and B trustees were increased and Erna Bekker became an A trustee while Johan Prinsloo, as CEO of The Golden Lions, was made a B trustee. Clause 16.5 stipulated that 'a Trustee shall be disqualified by his office from contracting with the Trust, either personally or on behalf of any partnership, firm or company in which he is interested, and all contracts entered into by or on behalf of the Trust in which a Trustee is interested shall be null and void.' The trust was subject to proper auditing by PriceWaterhouseCoopers and trustees were obliged to 'ensure that the trust funds are at all times clearly identified as the property of the Trust and kept separate from any of the Trustee's own assets, whether of a similar nature or not'. This remains unchanged to this day.

All my years in business had prepared me well for the unpleasant task of restructuring and turning around the TRFU and Ellis Park. I have always maintained that trying to buy popularity is a sure formula for failure. I had no other choice but to opt for harsh measures. Unless we rationalised and reorganised Ellis Park and the TRFU, I believed, we were doomed to repeat the costly mistakes of the past and sink deeper into debt and failure. In the process of chopping deadwood, a few nests dropped and the unhappy birds scattered all over the place, squeaking and squawking. Success did not come easy and it cost me dearly in terms of popularity.

I was, of course, prepared for at least some criticism, but I must admit that the campaign of calumny that followed in the wake of the so-called miracle at Ellis Park exceeded my worst expectations. No sooner had we steered the stadium and the TRFU away from the brink of bankruptcy to the road of riches when the attacks turned personal.

Some of the same member clubs and personalities who had come to me, begging that I save the TRFU and regain control of Ellis Park, were now lining up at the counter to collect 'their share'. My appointment of Rian Oberholzer, my son-in-law, and later my son Louis, to the management were held up as acts of nepotism. Results should have served as ample proof that family ties and much-needed loyalty were hardly the only reasons for their employment. Instead, their presence was portrayed as proof of the wild allegations that I was building a family empire at Ellis Park. Rarely was it mentioned that, in the dark days when the stadium seemed destined to go bust – and with it the TRFU – I had come to the rescue with my own money.

Above: Buck Shelford and Colin Meads of the 1986 New Zealand Cavaliers, pictured at Ballito.

Right: In pensive mood in 1980.

Below: Talking to Colin Meads at my home, Solitaire, in Saxonworld, Johannesburg.

*Above: Andy Dalton, captain of the 1986
New Zealand Cavaliers, speaks to the press
shortly after the team's arrival. His Transvaal
host stands in the background.*

*Left: My daughter Corlia, capped BA LLB
in 1983, when I received an Honorary
Doctorate (DCom), bestowed by the Free
State University.*

*I welcome the New Zealand Cavaliers at Jan Smuts airport in 1986. On the left is Ian
Kirkpatrick with Colin Meads the team manager.*

With his announcement in February 1990 of the scrapping of apartheid and the unbanning of the ANC and other previously outlawed political organisations, President FW de Klerk merely accelerated the negotiation process already underway in rugby since the 'unauthorised' contact with the 'terrorists' initiated by Doc Craven and I - an act that De Klerk and others in government had so vehemently condemned. In 1991, the ANC-approved South African Rugby Union (SARU) thus joined forces with the white-dominated South African Rugby Board (SARB) to form the new South African Rugby Football Union (SARFU).

While I accepted the arrangement as an unfortunate, but necessary *fait accompli*, Doc Craven had a hard time in coming to terms with the Patel conundrum. I was reminded of his reticence to get down and dirty in the ongoing 'transformation period' every time he asked me to stand in for him in matters involving the ANC. Even though I was passed over when Fritz Eloff was re-elected the deputy chairman of the SARB at its final annual meeting in March 1991, Craven continued to use me as his designated trouble-shooter and ANC go-between. Somehow, he must have learned a lesson in 1988 when his attempts to co-opt the Broederbonders in the process, failed miserably.

The officially sanctioned visits of the New Zealand and Australian teams to South Africa in 1992 are generally seen as the first steps in our long-awaited re-entry to international competition. Not so. Preceding these visits, there was another episode, which in effect signalled our return to the world of rugby.

It all started with a call from my good friend in New Zealand, Ivan Vodanovich, whom I had known since 1970 when he had coached the New Zealand All Blacks on their tour of South Africa. Ivan and his wonderful wife, Bettie, had been our house guests on quite a few occasions and I had visited them in New Zealand. In fact, Adri and I were on our way on a short vacation to Australia and New Zealand where we intended to meet with them and I assumed that Ivan was merely calling to confirm our arrangements.

Instead, he needed assistance in an unrelated matter. The All Blacks, he explained, needed six top South African players to include in the invitational international team scheduled to participate in the upcoming centenary celebrations. They wanted me to obtain 'permission' from the ANC-controlled National Sports Council for these South Africans to play. He needed my help, Ivan said.

'After all, what are friends for?' he asked in his typically charming manner.

I agreed to try my best on condition that Doc Craven first be consulted in the matter. That turned out to be unnecessary, as it was Craven who had apparently steered the New Zealand rugby bosses towards me. Craven was not about to ask favours from Mluleki George, chairman of the NSC, or any other ANC-approved sports administrator. As in the past, Craven bypassed his own deputy, Fritz Eloff, and others in calling on me to get the job done.

With my permission, Ivan Vodanovich handed my unlisted number to Eddie Tonks, Craven's counterpart in New Zealand. A few minutes later, Tonks was on the line. He apologised for the lateness of this request. New Zealand, he said, had waited to see how genuine the changes in South Africa were before it made its move. They were obviously still smarting from the opprobrium that had ensued during the 1981 Springbok tour and after the rebel Cavalier tour of 1986. This time around, the All Blacks wanted to have complete assurances that there would be no negative political fallout. They needed the written approval of the NSC. In the absence of any official representation in South Africa, the New Zealand High Commissioner in Zimbabwe, Doug Law, was asked to approach Mluleki George. Law was told that there was no objection, but he had been unable to obtain written confirmation.

'Louis, we desperately need your help,' Eddie Tonks said as if he was a long-lost friend.

When I phoned Doc Craven, he responded in a casual manner. It was evident that he had expected my call.

'Go ahead, Louis, help these guys,' he said. 'And be sure to pick the very best players to go out there. It is important that we make a great impression on our first reappearance in the world of rugby. And, by the way, send them our best, do you hear?"

I couldn't quite make out whether he meant the New Zealanders or the NSC, or both. I did, however, detect some sense of relief on his part for not having to go begging to Mluleki George and his comrades. Once again, the crafty Doc had me trotting out to the frontline while he managed to stay in the background, pushing the buttons.

Before I could approach George, I first had to find him. That proved to be quite a task. The numerous messages we left with Mthobi Tyamzashe, Secretary General of the NSC, remained unanswered. Tyamzashe would later move on to become Director General of Sport in the ANC government and assume a key role in the sordid battle that ensued between SARFU and the government, but at this time he was apparently trying his best to be helpful. I suspected that George was merely pulling our string and letting us know 'who is really in charge'. This tendency would surface frequently in future as we got to know each other, first as allies and later as foes.

I had planned to get away from it all after drawn-out and frustrating discussions with the Rupert Group over sponsorship of the Currie Cup and television rights for the international games. The deal was practically done – or so I was made to understand – and I finalised plans for a two-week vacation Down Under. But now I had been saddled with another pressing task – it was barely seven hours before Adri and I were to depart and we were still unable to reach Mluleki George. After several calls, Rian Oberholzer found out that he was practically under our noses at the Carlton Hotel in Johannesburg, awaiting the arrival of a delegation from the Federation Internationale de Football Association (FIFA). But when we contacted the hotel we were told that he had already left for the airport.

We thus proceeded to Johannesburg International airport at breakneck speed only to be told by a young reporter, Billy Cooper, who was still lingering there, that Mluleki George and his adjutants had left for a reception at the estate of Douw Steyn in Hyde Park. After being ushered through the security gate, we joined the milling guests on the expansive brightly lit lawn in search of the man. I had never met George but I had seen him on television a few times, proclaiming to the world that new times were upon us and that the old order had better watch out. He, I assumed, would also have no problem recognising me either. But on that day he was not exactly looking out for me at a reception of soccer officials and aficionados.

Mluleki George couldn't believe his eyes when I tapped him on the shoulder and he turned around to face me. What, he must have thought, is this wilful white rugby administrator doing at a soccer reception? Perhaps he also felt just a little embarrassed by his past public pronouncements about folk like me who had signalled our intent to resist political interference in our sport.

'Mr George,' I explained as I handed Mluleki the typed letter. 'Here is a document that we need you to sign to enable South African rugby to return to international competition.'

He read through the short document, took the pen from my hand and signed. When I returned home to join Adri and finish packing for our trip to Australasia, I called Doug Law in Harare to share the good news.

'That's great,' he said. 'I assume it is typed on the official NSC letterhead?'

It turned out that having the letter on an ordinary sheet of paper was insufficient. I immediately put the phone down and contacted Tyamzashe in East London. We agreed that a faxed version of the signed letter would be incorporated under the NSC letterhead and faxed, in turn, to Doug Law in Harare. Before I left, I also sent a copy of the Mluleki George letter to Law. When I called Tyamzashe to make sure he had received my fax, there was no answer. Time was running out, so Adri and I left for the airport. I then made one last call to Doug Law before we set off on our trip.

'Doug, I am afraid we are being made fools of,' I said, no longer hiding my anger and frustration. 'But I promise you, I will make one further attempt after my arrival in Sydney.'

'Don't worry, Louis,' he said, sounding equally exasperated. 'Give it one more try from Australia and if you don't succeed, I will issue the visas regardless. After all, I was made the same promises by Mluleki George. We cannot continue with this uncertainty.'

The players had all already been picked and were packed and ready. I had, as I promised Doc Danie, selected what I considered the cream of the crop – six men who would be great ambassadors for their country and the sport. They were André Joubert, Pieter Hendriks, Jannie Claassen, Naas Botha, Martin Knoetze, and Uli Schmidt.

Shortly after Adri and I had settled into the hotel at Sydney, I made contact with Tyamzashe. He had never received my fax, he claimed.

'Listen,' I said. 'We have one more chance to get this thing going.'

For obvious reasons I did not let him know that he and George no longer had the ability to stop the trip. I still felt it would be better if the New Zealanders could have the South Africans proceed with the full endorsement of the NSC, eliminating any chance of another fallout after the fact. They had had enough flak in the past and they certainly did not deserve yet another incident.

I thus arranged with Tyamzashe to watch the fax come through from my side while we both stayed in touch via the telephone. When he confirmed, I asked him to send the letter on an NSC letterhead to Doug Law and to copy one to me at the hotel. A half-hour later we had the new letter in hand, both in Harare and Sydney. I could now relax and enjoy my vacation.

From Australia, Adri and I flew to New Zealand where we were met by Ivan and Bettie Vodanovich. We had a great time together, sightseeing and talking about old times. When the conversation turned to rugby and the upcoming centennial game in Christchurch, Ivan heard that we did not have tickets to the game. He handed me two VIP invitations to the presidential box. I assumed these were courtesy of New Zealand Rugby Football Union President Eddie Tonks as a gesture of thanks for my efforts on their behalf. I was mistaken. Later, I would discover these tickets actually belonged to Ivan. After the game, when we attended the NZRFU reception at the invitation of another Good Samaritan, Tonks came to me looking rather embarrassed.

'I'm really sorry, I forgot,' he apologised, insisting that we accept invitations to two other games and receptions.

Adri and I had a good chuckle over a rerun on TV that evening showing the dignitaries in the presidential box. The camera zoomed in on Colin Meads, Ian Clarke and Eddie Tonks, with the announcer mentioning each name as it panned along. When it was my turn, the announcer simply identified me as 'another gentleman'. Only a few years later, Christchurch would carry big billboards proclaiming: 'New Zealand in luck. Louis Luyt lives in South Africa!' I had certainly managed to move from nincompoop to notoriety in no time, without any intermediate fame.

What I remember most fondly, despite all else that went wrong at the time, was the way in which our six players acquitted themselves both on and off the field. They contributed in no small amount to the World XV's victory over the

All Blacks. Pieter Hendriks scored two magnificent tries. South Africa was back in a big way. We made our statement.

The banner posters that greeted the All Blacks in August 1992, when they arrived for their first official test against the Springboks in 11 years, proclaimed: 'Welcome to your worst nightmare!' Instead, the nightmare turned out to be all ours. The contention that many years of isolation had done little to our ability to compete soon proved to be entirely wrong. An expanded Currie Cup competition was hardly a substitute for international experience. The All Blacks won the test 27–24 after we gave away two tries and too many penalties.

This historic test at Ellis Park Stadium on 15 August 1992 will, however, not be remembered for the play on the field or, for that matter, the score. It will always be referred to as 'The Day *Die Stem* Was Played'. Once again I found myself in the middle of a controversy so big that it made its way into three column reports in the *New York Times*, which normally gives rugby about as much attention as we do the Italian game of bocce. I was portrayed as the tough redneck Afrikaner who stuck it to the peacemakers in South Africa by obstinately rubbing the 'symbols of the past' in their faces.

For weeks leading up to the test, a debate raged in the press and over radio as to whether it would be appropriate to play *Die Stem* at Ellis Park before the game. I disagreed with newspaper pundits who strongly opposed the playing of our national anthem on this occasion while raising no objection to *Nkosi Sikilel' iAfrika* being played at soccer matches. After all, *Die Stem* was still our official anthem, as was the tricolour flag. What were we to do after we had played the New Zealand national anthem? I had told Rian that we should go ahead and play our anthem. And, even without the overwhelming support of the rugby public, I would still have pressed ahead. This was, in my view, an issue of principle. I was not about to deny the existence of a national anthem merely to please the ANC or any of the wimps who wished to roll over and play dead.

I spoke with Doug Law, who was still filling in from Harare for the New Zealand High Commission left dormant in South Africa. He was fully aware of the building controversy in South Africa and was not ready to be drawn into it, but had no problem in supplying us with the New Zealand anthem on tape. On the big day, many thousands of the 70,000 spectators packed into Ellis Park with flags they had purchased outside the stadium. I told NZFRU President Eddie Tonks when he joined me in the presidential suite that we intended to play the New Zealand anthem as well as ours. He nodded in agreement with the apparent approval of the New Zealand official who accompanied him.

'But did you tell our team manager, Ian Gray?' Tonks asked. 'He should be informed as well.'

'No,' I said, 'I don't think it is my role to inform him. Perhaps we should both go down to the locker room and tell him.'

I accompanied Tonks and the New Zealand government representative down to the change rooms where I left them and returned to the presidential suite to welcome the last few VIP guests. As I looked around me, I was reminded of a once-popular television show in America called *This is Your Life*: FW de Klerk, who had once threatened action against me and now had become so generous with the 'terrorists' he had previously so despised; Steve Tshwete, Ebrahim Patel, Craven and Eloff. Would the playing of *Die Stem* surprise some? Would it anger others? Would it please at least a few?

When the Springbok team appeared, a few voices near centre field started with *Die Stem*. Others soon followed. We were forced to request them to remain silent until we had the opportunity to play the New Zealand anthem. The announcement was greeted with a groan. The crowd had no way of knowing what was in store. After the All Blacks heard their national anthem, the loud-speakers fell silent. But only for a second. Then *Die Stem* started playing. Loud and clear. Most of 70,000 voices joined in. I looked around me. De Klerk looked genuinely moved. Even Patel's wife was singing along. It was the closest a rugby crowd in South Africa had ever come to matching the Welsh at Cardiff Arms Park in their spine-tingling rendition of Land of my Fathers.

Even the furore that followed could not quite dim the memory of that magic moment. It is one that will remain sharply etched in my mind for as long as I live – and, I am sure, in the memories of the many thousands who participated. To no one's surprise, least of all my own, I was portrayed by the press as defiant and obstinate. I had stood up for a principle and refused to let the would-be ANC government dictate to us. After all, we were simply playing and singing our anthem as it existed at the time, in the same way as we did later, with ANC approval, when we belted out renditions of the newly approved amalgamation of *Die Stem* and *Nkosi Sikelel' iAfrika*.

Barring a few individuals, including our rising new Transvaal captain, Francois Pienaar, who praised the moment, I cut a lonesome figure in rugby circles where the tendency had already developed to take the road of least resistance against outside interference. The ANC, of course, was livid. They threatened, as one would have expected, to reintroduce their 'ban' on rugby. I called their bluff and the press reported me as having told them to 'go to hell'. I might not have used those precise words, but the reports were otherwise correct. Danie Craven and Ebrahim Patel apologised in their capacity as joint presidents of SARFU. I stood firm. There was nothing in SARFU's constitution, I pointed out, that prohibited the host union from playing the nation's anthem at an international game. Calls of support were jamming our switchboard and our fax machines constantly ran out of paper as congratulations streamed in.

Joe French, the visiting chairman of the Australian Rugby Football Union (ASRFU), who was in South Africa to attend the next test against the Wallabies in Cape Town, stepped in to add his voice to the dissenters. Having known Joe as a good friend of South Africa, his criticism stung. He accused me of having acted with malice aforethought. While I would plead guilty to aforethought, there was certainly no malice intended – that came from the opposing side. French said he and his team were willing to return to Australia if the ANC wanted them to do so. A year later, at a pre-match lunch at Twickenham, he was not as brave when Carel de Wet confronted him about his remarks. In fact, he cowered before the pugilistic doctor and my respect for him quickly diminished. Yet, French was indeed an ardent South African supporter in his time and for that I have to give him due credit.

In the rather unpleasant aftermath of this magic moment, I was 'reported' to SARFU by my fellow executive members, Fritz Eloff, Johan Claassen, Hennie Erasmus and Nic Labuschagne for going against the South African Rugby Football Union dictates. An urgent executive committee meeting was requested to discuss the ramifications of this 'stupid' action. I thus sought the wise counsel of Fanie Cilliers, and suggested that I should not attend the meeting. But Fanie felt differently.

'Go and confront them – don't run away from them. This can be nothing more than a meeting because if they were to charge you with any misdemeanour they have to give you, according to the requirements of the law, proper notice of the charge, the place where you will be heard and an opportunity to state your case.' As usual, Fanie was quite right and I attended a meeting that was acrimonious from the very outset.

I was particularly harshly attacked by the Reverend Arnold Stofile who was quite personal in his vitriol and, in fact, libellous in the extreme – so much so that I had to warn him and suggested that he consult the galaxy of lawyers around the table before he uttered another word. That saw the quickest change of attitude I have ever encounterd in my life. Another eye-opener for me was Dr Craven's response after he listened to all my accusers and in particular those representing the old SARU.

Instead of remaining seated, Craven stood up and said: 'Gentlemen, I am sick and tired of hearing about us', looking at the former SARU representatives. 'What about us? Don't we have any rights any more? And let me tell you right now, I was a proud man on Saturday when that anthem was played and not only I; a mediocre Springbok team nearly beat the All Blacks! They were charged up.'

That was that – I was no longer the bad boy in the woodpile.

After a firm undertaking that SARFU would abide by the dictates of the ANC, the Australians stayed. On the instruction of Craven and Patel, there was to be no anthem. Instead the Western Province officials kept playing music until the teams had taken the field. Even those who wanted to sing were unable to because of the deafening noise of the music over the loudspeakers.

The Australian Wallabies thrashed South Africa 26–3, posting an all-time record victory over the Springboks. The fellows on the field proved to be as inept in dealing with international competition as we administrators were in standing up in the scrums against the increasingly intrusive politicos of the African National Congress.

In Johannesburg, after the New Zealand test, I observed another shortcoming that would continue haunting us right up to and beyond the World Cup. We had apparently lost our ability as a team to cope, off the field as well as on it. This became apparent as the New Zealand team was waiting impatiently for the South African team to make its appearance at a post-game reception hosted by South African Breweries. Merle McKenna of Breweries came to me on behalf of the hosts, complaining that the visitors had been standing around for more than an hour, waiting for the Springboks, and that they were now ready to leave. We thus drove to the Sandton Hotel where the South Africans were staying and found James Small and Pieter Hendriks in the lobby.

'Where is the rest of the team?' I boomed.

'They're in the Kontiki room,' Hendriks explained. 'Initiating the new caps...'

I flew through the door where manager Abe Malan and coach John Williams were conducting their team rituals while ignoring their obligations elsewhere.

'You have five minutes to get on the bus,' I announced. 'Five minutes flat.'

We just managed to save the day with the Springboks players filing into the reception as All Black manager Colin Meads and coach Laurie Mains were about to leave with their team. Was this inappropriate behaviour by the Springboks, I wondered afterwards, a simple lack of social graces due to years of isolation, or was there a need to correct the problem from the top? Surely some discipline was needed. Management could obviously do with a little shake-up. Discipline and good behaviour off the field are, after all, vital prerequisites for success on the field.

At the end of 1992 the Springboks went on their first tour since the lifting of the boycott. The trip to France and England was riddled with problems on and off the field. Not only did the South Africans show, as they had done in the two test defeats at home, that they had fallen behind on the field, but also displayed a disturbing lack of discipline off the field. They lost their very first match against an Emerging French XV and later went under against the French Universities and the French Barbarians. Surprisingly, they won the first test in Lyon before losing the second in Paris. But the big story was when Abe Malan led the team out of a dinner 'because the French were late in arriving'. With the Johannesburg episode still disturbingly fresh in my memory, I had hoped that something good might still come out of this. Perhaps the Springboks might now have learnt a lesson? During the World Cup in 1995, however, this proved to be a trifle optimistic.

After a good victory against England B there were high expectations for the test against England at Twickenham. I travelled to London to attend the game, but for some inexplicable reason, a fellow SARFU member, Hennie Erasmus, and I were given seats in the stands instead of being invited to the presidential suite, as would be customary. The president of the English Rugby Football Union, Dr Danie Serfontein, happened to be an expatriate dentist from Senekal who once went to school with Adri.

'We should place the bastard behind the posts when he comes to South Africa,' Hennie observed as we settled in, wrapped in thick overcoats to protect us against the damp chill.

Instead, I always saw to it that Serfontein received the best we could offer every time he visited his former homeland to attend games. He actually turned out to be a rather good fellow. But then my view of the man might have been skewed by the fact that he hailed from the same little Free State town that gave me a wonderful wife and partner in Adri.

Taking his place in the presidential suite next to British Prime Minister John Major was President FW de Klerk. The previous day, he was asked in a television interview whether he would sing if *Die Stem* were to be played at Twickenham before the game. No, he said with that disarming smile that had become his trademark in these stressful days of large-scale giveaways, *Die Stem* would probably not be played. And even if it were, De Klerk announced, he would not sing it as he did not even sing in church. To no one's surprise, *God Save the Queen* went unanswered as the two teams lined up before the game.

At half-time the Springboks led 16–11. In the second half, however, the English team dominated every phase of the game and trounced us 33–16. Particularly disturbing was the way in which the English took control at the front where we were once anyone's match. The Springboks were a team badly in need of some new techniques and proper training. The lack of cohesion, purpose and discipline in our management seemed to be felt on the field. Undoubtedly, the uncertainty over identity, symbols and the like, was also having a detrimental effect on the Springboks. While we obviously had the talent, we lacked spirit and sense of direction.

Evidently, I was not the only member of SARFU who felt that we needed drastic change at the top. Even Abe Malan concurred. He handed in his resignation as manager shortly after the team's return from the disastrous tour in 1992. John Williams, the former Springbok lock forward, signalled his intention to stay on as coach, but SARFU was determined to make a clean sweep.

Free State coach, Gerrie Sonnekus, was then selected to replace Williams. On the face of it, this was a good choice, given Sonnekus' reputation as an innovative no-nonsense guy who had had great success with the Free State team. Unfortunately, charges of fraud then surfaced and made his position untenable.

Sonnekus thus had to be asked to resign while the charges were pending and I was assigned to undertake this unpleasant task by Fritz Eloff. Having known this dedicated man for many years, this might have been the single most difficult task I ever had to perform.

Sonnekus was adamant. He wanted to stay on.

'Gerrie,' I explained, 'no one says you are guilty of anything. I certainly hope that these charges will all be proven false and that it willl all blow over. But in the meantime these charges are a distraction we don't need.'

I demanded that he send a letter of resignation by fax before four that afternoon. Otherwise, I explained, SARFU would have to fire you. It was sad to hear a grown man cry and I could fully appreciate why. This was Sonnekus' big moment and, to this day, I believe he would have made an excellent coach. Eventually, all the charges were dropped, but Gerrie was never given another chance. His resignation reached us five minutes before the deadline.

The search for a new coach resumed. There was a strong lobby in favour of the Natal coach, Ian McIntosh. A few diehards in SARFU were opposed to an English-speaking coach born in Zimbabwe who had never played rugby for the Springboks. I, of course, had no problem with McIntosh's failing of the Broederbond litmus test but my support for him was tempered somewhat by his past performance where it really counts – on the field. For several years he had tried unsuccessfully to coach Natal out of the B-Section of the Currie Cup into the A-Section. Eventually, Natal was elevated at Transvaal's insistence because we needed another large union in the A ranks to help defray the South African Rugby Board's costs, which rested largely on Transvaal's shoulders. Natal management went on a buying spree and built a winning team with players such as fullback André Joubert and flyhalf Henry Honiball and a host of other stars.

McIntosh – or Mac, as he preferred to be known – suddenly became the star coach when Natal managed to win the Currie Cup in 1990 and again, fairly luckily, in 1992 after this expensive facelift. The 1992 win was against Transvaal. In 1993, Transvaal would, however, turn the tables to win and beat Natal for the trophy at its home ground, Kings Park.

So Mac became the new Springbok coach. In the process, we might have broken the mould and opened the door to the appointment of an assortment of foreign coaches, including former All Blacks and Wallabies. But, unfortunately, we did not manage to make a clear break with past problems. Mac would not stay long. In my book, he wrote off more players than he made with his 'crashball' approach. But he simply was not good enough. Period.

In the meanwhile, the race for a suitable replacement for Abe Malan as manager continued. One day I received a call from Robert Denton, who had moved on to become marketing manager of SARFU after his forced departure from the TRFU when I took over the reins. I assumed, quite correctly, that the call was not social. Denton wanted a favour from me. He told me that he proposed Jannie Engelbrecht as the new manager and would appreciate it if I could see my way clear to nominate him at the next executive meeting of SARFU.

I did not know Engelbrecht all that well, but nevertheless agreed to look into the matter. While I was aware of his memorable – and not so memorable – moves on the field as a Springbok winger, I had little knowledge of his managerial skills beyond heading up a purportedly successful wine estate at Rust en Vrede in the Stellenbosch district. He was also fairly widely discussed in gossip circles, but I do not pay much attention to gossip. As a result, I contacted Fritz Eloff and found that he was 'thrilled' about the idea to have Engelbrecht on board. Next I phoned Engelbrecht at the number left by Denton and asked him whether I could put his name forward on behalf of the TRFU.

'Thanks,' he said, 'but Western Province has already asked whether they could nominate me.'

'Fine,' I responded. 'In that case, I will wait for Western Province to nominate you and then cast my vote in support of you...'

'No,' he interrupted. 'Coming from a big province like Transvaal can only help. Why don't you nominate me instead?'

For once, Denton managed to orchestrate the event without a hitch, even mustering adversaries like me on his side. That, however, would be the first and last time we found ourselves on the same side.

Jannie Engelbrecht's insistence on being 'his own man' apparently required that he oppose and criticise SARFU at every possible juncture, mostly in public through the media, who discovered in him a continuing source of good copy. Here was a jovial, free-spoken and likeable former Springbok star ready to do battle with the stodgy folks at the top without fear or trepidation. In his apparent attempt to gain popularity among the players, he assumed a relaxed attitude instead of applying the strict discipline so badly needed in the process of rebuilding our strength on the field.

Thinking back to an occasion in 1994 when Jannie Engelbrecht and his charming wife, Ellen, invited me to stay with them at Rust en Vrede, I can attest to the infectious charm of this rather debonair man. This was shortly before my election as president of SARFU and Engelbrecht had no hesitation in expressing his support for my candidacy to the post. I was asked to speak at the annual general meeting of the Stellenbosch University rugby club. Even though I was given the club's highest honour in 1970, when they awarded me their official blazer with the rugby emblem embossed with the silver star, I did not wear it that evening or ever in public. I just felt that it might have been interpreted as an attempt on my part to emulate Doc Craven. In any event, the weight gained as a result of physical neglect coupled with good eating, made it impossible for me to fit into the blazer.

Introducing me, former Springbok loose forward Boland Coetzee could not resist commenting on my 'stature': 'This afternoon, Jannie and I went to pick up Louis at the airport. And when I saw him stepping off the plane, I said to Jannie, this bugger looks as if he has swallowed the Currie Cup!'

When it was my turn to respond, I started by 'correcting' Coetzee: 'Boland says I might have swallowed the Currie Cup. But he only told you part of the story. I have also swallowed the Lion Cup, the Super-10 Cup and the M-Net Night Series Cup!'

In 1994, Transvaal had swept the competition aside both in South Africa and in the southern hemisphere. It was then that I was urged by my union to seek the presidency of the South African Rugby Football Union. Others seemed to favour the idea because there was a general feeling that my managerial and business skills might be useful as we approached the third Rugby World Cup scheduled to take place in South Africa in 1995.

Mindful of the furore that followed my bid for the deputy presidency of the South Africa Rugby Board (SARB) in 1991, I was somewhat hesitant when the TRFU urged me to go for the presidency of SARFU, which I had helped to form in 1991 as a replacement for both the SARB and the black-controlled South African Rugby Union or SARU. In the heat of battle, when I had challenged Fritz Eloff of Northern Transvaal back in March 1991 for the vice presidency of the SARB, there had been exchanges that served neither of us well. I had had a hard time coming to terms with Eloff's tendency to run for cover whenever the heat was on – as evidenced in 1986 with the rebel Cavalier tour and again in 1988 when Craven and I were attacked for having discussions with the African National Congress – so, shortly before the vote at the SARB annual general meeting in March 1991, I had withdrawn my candidacy for the sake of unity. But this had not prevented Eloff from launching a vitriolic attack, accusing me of 'making a mockery of the position'.

'It is my union's democratic right to nominate me for the position of vice president,' I reminded Eloff. 'I'd like a word with you afterwards,' I said.

After the meeting Eloff came to me: 'You wanted to speak to me...'

'Yes,' I said. 'You're a bloody coward, the way you attacked me.'

'In that case,' he replied, 'you and I have nothing further to discuss.'

'You're bloody right, we have nothing further to discuss,' I told him and walked away.

Eloff remained deputy president and, I must admit, acquitted himself extremely well. Doc Craven had him take up his seat in the International Rugby Board and when South Africa's turn came, the presidency of the world body. But Fritz was destined to serve for only a few months as executive president during the interim months between Doc Craven's death in January 1993 at the age of 81 and Ebrahim Patel's assumption of the post in March 1993 in terms of the agreement struck when SARFU was formed in February 1992.

In March 1994, Patel's one-year term ended and the presidency of SARFU was open to free election. Patel withdrew, citing pressing commitments elsewhere. During his year as president, we at the Golden Lions Rugby Union had made a new car available to him out of respect for the position. We even had a telephone installed. Patel insisted on any other colour but white. We gave him a top of the range Camry. Well after my election as president of SARFU and still also president of The Lions, Patel phoned me to inquire when he should return the car.

'Anytime, Ebrahim,' I said.

'Why not donate it to me? After all, I was one who helped unite the two unions. Come on, Louis, you can do it.'

'Take the damn thing,' I said in desperation with his callousness. Of course I had to report my gesture to the Golden Lions executive.

After all the lobbying and canvassing on my behalf by the Transvaal Rugby Football Union, André Markgraaff and Mauritz Meyer, I stepped into the position of president unopposed at a rather uneventful meeting at the Woodstock Holiday Inn in Cape Town on 11 March 1994. Fritz Eloff, who chaired the meeting the absence of Patel, was graceful in welcoming me to the post. Luyt, he noted, was a controversial man. 'But,' he added, 'we need a strong man to lead us on the road to the World Cup. Dr Luyt is that man.'

In my response, I returned the compliment. I could honestly say that, despite our differences of the past, Eloff proved himself to be a very able deputy president and, for that short period, a splendid executive president. His representation of our interests at the International Rugby Board was extremely valuable and should continue, I told the meeting.

Elected to serve on the executive committee were four members of the old SARU: Mluleki George and Silas Nkanunu of Eastern Province, Tobie Titus of Western Province and Arthob Petersen of Boland. From the ranks of the old SARB came Ronnie Masson of Western Province, Hentie Serfontein of Northern Transvaal, Keith Parkinson of Natal, André Markgraaff of Griqualand West and Hennie Erasmus of South-Eastern Transvaal.

Looking at the men chosen to serve on my executive, I recalled a meeting a few days earlier with Reverend Arnold Stofile, who was serving on the interim executive of SARFU and soon to become the ANC's premier of the Eastern Cape.

'I asked the reverend to pray for me,' I told the audience. 'And the reverend responded with, "Now more than ever!" But now that I see the executive you have given me, I don't think even that is enough,' I quipped.

What followed simply confirmed that many a truth is spoken in jest. But the trouble at executive level would only come later. First, there were other pressing issues to be dealt with – such as a manager who refused to accept any direction or, as he termed it, 'interference' from SARFU, and a coach who seemed unable to stop the bleeding on and off the field.

If you want to make enemies,

try to change something.

Woodrow Wilson

Chapter 12

THE ROCKY ROAD TO RECOVERY

In March 1994, when I was elected to the position as president of SARFU, I promised to work diligently round the clock for change. 'We are a rugby nation,' I reminded everyone, 'and we were the best. We need to become the world's best again.' No one or nothing would stand in my way to accomplish this goal, I pledged. In the audience there were those unfamiliar with my style of doing things, who dismissed this as nothing more than an empty threat. But there were also those who knew me only too well, who started building roadblocks and strengthening their own defences to maintain the *laissez faire* culture that had developed during the previous two years. With the lack of strong leadership as Doc Craven wasted away, and Eloff's inability to do anything in the short three months before he handed over to another interim caretaker in the person of Patel, everyone seemed to have done what they very well pleased. There were, thankfully, also a few who welcomed the idea of restoring authority to the post of president.

It did not take me long, however, to discover just how difficult it would be to restore discipline. One major obstacle turned out to be the very man I had so enthusiastically proposed as manager. Another happened to be the coach whom I had never regarded as the right man to repair and recondition our rusty rugby machine.

Much has been written about the squabbles between team manager Jannie Engelbrecht and me that eventually led to his firing as Springbok manager. I have also been pictured as the ruthless reaper who chopped Ian McIntosh from his post. Although I certainly accept responsibility for all my own actions, I find it strange that so few bothered to make any reference to the problems that existed well before I took over as president of SARFU.

During his very first outing as manager, when he accompanied the Springbok team to Australia, Engelbrecht felt obliged to openly criticise SARFU for its lack of organisation in accepting the schedule presented by the hosts. Fritz Eloff, who was serving as co-president with then executive president Ebrahim Patel, was instructed by SARFU's executive committee to reprimand Engelbrecht. I was not privy to Eloff's conversation with the out-of-control manager but, judging from Engelbrecht's continuing public criticism of SARFU during a subsequent tour of Argentina, one must assume that Eloff had failed to get our message across.

Patel, who was caretaker president of SARFU in 1993, accompanied the Springboks during the early part of their Australian tour and rejoined them before the final test. It was, of course, customary for the heads of international rugby unions to make such appearances during tours of their teams abroad. After the Australian tour, Engelbrecht came back complaining to me and others – in private – that Patel had been a great embarrassment to him when he had insisted on making the speech at the post-game dinner after the final test – a task, Engelbrecht argued, that was best left to the manager who knows more about rugby than the hapless president of SARFU. In public, however, Patel was held up by Engelbrecht as the very model of an ambassador for the game. As soon as I took over from Patel, I was worked over in the same manner. In public, I was held up as the new saviour of rugby and, in private, as the meanest of men to have held the post of SARFU president.

As early as 1993 there had been grumbling in the corridors of SARFU about Engelbrecht's tendency to use these tours as opportunities to further his own business abroad, taking off time to visit potential clients for his high-quality export wines when he should have, in fact, been with the team. Personally, I had no problem with occasional side trips as long as they did not interfere with his function as manager. After all, Engelbrecht took the job for the love of the game, without any remuneration beyond having his travel and accommodation expenses covered by SARFU. More troubling to me were recurring reports of lack of discipline among the players that had led to incidents and affected play on the field.

I also could not understand Engelbrecht's insistence that Robert Denton accompany the team to Argentina. As happened in the case of Ellis Park and TRFU, my arrival on the scene as the new president of SARFU in March 1994 signalled Denton's hasty departure. I simply could not see the reason for having a marketing manager who was unable to market, especially as we were fast approaching the 1995 World Cup in South Africa.

The first international encounter after my election as president of SARFU was supposed to be a celebration. After losing five games against our provincial teams, the English touring side facing us in the first test on 4 June 1994 was portrayed by pundits as a pushover. Unfortunately, not only the public but also our players seemed to believe these over-optimistic observers. The Springboks came out on Loftus Versfeld like a pride of lions ready to devour the visitors in a spectacle reminiscent of old Roman times.

The newly installed President Nelson Mandela had joined me in the presidential suite after having been introduced to the players on the field. It was his first attendance of a rugby international as South Africa's head of state and he certainly made an indelible impression as he moved about with the ease and grace that had become his trademark in the four years since his release from Robben Island.

This, however, was not my first encounter with this remarkable man. In 1990, he had been my guest of honour at a pop concert at Ellis Park and in 1991 he invited Craven and me to visit him and his colleagues at ANC headquarters in Shell House, Johannesburg. Mandela and Walter Sisulu were in the office into which Dr Craven and I were ushered. During a brief moment alone with Mr Mandela, I handed him a letter I had written that morning in which I, very sincerely, warned him against the continuous reference to nationalisation of certain assets.

I pointed out that the National Party government already 'owned' the bulk of industry through the IDC, Telkom, the South African Railways and Harbours, Sasol, the South African Broadcasting Corporation and a host of other examples. He read the letter carefully, folded it neatly and slipped it into his inside pocket. He shook his head in acknowledgement.

After a discussion in his office, he led us through to the conference room where he had assembled the rest of the SARFU delegation, with Patel and other members of SARU. Seated right next to him, I watched Mandela at the head of the table and marvelled at his ability to be both regal and humble at the same time. On this occasion, he urged us all to find a way to come together. He warned us not to, during our discussions, make remarks or insult each other that would only serve to make negotiations difficult.

In May 1994, I attended his inauguration but missed the state luncheon as I had to oversee final arrangements for the international soccer game to be played at the Ellis Park Stadium in his honour that afternoon. But I did receive reports about his kind comments regarding Craven and my efforts to promote dialogue and change in rugby.

On 4 June 1994, it seemed as everything had indeed come together. President Mandela was there as head of a rainbow nation, surrounded by a rugby administration of all colours and creeds. Seated on my left was Steve Tshwete, the Minister of Sport, with whom I had had the privilege to work in engineering the amalgamation of SARU and SARB into the single South African Rugby Football Union. All that we needed now was to celebrate this coming together with a resounding victory on the field.

The words of my speech after the England team easily disposed of a South

African A-team the previous Tuesday at Kimberley kept humming in my head. I had said that I was an extremely worried man after what I had seen that day. It was the first time England had played to its full potential, I had said.

My concerns, it seemed, had been well-founded. After 17 shocking minutes that left us all speechless, the English led 20–0 through two penalties and two converted tries. President Mandela stared straight ahead of him. So did I. There wasn't much to celebrate or talk about. Our team struggled back somewhat but as the day ended the score stood at 32–15 to England.

President Mandela looked at me.

'Louis,' he asked, 'what are you going to do about this?'

'Yes,' Steve Tshwete chipped in, 'what are you going to do about this?'

'Mr President, I don't know as yet,' I confessed. 'But you can rest assured that something will be done. I promise.'

It was now no longer merely rugby or my own ego on the line. It had become my mission to make it up to this kind man who had rescued South Africa from the brink of apocalypse only to be humiliated by the poor performance of his countrymen on the field. Looking back, I believe this was the moment that I finally decided that nothing or no one would stop us from handing him and South Africa the coveted World Cup exactly a year later.

But we still had a long way to go and time was running out. Just how long and difficult that road was became evident in the aftermath of our Loftus defeat.

That same afternoon Jannie Engelbrecht urged me to postpone the selection of the team for the second and final test until the Monday instead of announcing it that same evening, as was customary.

'Everyone is just too emotional to think clearly,' he argued.

I agreed wholeheartedly. Engelbrecht's undoubted experience showed and I was not going to ignore it.

Hannes Marais, the convenor of the selection committee, was, however, not happy with my decision. He was hellbent to pick the side immediately.

'The team will basically be the same,' he protested.

But I stood firm.

Monday morning, I assembled the coaches of all the major provincial teams at Ellis Park to get their views on how we might turn the tide. But, instead of being helpful, I witnessed an ugly display of provincialism at its worst. The Transvaal coach, Kitch Christie, wanted virtually the entire Transvaal team to be included, while John Williams reminded everyone that it was his Northern Transvaal Blue Bulls who had given an invitational team a sound drubbing in the curtain raiser at Loftus Versfeld. Why not include most of these guys?

Marais was not happy at the sight of all these coaches when he and the other selectors arrived.

'You said seven selectors were too many,' he remarked, 'Now we have 15.'

'They are not here to select the Springbok team for next Saturday's test,' I explained. 'They are simply here to express their views. In the end, you will pick the team.'

At noon I invited the coaches to join me for lunch and left the selectors alone. There were numerous changes. The one that irked me in particular was the replacement of Tiaan Strauss of Western Province at eighth man. Why? I inquired. He did not play well, came the answer. Both Engelbrecht and Dawie Snyman were in favour of the omission of this favourite son from their home province.

Only later would it become clear that Strauss had actually been dropped because of an injury that might have jeopardised his inclusion in the upcoming New Zealand tour. But I had to bear the brunt of this decision as loud booing greeted the announcement of my presence at the Newlands test that Saturday.

As I looked through the list of reserves, I reminded Marais and the other selectors that all these players would have to be included in the touring side unless they were injured or played particularly badly in the event that they went on as replacements. They asked for a few more minutes and then came back with a new list. The reserve bench had changed drastically. Slowly, it seemed, we were beginning to get organised at the top. Perhaps this might also percolate down to the field, I thought.

Before the second test against England at Newlands Jannie Engelbrecht asked me to speak to the players in the team room. Apart from François Pienaar, who captained the side, there were several other Transvaal players with whom I was quite familiar. It had become a ritual to entertain the team at my home in Saxonwold before every home game. The fact that these barbeque dinners almost always took the form of victory celebrations was ample proof of the value of building camaraderie and team spirit off the field.

I now appreciated the opportunity to meet with the other members of the Springbok team. My pep talk was an impassioned one. I reminded them that they were out there representing not only a sport but also a country that needed to be inspired to greater heights in every sphere. The youth of this nation look up to you as heroes, I told them. Our new president stands squarely behind you. Let's not disappoint any of them.

And they did not. The game ended in a resounding 27–9 victory for South Africa. Unfortunately, President Mandela was not able to attend but his two deputies, Thabo Mbeki and FW de Klerk, were there. So were Steve Tshwete and a bevy of other top ANC officials. Instead of booing, I was greeted with out-stretched hands and cheers as we wound our way through the milling crowds after the game.

I was then asked by Jannie Engelbrecht to speak at the farewell party for the English side.

'Please give Jack Rowell some of his own back,' he said, referring to the acid-tongued English manager who took every given opportunity during the tour to stick it to us. On one such occasion, a sarcastic Rowell described my office at Ellis Park as being so big that it could easily seat another 5000 spectators.

'Jack, you are a tall man,' I said when it was my turn to speak. 'Now, if you were to stand behind either the north or south pavilions at Ellis Park, I'm sure your head will protrude above the upper level. So all you have to do is open your mouth and we will be able to fit in another 20,000 people.'

Even though Rowell proved to be quite capable of taking it as well as he dished it out, the English press hardly appreciated my remarks. But, compared to the furore in the press that greeted a much milder speech after the World Cup final a year later, this was a mere storm in a tea cup.

The real bomb dropped after the party that evening when our selectors retired behind closed doors to select the Springbok team to tour New Zealand. A half-hour later when Ian Kirkpatrick, the secretary of the selection committee, returned and handed me the list, I immediately spotted a glaring omission.

'What the hell is this?' I asked, pointing at the name of Guy Kebble in the place of Japie Barnard, who had been on the bench as a reserve. 'Where's Marais?'

'He left,' I was told.

'And what about Johan Claassen?'

'They've all left.'

The press was waiting and I had no other choice but to announce the names as they were presented. Only later would I be told that coach Ian McIntosh had threatened to resign unless Kebble, a player from his province of Natal, was included. After the win, he had suddenly become very cocky.

The Springboks proceeded to New Zealand with high hopes of revenging the series loss in 1981. This time, there would be no flour bombs or tacks on the field or demonstrations in front of their hotel to keep the players awake. What's more, the All Blacks had just come off a humiliating 2–0 defeat in a home series against a visiting French team.

Surely, many thought, the Boks who had shown the cocky English a trick or two at Newlands were more than capable of dealing with a demoralised All Black side. They could not have been further off the mark. The 1994 tour of New Zealand turned out to be yet another bumpy ride on the rocky road to recovery.

In the blame game that inevitably followed in the wake of our disastrous defeat, I was tagged as the one who made life miserable for the team by 'interfering' with the happy-go-lucky manager Jannie Engelbrecht and his hapless coach, Ian McIntosh.

If I managed to spoil the joy of defeat by stepping in to try to restore some semblance of discipline, so be it. I simply could not sit by idly while some members of the team were travelling around New Zealand like a bunch of college kids out to have a good time. The night before the crucial test match in

Wellington, several of our players were seen living it up with young women at their side. I was back home in South Africa, and on my return a well-known Sprinbok – and one proud of that achievement – had no hesitation in informing me quite openly of this behaviour. After one game, I had walked in on coach McIntosh and James Small working diligently at trying to finish a bottle of scotch in the team room.

During the initial three weeks I spent with the tour, Engelbrecht was constantly on the move, making speeches and socialising elsewhere instead of staying with the team. In the end, Engelbrecht made 89 speech-making appearances, attended only two team practices and had his winemaker also make the tour to promote his Rust en Vrede wines.

My discovery that I had been booked into a two-metre-square room at Timaru while Engelbrecht enjoyed the comfort of a palatial suite hardly served to repair already strained relations between us. Springbok scrumhalf Johan Roux, apparently embarrassed by Engelbrecht's casual attitude when told about my discomfort, offered his own much larger room in exchange. I thanked him but declined. Before we moved on to the first test at Carisbrook in Dunedin, I arranged my own accommodation, away from the team. In a game of missed opportunities, the supposedly substandard All Blacks beat us 22–14.

Once again, I would be reminded of the lack of direction and discipline off the field that seemed to spill over into our game. Only after the fact would I learn that Engelbrecht and McIntosh took it upon themselves to have lock forward Phillip Schutte flown from South Africa to join the team as a substitute player. This was done without consulting Johan Claassen, vice president in charge of the selection committee. But, they argued when I challenged them, they had spoken with both Hannes Marais and Dawie Snyman.

'They are no longer selectors,' I informed Engelbrecht. 'In any event, your "terms of reference" are quite clear. It is spelled out in writing. You have to consult with Claassen.'

'I've never seen any such a document,' Engelbrecht insisted.

I discovered that Arrie Oberholzer, the SARFU general manager, had indeed failed to bring these rules to Engelbrecht's notice and I realised just how disorganised we were. But would Engelbrecht have acted in accordance with the rules if he had indeed seen it in writing? I had to wonder.

This was war, I decided, and if we were to win against the world in 1995 we had better get ourselves properly organised. Even if heads were to roll, I had a mission that was far more important than personalities and popularity.

During my three-week stint in New Zealand I had observed numerous instances of foul play by the New Zealanders that went unpunished and, on my return to South Africa, the topic naturally came up in a press interview. I remarked that it might be a good idea if we could follow the New Zealand example and cite opposition players wherever they see such infringements. In doing so, we would be protecting our own players and keep their spirit up. Engelbrecht could hardly wait to rebut me in public. The animosity between us ratcheted up a few notches.

Not long afterwards I received a fax from Engelbrecht, thanking me for my continued well wishes. With a president like this, he said, a team could only do well. I was reminded of the treatment meted out to Patel when he was in my post. Alternating attack and praise.

South Africa again went under in the second test at Wellington, 13–6. But the disappointing outcome of the game was soon overshadowed by the insistence on the part of the New Zealanders that Springbok prop Johan le Roux, who had been sent off the field for biting All Black Sean Fitzpatrick's ear, be disqualified and sent home.

Le Roux was from the Transvaal and the coach, Kitch Christie, was the first to call me after I finished watching the test on TV at my home in Saxonwold. He was more concerned about the incident than the provincial game that was to take place at Ellis Park that afternoon.

'Did you see that animal Le Roux bite Fitzpatrick's ear!' Christie shouted. 'Do yourself a favour and announce his immediate expulsion. I don't want him in my team ever again!'

'Kitch,' I said, 'calm down. I haven't even seen the incident. Let me first look at the video.'

Quite honestly, something that rested more heavily on my shoulders was the sight of a South African pack of forwards being pushed around like a bunch of lightweights. What in heavens name, I wondered, was McIntosh doing? Where's the coaching? Of course, biting or any other kind of foul play needed to be punished but, as always, we needed to hear the other side of the story before any action was taken.

Le Roux, as it turned out, was nowhere near the biting league of boxer Mike Tyson and there was hardly any blood or injury. Furthermore, it was obviously not done without some provocation. Might it not have been a good idea, I wondered, if we did cite the New Zealanders as I suggested? This might have put an end to their provocative play long before the Wellington test.

Engelbrecht would usually call to fill me in after every game. This time, though, he did not. Several attempts on my part to reach him, failed. Eventually, I managed to reach Johan Claassen, who had travelled to New Zealand with Mluleki George to watch the Wellington test and asked him to pass along a message to Engelbrecht to contact me. The next day Claassen informed me that Engelbrecht had received the note he had left under his door. His response was that he did not accept messages from third parties.

The Le Roux incident had reached boiling point without the president of

SARFU and his team manager even talking. The Springbok prop was expelled from rugby for 19 months by a New Zealand disciplinary tribunal who evidently took advantage of the lack of any defence on our part.

In a conversation with a senior member of my executive, Ronnie Masson, I mentioned that I might have to go back to New Zealand to try to restore some semblance of order. He thought it was a great idea. 'Take your wife along,' he suggested. I thanked him for the thought but declined. This was not the occasion for socialising or sightseeing. There was serious work to be done.

During my stopover at Sydney Airport en route to Christchurch, I ran into Johan le Roux on his way back to South Africa. I felt sorry for the man. While seeing the need to punish any kind of foul play, I felt that the punishment had been far too severe, especially as an All Black prop had received a suspension of only six months for eye gouging.

On my arrival at our hotel in Christchurch, I encountered Engelbrecht in the hotel lobby and I told him that we needed to talk. Immediately.

'In my room or yours?' he asked casually.

'Mine,' I said.

'What's on your mind?' Engelbrecht asked, no longer smiling, as the door closed behind us.

'A few things, Jannie,' I said. 'Why didn't you call me from Wellington? And why did you allow this terrible penalty to be imposed? I made certain statements at home and I wanted to discuss them with you so that we could find extenuating circumstances for Le Roux.'

'I think that penalty was deserved,' he protested. 'Anything else?'

'I thought the penalty was outrageous,' I told him. 'Particularly when you consider how they treat worse demeanours by their own players. You should still have called me. I wanted to talk to you before the hearing.'

'It was difficult, as the All Blacks asked us to join them. Time just ran out,' he explained rather sheepishly.

'Oh yes, there is something else, Jannie... Don't ever repudiate me in public again as you did when I queried our lack of citing players on opposing teams. Never again.'

'I'm sorry,' he responded in subdued fashion. 'Anything else?'

'No,' I said, 'that's all.'

'Well,' he said, 'I want to say something. I don't ever want McIntosh as a coach again.' That was the second time Engelbrecht had raised the McIntosh issue. A few weeks earlier, in the presence of André Markgraaff in the Ellis Park board-room, he had said exactly the same thing.

'We will look at that when we get back, but right now we have to support him,' I responded.

'And one other request...' Engelbrecht said as we stepped out of the room. 'Will you please tell the press that everything is okay? They will want a statement.'

'Why?' I asked. 'I came back here to try and repair the damage between ourselves and the New Zealanders – for no other reason. But I will tell them everything is fine with me.'

And that is exactly what I told the press. They did, in fact, ask me about McIntosh and I pointed out the need for everyone to get behind the coach. 'We have to win from now on. Everything!'

But surely, one reporter said in an aside afterwards, you must be aware of Engelbrecht's unhappiness with McIntosh? It's all over South Africa.

In the hotel foyer, I saw Okkie Oosthuizen, a former Springbok who had captained Transvaal and was still involved with club rugby until he fell foul of the law and left. He was in New Zealand following the Springboks around as a self-appointed analyst, running down the team at every opportunity.

Fired up and fed up with the state of affairs, the very sight of this man sparked my anger. I walked up to him and said: 'Can't you say something nice instead of just being plain bloody nasty with your remarks?'

'I can certainly voice my opinion without asking your permission,' he snarled back at me.

'You can bloody well do what you like, but I find it strange that anyone can be so utterly negative about his own team in a foreign country and wear a Springbok blazer at the same time.'

'I would like to come and talk to you in South Africa,' he said in conciliatory fashion, '... about rugby.' But I just ignored him and walked off.

That afternoon we played against Canterbury and beat them rather comfortably. After the game, a few Western Transvaal supporters, among them Ernest Claassen, brother of Johan Claassen, came over to talk to me.

'Now things will go better. The boss is here,' Claassen said.

But that apparently innocent remark worried me. What was wrong?

We then moved on to Eden Park for the final test. I had checked into the same hotel as the Springboks but hardly saw any of them. Engelbrecht, too, was nowhere in sight.

Friday, at breakfast, a reporter asked me what I thought of the test team. I was dumbstruck. Even though my hotel room was only two doors away from Engelbrecht's room, he had not had the common courtesy of passing along the names of our team to his president – which was the custom – before handing it to the press.

The final test ended in a draw, concluding the series with a disappointing 2–0 loss for the Springboks. Once again, however, the events off the field over-shadowed the game. Wynand Claassen, captain of the 1981 Springbok touring team, who followed the team as a newspaper columnist, expressed dismay over the lack of discipline as players lived it up on the eve of the test. Even though I saw very little of Jannie Engelbrecht, the rumour mill indicated that I was not completely out of his thoughts in his exchanges with the newsmen. Eventually, I would again be targeted in what became known as 'The Episode of the Empty Chair'.

I had received a hand-delivered invitation to both the after-match dinner on the Friday before the Saturday test and to the test itself. On the day of the test, I was among a busload of guests who had joined in at a meat-pie luncheon hosted by the New Zealanders before the game. Afterwards, we continued on to Eden Park where we were handed tickets. Two of the members of my executive, Keith Parkinson of Natal and Trevor Jennings of Eastern Province, were seated separately from me and I proceeded to a suite where I found myself in the midst of a group of people I had never met before.

It was, to say the least, strange that my counterpart, NZRFU President Eddie Tonks, did not, as was customary on such occasions, have me seated with him. This would have been a matter of procedure back home in South Africa. I had no idea whether this was yet another oversight on his part or a calculated snub engineered by my own management.

From where I had been seated, I had to make my way across the field to our team's changing room. Along the way, several people recognised me and wished to talk and get an autograph. When I got to our locker room, I was told they had already left. It had started to rain. One official pointed out the room where the reception was to take place that evening and I decided to hang around, but I was told that they were in the process of setting up tables and that I should wait outside. I was fuming not only over the humiliation, but the lack of respect shown to my office not only by New Zealand management but my own team management too.

'Where are you going?' I heard someone ask.

It was George Rautenbach of Megapro, the commercial sport organisation with which I have had extensive dealings on behalf of SARFU.

'I'm trying to find transport back to the hotel,' I explained.

'Why don't you join us?' he suggested. 'We are on our way to a reception arranged by South African Airways.'

I agreed. Along the way, I told him where I had been seated and he pointed out the suite where Tonks and special guests had sat. How odd, I thought. Almost unreal. Just imagine what the reaction would have been if SARFU president Luyt 'forgot' to seat NZRFU president Tonks in his suite during an international between the two countries in South Africa. But then his team manager might have raised the issue and the 'oversight' might have been corrected in time.

Rautenbach and his South African friends, who had rented their own bus, dropped me at my hotel. In the lobby I encountered Phil Saayman of *Rapport*, who was having drinks with photographer Hoffie Hoffmeister. Saayman lumbered towards me where I stood waiting for the elevator.

'May I ask you a few questions?' he asked.

On the way up, I told him that apart from the fact that our team had done its best, there was very little else to say. He followed me into my room. I offered him a beer and he took a brown envelope from his pocket.

'What can I write, Doc Luyt?' he asked.

'Write about the game,' I said.

'No,' he insisted, 'I mean what can I write about what happened between you and Engelbrecht?'

I was not, however, about to share any inner thoughts with this man in search of sensation for his Sunday paper. He, sensing my unwillingness to extend the non-interview, thus finished his beer and left. I then ordered dinner up to my room, and made a call to Adri before going to bed. As always, it was reassuring and comforting to be able to talk to my soul mate, the person with whom I could share my frustrations and, thankfully, also my triumphs. Her advice was both comforting and calming. I knew that there was no way in which this battle between Engelbrecht and me could continue without some detrimental effect on the team and South African rugby in general. But there was a right way to bring this all to an end and procedures thus had to be followed.

The next morning, Engelbrecht was all over the place complaining about the fact that he was about to be fired. How embarrassing, he told everyone who would listen, that he had to apologise to the president of the NZRFU because his own president had not turned up for the dinner. Where, I wondered, was his outrage about lack of a seat for his own president at the NZRFU presidential suite during the game?

The next day, as we embarked on the first leg of the long flight back to Johannesburg, Engelbrecht fired the first salvo.

'I hope you're happy now,' he whispered as he pushed past my seat towards Business Class.

Behind him was Daan Swiegers, a former Springbok selector.

'You've really got balls to do this,' Swiegers added.

'Wait a minute,' I said. 'What is the matter?'

Swiegers told me that my firing of Engelbrecht and McIntosh was all over the front page of *Rapport* in a report by Phil Saayman. Apparently, Engelbrecht's wife had called to tell him [Engelbrecht] about the story and it had spread rapidly through the ranks. The fact that I had refused to be drawn into a conversation with Saayman the previous evening hardly mattered. It was a story everyone wanted to believe, in any event, and Saayman had simply made it 'official'.

On our arrival in Johannesburg, I declined to be drawn into a press conference. Instead, I met up with Adri after passing through customs and left immediately for home. The next morning, as I was drinking my coffee, Jannie Engelbrecht appeared on *Good Morning, South Africa* together with Hennie le Roux, decked out in their Springbok blazers, ready to resume the battle. It was obvious that moderator Paul Ehlers had been thoroughly briefed beforehand to ask the right questions. Engelbrecht bore into me with a single-minded strength that had been strangely lacking when it was needed on the tour. He described in detail petty issues relating to small rooms, undue interference and empty seats at receptions. Absent was any reference to far greater issues concerning lack of discipline and the absence of deference to authority on his part. Le Roux was there in a mostly silent but supportive role.

I called Ronnie Masson in Cape Town.

'Yes, I've seen the interview,' he said. 'And I've told Joan all hell is about to break loose.'

'You're damn right, Ronnie,' I said. 'That SOB is gone.'

I then proceeded to Ellis Park and had my staff call a press conference, at which I announced that Engelbrecht would be asked to resign. When the news reached Cape Town, Engelbrecht was defiant. He insisted on a hearing before the executive of SARFU.

Before I left for Cape Town, there were ugly rumours about what might happen to me if I forced Engelbrecht from his post. The meeting on 10 August 1994 was shifted from our headquarters at Newlands to the Holiday Inn to avoid disruptions, but someone must have alerted the demonstrators. When I arrived at the hotel, 100 belligerent Engelbrecht supporters confronted me. When I stepped out of my car, the crowd surged forward. One man handed me a ballot with Engelbrecht's and my name on it, a check mark next to his and a cross next to mine.

'How does it feel to be the most hated man in the country?' someone shouted.

'I don't think Western Province comprises the country,' I replied.

I asked Mluleki George to act as chairman and took a seat with the rest of the executive. Engelbrecht was given the opportunity to state his case. It was a rehash of the now familiar complaints. Where, I asked, could I have interfered? I stayed with the team for only a few games and was treated like the proverbial mushroom – kept in the dark and fed manure. Engelbrecht even came armed with, among others, messages of support for him and McIntosh from New Zealand Minister of Sport John Banks and NZRFU President Eddie Tonks. Since when, I wondered, do we allow ourselves to be dictated to by the whims and preferences of our opponents? Perhaps I would also be afforded the opportunity in future to pick a coach and a manager for the All Blacks?

After his presentation, Engelbrecht asked to be excused from the meeting so he could participate in a television interview set before the meeting had been scheduled. Chairman Mluleki George specifically requested that he refrain from saying anything that might embarrass SARFU. Instead, Engelbrecht once again used the opportunity to attack me in public and when we reassembled, George found it necessary to voice his resentment from the chair.

Then it was my turn to state the reasons why I felt Engelbrecht was unfit for his post. I listed incidents during the tour that indicated a lack of discipline and dedication to the task and cited instances where he had challenged SARFU in public. I also recalled an episode when Jannie le Roux and a friend had overheard him saying, during a Transvaal-Western Province game at Ellis Park, that he would not recognise me if I dared show up in England for the upcoming Springbok tour. When I confronted Engelbrecht, he at first tried to deny it, but then apologised in the presence of the entire management committee of SARFU.

The consensus in the room seemed to be in favour of reconciliation for the sake of unity and peace on the eve of the important British tour. We shook hands, but we both knew that it was at best a temporary armistice. The rift was too wide to heal and our two personalities and approaches were worlds apart. It had long been evident that Jannie Engelbrecht saw himself as the rightful heir to Craven, even though not even his own province had seen fit to nominate him to SARFU's executive.

I had indicated before the Cape Town encounter that unless the team management stepped down, I would resign. In contrast to others, who seemed to flow back and forth like seaweed with the tide, I had always considered my word my bond. It was a matter of personal honour. On Sunday, 14 August 1994, the *Sunday Times* announced my decision in a banner headline over a report written by Dan Retief, with whom I had spoken about my plans. As the newspaper appeared on the news stands, the SARFU executive was congregating in Cape Town. In the end, almost everyone on the executive – with the exception of Keith Parkinson of Natal and Ronnie Masson of Western Province – implored me to stay on as president of SARFU.

Both Parkinson and Masson telephoned me, though, to 'explain' their voting against me. Masson had previously been very critical of Jannie Engelbrecht, whom he considered egotistical to the extreme. Both, however, assured me that their decisions had been based purely on 'internal rugby politics'. But Masson showed his true colours when, after he had agreed to the Edward Griffiths' appointment, he suddenly – during a management committee meeting to which he had been invited and where Griffiths' appointment was discussed – found the 'management style' too difficult to work with and resigned. The irony, of course, was that later in the year, he again made himself available to serve in that very same management, with whose style he disagreed. The unions, however, made him sit it out for another two years before he was allowed back into the fold. Today the same Masson serves as deputy president of SARFU and could still become president, although he has announced his 'retirement' quite a few times and has not hesitated to discuss with Harry Viljoen the possibility of joining Western Province with the Turnbull 'WRC' – or the 'World Rugby Circus', as it later turned out to be.

There have been numerous attempts to portray this episode as yet another example of a masterstroke on my part to strengthen my position at the top. The simple truth, however, is that my old-fashioned upbringing requires that you always do what you say you will do. In any event, the constant attacks on me were beginning to show their strains and effect on my family. I did not think it was worth putting my family at further risk – for this or anything else.

At the risk of sounding unctuous and self-serving, I might mention that the urgings of both Mluleki George and the Minister of Sport, Steve Tshwete, for me to remain and work for the sake of game and the country, did in fact have considerable bearing on my decision to withdraw my resignation. I would, however, question the hyperbole in Edward Griffiths' book, *One Team One Country*: 'While Tshwete's intervention had simply acknowledged the fact that, for all Luyt's lack of tact, this capable businessman was indispensable to South African rugby at that particular time. In terms of sheer ability and efficacy, of understanding the issues, Luyt stood head and shoulders above his colleagues. Who else would run the Rugby World Cup?'

There were certainly others who could have performed the job, but perhaps no one willing to take the abuse and insult that inevitably came with it. We were on the eve of one the greatest moments in rugby ever and we needed to throw everything into the battle – personalities, egos and self-interest. The man who had to make all these unpopular moves just happened to be the president of the South African Rugby Football Union.

The 1994 Springbok tour of the United Kingdom signalled the rebirth of South Africa as a formidable force in international rugby. This timely turnaround was largely, in my opinion, the work of coach Kitch Christie, whom I had assigned to take over from McIntosh at the conclusion of the Springboks' disastrous New Zealand experience. First, Christie's Springboks beat the Pumas at home, and then they travelled to the UK, where they convincingly defeated both Wales and Scotland. One of the highlights of the tour was, in fact, an astonishing display at St Helen's ground, where they humiliated Swansea 78–7. Our team returned with a proud record of 11 wins in 13 games, including a defeat by the narrowest of margins by the Barbarians.

The same 'experts' who criticised my replacement of McIntosh with Kitch Christie as a blatant act of provincialism and display of impulsiveness, now described it as 'a stroke of genius'. It was neither. It was a simple act of necessity. Not only Engelbrecht, but many others, too, had asked me to find a substitute for McIntosh, even though they pretended to support him in public. Personal feelings had nothing to do with my decision. If a CEO proves himself incapable of turning a company around, he is replaced. If a coach is unable to produce results, you end his contract and find another one.

Even though it gave me no pleasure to replace the wild-eyed Ian McIntosh after the New Zealand debacle, I knew that drastic steps were needed if we wished to become competitive before the World Cup in 1995. When I had to pick a replacement for McIntosh, I had no hesitation at all. Transvaal coach Kitch Christie was my first choice. I simply responded to the same gut feeling that had prompted me to recruit him for the Transvaal Rugby Union two years previously.

In 1992, when Transvaal was badly in need of a coach, Christie's name had come up. Harry Viljoen had left Transvaal abruptly after its narrow loss against Natal in the 1992 Currie Cup final and I filled in as coach for four games, while the union tried to find a suitable replacement and, in the process, won the Lion Cup. However, I must admit that my greatest thrill in coaching was when Transvaal beat the Shadow Springboks at Ellis Park in 1989.

After Avril Malan declined our offer to coach the team, I called in our manager, Johan Prinsloo, Rudi Joubert, as well as Avril for consultation. Joubert mentioned a fellow by the name of Kitch Christie, who, he said, had great talent but was entirely undervalued by Northern Transvaal. He once assisted John Williams but lately, he told me, had been relegated to coaching the second team at Pretoria Harlequins.

'Hell, why not?' I asked myself, as I picked up the phone and dialled Christie's number at his air-conditioning business.

'It's Louis Luyt here,' I said when he picked up on the other side.

'Who did you say you were?' Christie asked.

I repeated my name, then added: 'I want to talk to you about the head coaching job at Ellis Park.'

'This must be a joke,' he said.

'No, I'm serious,' I insisted. 'If you have any doubts, why don't you call me back at Ellis Park so we can talk further.'

'So, what do you propose?' Christie asked, still a little suspicious.

'When can you come over to talk?'

'How about within the next half-hour?'

Christie then joined me at my Ellis Park office and we left for lunch at LM Prawns. Between the shells and the wine, we talked. I wanted a coach who could share my enthusiasm and I had found one. But I knew so little about the man – so we talked some more. Finally, I raised my glass.

'Kitch, let's give it a try.'

'Sure,' Christie said. 'But on one condition. I want Ray Mordt to assist me.'

'Call him right now,' I suggested.

He called the brilliant former Springbok winger at his office and, after a brief discussion, Mordt agreed. Ray was to become one of my closest friends. He remained a true supporter in later years when others ran for cover in the face of government intimidation.

'So, when do I start?' Christie asked.

'Right now,' I answered jokingly.

On the way back, we stopped at the hotel where the Transvaal team had convened for the semifinal of the Lion's Cup against Northern Transvaal at Ellis Park. I introduced Kitch Christie as the new coach and invited him over for the game. We won and Hentie Serfontein jokingly offered me the coaching job at Northern Transvaal. In the change rooms afterwards, with perhaps a little more gusto than was needed, Kitch gave scrumhalf Du Randt a piece of his mind for not following a game plan in which Christie himself had had no input or, for that matter, any knowledge about.

As we left, he apologised. 'Must be the wine,' he explained. 'I hardly ever drink.'

In one of his few complimentary remarks about me in his book, Griffiths argued that I 'deserved enormous credit' for my decision 'to bring Christie in from the wilderness'. According to Griffiths, 'Luyt had the courage of his convictions (not a common trait among rugby officials) and was richly rewarded'.

While the players readily accepted Christie, the TRFU executive was far less obliging. They made it clear that I would personally be held responsible for Christie's performance. My deal with him did not involve a salary. Instead, he was paid match fees and I gave his company a suite at Ellis Park in which to entertain customers.

Kitch more than fulfilled his end of the bargain. Transvaal defeated Auckland at Ellis Park to win the inaugural Super-10 final in 1993 and, later that season, overcame Natal in Durban to win the Currie Cup for the first time in 21 years. In 1994, the Super-10 final was lost to Queensland, but Transvaal retained the Currie Cup – with Ray Mordt in charge – by beating Free State at Springbok Park in Bloemfontein. In a matter of two seasons, Kitch had helped to build Transvaal into an almost invincible team. In only 22 months, Christie had moved from relative obscurity to the highest coaching post in South Africa. He accomplished this with outstanding results.

While Christie went to work with what he called his 'hospital job' on the demoralised and disorganised Springboks, Engelbrecht pressed ahead with his own agenda. On 10 October 1994, two days after the test against Argentina's Pumas in Port Elizabeth, a memorandum from him landed on my desk, urging us to expel James Small from Springbok rugby. While I could sympathise with Engelbrecht's concern over Small's tendency to become involved in altercations off the field, I found the team manager's unforgiving condemnation of this meteoric player's 'disregard for discipline' rather ironic. SARFU, Engelbrecht insisted, should 'recommend unanimously that [Small] is beyond rehabilitation and no longer a member of the national team'. Instead, I chose to follow the advice of Christie and his assistant, Gysie Pienaar, who scribbled and co-signed the following comment: 'I think any person can be rehabilitated, including James Small.'

If I banished for life every rugby player who landed himself in an altercation off the field, we would have lost the talent of several of our superstars during the World Cup in 1995 – not least among them, Transvaal and Springbok captain François Pienaar who, on his own admission, had to be reprimanded by me after several bar-room scraps in his formative years as a provincial rugby player. He changed his ways to the extent that I could reward him with the captaincy of Transvaal to help lead our team into mopping up all the competition in sight. His able leadership of the Springboks during the World Cup series is a further example of how rehabilitation can work.

In response to general criticism that Engelbrecht was – in his speeches during tours – unable to span the gap between the old days and the present, I appointed Edward Griffiths, both as a speechwriter and press liaison officer. With his experience as a sportswriter, the British-born Griffiths managed to turn around the negative image of the Boks during their tour of Britain. Engelbrecht, however, disregarded Griffiths' texts and continued in his official speeches to dwell on his own experiences as a leading player during the sixties. It was on one such an occasion that he once again tried to humiliate me in public.

The event was the dinner reception after our test against Scotland in Edinburgh. Engelbrecht, who was seated next to Princess Anne, with François Pienaar on her other side, praised Danie Craven in his reply to a toast and stated that 'no one could follow in his footsteps'. From where I was seated at the next table, furtive glances in my direction around the room made it clear that the other guests knew exactly what Engelbrecht meant to convey. Steve Tshwete, angry as a rattlesnake, shifted uncomfortably in his chair next to me.

That very afternoon Tshwete had been in the middle of another incident involving Engelbrecht and me. Before the game, he wanted to visit the team to wish them well but Engelbrecht would not allow it. I told Tshwete to come with me and took him to the Springbok locker room where he had the opportunity to convey his own and President Mandela's best wishes. The team appreciated this gesture, but Engelbrecht was once again livid at my 'interference'.

On my return to South Africa, I then set about finalising plans for the removal of Engelbrecht. He had, as far as I was concerned, used up all his chances. In January 1995, my dismissal of Engelbrecht and his replacement with Morné du Plessis was fully endorsed by the SARFU executive. My personal choice to replace Engelbrecht had been Carel du Plessis, but for some reason or another Masson of Western Province remained entirely unconvinced regarding the abilities of what I saw as an outstanding wing. Although Masson also took a stand against Morné du Plessis when he had been nominated to replace John Gainsford, when the latter had decided to retire from the Western Province executive and was urged to remain on board, he now suddenly supported Du Plessis' nomination. At the time, Morné du Plessis was simply *persona non grata* at Western Province.

More than 40 years after Uncle Felix had given me the opportunity to play for

Free State, I called on his son to help lead the Springboks in their tough fight for the coveted William Webb Ellis Cup. Morné came, of course, with impeccable credentials – as well as some baggage of his own. He, with Cheeky Watson, had tried to form a splinter group called the Veterans in an effort to break away from SARFU. The effort had, however, failed, and he was refused affiliation by the NSC.

When Morné, Christie and Gysie Pienaar were selecting the team to represent South Africa, Christie's first choice as hooker was Henry Tromp. Tromp, who was jailed for killing a black youth during the course of executing some sort of punishment, served four years and was then released. Griffiths came to me while I was watching a game from the presidential suite at Ellis Park. The selectors were busy with their task and Griffiths said: 'They can surely not pick Tromp. He killed a black boy. You agree, don't you?'

'I certainly do not,' I said. 'Tromp has served his time and he's been playing Interprovincial rugby for how long now! They may well pick him.'

But when I entered the room where the selectors had gathered the atmosphere was sombre indeed. The team they gave me did not include Tromp.

'We decided on Chris Rossouw,' Christie said meekly. 'He's better than Tromp.'

I knew he was lying because I knew how much he liked Tromp, but decided not make an issue of it. Much later, Christie would confess to me that Griffiths and Du Plessis had pressured him. Du Plessis had even threatened to resign as manager, Christie told me.

In the meanwhile, I knew Griffiths was at work, because the next noise came from parliament where Mluleki George declared that a murderer could not be included in the Springbok squad. How did he know what had gone on behind closed doors among the Springbok selectors? This was certainly Mr Griffiths at his best and involved my deputy president as well.

Du Plessis, a former Springbok captain, like his father, had always been respected for his tact and calm demeanour in the heat of battle. He was, apart from Carel du Plessis, ideally suited for the task. I was thus looking with renewed confidence at the upcoming World Cup. We had assembled a team in Morné du Plessis, Christie and François Pienaar that would prove to be invincible. We were at last ready for the challenge on the field.

But, as hosts of the 1995 World Cup, we had much more on our plate than simply the deep desire to win the world championship from which we had been barred in 1987 and 1991. We had to actually organise the event. And I was determined to prove that we could spin a handsome profit, instead of having to beg governments and participating unions for a bail-out as had been done in the past.

President Thabo Mbeki welcomes me to Parliament in 1999.

Transvaal were the Currie Cup Champions in 1994. Here I am pictured with the team captain François Pienaar.

The International Rugby Board joins the Olympic movement at Cardiff in 1994.

Adri and I celebrate our Silver Anniversary with, from left to right, Lucien, Adri Junior, Louis Junior and Corlia.

To the victors belong the privilege of
fighting over the spoils.

Anonymous

Chapter 13

THE SPOILS OF VICTORY

In 1992 the International Rugby Board assigned the 1995 Rugby World Cup competition to South Africa. The formal announcement was made at its meeting in Wellington, New Zealand. Following in the wake of meaningful steps towards the formation of a new non-racial government and the ANC's lifting of its 'ban' on overseas contact between South Africa and the outside world, the IRB's decision was portrayed by many in the media as a mere formality. But, in doing so, they overlooked the crucial role played by Nic Labuschagne and Fritz Eloff in mustering support from the five home unions in Europe beforehand.

Although serious differences would develop between Nic Labuschagne and myself over what I saw as a tendency on his part to favour the IRB over South African interests, his initial input was invaluable. After he lost the presidency of the Natal Rugby Union to Keith Parkinson in 1994, Labuschagne continued to represent South Africa on the board of Rugby World Cup Limited (RWCL), the entity formed by the IRB to administer the quadrennial event. A former England rugby international, Labuschagne replaced the ailing Danie Craven as one of the SARFU delegates on the International Rugby Board and was nominated to serve as a director of RWCL. From this vantage point, Labuschagne was able to push our application to the top of the pile.

Prior to the IRB's Wellington meeting in 1992, where it was to make the final announcement, I travelled with Labuschagne and Ebrahim Patel – then serving as Craven's deputy in the newly formed SARFU – to a southern hemisphere rugby indaba in Sydney, Australia. I was asked by Doc Craven to do so in my capacity as head of SARFU's financial committee. During the deliberations, chaired by the very able head of the Australian Rugby Football Union, Joe French, both New Zealand and Australia expressed their support for South

Africa's bid. Their endorsement, together with the commitment of the five home unions, made it a shoe-in. My role was a minor one in nudging Argentina to come to our support as well.

Little did I know during that relaxed trip that I would soon be handed the task of running the World Cup competition. As had happened in the past, Doc Craven once again passed the ball and I had no choice but to run with it as best I could. It was definitely not the job for anyone who sought to win popularity contests. Eventually, it caused a rift between Labuschagne, who had played such a pivotal role in getting us there in the first place, and me. Also, Patel and I would soon forget that pleasant encounter in Australia as we found ourselves on opposite sides of the fence over RWCL matters.

This final assignment from Doc Craven to take charge of SARFU's organising committee turned out to be the toughest. As fate would have it, he would not be around to witness the outcome. One of my greatest disappointments is not having Doc Craven at my side on that June day in 1995 when South Africa and the rugby world stood in awe of the Springboks as they beat New Zealand to become the world champions. He would also, I am sure, have grinned with pleasure as the sponsorship monies rolled in to stuff the coffers of both SARFU and the IRB. But he was at least spared all the unseemly battles over the spoils that followed.

The only amusing incident after the meeting in Australia was when I invited Nic Labuschagne to my 'suite' for a drink. Nic took one look at my abode and remarked, 'But this isn't any bigger than my room, are you sure this is a suite?' Then he laughed.

'Have you seen Ebrahim Patel's suite?' He inquired. 'I can swear he got yours. Let's go and visit him and you can see for yourself.' That we did and, low and behold, it was a huge suite with two liquor cabinets and all the niceties that Au\$500 a night could secure.

After inquiries, it emanated that the management had made a mistake and allocated my suite, for which I had to personally pay, to Patel.

That's where Nic and I decided to cause a little embarrassment to Ebrahim Patel. We thus returned to his suite and emptied his liquor cabinets, much to the obvious unease of this devout Muslim. But, he was, in effect, living in luxury at my expense.

After the Wellington meeting of the IRB, at which South Africa was allocated the 1995 World Cup, Patel rather furtively suggested that we tell no one that South Africa had been honoured with this prestigious event because he would make the announcement himself when back in South Africa.

'Ebrahim,' I suggested, 'if you think that South Africa doesn't know by now that it got the World Cup, you are kidding yourself. It has already been all over New Zealand television and unless the international media representatives haven't done their job, we're going to look stupid.'

Doc Craven's death on 13 January 1993 came as a huge loss to rugby, the country and me, personally. It was, however, not unexpected. Even though he was too proud to admit it, Craven knew by 1992 that he was too sick to carry out the increased workload that had resulted from South Africa's re-entry to international rugby. My suggestion during the November 1992 annual general meeting that we create an honorary presidency for Craven and leave the administration of SARFU to an elected chairman was eagerly misconstrued by outsiders as an attempt on my part to push Doc aside and take over. I went to see Dr Craven at Stellenbosch to clear with him whether he would acquiesce to becoming a president with a chairman who would attend to run-of-the-mill matters. He agreed, but later, according to Arrie Oberholzer, he changed his mind because he firmly believed we wanted him out of rugby.

I find it somewhat ironic that some of the very people who constantly complained about Doc Craven's lack of energy and involvement during his final days, would step forward as his prime promoters the day after he died. Having known Doc Craven through the years, not only as a director of my company but as his surrogate in serious matters, as well as a friend, I do confess to good as well as bad times. That is what friendship is all about – willingness to honestly admit differences while at the same time shelving them and standing united when it really counts.

The claim by some – after my election in March 1994 to the post of president of SARFU – that I would never be able to fill Craven's shoes was pathetically misguided. Never once had I indicated any such intent. In fact, I wanted Fritz Eloff to become the president, but he steadfastedly refused to remain involved in the day-to-day matters and André Markgraaff, together with Mauritz Meyer, worked round the clock to make sure I got the vote as the next president. It was never my wish to stay in the post for 30 years. Given the stresses and strains of the job as it evolved in the nineties and my age when I was elected, I had little chance of living long enough to do so, in any event. Furthermore, even though there was much that I admired and emulated in Doc Craven's long career, the presidency in these modern, materialistic times set entirely different demands. Rugby had become more than merely a sport. It had evolved into a business. Sad as it was for us, who grew up playing the game for its own sake and the glory of our country, money was becoming a prime object.

In fact, money was very much on the minds of the RWCL delegation when they first visited South Africa towards the end of 1992 and called on President FW de Klerk to seek an underwriting from the South African government. I was told afterwards by the Secretary of Sport, Jood Bodenstein, that the RWCL mission, led by Sir Ewart Bell and including Marcel Martin of France and Nic Labuschagne, received assurances from De Klerk that South Africa would advance the equivalent of £2 million to enable the 'cash-strapped' RWCL to proceed with the play-offs leading up to the World Cup tournament.

In the meantime, Doc Craven and the executive committee had appointed me as chairman of the South African organising committee and selected to serve with me Ian Simms, the former managing director of British Petroleum; advocate Lex Mpati, who was later appointed a judge of the Supreme Court of Appeal; Silas Nkanunu, a member of SARFU's executive, who eventually became its president; SARFU secretary Arrie Oberholzer; and Robert Denton, who was marketing manager at the time.

I found it odd that our government should be asked to underwrite the play-offs, especially after I discovered that the RWCL had ample funds of its own in offshore accounts. Such support had not been required of previous host governments. As it turned, out this was only the first of many new conditions to which South Africa would be subjected before the RWCL would 'finally' agree to award us the competition. Eventually, I had no other choice but to step in and put an end to the endless demands, bordering on extortion. In doing so, of course, I did not make many friends in the ranks of the RWCL and I soon earned the reputation of being 'difficult to work with'.

During our first encounter with the RWCL delegation at a meeting at Ellis Park, Ebrahim Patel insisted not only on being present but acting as chairman. When the visitors submitted their *pro forma* agreement, Patel announced that he had his own attorney on hand to look it over. To my surprise, I discovered he had hired my daughter, Corlia Oberholzer, for the job on the basis of work that she had done for him in a libel case.

During a break, I cornered him in the gents.

'Ebrahim, you're not supposed to be here. You're not even on this committee and you are embarrassing me by dragging Corlia into the discussions,' I whispered in Afrikaans.

'No, Louis,' he insisted, 'let me see this through. These buggers are out to take us to the cleaners.'

We reassembled after Corlia had had a chance to work through the proposed agreement. It was a useless document, and the RWCL delegation offered to go back and then submit another proposal.

For several months after Doc Craven's death in January 1993, I continued largely on my own. There was not much our committee could do until the next visit of the RWCL directors. When they returned to South Africa towards the middle of 1993, they first called on Nelson Mandela and Walter Sisulu before resuming discussions with SARFU, now under the caretaker presidency of Ebrahim Patel. In the meantime, the South African treasury had informed us that they needed a guarantee from SARFU before they could advance £2 million promised by De Klerk to the RWCL.

I invited Sir Ewart Bell and his RWCL delegation to meet with me and my committee at my home at Saxonwold. At my insistence, the RWCL produced records showing a balance of £3.6 million in its offshore account at the Bank of the Isle of Man. Why then, I wondered aloud, was it necessary for South Africa to underwrite the play-offs? The explanations came fast and furious, none of which made any real sense. Another sticking point was still the contract between the RWCL and SARFU. I demanded that we spell out clearly how the profits were to be split after the World Cup competition. At this point, Sir Ewart Bell concluded the meeting with a shocking announcement.

'I'm not even sure we should be negotiating with you,' he said. 'We have no assurance that you have the necessary authority.'

This statement caught me completely off-guard.

'I don't know what you are talking about,' I protested. 'This is the committee appointed by SARFU to take care of all arrangements.'

'No,' Sir Ewart Bell insisted, 'We are not going any further until we have written confirmation.'

Present with me at this gathering at Saxonwold were the CEOs of the big provincial unions, as well as Arrie Oberholzer, Robert Denton and Rian Oberholzer, who in 1994 would officially be appointed by me as the official tournament manager. Although Rian Oberholzer was completely inexperienced in running such a huge event on his own, I had all the faith in him that he would listen and learn. I surrounded him with people I trusted and he reported to me on a daily basis so that we could immediately resolve any problem that surfaced. It did, then, come as a surprise to me that, in the end, Rian Oberholzer really thought he had run the tournament single-handedly! But part of that was my fault because I had heaped lavish praise on him at every opportunity.

They had all been duly authorised by SARFU to replace Doc Craven's original committee. It was my idea to have representation from the larger unions. Now I found myself at a complete loss to understand why the leader of the RWCL delegation should raise questions about our authority.

On one hand, I was willing to dismiss Sir Ewart's questioning of our standing as the action of a man anxious to extricate himself from a difficult meeting by any means. On the other hand, I simply could not let go of the feeling that there was something more sinister lurking behind all this. A call from Leo Williams from Australia shortly after our abbreviated meeting helped solve the mystery. I had got to know Leo as the chairman of the Australian Rugby Union and had taken an instant liking to this straightforward, no-nonsense man. Now, as a member of the RWCL directorate, he felt he owed it to me to forward some crucial information.

'Louis,' he said, 'I don't think your president is doing you any favours. The day before [the RWC members] went to your house, they invited Patel to a meeting at the Sandton Sun. It was he who told them you did not have any authority to negotiate on SARFU's behalf.'

Then I heard from Steve Tshwete that Patel had also asked him to raise doubts about my fitness to serve as chairman of the organising committee. Tshwete had refused to do so but thought it proper to let me know. Barely two days after these revelations, I had my opportunity to face Patel in person at a meeting of the SARFU executive.

'Mr Patel,' I asked, 'when did you last see the RWCL delegation?'

'You know,' he retorted indignantly. 'When we both met with them at Ellis Park, some time ago.'

'What would you say if I told you you're lying?' I asked.

'What do you mean?' he protested, eyebrows arching.

'You saw them on Thursday at the Sandton Sun, before the Friday meeting at my home,' I announced. 'Now tell me, did you or did you not?'

'Well,' he replied, shoulders slightly slumped and the eyebrows no longer arched, 'I merely had a cup of tea with them.'

'But I thought you had not seen them since Ellis Park. That's why I asked the question. But let me go further and tell you what you said to the RWCL directors at the Sandton Sun. You told them that I did not have the authority to speak on behalf of SARFU...'

'I did nothing of the sort...'

'You did!'

Patel switched into attack mode.

'Gentlemen,' he said as he glanced across the room at the other members of the executive, 'I think the SARFU executive should play a much larger role in the running of the World Cup...'

'I agree wholeheartedly,' I interrupted. 'Here are all the files on what has been done so far. You can hand this to the next chairman of the organising committee, because I'm resigning.'

Patel sat silent. *En masse* the rest of the executive committee turned on him and urged me to stay on. No one else could do the job at this time, they argued. Others spoke up and condemned Patel's actions. In the end, I agreed to remain in the post on one condition: I should be given full authority to restructure the organising committee. They agreed.

'Both Denton and Oberholzer should immediately leave the committee,' I said, looking across the room at them where they sat as observers. 'You both knew when my authority was brought into question that I had been authorised by SARFU to do the negotiations, yet you sat silent throughout the meeting at my home and did not murmur a word and, in particular, you, Arrie Oberholzer, who took the minutes of all these resolutions.'

Afterwards, I had Arrie Oberholzer send a fax to the RWCL confirming SARFU's full backing of a new, smaller organising committee under my chairmanship. I had both Patel and Fritz Eloff sign the fax. Now we could get to work and try to tie up the loose ends, button up the contracts and find the necessary guarantee to back up the government's £2 million advance to the RWCL.

Rian Oberholzer, who I had picked to serve as my full-time organiser on the committee, accompanied me to the offices of ABSA's managing director, Dr Danie Cronjé. Flanked by his public relations director, Jan Snyman, this Cronjé turned out to be much less cooperative than his now retired, unrelated namesake, Frans Cronjé of Nedbank, who had come to my assistance at several crucial junctures in my early business career.

'Why can't the RWCL use their own money?' he kept asking.

I tried as patiently as I could to move him beyond this point.

There was nothing that we could do about it, I explained. The RWCL did not want to spend their own money. This was the reality - and we would have to find the equivalent of £2 million to guarantee the government's involvement. I added, however, that there was no doubt in my mind that the gate money at these play-offs would exceed the amount by far. In fact, I said, our money would be put in an escrow account.

Cronjé frowned.

'But I still can't see why the RWCL can't use their own cash.'

The hard facts were that Cronjé did nothing more than echo the same reservations aired by the South African Treasury Department when they asked me the very same question – the same gnawing query I was still unable to address myself. In fact, it was the same question De Klerk should have asked if he had had any knowledge of what he had so easily acquiesced to without much consideration. Instead, of course, De Klerk had wanted to come across as the 'nice guy'.

Worse, however, was to come when the Treasury also informed me that Marcel Martin and Nic Labuschagne wanted the loan paid over directly to the RWC account on the Isle of Man, which, of course, they firmly had to refuse. They were making the money available through SARFU and nobody else. Only, we hadn't had the faintest inkling that they would need a guarantee. It was infuriating that the WRC directors thought so little of SARFU – under Dr Craven – and the rest of us to approach the government directly.

I thus stood up with the 'authority' of someone who had many other eager lenders in the pipeline.

'It is obvious that I am wasting your time and you are wasting mine,' I said.

As we stepped out of the elevator downstairs, Oberholzer turned to me.

'So where will we get the money?' he asked.

'I'm going to try one last thing – we're going to our sponsors. If this one fails, we're in trouble.' I could just see myself once again putting up a guarantee for rugby to ensure our hosting of the coveted Rugby World Cup.

In 1992, I had managed – as chairman of SARFU's financial committee – to sell the television sponsorship rights to the Currie Cup competition to Bankfin for R96 million over a six-year period. There were still four years left, so I called on Dolf Wright, chairman of Bankfin.

'Dolf,' I asked, 'would you have any problem if we at SARFU ceded the remainder of our contract to the South African government as a loan guarantee?'

Fortunately, it was a short meeting that ended in smiles and a handshake. Bankers like no-risk proposals. I turned around and informed the officials at the treasury about this arrangement and they, in turn, transferred the required £2 million to the RWCL. At my insistence, however, it went with a rider. I inserted a clause in our lending agreement with the RWCL that gave me full access to their books not only at the Isle of Man but to another account in The Hague in the Netherlands.

In the end, the RWCL never used our money. Had they simply been pulling our chain? I would never know for certain. A few years later, the advance was returned, and we had made a profit of R500,000 in exchange control gains and interest. In the process, however, much acrimony erupted as I insisted on exercising my oversight rights to keep tabs on the RWCL's books in order to protect our interests.

In view of the ANC government's subsequent generosity in pursuit of the Olympics and the Soccer World Cup, with a reported total donation of R100 million in taxpayers' money, this insistence on a guarantee from SARFU to back up the loan seems odd. Recently, our government once again saw fit to donate R10 million to Mali to help it make the African Soccer Cup competition a success.

In the middle of 1993, I set off for the IRB offices in Bristol, England, to meet with the RWCL directors and negotiate a final agreement between us. At that time, we were on probation and the RWCL took every opportunity to remind us that it could still relocate the 1995 World Cup to New Zealand or Australia, if necessary. I was, to say the least, beginning to grow tired of the RWCL's endless whining over crime and other 'negatives' in South Africa that might force them to make the switch at the last minute. At the same time, I was made out in public as being entirely unreasonable and too demanding as I tried to protect SARFU's interests. It was time, I decided, to finalise matters and put an end to all the threats.

Silas Nkanunu and my daughter Corlia, who was originally brought in by Patel, accompanied me to the meeting, where Marcel Martin, Keith Rowlands, the RWCL secretary, with an attorney whose name escapes me, awaited us. However, I still vividly recall this gentleman's demeanour, which reminded me of an undertaker ready to close the lid on a corpse.

It was evident that the attorney was acting independently. Every time a new point came up, he would excuse himself from the talks and call someone for advice and guidance. When it came to the clause on arbitration, I offered to write it because my doctoral thesis had been on arbitration and I had a reasonably extensive knowledge of the subject. For once, the RWCL's attorney stayed in his seat and had me dictate the terms. In the next few weeks, both sides signed.

One of the first issues we needed to settle was the matter of venues. Arrie Oberholzer, who had earlier accompanied the RWCL on an inspection tour of South Africa to pick sites for the games, succeeded in having rustic Rustenburg, the headquarters of his small union, Stellaland, included as a venue. As a director of the RWCL, Nic Labuschagne had managed to have Pietermaritzburg placed second on the list of venues in his home province of Natal, after Durban. Now we were faced with 14 separate venues, which made no logistical sense.

I argued in favour of double headers at major venues as it would cost less and bring in more revenue. But the RWCL stuck to its guns. No self-respecting country, they insisted, would want to play in a curtain raiser. The competition had to be spread throughout the country. After much haggling and an ongoing heated argument we finally, at the beginning of 1994, agreed on nine venues. Pietermaritzburg was among those that had been dropped, but Rustenburg remained. Danie Craven Stadium in Stellenbosch was added to the roster in deference to the late South African rugby legend. In the end, however, the town fathers declined as tight schedules required Stellenbosch to stage a game on a Sunday, which would be considered by many as a denigration of the Sabbath. I respected their decision, but there was little we could do about it.

At the beginning of 1994, a tournament director had to be appointed. My personal choice was Jeremy Nel, a former Springbok from Stellenbosch, who had just retired from the board of directors of JCI, a major mining house. Nel not only knew both rugby and business, but found himself equally at home speaking Afrikaans and English. I had the full support of SARFU in submitting Nel's name to the Cape auditing firm that handled the applications. But, to my own surprise – as well as the folk at the auditing firm – Craig Jamieson of Natal was appointed to the post by the RWCL instead. John Bester, from the auditors Ernst & Young, who handled the applications, told me afterwards that Jamieson's name had never even featured on the list of 130 applicants. It was evident that Nic Labuschagne had used his influence to secure the position for his friend from Natal.

When I made inquiries, Sir Ewart Bell told me that Jeremy Nel would have been too expensive. As it turned out, however, Jamieson doubled Nel's requirement of R150 000 per annum when he insisted that this amount be changed to US dollars instead of South African rands.

In a fax to Leo Williams at the RWCL's Isle of Man office, I expressed SARFU's opposition to the way in which the appointment had been handled. 'This whole appointment has been handled in a clandestine and most unsatisfactory way and, in our opinion, completely against the spirit of our agreement,' I wrote. In the end, Jamieson would be no more than an errand boy for the Rugby World Cup directors.

But equally objectionable was the way in which the RWCL had tried to ram through the appointment of Deon Viljoen as the media liaison officer. In yet another confrontation, to the apparent unease of Fritz Eloff, who was present, I told the RWCL that I would not accept Viljoen's appointment. Deon Viljoen, in my view, was the man least suited for the job, as he had been a constant critic of SARFU and South African rugby in general. Would anyone dare appoint me as media liaison for the Pan African Congress? I don't think so. The present Minister of Sport, Ngconde Balfour, was also one of the applicants to this position but the entire SARFU executive had summarily rejected his application.

In January 1994 a special meeting was called in Paris. Naturally, it was portrayed in the press as an occasion for the RWCL to haul me onto the carpet. Apart from the Viljoen appointment, we were still at loggerheads over venues and several other more important issues. On his way to Paris from Australia, Leo Williams stopped over in Johannesburg to appeal to me to help him get the others on board. He put his legal and personal skills to work and I promised to do my best. When Rian and I entered the meeting, it was evident that Leo Williams had also coached the other side. Sir Ewart Bell started in a surprisingly conciliatory fashion.

'You cannot do the six venues, you know,' Bell said in a subdued manner.

'We have come to realise that we should do what you say,' I replied in equally sympathetic fashion. 'We will do what you say. But I would be remiss if I don't point out the follies of your ways. Here is a letter I should like you to read out loud to the committee.'

Sir Ewart read the letter but refused to read it out loud.

'We have an agreement, which you have signed,' I pointed out. 'You promised to provide us with regular management accounts. I want to put the RWCL on notice that we need these on a monthly basis. In fact, I would like to have the latest management accounts right now.'

'Why?' Sir Ewart asked, his refined English voice now raising a decibel or two.

'Because you gave that undertaking and you are working with our money. Surely, either your offices in the Isle of Man or The Hague should be able to fax it through at a moment's notice?'

During the break, Bell went into a huddle with Marcel Martin who proceeded to make a few phone calls. When we reconvened, Martin handed me a set of hastily scribbled figures. I looked at it and handed it back to him.

'No,' I insisted, 'I need proper and detailed accounting.'

Then Leo Williams stepped in.

'I think this is a little unfair, isn't it?'

'Leo,' I responded, 'how can this be unfair? How can you not expect someone who lends you £2 million not to be interested in knowing exactly how it is spent? We are entitled to it in terms of our contract.'

The RWCL asked for 10 days to come up with the proper documentation and I agreed. Instead of hauling me onto the carpet, the RWCL had found itself on the defensive. At the same time, I had made a major concession with regard to the venues. Still, it was obvious that we parted not with a lasting peace but merely a temporary ceasefire.

Then we were approached with a very strange request. Conveyed by Leo Williams, the RWC directors pleaded that I issue a notice of support for them. Up front as always, Williams confided in me and told me that a press report written and syndicated by the straight-shooting John Reason, had seriously damaged, in particular, the character of Marcel Martin. I firmly believed that Reason, no slouch on facts, had cut dangerously close to the bone but nevertheless issued a toned-down statement to help them because I did not have the facts that were clearly in the possession of Reason. I simply stated that I had no evidence to doubt their integrity. That was construed by the press as me kowtowing to the board after I had been roasted by them. Fortunately, Rian Oberholzer had been privy to all these discussions.

The next battle was over tickets. In terms of our agreement, there would be an even split of the 1.4 million available tickets between SARFU and the RWCL. Somehow, the RWCL seemed to have assumed that they were in a better position to decide on the pricing than SARFU with its intimate knowledge, backed up by extensive research, of the local market. Next, our tally of the number of seats available at Ellis Park, where the final was to be held, was questioned. For some reason, the RWCL believed that our count of 62,000 was an under-reporting in an effort to short-change them. The exchange of faxed letters between Sir Ewart Bell and myself reflects the atmosphere at the time:

'[From:] RUGBY WORLD CUP LIMITED, [To:] Dr Louis Luyt, President: South African Rugby Football Union. 3 February 1995. Host Union Agreement – Ticketing...

'It is with grave concern that the Rugby World Cup Limited (RWCL) Board received the report of our Tournaments Coordinator on the ticketing meeting that he and the Rugby World Cup Tournament Manager held recently with representatives of your Rugby World Cup Organising Committee and support staff at Ellis Park. As a result it is clear that:
- The "audit" conducted by your Tournament Auditors on the seating accommodation involved in staging the Rugby World Cup Tournament is seriously flawed.
- The complete breakdown by price category required in certain stadia has still not been undertaken.
- The diagrammatic placing plan by category called for in the Host Union Agreement is still not available for some stadia, and

- The "blind" boxes-seating contracted out has not been calculated on a similar basis to that of the private suites/boxes category as agreed in the formula of allocation of placing to Rugby World Cup and SARFU.
- We are further advised that the figures tabled at that meeting from direct consultation with the individual venue managers are now being disputed by SARFU.

'The result of this process brings into serious question either the conduct of the audit by your Tournament Auditors or the specific brief with which they were provided when instructed with this assignment several months ago.

'The report also raises doubt that the media positions that SARFU were contracted to provide under the terms of Host Union Agreement have been satisfactorily considered. The standards for such positions have been supplied to SARFU by RWCL. It is accepted that this is an internal matter for SARFU but we would wish to point out that if at this stage these places have not been catered for serious consequences could result. Neither of us would wish SARFU or RWCL to be embarrassed.

'The terms of our agreement on ticketing are set out quite clearly in the Host Union Agreement, namely that RWCL and SARFU should share equally the positions available at each stadium, category by category. Where specific categories of accommodation have been pre-contracted then an equal number of placings will be allocated to RWCL, with the resultant balance by category to be divided equally between RWCL and SARFU.

'We are aware of the practice in South Africa of selling additional places in private suites and boxes for major matches. This fact was confirmed by all but two of the stadia management representatives who were consulted during the recent meeting in South Africa. The prices charged for such additional places are the same as those charged for the seating within the private suites and boxes as demonstrated in your calculations of all the estimated gate monies.

'Your Committee's inability to provide the required ticketing information places SARFU in serious breach of the Host Union Agreement (Clause 4.2 and Schedule 10).

'We urge you to instruct your staff to remedy this situation immediately by:
1. Complying with the requirements of Clause 4.2.
2. Reviewing the actual stadium capacities so that either the data are corrected or we are given an explanation of the reasons for some large variances between your latest figures and your original ones on which you based estimated gate monies and we prepared our commercial programme.

'RWCL reserves all its rights in line with the Host Union Agreement in giving you notice of this default. We are also considering steps to protect our rights to control the number of tickets such as a proper audit trail in your computer programme and physical checks at the stadium gates.

'We are sure that you will understand that at a time when your sales pro-gramme is reported as highly successful and our commercial programme is requiring its final ticket allocation, it is important that we can work from an undisputed base for the benefit of all concerned.

'We trust you will give the above the utmost priority and that we will hear from you by return.

'Yours sincerely, Sir Ewart Bell – Chairman, Rugby World Cup Limited'

My reponse to Sir Ewart's fax was as follows:

[From:] The South African Rugby Football Union, [To:] The Chairman, Rugby World Cup Limited. 4 February 1995. Host Union Agreement – Disputes...

'*The intemperate allegations in your letter of the 3rd instant are regret-table. Coopers & Lybrand are a universally well-respected firm of chartered accountants. They are not SARFU's official chartered accountants. Yet we had appointed them to garner the information which we were obliged to furnish to you in terms of Clause 4.2 of the Host Union Agreement, specifically to ensure that there could be no doubt about the professionalism and impartiality of their work.*

'*Thus I dispute the charges levelled either at them, or at SARFU, in your letter under reply. It is clear from the wide-ranging allegations in your letter and from our disputing of each of them, that disputes as envisaged in Clause 13 (Arbitration) of the agreement have arisen in regard to the parties' respective rights and obligations. I return below to the procedure for their determination.*

'*Apart form the disputes raised by you in your letter, SARFU has become per-turbed at your recalcitrance in complying with obligations in terms of Clause 3.1 of schedule 9 to the agreement. Despite having been requested in writing to furnish the information referred to in that clause, you have failed to do so.*

'*SARFU requires this dispute to be resolved forthwith.*

'*The disputes which SARFU submits to arbitration are whether it has com-plied with its obligations in terms of Clause 4.2 of the agreement; and whether you have complied with your obligations in terms of Clause 3.1 of Schedule 9 to the agreement.*

'*Both issues clearly concern primarily questions of interpretation of the provisions of the agreement and its schedules, and therefore are of a legal nature. Considering the weight of the matter, the arbitrator should be a Queen's Counsel.*

'*We shall advise you shortly of some silks that will be available. In the absence of agreement in this regard by next Saturday, we shall request the President of the Law Society to designate an arbitrator.*

'*Yours faithfully, Louis Luyt.*'

Sir Ewarts's reponse, in turn, read as follows:

'*From: Sir Ewart Bell KCB MA, Chairman: Rugby World Cup, [To:] Dr Louis Luyt, President: SARFU. 7 February 1995.*
'*I have your letter of 4 February 1995. Firstly, I would like to reply to your allegation of our non-compliance with the Host Union Agreement – Schedule 9, Clause 3.1. This allegation does not stand. You were sent quarterly reports about the loan usage – these reports never drew an adverse comment from you. Before the loan was fully used, you asked to audit our books and this was also done to your full satisfaction. In September we put in place the Tournament insurance cover and the loan was no longer used. Finally, you know that this loan and its corresponding counterpart are identified in our balance sheet and we will be glad to give you an audit statement to that effect. We are therefore at a total loss to understand your allegation. Perhaps you can identify the problems so that we can know what we should remedy before you seek arbitration.*
'*Secondly, regarding the auditors – I would like to put the record straight in pointing out that they are part of your Tournament organisation and that it was at your request that they were nominated.*
'*Finally, your letter does not address the points I raised but merely disagrees with them. According to the Host Union Agreement, remedy should be sought to default before arbitration is invoked. The whole dispute is about proper accounting of the standing seats in the boxes, where any decrease of your previous data directly impacts on our share of the seating capacity. You will understand Rugby World Cup cannot accept such a situation that affects our programme.*
'*I therefore reiterate my request that you remedy the situation by either verifying the submitted data or giving us proper explanation about the variances.*
'*Time is running against us and I do not want to find ourselves in a situation where it appears that lack of cooperation makes the Tournament in South Africa unmanageable.*
'*Yours sincerely, WE Bell: Chairman.*'

'*From: Dr Louis Luyt, President: SARFU, [To:]. Sir Ewart Bell KCB MA, Chairman: Rugby World Cup. Host Union Agreement – Disuptes. 7 February 1995.*
'*... I do not understand why the issue is being avoided. Disputes have arisen, and the provisions of the agreement are clear. The disputes are to be resolved by arbitration in terms of Clause 13 of the Host Union Agreement.*
'*A "default" as envisaged in Clause 12 is not a prerequisite for an arbitration pursuant to Clause 13. The one dispute relates to your pertinent contention that we are in "serious breach" of our obligations in terms of Clause 4.2 of the agreement. We have disputed this, and have contended throughout that the auditor's report is correct. There is no room for further debate in correspondence.*

'...*The second dispute relates to the loan. I must record that we were never sent quarterly reports as now contended by you. The only report was an unaudited report under cover of your letter of 14 April 1994. We did ask for access to the books in order to have your books audited. However, it is incorrect to suggest that the result was to our "full satisfaction". I specifically reserved our position and stated that we would raise the matter at the IRFB.*

'*There is no relationship between the tournament insurance cover and the loan. The insurance cover relates to your risk of loss should the tournament be abandoned. Also, the mere identification of the loan in your balance sheet bears no relation to your contractual obligation to make available "... documentation and books of account relating to the application of the loan for the tournament...", especially in the context of the loan application clause as embodied in Clause 1.2.*

'*However, despite this response we must not be taken as exhaustive as we do not intend litigating the disputes by way of correspondence.*

'*The arbitration proceeds. We are scheduling the arbitration to take place on Monday and Tuesday, 13 and 14 February 1995, in London. We have established the availability, and recommend the appointment as arbitrator, of any of Alan Heyman, Eben William Hamilton, Nicholas Chambers, Jonathan Hirst and Mark Cran. They are all Queen's Counsel. Please revert within 24 hours failing which we shall approach the President of the Law Society on an urgent basis to designate an arbitrator.*

'*Finally, we reject out of hand your suggestion that there is a lack of cooperation, and that the tournament might become unmanageable. There is no substance in these allegations. In fact, the contrary is true. Our actions are aimed at resolving the disputes that have arisen. The tournament planning is on schedule.*

'*Yours faithfully, Louis Luyt.*'

The RWCL thus finally surrendered and we managed to avert what would have been a major confrontation. In the 'Settlement Agreement' signed by both sides on 10 February 1995, the RWCL 'accepted as correct' the audited total capacities submitted by Coopers and Lybrand and both sides withdrew the correspondence that passed between Sir Ewart Bell and me. This time the peace would last at least until after the Rugby World Cup when, to my surprise, the RWCL, instead of a handshake of gratitude, clenched one fist while grabbing its lion's share of the record profits with its left. We had fulfilled our promise to make record profits from the event, but that did not seem to matter as new turf fights broke out.

Throughout the many major arrangements and multitude of minutiae that precede an event of this magnitude, we found ourselves locked in a legal tussle with First National Bank over its advertising rights at Ellis Park. In accordance with our host nation agreement with the RWCL, every stadium that was to stage an event had to be swept clean of advertising. Ellis Park was designated not only as the site for several play-offs but for the final, too. Television and sponsorship rights belonged to the world body and we had no say in the matter. FNB, however, demanded that we compensate them for lost advertising if they had to remove their banners around the field. I responded by letter, arguing that their advertising rights were not in perpetuity and suggested that we come to a compromise. Unless we complied with the RWCL's request, I pointed out, there would be no matches at Ellis Park.

In a meeting at my office with FNB's senior manager, Norman Axton, and two of his colleagues, Phillip Canton and Johan Meiring, we agreed that, in the interests of the nation, nothing would be done by either side until after the World Cup. Flanked by Rian Oberholzer and my son Louis, I concluded our discussions by saying: 'Gentlemen, please don't jump any surprises on me.' They promised they wouldn't and, to show our goodwill, I promised to provide them with the additional tickets they had requested for the games at Ellis Park.

In the middle of the December 1994 holiday season, I was jolted out of my relaxed mode at Ballito by a call from Ellis Park. The guards at the gate of the deserted stadium, I was told, had been served with a summons from FNB demanding performance in response to their claims. In the following encounters, FNB would vehemently deny our verbal agreement. Although I had all the facilities to record this conversation, so much was my faith in Axton as a senior executive of FNB that it had simply not occurred to me that he would not follow through on what I understood to be our agreement. This unpleasant experience would, however, mean that from then on I recorded every discussion of importance that took place in my office – simply to circumvent a repetition of this sad instance.

On one hand, as president of SARFU, I was fighting off interference from RWCL, and on the other, as president of the Transvaal Rugby Football Union and chairman of Ellis Park Stadium, I had to try to make FNB comply with the RWCL's rules. In the meantime, we were involved in ticket sales, security arrangements, and emergency and contingency planning – from back-up airforce planes in the case of a commercial airline strike to stand-by generators in case of power failure. Together with the managers of the various venues, Chris Dirks and Rian Oberholzer were also overseeing extensive improvements at stadiums around the country.

Try as we could to dispose of it, the FNB matter clung to us like clay to a cleat. Our response to FNB claims was eventually served at Justice Piet Schabort's house while he was watching the Springboks play the Australians at Newlands in the first match of the 1995 World Cup. One would never know whether this rude intrusion played a role when a noticeably irate judge faced Wim Trengove, acting for FNB, and Schalk Burger on our behalf in court a few days later. This case, he decided, should never have been brought to court. It should be settled out of court within the hour. Our respective counsel returned and promised to seek a compromise. But FNB chose to press on. They subsequently won before Acting Judge Phillip Borokovich and we appealed. Two years later, the Appellate Division unanimously overturned his ruling in Bloemfontein and granted us court costs, even though we had not asked for it.

While we sold all of the 700,000 tickets allocated to us as the host country, the RWCL was still sitting with 400,000 tickets, mostly to minor games, a few weeks before the start of the World Cup. Instead of selling tickets in packages, including both major and minor events as we did, the RWCL's agents had linked their best tickets to expensive hotel accommodation. By doing this, they not only precluded overseas rugby enthusiasts who wished to make their own hotel arrangements or stay with family or friends, but the less desirable tickets were also left unsold. We also discovered that the overseas agents had been involved in the black-market sale of tickets. In terms of our agreement, all the unsold tickets were thus returned to us and it took a massive effort on the part of our agents to sell them.

Apart from ongoing last-minute renovations at a few stadiums, we were set to roll as we hosted 16 rugby squads and the world's top officials at an opening lunch at the Groot Constantia wine estate in Cape Town on 20 May 1995. Even though some might have pretended to have the power to do so, no one could control the weather. But the steady autumn showers failed to dampen the festivity. My brief welcoming speech was followed by lavish praise from the RWC directors for all that SARFU had done.

Through all the speeches, I fixed my eyes and my thoughts on the Springbok squad. In a way, I felt sorry for them. Here they were, with all the weight of the world on their shoulders. South Africa expected them to show that they were the best. Anything short of a World Cup win would be considered a national tragedy. I believed that they had the capability, but then I also knew that many a game could be lost through a bad break, the bounce of the ball or even a questionable call by the referee.

Absent from the South African squad was one player I felt quite strongly should have been there. In my view, Tiaan Strauss of Western Province was among the best in the world and a certain choice for the national squad. But coach Kitch Christie felt that he and Springbok captain François Pienaar would not compliment each other and insisted that Strauss be left out. I begged to differ, but left the final decision to Christie. I did, however, call Strauss to commiserate with him. As had happened before, when Engelbrecht and Snyman decided to leave Strauss out of the Springbok squad, I proceeded to Newlands as the one accused of being the reason for Strauss' absence.

It is indeed true that most of the Springboks came from the Transvaal. But that had not been my choice. Although I certainly had something to do with bringing top players to the Transvaal, even if it required some form of remuneration, I was not responsible for securing their places in the national team.

Looking at the Transvaal Springboks from the head table where we sat, flanked by the IRB and the RWC and other austere representatives of world rugby, I remembered numerous pre-game barbeques at my home in Saxonwold where these players had become part of my extended family. Since I became president of SARFU in March 1994, I had tried to cultivate the same relationship with Springboks from other parts of the country. I felt for these young men the same way as anyone would on the eve of a major challenge facing his own family.

As is customary, we – as host nation – were scheduled to play in the first game against the defending champions. This pitched us against Australia, the winners of the 1991 World Cup. Having lost to the Wallabies at Newlands 26–3 only three years earlier, we were thus going into this vital match on Thursday, 25 May 1995, as the decided underdogs. The not-so-quiet confidence of the Australians meant that everyone naturally anticipated a repeat perfomance of their victory in 1992.

The Springboks had the entire country behind them and had much to prove, but were they really up to the task? Kitch Christie seemed dour and determined; Morné du Plessis calmly confident, and I tried to hide the few lingering fears I might have had. But ultimately, I believe, it would be the enthusiastic support and encouragement of President Mandela that helped them pull through.

Much has been made of Nelson Mandela's visit to the team training at Silvermine military base – and justifiably so. The impact of this gesture by Mandela, moving along the line, shaking the hands of his 'boys' and wishing them well can hardly be overestimated. Here was the new leader of the so-called Rainbow Nation, setting the example in pushing aside the differences of the past and standing behind his team, regardless of colour or creed.

There have been many reports on how the Springboks turned around the game from a 13–9 deficit to a 27–18 victory but it was, from my perspective, more than just a win. South Africa served notice that it was back in world rugby. The long, agonising preceding months, with all its acrimony, seemed well worth it. Long after the details of the game have been forgotten, one lasting impression remains: determination and inspiration. These were Springboks playing for the glory of their country. They would do so throughout the World Cup series.

One incident that was never reported, however, was the fact that the pasta – dished up to the Springboks for their required fill of carbohydrates – had a terrible effect on the stomachs of the team and, at one point, we were afraid that they were all suffering from severe food poisoning. But we never breathed a word. The only casualty at the end of the day were the chefs, who were replaced by our hoteliers, Southern Sun.

Even though I had acceded to Kitch Christie's request to provide the Boks with additional monetary incentives, I believe that these payments served only as the icing on the cake and had no real effect on the players' performances. It is only after the World Cup that money seemed to become the main object.

When Kitch approached me during the early days of the World Cup, we were paying the Springboks about R3,000 per game, and he asked whether it would be possible to give the team R400,000 if they only won the quarterfinal, up the amount to R800,000 if they won the semifinals and pay them a total of R1 million if they won the final.

'Kitch,' I responded, 'I tell you what, instead of waiting to see how far the team goes, let's make a different deal. If you win the quarterfinal, I'll give the team R400,000, when they win the semifinals, they get another R800,000, and when they win the final we give them another R1 million. That is a total of R2.2 million if they win the Cup.'

'Hell,' Kitch gasped, 'I've never bargained as easily as this! But thanks a lot!'

I found it unusual to be praised as a pushover and hoped secretly that Christie might spread the word to all those who still insisted on labelling me the 'bastard' after having dealt with me in business and sport. Judging from what was to follow later, Christie either kept his mouth shut or no one believed him.

Arrie Oberholzer proved to be as impotent to run SARFU as general manager as had been the case with his union Stellaland when he was still their president. The executive thus decided to ask him – through Ronnie Masson who I had put in charge of administration since he was domiciled in Cape Town – to resign. To my utter surprise, Masson then asked me to attend the meeting at which he was to break the news to Oberholzer. At the meeting in the Western Province offices, I waited in vain for Masson to make his pitch. It was then that I realised that Masson was as scared as a rabbit being stalked by a greyhound. He looked pleadingly at me and I wasted no time in getting the process under way. To his credit, I must say that Arrie Oberholzer was extremely decent about it all, almost as if he expected to be relieved of his obligations. He asked to announce his request to be released of his duties and I had no hesitation in agreeing to this humble and dignified approach.

By this time, Edward Griffiths had assumed the role of public relations officer for SARFU, the team and myself, writing speeches and communicating with the media. Having appointed him as chief executive officer out of more than 100 applicants for the post, I soon discovered that his talent for writing and communicating was certainly not matched by managerial skills. When I had picked Griffiths for the job – in the wake of his outstanding job as media liaison during the 1994 Springbok UK tour, and over the objections of most members of my executive – I chose to ignore the headhunter's note about his lack of administrative experience. This turned out to be a big mistake. It was right there, in cold print:

'It would appear that [Edward Griffiths'] input to the media relations during the recent tour of Scotland, Ireland and Wales and, in addition, the handling of events in January this year, indicate his well-developed skill in that area. Our only concern remains his lack of management experience and ability and the [South African Rugby Football Union] executive need to be aware of the risks involved in such an appointment.'

Another characteristic that would only reveal itself after his appointment was Griffiths' tempestuous moods. During the first few months of his short tenure as CEO, I assigned him to act as media liaison officer for the Springbok team. But it soon became evident that he was not content with being a press spokesman, and repeatedly entangled himself in team issues and matters way beyond his job description. In the process, he landed himself in shouting scraps with Ronnie Masson and Dawie Schoonraad, as well as other SARFU executives, and ran foul of team manager Morné du Plessis in a heated public debate in the SARFU offices over fees. He also clashed with coach Kitch Christie, most notably on his hands-free cell phone – but that's another story entirely...

At Durban's Kings Park, where we faced the distinct possibility of a cancelled semifinal as a result of a flash flood, which would have given France a win by default – I had my own taste of Griffiths' excitable nature. Exasperated by his ranting and raving over the 'negative' world image portrayed by a hastily gathered emergency team of Zulu women sweeping water from the field, I had no other choice but to summarily order him off the field, ignoring his claims that he was SARFU's CEO and thus had a right to be there. Only a few weeks later, Griffiths found himself on the verge of being ordered off a SAA flight when he insisted on placing the World Cup in the cockpit over the objections of the pilot.

When he eventually returned to his duties as CEO, Griffiths found himself out of his depth, and began leaving a trail of unkept promises and unauthorised contracts on behalf of a growingly restless SARFU executive. On several occasions, he spent SARFU funds without consulting the executive and in at least one instance we had to order him to repay unauthorised personal expenses. In January 1996, less than a year after his appointment, I finally had to admit to myself and others that my appointment of Griffiths had been a mistake. I wrote him a letter, instructing him on specific issues. This was met with a typical Griffiths reaction; he was extremely rude to my secretary and sent me messages while I was conducting discussions with other people. I asked my secretary to tell Griffiths to wait at his telefax machine, and I faxed his dismissal 'for his eyes only'. He was fortunate that it was just not possible for me to simply up and leave for Cape Town, or I would have physically evicted him from his office. I expected Griffiths to be unhappy with his dismissal, but I never quite anticipated the depth of his resentment. I would pay dearly for my underestimating this character, but quickly learned much about the make-up of this opinionated man.

244

After the magnificent victory over Australia, the next few matches against Romania, Canada and Western Samoa were supposed to be sure wins. This was the occasion to open up the game and to experiment with the second-string players in our 29-man squad before we reached the semifinal. On Tuesday, 30 May, however, we posted a lacklustre 21–8 win over Romania at Newlands, barely five days after the impressive defeat of Australia at the same ground. The following Saturday we scored a brawling 20–0 win at Port Elizabeth over a Canadian team intent on trying to keep the Springboks at bay with foul tactics. One encounter resulted in two Canadians, as well as our hooker, James Dalton, being sent off the field. Another Canadian and Pieter Hendriks, from our side, were cited in the same match.

Apart from losing the services of key players, expulsion had further implications for the World Cup. In terms of tournament regulations, the team that had the least number of players sent off the field in preceding games became the automatic winner in the case of cancellation or the inability to break a tie.

In the early morning hours of Sunday, 4 June, word reached me that RWC Match Commissioner Ray Williams, after hearing the referee and touch judge's version of what happened, suspended James Dalton for 90 days. The suspension of two Canadians for 30 days was thus not only indicative of the double standard that was applied, but also purely academic as their team was already out of the running. At another disciplinary meeting on Monday, Hendriks was found guilty of kicking and punching and he, too, also suspended for 90 days. This was after I had forcefully rejected Marcel Martin's offer on behalf of the RWC not to have any other players cited if we agreed not to appeal against Dalton's expulsion.

While I felt that Hendriks had clearly lost his cool and was justly punished, I could see no reason why Dalton should have been suspended. He evidently came in to try to stop the fight. I asked Fanie Cilliers, a brilliant advocate with a long-standing and proven record of excellence in such matters, to handle Dalton's appeal. But, in the end, Morné du Plessis insisted on facing the three-man panel appointed by the RWC alone, in the belief that he, as a former player, could more effectively appeal to their sense of fair play. Afterwards David Moffett, a member of the disciplinary panel, confided in me that Dalton would have been exonerated were it not for Morné du Plessis' insistence on playing another tape he had acquired. Morné's tape created grave doubts in the minds of the panel and even though referee David McHugh conceded that he had mistakenly identified Dalton as 'the third man' the panel refused to overturn the original decision, and James Dalton was out for the rest of the tournament.

After a hard-tackling, bruising 42–14 win in the quarterfinal against Western Samoa at Ellis Park, the Springbok team was not only minus two first-string players but also had several on the injured list. Eventually, in an exemplary show of patriotism and pure guts, fullback André Joubert stepped onto the field for the semifinal in Durban with a bandaged fractured hand. Kobus Wiese, Ruben Kruger and Joost van der Westhuizen, who had also been injured in the scrap with Samoa, made their appearances too.

Between a seemingly never-ending string of administrative duties and receptions, I tried as best I could to squeeze in a few hours of rest at my home at Ballito, the day before the semifinal at nearby Kings Park, Durban, on Saturday, 17 June. The busy schedule – mercifully – helped take my mind off the crucial upcoming semifinal against the unpredictable and always-dangerous French side and the increasingly ominous weather. The field was wet after some morning showers when the Springboks had their final light practice at Kings Park on Friday. The weather forecast predicted some clearing overnight.

When I woke up on Saturday and pulled away the curtains, it was evident that the weather prophets had been way off target in their predictions. I could hardly see the Indian Ocean below my balcony as the rain pelted against the window. Playing the French in dry weather is a formidable enough task, but facing the opportunistic, agile Frenchmen in wet conditions is a huge risk, to say the least. Suddenly, our chances of reaching the final seemed to be diminished by unseasonable June showers.

By noon, when Adri and I set out on the half-hour drive to Kings Park stadium there was still no let-up. We were deeply immersed in our own thoughts as we joined the heavy traffic in the pelting rain. Quietly, I said my own prayers and so did Adri. Only the same God who controlled the skies could now come to our rescue and save us from seeing all our hopes to glory drowned. The French team, I also knew, could move on to the final without touching the ball or even leaving their locker room. If the game had to be scrapped because of the weather, they would be victors by default. We had had one man sent off the field while the French had had none.

I encountered Marcel Martin on the playing field. He was clearly trying to influence the referee, Derek Bevan, to call off the game. I walked up to him and also ordered him off the field.

'I am a World Cup director,' he protested.

'That much I know, but you're not part of the organising committee,' I said, 'so get off the field.'

To the Welshman Derek Bevan, I said, 'Mr Bevan, you are the only person who can decide on this game, but whatever you decide, I will accept. I hope that you would not have been influenced by Martin or myself in making your final decision.'

Ideas on how to remove the water were bouncing from all directions. Helicopters. Golf gear from nearby Durban Country Club. Vacuum cleaners. I settled, however, for the nearest and the quickest. We called in the help of a dozen Zulu women who managed to mop the water up during a brief lull in the rain.

But the minute the field was finally declared ready, another hitch developed – John Jaevons-Fellows appeared at the Springbok locker room to inform us that no one would be allowed to go onto the field with any other number but the numbers against their names on the official programme. Anticipating better weather, several of the Springboks had cut the sleeves off their original jerseys and then exchanged them for the spare jerseys with different numbers.

Jaevons-Fellows was simply enforcing the regulations that players had to be properly numbered. Morné du Plessis balked. He was not going to tell the players to change jerseys once again after all that they had been through. In that case, Jaevons-Fellows warned, South Africa would be disqualified.

I stepped in and told Morné that we had no option. He went back into the locker room. 'Sorry, boys, we have to comply,' he said. There were murmurs, but they made the switch back to their original jerseys. I then wished them well and walked up to the presidential suite in time to see the teams running onto the field with a downpour greeting their every step.

Even though the teams were on the field, playing, there was no certainty that the game would be completed. According to the rules, should a semifinal be stopped due to bad weather, the number of tries scored until then would be the deciding factor. In the 27th minute of play, Kobus Wiese and Ruben Kruger jointly crashed over the French line and, even though the try was later officially recorded as a score by Kruger, I much prefer to think of it as a joint accomplishment. This try and conversion put South Africa ahead by 10–6 at half-time. This had bought us some insurance, but the French refused to give up. After a few more penalty kicks on both sides and several narrow escapes on our part as the French pushed towards our line with all their might in the dying minutes, the game ended with a final score of 19–15 in our favour.

South Africa had earned its place in the final. All that remained was to determine who they would face. And that did not take long. The very next day, on a dry and sunny Sunday afternoon in Cape Town, the All Blacks kicked off against England. From the third minute of the game, when All Black wing Jonah Lomu trampled over the opposition to score a 35-metre try, the English looked like a defeated side. New Zealand's runaway victory of 42–29 included three tries by the speedy giant, Lomu.

On Monday, 19 June, British pundits were describing South Africa's chances of beating New Zealand from slim to none. Lomu, they decided, was unstoppable. The match-up in the final was generaly considered to be between the Springboks and the All Black. Unless the Boks could find a way to throw this Jonah overboard, their ship was certain to sink. But how?

There was no shortage of advice from the South African public, who sent reams of faxes to the Springbok team. With Kitch, however, I had no doubt that we were capable of neutralising the Kiwi flyer. The secret was not to give him any room in which to gather speed. It was decided that James Small, Lomu's much smaller opponent, would force him to the inside where our loose forwards would be ready to go in for the kill. My worry, in the meanwhile, was not stopping Lomu, but rather the possibility that we would become so fixated on this one player that we would forget about the other 14 equally dangerous opponents.

With the harrowing experience at Kings Park something of the past, I had many doubts about the outcome of this World Cup final. We were up against, in my book, the most complete side of the tournament. Awesome! While others – including some of our own sport writers – were giving the odds to the All Blacks, I fervently hoped that our day of greatness had dawned. Ours was a team inspired – one with the ability to respond to the massive home crowd at Ellis Park. I tried hard not to entertain any negative thoughts as we approached the crucial day. In any event, during the week leading up to the big game, I had another urgent and momentous task to distract me.

Accompanied by my son Louis, I left for London on Sunday, 19 June, to conclude a deal that would finally end amateur rugby. After over a month of secret negotiations we had reached the final stages of a binding contract with Rupert Murdoch's News Corporation. The 'we' was SANZAR, a newly constituted entity representing South African, New Zealand and Australian rugby.

It was only fitting, I thought as we settled in for the overnight journey on South African Airways to London's Heathrow, to have my 27-year-old son with me on this mission. Rugby as I used to know it was about to become history and we were entering a new era that might seem more acceptable and normal to his generation than mine. We were, in a sense, passing on the baton. Never again would rugby be the same.

There are, of course, those who could argue that what I was about to do in London was merely bringing rugby out of its double existence into the open. What many referred to as 'shamateurism' was practised widely in all major rugby playing countries, including South Africa, although Argentina was an exception. Every province in our country that could afford it, was buying players and some-times this bidding war had taken on nasty proportions. We might as well start making real money, as we would soon need it to be able to afford increasingly demanding superstars.

The possibility of a deal with Murdoch had first come to my notice on Sunday, 7 May 1995, when I joined my counterparts from Australia and New Zealand – Leo Williams and Richie Guy – at the Park Royal Hotel in Sydney for discussions on the eve of the World Cup tournament. Also in attendance were Williams' deputy chairman, Ian Ferrier, and Guy's sidekick, Rob Fisher, as well as David Moffett, the executive director of the New South Wales Rugby Football Union, and Bruce Hayman, the CEO of the Australian Rugby Union.

Even though the chemistry around the room was excellent, I knew that I was not there simply because I would have made good company. Until 1994, we had the so-called Super-10 competition, which included our four top Currie Cup teams, four teams from New Zealand and two from Australia. When the SABC, who sponsored the series, decided not to take up the option to renew beyond 1995, Australia and New Zealand indicated that they would instead establish a Super-Eight between themselves. I announced that we might go into a series with England, France and Argentina. Then came the call from Richie Guy, asking me to join them for talks in Sydney.

'So why are we here, then?' I asked after Leo Williams welcomed us all from the chair.

'We don't see our planned Super-Eight series succeeding,' Williams explained. 'We had the Super-Six between our two nations before and it was never really successful. South Africa has the money for rugby. There is no money in New Zealand and Australia is definitely not a rugby country.'

The bottom line was that they needed South Africa to become part of a television rugby package that could be sold to either Rupert Murdoch or his rival, Kerry Packer, for big bucks. Even though Ken Cowley, the managing director of Murdoch's News Corporation in Australia, had virtually shut the door on them after their initial meeting, they were confident that there would be interest on his part once he found out that South Africa had joined.

'So, what are we going to sell?' I asked.

It soon became clear to me that their approach was terribly flawed. Based on the formation of a corporation relying on a US$2 million (NZ$4 million) underwriting and a meagre $140,000 from Australian television, players would become shareholders and be paid in dividends.

'Gentlemen,' I said, 'we're wasting our time. I don't know a single player who would go along with the idea of earning dividends. We need to pay them – and much more than they are currently getting.'

We all agreed that the really big boys in television would only bite if the competition they were getting was spectacular enough to translate into millions of viewers. What we needed was a package that combined provincial team competitions with a tri-nation series of internationals between South Africa, New Zealand and Australia. It was crucial, then, that we in rugby union offer a product that far exceeded either Packer's League Rugby or Murdoch's Super League in viewership potential.

Encouraged by the prospect of adding South Africa to the equation, Guy and Fisher reworked their original plan and went back to Cowley at News Corporation with the revised package. There was consensus among us that Packer was an unlikely candidate because of his heavy involvement in cricket and rugby league. This opinion was further strengthened by a meeting I had had at my hotel with former South African cricketer Tony Greig, who had close ties to Murdoch's archrival. In reply to my casual question whether Packer might in future branch into rugby union, Greig said: 'No, never. He is all league.'

At the time, we were blissfully unaware that barely a few blocks away from the Park Royal, another expatriate South African, Geoff Levy, together with a certain Ross Turnbull and others, were plotting with Packer's men to move onto our turf.

The second time around, Ken Cowley seemed to like what he heard – in fact, so much so that he suggested a delegation fly to London to meet with Sam Chisholm, who handled international sport contracts for News Corporation. Guy and Fisher, accompanied by David Moffett and Dick McGruther, another senior ARU official, embarked on their long journey for London as I left for Johannesburg to reapply myself to the upcoming World Cup. Ian Frykberg, yet another expatriate South African who had taken a personal and professional interest in the matter, met them.

I knew Frykberg as the CEO of Communication Services International (CSI), which acted as SARFU's international agent for television rights. A likeable fellow who had been born in Johannesburg and gone to school in Welkom before moving to Australia via New Zealand, Frykberg now found himself straddling the divide and acting for both sides. In my view, it was clearly a conflict of interest. Once I was asked to take over negotiations, I conveyed this message to CSI's owner, Michael Watt, and his deputy chairman, Jim Fitzmaurice. They thus decided to take Frykberg off Chisholm's account and instructed him to join our side. He would prove to be quite helpful, as he obviously knew Chisholm's thinking and style. At the same time, however, I suspect that he continued to feed the New Zealander with tips about us to help the process along.

Instead of returning to New Zealand, Richie Guy flew from London to South Africa for the impending kick-off of the 1995 World Cup. On 19 May, the day before the opening game between South Africa and Australia, we assembled at SARFU's Newlands offices to get a report-back from Guy and to plan future strategy. Present, apart from Guy and Moffett, were Leo Williams and Bruce Hayman from the ARU. I had Griffiths sit in with me on behalf of SARFU. Guy, as it turned out, had found sufficient interest on the part of Chisholm to suggest that we move forward.

A company was established. The name, Southern Cross, which we originally bandied about, had already been taken, so we needed to find an alternative. SANZAR – South African New Zealand Australian Rugby – seemed a logical option. Each of the three nations was to be represented by two directors. Williams nominated me as chairman and I in turn proposed Moffett as the CEO.

I, in the meanwhile, discovered that David Moffett was one of the most volatile personalities I had ever come across. He resigned no fewer than three times during his short term as CEO of Sanzar. The third time, I accepted his resignation and asked the other directors for their support to appoint Rian Oberholzer in his place.

Oberholzer moved to Sydney with Corlia and the children in order to fulfil his functions, but soon discovered that John O'Neill of the Australian Rugby Union virtually ignored his existence and carried on as if he was solely in charge. O'Neill, who had come to the ARU thanks to Leo Williams, who had given him a job when he did not succeed as a banker, was an extremely irritating individual, particularly as he knew next to nothing about rugby.

After Griffiths had been given his marching orders – and not a minute too soon, I might add – Hentie Serfontein and André Markgraaff solicited and received the necessary support to bring Oberholzer back as CEO of SARFU. Because Rian was my son-in-law, I refrained to involve myself with his appointment although I knew he was eminently qualified and the right person for the position – after all, I was his mentor. I taught him everything he knows about rugby administration, although I had not taught him everything I know.

It had already been decided in Sydney that the Super-12 competition would include five teams from New Zealand, four from South Africa and three from Australia. Even though Australia only had two unions – Queensland and NSW – they assured us that they could form a third with the players who did not make it to either of these teams. Soon this new union, Australian Capital Territories (ACT) – nicknamed Brumbies – became a dominating force in the competition, proving, once again, that it is not the individual superstar but the team as a whole that wins games.

The only serious hitch turned out to be in devising a programme according to which the Super-12 competition could be fairly conducted. At Moffett's suggestion, the problem was passed along to the mathematics department of the University of Sydney. After several days of number-crunching in Sydney, we seemed no nearer to a solution and I handed the problem on to my son Louis and his secretary, Maelen Hart. In about four hours, they came up with the formula that remains in use today.

The other part of the package, the so-called Tri-Nations competition, was much easier to schedule, but it did nevertheless leave me with a certain measure of melancholy. We were, in effect, doing away forever with the long international tours that had become such an integral part of rugby since the early 1900s. In a subsequent interview, All Black fullback, the late Don Clarke – who, until his death, lived in South Africa – expressed a longing for the old days when players had had the opportunity to build some sense of camaraderie and form lasting friendships while on tour. I could fully sympathise with the sentiments of a man whom I first faced in 1960. In that game in Bloemfontein, Clarke's boot turned mercifully cold and allowed us to score a narrow win against the All Blacks. Now, however, we had no choice in the matter. South Africa's already scheduled 1996 tour of New Zealand would be the last of its kind.

When it came to deciding on who should lead the follow-up talks with Chisholm, the group selected me. I gathered that both Guy and Moffett found Chisholm's attitude too abrupt and intimidating and needed someone equally brusque to carry the concept back and set a decent price. There was no discussion about pricing at the first encounter. Moffett would accompany me, but first we had to put a price on the package. We felt that US$550 million over 10 years might be reasonable, but decided to add another US$100 million to give us some room for negotiation. Guy was originally opposed to the idea of selling rights for more than five years, but the rest of us prevailed in our argument that 10 years made it more attractive for the buyer, who would have to spend both time and money in building viewership.

The name Ross Turnbull surfaced briefly during the meeting at the offices in Newlands. By now it had become known that this former Australian prop and ex-chairman of the New South Wales Rugby Union had joined former South African Geoff Levy in talks with Kerry Packer's men with a view to selling their own world rugby product. Although I had met Turnbull some years previously and even found his brash, ebullient manner appealing, I also knew about the financial fiasco resulting from his effort to turn a modest Sydney site into a great rugby stadium. While I had never met Levy, his name was familiar to me, as he had assisted me in obtaining the books from Australia, which I needed for my comparative legal studies in company law towards an LLD degree at the University of Pretoria.

Turnbull, everyone decided, hardly deserved our time. He had no money of his own and Packer was certainly not interested in rugby union. On top of that, we all believed that we had a lock on our players. No one would sign up unless they were assured of being paid and we were the only ones who would be in a position to give that assurance. As it turned out, we sadly underestimated the bulldog in Turnbull and the naiveté of our own players.

When I ran into Ross Turnbull at the Sandton Sun in Johannesburg after I had had lunch with Richie Guy and David Moffett at The Touchdown Restaurant at Ellis Park, I failed to recognise him. It had been many years since we had seen each other, and it was only afterwards that Moffett identified the friendly fellow who had pushed forward to shake my hand. I did not find it strange at all to see him around as all and sundry with any interest in rugby had converged on South Africa for the World Cup. I also did not know that, at just about that time, Harry Viljoen – who later became Springbok coach – and François Pienaar were in the process of plotting with Turnbull and his associates, and that Pienaar had commanded a whopping performance fee of US$300,000 for himself.

So, in the days following the Newlands meeting, we had to sort out the relationship between the three partner nations. There was no doubt in my mind that South Africa deserved a larger slice of the pie as we obviously offered more by way of revenues. We were ready early in June, and Moffett and I set off to London to present our package to Chisholm. Our meeting was at his offices at BSkyB. I found myself towering over the shortish New Zealand media manipulator as we settled around the table. His businesslike demeanor, which had so intimidated others, rather appealed to me. We handed him our document. He flipped through the pages until he found the bottom line: US$650 million.

He looked at me, slapping his chest, feigning a heart attack.

'This is going to kill me,' he said, abruptly. 'We're not going to pay that much.'

Moffett looked at me.

'All right,' I said to Chisholm, 'why don't we think about it and if you find that you are interested later, give me a call. In the meantime, I'm certain you won't mind that we look around for another possible taker. But thank you very much for your time.'

You have to know just when to make your exit.

This was probably the hundredth time I had found myself in a similar situation both in business and, more recently, in sport. If the product is good enough, they will always come back – especially if there is another strong competitor waiting hungrily in the wings. In this case, however, even though it suited us to pretend otherwise, I still believed that Packer was not really a contender. But Frykberg, anxious to seal the deal, continued to play this card in his ongoing talks with Chisholm.

When striking a deal with Bankfin in 1990 – one that tripled our original asking price – I had also played the take-it-or-leave-it tactic by first securing another firm buyer. A SARFU committee, under the chairmanship of Jan Pickard of Western Province, had already reached an understanding with Bankfin to sell to them the television and sponsorship rights to the Currie Cup for five years for a mere R33 million. As president of the TRFU, I immediately contacted Doc Craven to express my unhappiness with this giveaway. After all, it affected all of our pockets. I was told that the deal had been struck by a very able team that included Jan Pickard, Nic Labuschagne of Natal and Pietman Retief, then the general manager of SARFU. But I threatened to pull Transvaal out of the Currie Cup unless we renegotiated. On this issue, Steve Strydom of Free State and Professor Koos Vermaak of Eastern Province joined me. I was thus challenged to re-open discussions with Brink Botha of Bankfin. But first I went to see Hein Jordaan of the SABC, who agreed to pay R96 million for the same contract. M-Net was also willing to compete for the rights at this price, so Bankfin, who had first right of refusal, had no choice but to match this amount and sign on the dotted line.

Somewhat more controversial was the deal I had struck with Barry Smith and

Tobin Prior of South African Breweries.

For the right to display their emblem on the Springbok jersey, SAB agreed to pay a hefty annual fee. Even though it gave me no joy to see commercialism encroach on the green and gold for the whole world to see, we had to move with the times or be left behind. SARFU certainly needed the money to meet the increasing demands not only from its own players but also for development programmes involving black and coloured players. Still, I had to respect the sentiments of the Springboks, who let us know through then manager Abe Malan that they refused to play in the new colours with a 'Christmas tree' on it. I asked Malan to come and see me and we finally settled on a smaller SAB logo, which the sponsor kindly accepted.

As I shifted about in my seat, trying to settle down and catch up on some sleep on the way back from our brief encounter with Chisholm, I kept thinking about the good old days when rugby was merely a sport. With the money already floating around, plus this valuable new contract – which, I was certain, would come to fruition – we were about to open a Pandora's box that could never be closed again, even if we wanted to do just that.

Even before we managed to conclude the deal, there were already quarrels between the three partners of Sanzar over how we were to split the spoils. We could expect more of the same as the dollars started rolling in and the handsome cheques were written. And our players would be right there to claim their share. The European unions, which had been excluded from this lucrative deal, were bound to accuse us of blatant professionalism even though they themselves had long abandoned amateur rugby. Big money, I knew, was about to sow disunity and unhappiness in the ranks of world rugby. But I had no idea just how nasty it would become.

Not long after my return to South Africa, Frykberg was on the phone.

'Chisholm is definitely interested,' he reported. 'But he is not going to pay $650 million. From now on, however, he wants to deal with you alone. He does not want Moffett along.'

'Fine with me,' I replied.

'Oh yes,' Frykberg continued, 'Murdoch wants your *curriculum vitae*.'

'No problem – as long as he sends me his,' I quipped.

Next came the call that prompted me to leave for London that Sunday before the World Cup final. My son Louis and I managed to slip out of the country without the media getting any wind of it. The only one who knew, apart from Adri, was my trusted assistant, Susan Kruger. It was not too difficult to make a quiet exit as the media were, in any event, so focused on the upcoming historic clash between New Zealand and South Africa that everything else seemed to escape their attention.

When Louis and I, together with Frykberg, were ushered into Chisholm's apartment on the morning of Monday, 20 June, we found Murdoch's man surrounded by a bevy of executives and ready to do business. I introduced my son:

'Louis's come along,' I said, 'to get some experience of how you men operate, to get a feel for how business is done at this high level.'

Chisholm chuckled. He was in a cheerful mood, obviously buoyed by the spectacle between England and New Zealand at Newlands, which he had watched on TV the previous week from the comfort of his London home. If this was the kind of stuff he was purchasing, he seemed to have decided, it was definitely worth a pretty penny.

'Tell me what you have in mind,' I said, as we settled around the table. 'We don't have much time.'

Chisholm nodded in agreement. I gathered he also wanted to get things done in a hurry.

'We were thinking of $550 million.'

The offer was $550 miilion, exactly $100 million below our asking price. Considering that Frykberg knew that this was the precise amount we had initially agreed upon as the real asking price, I had to assume that he had used his foreknowledge to help the negotiations along.

'No, I'm afraid not,' I said, 'we need a little more than that, say $555 million. That would do it.'

Chisholm looked as if he might feign another heart attack. I felt, however, that I simply needed to make sure that he paid a little on top of his original offer. After a few minutes of back-and-forth, Chisholm concurred. Yes, he would sweeten the deal with an extra $5 million and make it a 'nice-sounding triple five' over the following 10 years.

What my son witnessed for the rest of the day was hardly your run-of-the-mill boardroom business meeting. Chisholm's attorney, Bruce McWilliam, tapped away at the keys of a laptop computer as we talked around the dining-room table. Every now and then, McWilliam would print out a few pages and hand it to us for review and editing.

By lunchtime, we had cobbled together an agreement. For the total amount of $555 million, News Corporation (Newscorp) acquired exclusive worldwide television, radio and video rights for all international and representative rugby union matches played in Australia, South Africa and New Zealand for the following 10 years, starting in 1996. Annual payments for the year escalated from $32 million in 1996 to $78 million in 2005. Each of the three participating nations undertook to do its best to sign up their own players and keep them to the contract.

Louis and I left with Frykberg for ribs at the Carlton Grill Room, while Chisholm made his calls to run the proposed contract by Rupert Murdoch. When we returned to the apartment, the Heads of Agreement was ready. I signed and initialled every page on behalf of Sanzar and Chisholm countersigned on behalf of News Corporation. Rugby in the southern hemisphere had just become a half-billion-dollar business. No fanfare. No celebration. Merely a handshake and a hasty departure for Heathrow to make the early evening flight back home to Johannesburg.

At the airport, I leafed through the newspaper and came across an article by a Miss Battersby who described New Zealand as a team from another planet – and, I must admit, I almost agreed with her – in their destruction of the England team at Newlands. When I made a joke of this in my much-maligned speech at the closing function, I was apparently the only person who had read the article.

On my return to South Africa, I handed copies of the Heads of Agreement to the other two partners for their approval. Both Leo Williams and Richie Guy concurred and we decided to call a press conference on the Friday before the final at Ellis Park.

There were gasps of surprise around the room as I read off the fees involved. Rugby had made a sudden bold move from performing for peanuts to playing for big bucks. Instead of the total of US$5.7 million the three member nations were currently earning in television rights, we had now signed up for $32 million in 1996, escalating to more than double that amount in the 10 years that were to follow. A six-fold increase on a single year!

I was asked why we had decided to team up with News Corporation.

'There is no one single reason, but rather 555 million reasons,' I said and no further questions were asked.

As Ian Ferrier observed, the Australian Rugby Union's share of the Murdoch millions ballooned from a payment of a mere A$200,000 for its television rights in 1991, when it had won the World Cup, to a hefty A$11 million in 1996, when the News Corporation contract came into effect.

Mindful of the sensitivities in the International Rugby Board and the resentment of those in the northern hemisphere, which had been left out, we tried as best to deny that this actually meant a unilateral step on our part to end amateurism in rugby. I am afraid, however, that we were somewhat disingenuous in this respect.

My insistence that the money was largely earmarked for 'rugby development' also left our audience unconvinced. I knew, right from the beginning, that a good part of these earnings would have to go to the players. It was, however, still too early to broach this question openly. Little did we know that Pienaar and his squad, as well as many of their counterparts in New Zealand and Australia, were already having salary talks with Turnbull's so-called World Rugby Corporation. It turned out later that, as we spoke, Turnbull was in Harry Viljoen's office, going over the details of his offer to the South African team. After all, Viljoen was the man – with the very willing assistance of Ian MacDonald, who would blow the whistle on the whole affair later – who put the Australian in touch with Pienaar in the first place.

A crisp, clear daybreak on Saturday morning, 24 June 1995, found me at my office at Ellis Park Stadium taking care of last-minute preparations for the big game that afternoon. The country had come to a standstill. Everyone was involved and pulling for his or her team. People of all races were smiling at each other and exchanging greetings: 'Amabokoboko!' they shouted, using the Springbok name in native tongue that became as much a trademark as the 'Vrystaat!' of old. It was Rainbow Nation united in full support behind President Mandela and 'his boys'.

As I gave instructions and made calls, it occurred to me that if there was such a thing as 'real happiness', this must surely be it – or at least as close as it gets. I had had many highs to compensate for the lows in my business career, but nothing like this. Knowing that you had played a part in making this historic and glorious event a reality, all those years of bitter in-fighting over Craven and my excursions abroad, the vituperation whenever I made a change in management or coaching staff, and the recent arguments with the RWCL, all seemed well worth it. The only detail that remained was South Africa winning the coveted William Web Ellis Trophy. But that, I was convinced, would only be a matter of time. My script simply did not allow for any other ending.

Then a call came in from President Mandela's office. It was his secretary, Mary.

'Dr Luyt,' she explained, 'The president would very much like to wear the Springbok jersey today.'

'Sure,' I said. 'It would be an honour.'

'Only one problem, however,' Mary continued. 'He seems to have left the one he received from François Pienaar in Cape Town. Would it be possible to get him a another?'

'Of course.'

I called in my son Louis and Chris Dirks. As it turned out, we had the facility downstairs to make up a new jersey, replete with the World Cup emblem and Pienaar's number 6 on the back. The jersey, as well as a cap, was thus delivered to Mandela's home in Houghton within the hour. When he arrived at the stadium at 2.30 that afternoon, the president cut a dignified figure despite the unstatesmanlike apparel consisting of a rugby jersey draped, pullover-style, over his grey pants, and a peak cap on his head. I am sure I was not the only one in the presidential box who envied this unusual man his effortless ability to cut such a regal figure in just about anything he chose to wear.

'Mr President,' I asked, 'don't you think it might be a good idea to have you go down and visit our players in their locker room?'

'Sure, Louis,' he said. 'I would like to wish my boys the best of luck.'

In his short speech, Mandela reminded the players that they were playing for the nation and that everyone depended on them. The electrifying effect of the man's presence and his words clearly had a visible effect on the men in the locker room.

We were back in the presidential box in time for the surprise flyover by a South African Airways Boeing 747 dragging a huge banner that read, 'Good luck, Bokke!'. The sudden, thundering swoosh of the low-flying giant had several around me instinctively duck, including Mandela.

Next, I accompanied President Mandela and Ewart Bell onto the field to be introduced by the respective captains to the members of their teams. The two national anthems were played and we returned to our seats. The All Blacks then rounded off the formalities with their customary haka as the Springboks stared them down as nonchalantly as they possibly could. Ed Morrison of England, who had once sent off James Small in Australia, had been selected to handle the game over Derek Bevan, whom, in fact, we would have preferred after his very able handling of the difficult semifinal in Durban.

The capacity crowd at Ellis Park certainly got full value for their money, as did the hundreds of millions around the world who watched the titanic struggle on television. I could actually picture Sam Chisholm, sitting in his apartment with friends and colleagues and patting himself on the back for having clinched the rights to this magnificent sport. Throughout the game, President Mandela, with Steve Tshwete as an interested onlooker, kept asking me for explanations about penalties and other rulings.

There was at least one instance where I was at a loss for an explanation when Morrison refused to award a try after Springbok loose forward, Ruben Kruger, barged across the All Black line. Pienaar later commented that you can always see whether you scored or not by looking at the facial expressions of your opponents. I agree. In this instance, the All Blacks on the scene certainly appeared resigned to the fact. But Morrison decided otherwise.

Twelve minutes into the game, Jonah Lomu was sent into action on the field. His effort to crash through centerfield came to an abrupt end when Springbok centre Japie Mulder brought him down with a ferocious tackle. Every time he received the ball, Lomu was dealt with swiftly and effectively. The plan was working. By half-time, we were leading 9–6, with two penalties and a drop kick by flyhalf Joel Stransky against New Zealand's two penalties by his counterpart, Andrew Mehrtens.

The tight struggle between the world's best teams continued with neither side able to cross each other's line. When regular play ended, the two teams stood even at 12–12, after a few additional penalties. The highly improbable and entirely undesirable ending we on the Springbok side had all so feared had become a distinct possibility.

As in the semifinal in Durban, the Springboks had once again started off with a clear disadvantage. According to the rules, a draw at full-time would be followed by 10 minutes of extra time both ways. If the two teams still found themselves deadlocked, the one who had scored the most tries in the final would be declared the winner. If both scored an equal number of tries, the team who had the least number of players ordered off the field during the tournament would be the victor. The Dalton factor had thus come back to haunt us. I felt sorry for the hooker watching from the sidelines, Chris Rossouw playing in his place, and felt equally sorry for us being at an unjustifiable disadvantage. If only Fanie Cilliers had been allowed to put his skills to work in the Dalton case instead of us throwing ourselves at the mercy of men who refused to be confused by the facts.

Then, deep into the nail-biting 20 minutes of the game's overtime, Joel Stransky launched a perfect drop goal through the goal posts. From where I sat, I thought we might be lifted out of our seats by the huge roar from the thousands of supporters who packed the stadium down below. I looked over at President Mandela and smiled. He smiled back. But we all realised that anything could still happen before that final whistle blew and signalled the end of the game. Even though we had succeeded in taming Jonah Lomu, there were still 14 other players who could snatch victory away from us – not least of them Mehrtens, with his magic boot. One infringement and it would be even again. Two and we would lose. And, to cap it all, Stransky missed the easiest of penalty kicks at goal minutes later. Fortunately for him, his bad miss would be despatched to oblivion considering his unforgettable drop kick just minutes before. In fact, the very fact that Stransky was indeed playing was nothing short of a miracle in itself. Christie had already decided that Cameron Oliver, that magnificent former Natal and Transvaal flyhalf, was set to be his man in the World Cup, but Oliver had died tragically in a freak road accident.

The final whistle blew. For once, President Mandela seemed to have lost his regal demeanour and became just another overjoyed fan. We grabbed each other and I instinctively lifted him off his legs as we embraced. We were big men acting like boys.

Then we were, on our way down to the field, where Mandela handed the William Webb Ellis trophy to François Pienaar. I stood back, savouring the moment. This was the dream that had kept me going despite all the unpleasantness of the past. I had fulfilled my promise to Mandela after that disastrous game against the English at Loftus Versfeld.

The only sour moment of that memorable day, quickly forgotten in the joy of victory, was when Meads, Guy and Brian Lochore pretended not to see my hand outstretched to them in congratulations and walked right past as if I did not exist.

The festivities continued on and off the field, in the streets and all over South

Africa. Afterwards, Adri and I embarked on the slow journey back home, my car was repeatedly stopped along the way by the throng in the streets as black and white well-wishers insisted on shaking my hand.

After a hasty shower and a change of clothes, Adri and I set off once again, this time for Gallagher Estate off the main road to Pretoria, where the final reception was scheduled to take place.

From the outset, I had been dead set against this event. Why would the losers want to sit down to dinner and see the winners gloat in their glory? Why would tired and beaten-up rugby players want to spend their time listening to boring speeches by administrators patting themselves and each other on the back for a job well done? It was, I told the RWCL, a sure formula for disaster, but they insisted on having it and we went along, facilitating as best we could, a reception fitting for world champions and would-be champions.

We had finished our cocktails and were already seated, but there was still no sign of the Springboks. The All Blacks were shifting impatiently in their chairs, glancing at the doors, growing visibly irritated. I could not blame them. Blood was rising to my cheeks too. In their greatest moment, Pienaar's men were showing themselves to be no better than teams in the past that had showed the same lack of respect for their guests. I clearly recalled the occasion in 1992 when I had had to drive with Merle McKenna of South African Breweries to the Sandton Hotel to herd the team onto the bus so that they could attend the reception for the All Blacks.

All Black manager and long-time friend Colin Meads turned to me:

'Where the fucking hell are your Springboks?' he asked.

'I honestly don't know, Colin,' I replied.

'If we had won the Cup, we would have been here at seven o'clock,' an angry Meads said to me.

'But you didn't, Colin,' I responded and he came close to punching me.

It was still my hope that there might be a good excuse for the Springboks' delay. Perhaps the bus had broken down? But when they filed in as the food was being served, I learned that they had simply been detained at the hotel for talks. Later, it would become clear that these 'talks' were about a deal with Turnbull. The convenor of the meeting had been none other than Springbok captain François Pienaar who stood to gain a whopping $300,000 performance fee by selling his team in secret.

The speech-making began. I called over Edward Griffiths and asked him for the script he was supposed to have prepared for the occasion. He told me he had not had the time, and instead produced some hastily scribbled notes I was certainly not able to read. I shoved it back at him with a choice expletive. In the meantime, Sir Ewart Bell was at the microphone, lavishing praise on his RWC team who had made it all possible and thanking SARFU for 'assisting'.

260

Earlier in the evening, our Transvaal CEO, Johan Prinsloo, had handed me a watch, neatly gift-wrapped, with the request that I hand it to referee Derek Bevan. 'The referees asked me to have you present this to Derek as he has been voted the best referee of the tournament,' said Prinsloo. In hindsight, this was perhaps the dumbest thing I had ever done. Instead of asking the referees to do it themselves, I obliged and paid a terrible price for this mindless and utterly foolish gesture.

Now it was my turn to speak, and I was still without any script. Under normal circumstances, I would have had little trouble ad-libbing my way through it all in gracious fashion. But here I was, hot and bothered by the catastrophic events of the evening and Bell's presumptuous remarks. What followed would be referred to in numerous news reports as 'The Speech' for all the wrong reasons. While it hardly ranks among the great speeches of our time, I do think I managed to contain my emotions and to introduce a little humour.

This was the South African Press Association's reconstruction on the basis of an apparently poor recording:

'Before I speak, I would like one man to come up here, Rian Oberholzer. Ladies and gentlemen, of course for us South Africans, this is a great day. This is what we have been waiting for for so many years. We boasted in '87 that the real World Cup was not won by New Zealand, because we were not there. Then again in '91, we boasted again. We were not there. Then in '95 we proved if we were there we would have won.

'I want to say one thing. So much has been said about Rugby World Cup. If ever one man made all this possible, one man who worked round the clock, one who did everything for South Africa [background noise makes the tape almost inaudible but it sounds like "it was Rian Oberholzer"].

'I want to thank you all for your support: Brian [almost inaudible], Richie Guy, Colin, all of you. I want to say thank you. It was wonderful to play against the All Blacks. I believe today we saw the two best nations on this planet.

'Tuesday, in London, I read in a newspaper, a lady called Miss Battersby [almost inaudible]. She said, "If there is a better team on this planet I would like to see it". And she also said [that] if there are other planets with teams, they would lose to the All Blacks.

'So we are from Mars. From Mars, we would say thank you. The All Blacks are the greatest rugby nation with us – not next to us, with us – because next time they will beat us and next time we will beat them. But today was a perfect script, the perfect script written by whomever. South Africa played New Zealand. The Springboks against the All Blacks.

'And I would like to say thank you to those magnificent Springboks. You have done our country proud. You have brought this magnificent trophy home.

'I heard that my coach, Kitch Christie, today told his players he was not available henceforth. I want to tell you [that] you haven't spoken to me yet, pal. You will be available. So will you be, Morné du Plessis. You will be available. We built the perfect team around a perfect manager. The manager, Morné; Kitch and the team. [Applause, tape inaudible.]

'François, I want to talk to you, I want to talk to you [tape inaudible]... I heard that Murdoch's name was mentioned here. Sir Ewart Bell said we must never lose the rugby culture. Sir Ewart, we today assure you we would never lose it. Rugby Union is part of our culture; it will always remain part of our culture. And this is the way to show league that we are there.

'I thank you for your support and I thank you for coming here. I thank you for supporting this country. We went through very tremendous periods, tumultuous periods. There was a time when the Rugby World Cup could have been removed from South Africa.

'We fought for it, we kept it here, and we showed the world that we can host it, host it in a way that will be very difficult, may I say to Wales, to emulate. Thank you very much...' [Tape ends.]

The next morning, reports about this disastrous dinner vied for space with accounts of the game in the Sunday papers. The report of the late Barry Glasspool was typical of the approach. I found myself targeted and blamed for everything that had gone wrong. Most aggravating was the spin put on my words to make me fit the image of a bad winner and terrible host.

'Rugby officials have moved fast to defuse the furore over controversial Louis Luyt's victory speech, which led to the All Blacks walking out of Saturday night's official farewell World Cup dinner,' wrote Glasspool under the headline, 'Bid to defuse walk-out furore'. Instead of placing the blame where it belonged – the late arrival of the Springboks – Glasspool claimed that Colin Meads had led the exit of the All Blacks before the end of the banquet, 'angry at the tone of the remarks'. Griffiths gave further credence to this fabrication by conceding that there had indeed been 'some misplaced remarks'.

'The New Zealand team managers yesterday tried to defuse the situation after Luyt had told the guests of honour – which included the World Cup squads and rugby officials from South Africa, New Zealand, France and England – that the Springboks would have won the last two tournaments in 1987 and 1991 if they had played,' Glasspool wrote, relying on a partially inaudible recording which turned my 'could' into a 'would'.

At a loss to explain the early departure of semifinalists France and England, who were apparently equally fed up at having to wait around for the late arrival of the Springboks at a dinner that was of no interest to either, Glasspool simply stated that they 'would not comment on whether they too were reacting to Luyt's speech'. My awarding of the gold watch to Derek Bevan, as requested specifically by Prinsloo on behalf of the other referees, became another *faux pas par excel-*

lence. The watch, it was claimed, was intended for Morrison as he had refereed the final. Even the rude behaviour of a certain All Black loose forward, Mike Brewer, who had stumbled to the head table to insult me, was my fault. The only consolation I had from this altercation was to tell Brewer exactly where he could get off because he was such a bad loser.

At the bottom of all this lies the fact that farewell dinners of this kind are entirely inappropriate. To sit around waiting for more than an hour at the convenience of the victors simply serves to rub salt into the wounds of the defeated. And add to that the fact that New Zealanders have never been gracious losers, coming from a country where rugby arouses the same fervour as soccer does in South America – no wonder, then, that the 1995 All Blacks had to come up with food poisoning as an excuse for their loss. If that were indeed the case, I thought to myself, they – judging from the way these 'poisoned' players had performed for 100 minutes without any let-up – certainly succeeded in breeding a superhuman race in New Zealand. But this, apparently, was not a novel excuse – the All Blacks had, according to a senior Australian rugby official, used the same reasoning for losing the Bledisloe Cup against the Wallabies a few years previously. Needless to say, I was extremely disappointed with this attitude because, I had to admit – I said as much in speeches at numerous functions – that the All Blacks were the best coached, most complete and strongest side to have played in the 1995 World Cup tournament. I called them 'awesome' – the final had simply not been their day.

Former Springbok captain, Wynand Claassen, was one of the few in the media who refused to join this feeding frenzy and stuck to the facts. In his column, *A Touch of Claassen,* he wrote:

'There was one sour note about it all. The poor sportsmanship from the New Zealanders before and after that final. Let's face it, the All Blacks were beaten fairly and squarely despite amazing excuses to do with food poisoning two days before the final and insinuations regarding the bribing of the referee.

'The furore which erupted from the All Black camp can only be described as sour grapes. They are bad losers and it seemed they would do anything to take the glory of victory away from the Springboks.

'This was clearly evident at the after-match banquet when the All Blacks apparently walked out of the function because of some remarks made by Louis Luyt, SARFU's president, in his speech.

'People may say and believe what they like about Dr Luyt, but I believe his remarks that South Africa would have won both the 1987 and the 1991 World Cups was said with tongue in cheek.

'I have been to hundreds of similar post-match functions and listened to hundreds of after-match speeches. They are all held in good spirit and humour has always been part of the occasion. Win or lose, the formalities always include

There are lies,

damned lies and... honest lies.

Mark Twain (with apologies...)

Chapter 14

HONEST LIES

On 19 March 1998, State President Nelson Mandela stepped onto the witness stand noticeably irritated and short-tempered. 'I'm the president of this country,' he had told a battery of local and foreign journalists who awaited his arrival outside the Pretoria Supreme Court together with a rowdy crowd of supporters in ANC colours. 'I'm not only concerned with the problems of SARFU, I'm concerned with the problems of the country and the world.'

He had it right, in part. It was also our argument that the government had no business sticking its nose into SARFU's affairs by appointing a commission of inquiry and that Mandela – by giving his Minister of Sport, Steve Tshwete, *carte blanche* to pursue a political witch-hunt on the basis of wild accusations and rumour – had acted unconstitutionally. I had tried as best I could to avert this very confrontation in meetings with Tshwete, with whom I had cordial relations until he became a prisoner of the political forces that wished to see so-called white control of SARFU replaced at all costs. I also urged Mandela at a private meeting – initiated by him at his home – to use his influence to stop the madness. But he too found himself unable to go against the tide.

Now, watching the 79-year-old icon snapping at our counsel, Mike Maritz, while wiping his brow, gave me no comfort or pleasure. He had refused to take the seat offered to him, as if to preside over the proceedings while under cross-examination. Here he was trying to cover for his Minister of Sport, Tshwete, and his Director-General, Mthobi Tyamzashe. The latter had actually managed, in his own testimony before the court, to broaden the South African political vernacular by explaining his talk as 'honest lies'.

'I am getting irritated by Mr Maritz asking the questions in different forms,' Mandela bristled. 'He assumes the president of this country has told lies. I have told the court what I have said and I stand by that.' Instead of addressing Judge William de Villiers in the customary respectful 'My Lord', Mandela simply called him 'Judge'.

But the worst tongue-lashing was reserved for me. Referring to our questioning of the validity of his affidavit, which had prompted Justice De Villiers to sub-poena him, Mandela told the court: 'I would never have imagined that Louis would be so insensitive, so ungrateful to say when I gave my affidavit [that] I was lying. Dr Luyt is a pitiless dictator. No leader can stand up to him. You cannot talk of democracy.'

Here was the man who I respected and admired, dismissing me as a 'pitiless dictator' while the world sat in attendance. What had happened to the kindly statesman I had truly and honestly placed a notch above that other great South African, Jan Smuts? I was hurt, stung by the suddenness and severity of his remark. It sounded almost unreal, coming from the same man who had walked over to me during a tea break to discuss the case. Fearful that the press might be listening, his aide, Rory Steyn, suggested that we retire to a secluded corner.

'Louis, we can solve this in an hour,' President Mandela said.

'Mr President,' I replied, 'today you were a statesman but yesterday you were not.' Then, pressing forward at the prospect of setting this all aside, I added: 'Why don't you go back on the stand and tell the judge that we have decided to resolve it? I will give you what you wanted.'

Mandela frowned and remained in deep thought for what seemed to be at least a minute.

'Louis, I don't think it is politically the right time.'

There was a hint of sadness and even hopelessness in his voice.

So, here we were, facing off in court barely three years after that momentous day at Ellis Park when we hugged in victory celebration. How had it come to this?

The souring process was not one of my making – or Mandela's, for that matter. We were merely the two main actors in a political drama with many parts, people and plots. He had around him men who served him badly and I surely had my fair share of them too. But he had one distinct advantage over me. In the public eye, Mandela walked on water – and deservedly so – while I was constantly struggling to stay afloat in waters muddied by men in search of personal and political power and money.

During the first weekend of July 1995, after a victory parade through the streets of Johannesburg, the triumphant Springbok team and their wives slipped away to the sumptuous Palace of the Lost City at Sun City for two days – courtesy of SARFU and Sun International. I could not imagine in my wildest dreams that this would be the opportunity for captain François Pienaar to continue doing his bidding in secret on behalf of Ross Turnbull's so-called World Rugby

Corporation (WRC). Pienaar, I learned only later, went to Lost City armed with the WRC contracts he needed signed by the team to be able to collect his 'success fee' of $300,000.

When I first heard about the conspiracy, I likened Pienaar to Judas Iscariot, having sold out South African rugby for what might have amounted (considering inflation since biblical times) to 30 silver pieces, while enjoying the hospitality of the very SARFU he was circumventing in the process. Edward Griffiths was there as CEO of SARFU to mix in the merriment, but later claimed to have been entirely unaware of these momentous developments behind closed doors. The Pienaar affidavit in the Cape court, however, told a very different story.

All the Springboks signed, with the sole exception of Brendan Venter, who, in contrast to the other players, who merely wanted to know about the money, read the fine print and declined. He only signed later. For the sake of secrecy, Pienaar insisted, all the signed contracts had to be returned to him for safekeeping.

Apparently emboldened by these supposedly lucrative contracts, the 13 Transvaal Springboks returned to Johannesburg with demands for an increase in pay from the Transvaal Rugby Football Union, renamed first the Gauteng and afterwards the Golden Lions Rugby Union (GLRU). I got wind of this mutiny when Uli Schmidt, who handled players' affairs, called to tell me that the players refused to play until certain demands were met. Our coach, Ray Mordt, who succeeded Christie in the Transvaal, then conveyed the same message. This brilliant Springbok wing turned out to be an outstanding coach and a loyal friend. In 1994, he had chalked up a 57–23 victory over a strong Free State side in the Currie Cup final at Bloemfontein.

'These bastards don't want to play,' Mordt fumed. 'I've had it with them.'

'Go ahead without them,' I decided. 'Let's play with the youngsters.'

The story spread quickly. That same evening, a radio journalist conducted a telephonic interview with me. What about the Boks? He asked.

'You mean the ex-Boks,' I corrected him.

Mordt had sent Pienaar and his co-conspirators packing and tried as best he could to prepare an untested team for the upcoming clash against Eastern Province in Port Elizabeth. In the end, our young team acquitted themselves very well by managing to escape with a narrow defeat at Boet Erasmus stadium – better known as 'the graveyard' because the hopes of many a visiting team lie buried there.

Leading the 'revolt' was Hennie le Roux, who as sports director at Rand Afrikaans University, received a salary in the form of a bursary from the GLRU, and a free car. At my instruction, Le Roux was told that his services were no longer required and that he had to return the car. The debate continued in public, with François Pienaar complaining about the measly R3,000 he received from RAU each month. In reality, Pienaar and his colleagues all received an additional R14,000 per month plus a car from the Transvaal Trust. We also took care of their medical expenses. It was all there for everyone to see, even though our general manager, Johan Prinsloo – mindful of the growing uneasiness in the International Rugby Board over professionalism – refrained from calling it 'salaries'. On top of this, each of the Transvaal Springboks had received R119,000 – after tax – for their part in the World Cup victory, and Pienaar and several others were raking in appearance money at celebrity events. In fact, in Pienaar's case, this was true of charity events, too, where he insisted on his fee.

It was with no small measure of surprise, then, that I read a statement in the press by the late Professor Johan Gouws claiming that Le Roux worked for Rand Afrikaans University and could therefore only be dismissed by that institution. Was it ignorance on his part or did he simply choose to ignore the fact that the bursary that kept Le Roux at RAU was paid in full by the Golden Lions Rugby Union? It seemed to be my bad fortune to once again find myself at loggerheads with a prominent member of the Broederbond, the 'true' Afrikaners with whom the English-language press had tried to associate me on many an occasion.

Early one Saturday morning, Griffiths appeared at my house in Saxonwold. He had an urgent matter to discuss, he said.

'What if the players are willing to apologise?' he asked. 'Would you be willing to take them back?'

'Edward,' I said, 'you are out of your domain. You work for SARFU, not for Transvaal. In any event, I am not willing to negotiate with a sword over my head. As far as I am concerned, Pienaar and the whole World Cup lot can go to hell.'

Edward Griffiths came back again and told me that the players had decided to drop their demands and wished to settle. This was no surprise as it was an open secret that dissension was growing among the players once they realised that they might lose the very income they denied receiving. I accepted a settlement on one condition. They should apologise in public for their actions and return to the *status quo* with the promise of review. In my view, the Transvaal Springboks had much to apologise for, not least of which was the poor example set for younger players.

We thus reinstated the leaders of the mutiny and all the others returned. But the atmosphere had already been sullied. Never would we experience the good old days again when we got together as one large family during pre-game bashes at my house, Solitaire, with everyone honestly concerned about the other's family and well-being. A once cohesive team had become a group of individuals jealously guarding their own financial interests. It was 'management against workers', and even the workers were fighting among themselves for the biggest slice of the pie. Rugby had finally become a cut-throat profession.

Rumours were flying about regarding Turnbull's and Kerry Packer's plans to pre-empt counterparts in Australia and New Zealand. We all knew Turnbull had neither the money nor the reach to put this together. Packer, we kept telling our-selves, was not about to get involved. In the meantime, Sam Chisholm claimed to have received a 'warm letter' from Pienaar congratulating him on the Sanzar deal.

Towards the middle of July, I received a call from Frikkie Erasmus, a Cape Town attorney who represented the interests of Chester Williams, the celebrated Springbok wing from Western Province. Erasmus requested an urgent meeting and flew in the same day to meet me at my Ellis Park office.

'I'm afraid your CEO, Griffiths, is deceiving you. He is fully aware of these developments and is not informing you,' Erasmus said as he pulled a document from his briefcase. The document looked lile a patchwork quilt. It was the contract Williams had signed and then requested back on the advice of Erasmus. Pienaar, instead of handing it back, tore it into small pieces. With the help of his staff, Erasmus had painstakingly reconstructed the document. Finally, we had the smoking gun. Equally alarming was Erasmus' revelation that he had tried to meet with Griffiths about this but had been given the cold shoulder.

Today I know that Griffiths, despite his protestations to the contrary, was privy to the plot when he joined the team at Lost City after the World Cup. While professing to me that he would never have allowed an Australian to hijack South African rugby, he blurted out how Brendan Venter – the one player who had demurred – had paced up and down the lobby of the Palace complaining that the Boks were signing away their future. As CEO of SARFU, his first duty was to report this incident back to me, which he had not.

By then, it had already become abundantly clear that Griffiths' pecuniary prowess fell way short of his ability as a wordsmith and that he was prone to act impulsively without informing me or the board. It was only after the event that I would learn that Griffiths had undertaken to pay Morné du Plessis a whopping R70,000 a month for managing the Springboks during the World Cup. On another occasion, he had committed SARFU to R15,000 in 'pay-off' money to have Peter Hendriks drop his appeal against his suspension after that fateful Port Elizabeth test against Canada.

Now several other things had fallen into place. First, there was Ray Mordt, who had pulled me aside in the presidential suite with a word of caution during the World Cup.

'Doc,' he said, 'I've been offered a contract by François Pienaar. Big bucks. I did not accept, but I think you should know about it.'

I dismissed the thought at the time. Why on earth would Pienaar be doing this? Then there was Pienaar's insistence, when we settled our differences, that the players' contract with the GLRU be limited to six months and then be reviewed. Instead of picking up on this, I simply accepted it as part of a good compromise. Now it turned out to have been a crafty play in preparation for the time when the Turnbull-Packer WRC plan ripened.

Pienaar had even gone so far as to sign a document in which he stated he had not signed or done nothing to harm South African rugby. Considering the firestorm that followed his secret rendezvous with the Packer plotters, this statement was disingenuous at best – as were many other pronouncements and explanations that followed.

Instead of a routine meeting, the gathering of the Sanzar partners in Sydney on Friday, 28 July 1995, turned into a damage-control exercise. The morning newspapers had reported that the World Rugby Corporation had already signed up most of the Australian and New Zealand rugby stars playing in the following day's Bledisloe Cup game – as well as the Springboks.

I found myself around the table at the Australian Rugby Union's offices with, among others, Leo Williams, Richie Guy, Ian Ferrier, and David Moffett – all looking quite grim. Ian Frykberg had the floor. Clearly animated – and forgetting his own bluster that he 'knew' Packer and company and that they would never contract with rugby union – Frykberg contended that 'the nasty stuff had hit the fan'. He was now 'fucking concerned' about this apparent coup by Turnbull and company.

Next we found ourselves at Chisholm's home in Sydney, where the diminutive man was throwing a fit. It was imperative that we honour the contract and sign up the players as we promised – or there was no deal, he warned. I looked around the room at the others who sat in silence while Rupert Murdoch's man jumped all over them. It was time to intervene and put Chisholm in his place. The contract I had signed simply stated that 'we shall use our best endeavours' to sign up the players.

'Listen,' I said in a gruff tone, living up as best I could to my ill-deserved reputation as a bully, 'you will stop talking to us as if we are a bunch of schoolchildren. You'd better hold your horses. If you want to take legal action, get your little lawyer standing behind you to send us a letter.'

Napoleon, it seemed, had met his match in Sydney and was now on the retreat. Chisholm's tone changed immediately.

'Louis, you've got to get the Springboks signed. After all, they're the world champions,' he pleaded.

'Sam,' I said, 'you'll get your players. Even if we lose some, we have a replacement for everyone that may be even better.'

That very same evening I made a call to South Africa and arranged for the Transvaal Springboks to meet me at my home on the Sunday morning of my return from Australia. Until my departure after the game on Saturday and during the long flight back to Johannesburg, I kept replaying in my mind the possible scenarios. While there was no doubt in my mind that I would be able to bring the Springboks back into SARFU and Sanzar, I also realised it would exact a heavy toll.

It was not the money that bothered me. I have, over the years, been the most generous administrator in the country and perhaps even the world. Players, in my view, need a decent income as much as anyone else. But in this instance I knew that no amount of money would ever succeed in healing the rift that had developed.

I felt that François Pienaar, whom I had pulled out of relative obscurity to take over the captaincy of Transvaal, had betrayed both rugby and me. Later, Harry Viljoen – Pienaar's co-conspirator – would claim to have been the one who 'discovered' Pienaar. Instead of taking me into his confidence after Turnbull had approached him, Pienaar had chosen to concentrate on his personal gain. This was clearly a relationship of trust that could never be restored. Most of the others, I believed, with the exception of Hennie le Roux, who even the tolerant Springbok coach Nick Mallet described as having an 'insidious' presence in the team, had obviously been victims of their own naiveté. They refused to recognise, as did Venter, and eventually Williams, that money conditioned on a sale is not cash in the bank.

On Sunday, 30 July, I stepped into my study at Solitaire where François Pienaar, Kitch Christie, Rian Oberholzer and Edward Griffiths were waiting. I barely had time to take a shower and change clothes after the long flight from Australia. I was tired out, but fired up. Next door, in another room, 10 other Transvaal Springboks were waiting. Kobus Wiese and Chris Rossouw had been unable to attend.

Finally, slightly more relaxed after venting my anger at the man who had betrayed me, I said: 'Francois, I'll match Packer.'

On this occasion, Kitch Christie indicated that he had had no advance knowledge of all the goings-on between Pienaar and the other players. Why, he asked, had we not also made him an offer? Only afterwards would I learn from reliable sources that Christie had indeed been part of the plot. Even though this rather unassuming man, whom I had trusted so implicitly, denied until his dying day that he had anything to do with the Packer scheme, the overwhelming evidence indicated otherwise.

I repeated my offer to the group waiting in the living room. From there they would take my offer to the rest of the Springbok squad, scattered across the rest of the country. Fanie Cilliers, as ever a true friend, was there to advise the players on their contractual rights – except, of course, for Pienaar, whom he advised to obtain the services of another counsel as he could face other problems regarding his Packer commitments. As I stepped out to allow the players to talk among themselves, Griffiths followed me. He became animated.

'We're paying too much,' he insisted.

For some reason, he still seemed to believe that we had the luxury of signing up players at bargain-basement prices. Or he did not understand the Packer agreement. Even though I knew that the WRC contracts weren't worth the paper they had been written on, we did not have the time to allow the players to find this out for themselves. It could take months and, in the meantime, Sanzar remained in limbo. Whatever happened here today, I knew, would determine the future of rugby not only in South Africa but also in the rest of the southern hemisphere. New Zealand and Australia were waiting. Only later did I learn that Chisholm had called Pienaar shortly after our Sydney encounter, and had made the same offer, promising to honour the $300,000 'success fee' offered to Pienaar personally by the WRC if he delivered his team.

This interference in South African rugby irked me as much as Packer and Turnbull's attempt to hijack our national sport for their own gain. Later I would learn that Ian Frykberg had also dabbled into deals of his own making without our permission or approval.

That same evening I received a fax from Griffiths – yes, he started the faxing - that accused me of taking over 'his' executive responsibilities at SARFU. He seemed blissfully unaware of the fact that, as chairman of the executive committee, as well as the finance committee, I had the authority to overrule and override him when needed. And, in this instance – as in many others, such action was definitely needed. In fact, Griffiths had no authority whatsoever.

On this Sunday in late July I found Griffiths' sudden concern about the amount of money offered to the players, whose cause he had so ardently promoted during our Transvaal stand-off, rather strange indeed. Finally, now thoroughly tired of his constant whining when he raised the issue yet again during lunch at Ellis Park Stadium's Touchdown restaurant just a few days later, I told him: 'Edward, do you really think that the world's top rugby players will play for peanuts? Get real.'

Griffiths then dropped the subject only to raise it one more time in his personal memoirs a few years later. I am always extremely wary of people who, having never conducted any meaningful business before, suddenly proclaim to be some sort of financial genius. Granted, we did indeed buy these players at a premium – at a price that was definitely too high (almost three quarters of our first year's earnings from the News Corporation contract went directly into their salaries) – but we had no alternative. By hanging tough, we would have caused interminable disruptions in rugby and thus jeopardised our contract with News Corporation.

There was, however, a remarkable improvement in the balance sheets of the Sanzar partners as News Corporation's payments to us in US dollars ballooned with the drastic devaluation of our currencies. Even though the NZRFU and ARU, with their misplaced belief in the strength of their own currencies, initially complained about this arrangement, they soon came to praise my 'foresight' as the Australian and New Zealand dollar suffered the same fate as the rand.

Understandably, not everyone was enamoured with our contract, however. After the announcement of the News Corporation deal on the eve of the World Cup final, I had received a call at home from Koos Bekker of M-Net. This local network had approached me when rumours first surfaced about negotiations with overseas entities, and begged me to keep their interests in mind. I did so by specifically mentioning M-Net in the contract with Chisholm as the preferred buyer of South African rights from News Corporation. Now Bekker accused me of having acted in bad faith because, according to him, I had 'promised' the primary rights to M-Net's Supersport director, Russell McMillan. His cable network would not sign up with News Corporation, Bekker told me, because Murdoch was likely to leave it out in the cold after a year once he had had time to establish his own satellite feed to South Africa.

'Then don't sign for a year,' I suggested. 'Make it a long-term contract.'

I was, of course, blissfully unaware of the purported talks at this time between Bekker's big (now former) M-Net shareholder Johan Rupert and Ross Turnbull, aimed at circumventing SARFU through a Packer-backed WRC contract. Predictably, Turnbull received the cold shoulder as soon as it became apparent that M-Net might be barking up the wrong – empty – tree.

In February 1996, M-Net signed a five-year contract with News Corporation, buying the South African rights for the Sanzar games – in other words, they had done exactly what I had suggested. But they did so only after almost dragging me into court. They did, however, drop their frivolous lawsuit and eventually paid all the costs. My previously cordial relationship with M-Net thus suffered in the process. I suspect that the acid remarks in an article in the *Mail & Guardian* by one of its commentators, a former English Post Office employee, Andy Capistagno, about me having 'given away' the rights to News Corporation for 'a mere 50 million dollars' a year, was part of a planned campaign – or, at best, not written with the basic financial skill and business knowledge necessary for such an analysis. He also claimed that M-Net would have paid much more than News Corporation. Afterwards, however, the powers at M-Net would confess to me that they could only have matched an offer for the South African rights with payment in rands.

I thus received a call from the Reserve Bank for full particulars about the News Corporation agreement and I went to see them, rather upset at their involvement because we were bringing money into the country, not taking it out. I asked Bruce Brand of the Reserve Bank straight out whether M-Net had had anything to do with this query from his office, but he vehemently denied their involvement. I, however, made the same accusation in my reply to M-Net's court application and, in reply, M-Net admitted that they had indeed alerted the Reserve Bank. Today, I am very pleased to report that my relationship with M-Net has been happily restored.

274

Back in 1992, M-Net – in collaboration with the SABC – had tried to purchase the upcoming New Zealand and Australian tests in South Africa for a mere R800,000, even though we had been offered three times that by the French for the single test against the All Blacks. Doc Craven and Fritz Eloff, finding themselves under severe pressure from the South African public who did not want to miss these games, were ready to cave in. I insisted that we stand strong. In a last-minute make-or-break session between Gerrie de Villiers of M-Net and Piet Theron of SABC, I managed to strike a deal at 3.30 in the morning, requiring the two networks to cough up R1.6 million – twice the amount they originally offered.

On Friday morning, August 4, the Springboks gathered at the Midrand Protea Hotel, halfway between Pretoria and Johannesburg, to make their final decision. While they were meeting, my daughter Corlia was waiting in an adjacent room with contracts should they decide to accept our offer. The vast majority voted in favour of signing up with SARFU and News Corporation instead of Turnbull's WRC. Pienaar, Hennie le Roux and James Small, who had initially raised their hands in opposition, joined the rest of the gang and signed a three-year contract with SARFU.

On hearing this, the Australian and New Zealand players had unkind and uncouth words for their South African brethren – before they, too, followed suit. A major crisis had thus been averted and the show could go on. But Pienaar's New Zealand and Australian counterparts would never trust him again.

Pienaar later recounted how Johan Rupert had called him in the midst of it all. The younger Rupert seemed to have inherited his father's penchant for trying to obstruct anything or any cause that had the name Luyt attached to it. In fact, in 1996, Rupert, in a message conveyed by Edward Griffiths, invited André Markgraaff to a game of golf to discuss ways in which to replace me as president of the South African Rugby Football Union with Morné du Plessis. This invitation was never repeated.

While I had little trouble in having the final agreement passed and endorsed by SARFU's executive committee at our annual general meeting in November 1995, the preceding process had been painful and complicated. To facilitate South African rugby's bold entry into the brave new world of professionalism, we needed to drastically reduce the number of SARFU member unions from its all-time high of 23. While quite substantial, the income from News Corporation was hardly sufficient to support so many provincial unions. After tough and, at times, trying talks we ended up with 14 unions.

The four major provinces – Transvaal, Natal, Northern Transvaal and Western Province – were each allocated R4.14 million rand to pay their players, while

Eastern Province and Free State received R3 million each from SARFU. Griqualand West, Border and Western Transvaal were paid almost R2.5 million each and the other provincial teams – Boland, South Western Districts, Eastern Transvaal, South Eastern Transvaal and Northern Free State – each R2.24 million. In return, member unions were required to pay SARFU R360,000 for each member of the World Cup team in their ranks. This meant that Transvaal, with 13 players in the national team, actually paid more than it received from SARFU. Future Springboks would receive a lump sum per test match, set at a figure substantial enough to ensure that this fee, together with their provincial pay, added up to roughly the amount paid to the World Cup squad.

Soon after the conclusion of these contracts, Pienaar turned up at my office. He was there to collect the $300,000 'Packer money', which Chisholm had apparently promised to pay. Strange, I thought, that he should insist on being paid by us for his failure to live up to his undertaking with WRC. Here was the man who resisted signing up with SARFU and News Corporation to the very end – until he was over-ruled by a majority of his own players – now demanding to be rewarded by the very people he had fought against.

'François,' I said, 'there is no Packer money. How can you expect SARFU to pay you this?'

He looked in shock from me to Griffiths, who was present on this occasion.

'Dr Luyt is right,' Griffiths said, 'you can hardly expect SARFU to pay out this amount to you now.'

'But Chisholm promised to make it good to me,' Pienaar insisted.

'I'll tell you what I'll do,' I said. 'I'll talk to Chisholm and ask him to stick to his end of the bargain if what you've told me is true.'

As it turned out, Chisholm had given Pienaar the undertaking and had no choice, so he transferred the $300,000 to SARFU and I made out a cheque in the equivalent amount in rand. I also insisted that Chisholm send an additional $7 million to compensate for the escalation in players' fees.

Eventually, we received only $5 million, which included the $300,000 for Pienaar. Afterwards, News Corporation requested an IOU from SARFU for this amount as the other two nations had borrowed money for the same purpose and declared themselves willing to pay it back. Good try, I said to Bruce McWilliam, the News Corporation lawyer, but this is not the way things work in this part of the world. He thus dropped the topic.

Less willing to face reality was Ross Turnbull. On Saturday, August 5, he went before Justice Van Reenen at the Cape Supreme Court charging that SARFU and I had 'brought enormous pressure to bear' on the Springboks to negate their undertaking with the WRC. Van Reenen acceded to Turnbull's request and granted an injunction forbidding SARFU from having further contact with any players in South Africa already committed to the WRC. Coincidentally, it was in this same court, in an admission under oath, that Pienaar admitted that he and the rest of the team – as well as Griffiths – had met after the World Cup final to discuss the WRC offer, keeping their guests at the farewell dinner waiting in the much-publicised debacle that followed.

Turnbull then went scurrying around the country to sign up provincial players who had apparently felt betrayed by being left out of SARFU'S millionaires' club. In fact, so deep was the resentment among some of the players that they changed the slogan, 'One team, One country', which had served us so well during the World Cup, to a cynical 'One team, One million'. After signing up top provincial players in Eastern and Western Province, Northern Transvaal and the Free State, Turnbull boasted that he had successfully isolated the Springboks.

It took the judge, Justice Van Reenen, exactly a week to come to a decision. The injunction against SARFU was lifted and the application struck from the roll. True to form, 'Mad Dog' Turnbull, as he was known Down Under, refused to concede defeat. The week's moratorium, he claimed, enabled WRC to broaden its base among the provincial players. Later we would learn that Ross Turnbull still had high hopes of recruiting Johan Rupert to his side. But that pillar soon crumbled too.

Turnbull went on the nationally televised show, Talking Sport, to share his bullish feelings about the future of the WRC. He dismissed the court decision as a stand-off and waxed on about the many provincial players who had signed up with the WRC. I decided the time had come to confront this foreign intruder with the facts and to reveal his true motives. I picked up the phone and called in. Not surprisingly, I was immediately put through to the studio – this was to be the kind of confrontation that makes for good television ratings. I then challenged Turnbull to come clean about what the judge had really said in his ruling.

'I think we're going to be wasting each other's time if we are going to talk about courts,' Turnbull said, defensively. 'What you and I should be doing together is having lunch tomorrow and trying to sort this out, so don't go on with what happened in the court.'

'Let me be frank, Ross,' I said. 'I don't want ever to sit down with you.'

'Well, look, there has to come a time, Louis, when we have got to sit down and talk,' he shot back.

'Not with you,' I repeated.

At this point, the moderator intervened to give me a chance to speak my mind. It was time for me to become formal and send Turnbull a clear message.

'The fact of the matter is, Mr Turnbull, we do not need you in our Currie Cup; we do not need you in South Africa. Let me tell you right now that while Murdoch bought television rights, you bought the souls of the players – the bodies and souls of the players. You can tell them what to do, what they cannot do, when they can speak and when they cannot speak, what they have to wear, what they have to do, that's what you have bought.'

I never saw or talked to Turnbull again after that episode, although he would later claim in a conversation with a local sports reporter that he saw me and stared me down 'like you do with any bully'. 'And you can write it,' he told the reporter who then took this lie into print without confirming Ross Turnbull's claim with me.

That, however, turned out to be the last salvo. Within a matter of weeks, the WRC became history.

Later, Pienaar would tell people that I complained that I saw his face on every cheque I signed for a player. I cannot remember ever having made this remark to Kitch Christie, who was involved in a business venture and close friends with Pienaar. While I have never begrudged the players their fair share of the millions we had, after all, earmarked for them, I certainly had trouble coming to terms with the way in which Pienaar had set about selling out his team-mates and South African rugby to a mercenary group for self-gain.

South African rugby took the backseat in the plans of Harry Viljoen, François Pienaar and Hennie le Roux. In terms of the WRC contract offered by Kerry Packer and Ross Turnbull, they would not play as South Africans or Springboks but in 'conference teams' with other nationalities all over the world. Yet, Pienaar continued to insist that he had done it all for the benefit of South African rugby. Pienaar had been as much a mercenary as his counterparts in New Zealand and Australia who opted to sell out their team-mates and countries to an amorphous international league envisaged in the Turnbull scheme. This stands out in the Agreement and cannot be argued. The Springbok, Silver Fern and Wallaby were not considered at all.

But not every problem related to player demands. Within Sanzar, there were several divisive issues and News Corporation added a few of its own. Money always has that effect, it seems, especially on those who for the first time find themselves on the verge of unexpected new wealth. Australia, which made do with a measly $140,000 in the past, did not like the idea of receiving a smaller share of the millions than its two partners – and least of all the fact that South Africa, as the major rugby market, stood at the top of food chain. As a result, they 'ganged up' with neighbouring New Zealand and enlisted Chisholm's support in their effort to change the original agreement to an equal three-way split. I would have none of this, I told Chisholm. If necessary, we would go to arbitration. Eventually, this proved unnecessary as Australia became more reasonable and accepted a 28 per cent share while New Zealand settled for 34 per cent against our 38 per cent.

Even though the Australians and New Zealanders formed this temporary alliance in an effort to squeeze us – the third party – out of our major share of the contract, they were also at each other's throats. After one Sanzar meeting in Sydney over which I presided, I felt obliged to caution the CEO of the Australian Rugby Union, John O'Neill, to stop calling Richie Guy of New Zealand a 'block-head'. This, I told him, would not be tolerated in meetings under my chairman-ship. He apologised but I advised him to direct his apology where it was most needed – to Guy, whom he had offended.

On a pleasant spring day, Rian and I stepped out of a cab in London and made our way to Chisholm's headquarters. It was evident that Chisholm was not well and he sneezed and sniffled through another problem-solving session with us. Also in attendance was Ian Frykberg. At one stage, Chisholm asked Oberholzer and Frykberg to leave so we could speak alone. As the door closed behind them, he immediately got to the point.

'Communication Services International has just fired Fryburg,' he said. 'They have not treated him well. If we cancel them out, we can pay Frykberg 5 per cent in commission instead of their standard 10 per cent. That means 5 per cent more to you guys in South Africa, Australia and New Zealand.'

'No,' I said. 'This I will not do. CSI has been very good to us – long before you came onto the scene.'

Some time later, Michael Watt, the chairman of CSI, asked me straight out about rumours that we were about to drop his company, and I related the gist of my conversation with Chisholm in London. He seemed to appreciate my loyalty.

'Frykberg,' he noted, 'came out of it quite well. We paid him US$3 million in severance pay when he left.'

Everyone has a price. The once noble amateur sport of rugby had turned into a melee of millionaires – on and off the field. But other members of the Inter-national Rugby Board (IRB) were obviously not enamoured at seeing South Africa, Australia and New Zealand raking in the Murdoch millions with them as mere bystanders. Suddenly, professionalism had become a burning issue in the world body and I provided a convenient lightning rod for their frustrations.

At the 1994 Vancouver meeting of the IRB, I had – in my absence – been attacked for having had the temerity to state that the World Cup of 1995 could mark the end of 'shamateurism'. There had even been talk of disciplinary measures. On that occasion, both Fritz Eloff and Johan Claassen had sat in silence, while I was berated for suggesting that the great pursuit of rugby might fall prey to Mammon, as did most other sports.

In Paris on 27 August 1995, at the first IRB meeting since the signing of the News Corporation contract, the late Vernon Pugh of Wales – who had been appointed chairman of a committee to investigate professionalism in rugby and who had wanted to suspend me during the IRB meeting in Vancouver in 1994 for breeching the 'Amateur Code' – announced that Rob Fisher of New Zealand, who later became his deputy, would address the issue of professional rugby. Fisher flipped the ball over to me.

'I don't think I'm the right person to do so,' he explained. 'Dr Luyt should take the floor instead.'

A heavy cloud hung over the room and everyone's eyes turned to me. Perhaps they were hoping that I would – as they did – tiptoe around the issue and save everyone embarrassment. Instead I decided to tackle the 'Pro' word head-on. The time had come, I felt, to talk honestly and openly about professionalism instead of hiding behind euphemisms and obscurantisms.

'First of all, Mr Chairman, I am here today to declare SARFU and South African rugby as professionals to your organisation,' I said. 'But now, if I have the chairman's permission, I would like to go around the table and ask each and everyone whether they have ever paid their players in one way or another. Let's start with England...'

You could hear a pin drop in the ornate conference room. Several board members shuffled in their chairs and rearranged the papers in front of them.

The first answer. Yes, England did, in fact, pay its players. But, it was through a trust fund...

'Does it matter?' I asked. 'The end result is the same.'

Next, Scotland in the affirmative. One after another, everyone admitted to some form of payment – except Argentina, where a rare breed of players was still willing to be bruised and battered for the sheer joy of it. In fact, I was actually surprised at the amounts paid by some of the nations. It had always been my impression, judging from the constant criticism heaped upon us, that South Africa led the field. But we did not.

When Syd Millar of Ireland took his turn, he remarked: 'Yes, Louis, we do pay, but only a few thousand pounds a year. Nothing like the big money that some others are throwing around.'

'Syd, with all due respect,' I responded, 'there is no such thing as being "a little bit pregnant".'

The young lady who provided the simultaneous translation into French sniggered, but Millar and the others were not amused. I had cleared the air, but muddied the waters. No one likes to be shown up as a hypocrite and, in a single session, I had succeeded in sullying every single 'shamateur' who had managed to hide behind the door while taking cheap shots at SARFU and me.

The Paris parley on professionalism was still fresh in everyone's memory when I faced the Rugby World Cup directors in Tokyo to hand over our final report on the 1995 event. While they had no problem in accepting their share of the £28 million in profits, they refused to hear or read about questionable practices on the part of their appointed travel and ticket agents. In fact, they had their own report ready for adoption, one that was highly critical of SARFU and me, personally. I found it particularly strange that Nic Labuschagne, who represented South Africa on the RWCL, went along with this rather personal attack, but even more painful was RWCL chairman Leo Williams' endorsement of the indictment – although, it must be said, he did seem to change his mind after his retirement when he praised me for having taken world rugby to new heights in 1995. I still have the highest regard for this man, who saved the Rugby World Cup when he intervened to end the impasse reached before the Paris meeting in 1994.

I, however, hardly had to go abroad in search of enemies and enmity. There were plenty to go around right here on my own doorstep. Just about everything that could be remotely described as a negative in South African rugby was laid at my doorstep.

While I have never feared open confrontation, I found myself in a situation in which the enemy moved almost invisibly within my own ranks. In the South African [Anglo-Boer] War, we called them *hensoppers* or 'hands-uppers' – the ones who surrendered. These were Afrikaners who talked bravely but threw their hands in the air and surrendered as soon as the shooting started. In the drama that unfolded – and led to my resignation from the presidency of SARFU – I encountered not one or a few, but a host of *hensoppers*.

Reams have been written about the break-up of the triumphant triumvirate consisting of Springbok coach Kitch Christie, manager Morné du Plessis and captain François Pienaar. Most accounts picture me as the mastermind behind a so-called midnight massacre of the very team I had so carefully assembled to lead us into the World Cup. Oddly, those who accused me of having disbanded this winning combination were mostly the same people who had earlier crucified me for axeing former manager Engelbrecht and coach McIntosh to make room for them in the first place. They simply refused to accept the fact that coaches and captains do not have lifetime tenure.

It came as no surprise, then, when Edward Griffiths, who I had fired as SARFU's CEO in January 1996 with the full support of the executive, joined the ranks of those who tried to lay the blame for the break-up of the 'dream team' squarely on my shoulders. Mustering all his writing skills and media contacts, Griffiths went about seeking revenge by portraying me as a ruthless megalomaniac bent on getting rid of these men after they had served their purpose. At the same time, however, he remained conspicuously silent about his knowledge of the 'Big Sell-out' orchestrated by Pienaar.

While taking full responsibility for the departure of Edward Griffiths, I can hardly be fingered as the sole reason for the departure of Christie, Du Plessis and Pienaar. I did not concede to Kitch Christie's wish to be brought back to coach both Transvaal and the Springboks, and when the lymphatic cancer, which Kitch fought for many years, reared its ugly head yet again, I advised him that it might be better for him to retire. Christie went ahead, though, to fulfil his lifetime dream and coached Northern Transvaal in the Super-12 competition, albeit with disastrous effect. This potent union drew one game and lost the remaining seven, giving Kitch Christie the worst coaching record the union had ever seen. So, while sympathising with Christie's plight to keep going despite his debilitating illness, it had become evident that he was no longer able to keep up with the rigours of the job.

Morné du Plessis, on the other hand, had made his own decision. Instead of facing a let-down after the great excitement of the World Cup, he apparently decided to move on. But if he had not made this decision on his own, I would probably have asked him to resign. Du Plessis, in my opinion, had become more interested in his own future than that of the players or the South African Rugby Football Union.

But it was François Pienaar's exit that proved the most controversial and widely publicised of the three. André Markgraaff, whom I had brought in from Griqualand West to take Christie's job as Springbok coach, felt that, in his scheme of things, Pienaar did not feature as captain. Instead, he settled on Gary Teichmann for the position of eighth man and captain. I respected Markgraaff's judgment. In fact, I consider André Markgraaff the coaching peer of both Kitch Christie and Nick Mallett. I had never overruled selectors or coaches and was not about to start doing so. In any event, my relations with and respect for François Pienaar were such that I had no desire to put up a fight for his sake. But I did warn Markgraaff and his co-selectors, Ray Mordt and Francois Davids, to buy all the lead they could lay their hands on to protect themselves from the 'radio-active fall-out' that would follow the atomic explosion with the axeing of Pienaar. Ray Mordt also warned Markgraaff to advise Pienaar before he axed him but Markgraaff decided to do it his own way.

Although I anticipated a huge public outcry, the uproar that followed took me by surprise. Even President Mandela's voice was among those who clamoured for Pienaar's reinstatement. While I respected Mandela's qualities as a statesman, I felt that Markgraaff was better suited to decide questions relating to rugby. Ignoring the facts, both Pienaar and Griffiths – who helped write Pienaar's memoirs – would insist that I was the one who had instructed Markgraaff to drop Pienaar. Yet, in an affidavit under oath, Markgraaff told Michael Katz that I had no part in Pienaar's axeing or, for that matter, the selection of teams in any way whatsoever.

When I finally acceded to pressures within SARFU to terminate Griffiths' services, I hoped that he would find a way to leave without making a fuss. Revisiting the many instances in which he came up short in his job as CEO of

SARFU would, I felt, simply be grist for the media mill and serve neither Griffiths nor us. It had become obvious that his lack of managerial and business skills – coupled with a penchant to ignore authority – could no longer be tolerated. Even though it was I who had originally appointed him, I had to concede that I had made a major mistake in thinking that this media liaison man could develop into a sound manager. After the World Cup, he told me that Morné du Plessis should go and that he was already preparing the press for such an event. In fact, he even insisted that Du Plessis had told him of his unavailability and, when I confronted him with a written letter from Du Plessis where he made himself available for re-election as manager, he claimed he had only learned of Du Plessis' availability the previous day. Markgraaff told me later, however, that he had been seated next to Griffiths on the flight to Durban and that Griffiths had also told him that Morné du Plessis would not be available. When confronted with Du Plessis' letter of a month earlier, he thus decided to just lie. But Markgraaff told him straight to his face that this would cost him his job if he carried on in that way.

At an executive committee meeting at my Ballito residence, Griffiths also assured the executive that he had informed Gysie Pienaar, assistant to Christie, that Christie no longer wanted him because – to use Christie's own words – 'he did not need an assistant who is only good to kick back balls for the place kickers'. This, it seems, was never done – or Gysie Pienaar conveniently forgot about it – because, to this day, Gysie still blames me for his axeing.

After a general meeting of SARFU, I sent Griffiths written instructions on how he was to handle his job in future. For once, he had a clear job description. He called my office and insisted that my assistant, Susan Kruger, call me out of a meeting so he could speak to me. She refused, and he became abusive and left a rude message. When she relayed the episode to me, I had little choice and dictated a letter of dismissal. I instructed Susan to send it to him, but to forewarn him that a message might be forthcoming. This fax became the topic of heated discussions and much furore in the press in the ensuing weeks.

'So, what am I going to do?' he asked when we eventually spoke and I told him his services would no longer be needed.

'Do what you do best,' I told him, offering him a six-month severance. 'Go write. Write articles and books.'

He did. But what he wrote was hardly what I had had in mind. Much of it was about me. Unflattering stuff. He appeared on television and radio to launch a vendetta against both SARFU and me. I, however, kept silent. Let him have his day, I decided. The media would soon be bored with the story and move onto other more interesting news. I left it to Hentie Serfontein and other members of the SARFU executive to do the talking.

A year after Griffiths was sacked, I finally decided to break the silence. He had come up with the far-fetched accusation that I had tried to have him deported. I was in Sydney on Sanzar business when Mark Keohane of *SA Sports Illustrated* confronted me with this latest fabrication.

When I appointed Griffiths as CEO of SARFU, I told Keohane (who would in 2003 play a key role in the Geo Cronjé/Rudolf Straeuli fiasco), he informed me he did not have a work permit – although, oddly enough, on his job application his nationality was indicated as South African. When asked how he could have worked as a journalist at the *Sunday Times* without such a permit, Griffiths told me that no one had picked it up before and that he did not think it would be a problem. I insisted, however, that he apply for a work permit as it would be a source of great embarrassment for SARFU should this become public knowledge.

Later that same year, when illegal immigration became a focal point in the South African media, I again asked Griffiths whether he had obtained the necessary work permit. He told me he had not and I informed him that both he and I were at risk. On 5 January 1996, I decided to change his contract with SARFU to that of consultant. Even though he kept his CEO title, this new status would allow him to perform his task without running foul of the law. In the meantime, I wrote letters to the Home Affairs Minister Mangosuthu Buthulezi and left several messages.

'After all this,' I told Keohane, 'Griffiths is now accusing me in public of trying to have him deported. Perhaps the time has come to provide you with a list of reasons why he was asked to leave SARFU.'

A document listing 21 reasons, ranging from petulant encounters to downright irresponsible behaviour, was sent from my office. While there might well have been a funny side to Griffiths lashing out at an SAA pilot for refusing to squeeze the heavy William Webb Ellis World Cup into the cockpit of an Airbus carrying the Springbok road show to Cape Town, his verbal attack on Kitch Christie, which prompted the coach to call me from his car, was far more serious. On the way back from practice, an aggravated Griffiths had been heaping such abuse on Christie over his hands-free cell phone in the car that he felt obliged to call me. 'No one talks to me like this in front of my wife and son,' Christie complained, 'no one.' Several others seemed to share this sentiment, including Morné du Plessis and Ronnie Masson of Western Province who had been targeted for the same treatment.

The clash in Christie's car had erupted over Griffiths' insistence that James Dalton – who, he claimed, had signed a contract with Reebok in contravention of his agreement with SARFU – should be expelled from the team. In response, the entire team walked off the practice field and Christie sat with a serious dilemma on his hands. As it turned out, Dalton had not signed with Reebok.

Ultimately, however, it was not Griffiths' lack of self-control or talent for the task that prompted his firing. He rode roughshod over SARFU in his belief that it was his mission to 'set rugby ablaze across this country' and transform it from a mostly white game to a mostly black game. In his own inexperienced and somewhat misguided way, he had become the unwitting agent not of true reform and development but of political forces who sought to hijack rugby. He pictured SARFU's management as an unbending remnant of the Afrikaner establishment, intent on preserving the 'racist' rugby practices of the past.

In the meantime, not a single member of SARFU's executive was against development of rugby among coloured and black South Africans – although most, if not all, were opposed to the enforcement of a quota system dictated by politicos instead of teams selected on merit.

In this regard, Griffiths went around the country making commitments on SARFU's behalf without checking whether we had the money to back him up, and only after he had left did we discover the full extent of his promises as black administrators started calling us to collect. Mark Keohane went to the trouble of talking to some of them to get the full story.

'Griffiths came to Soweto after the World Cup and promised us heaven and earth,' Nelson Botile, chairman of the Soweto Rugby Club, told Keohane. 'We had been put in contact with him through the Soweto Olympic Sports Council, and he was eager to develop rugby in Soweto.'

'We told him our needs for facilities and he visited various sites with us,' Botile went on. 'We settled on developing fields in Orlando East, Jabulani and Dobsonville. We received a cheque for R106,000 for the Orlando East project with promises of much more later on.'

'[But] it never materialised,' Botile said, 'and when we heard Griffiths had been sacked, we contacted Dr Luyt at the Transvaal Rugby Union. He was very surprised by our phone call and had no knowledge of any plans to develop the stadiums. It then became apparent that Griffiths came to Soweto without having first consulted with his executive, although the impression he gave us was that all the plans had been approved. It was as if the money had already been allocated to Soweto Rugby Club. It had not and now we are negotiating with the TRU.'

These stadiums in Gauteng would have cost SARFU in excess of R5 million, on top of another unauthorised commitment of R9 million to the Eastern Province Rugby Union. At the same time, Griffiths had been antagonising the very sponsors on whom we relied for funds to run development programmes in underprivileged areas. Numerous complaints were received from corporate representatives who resented the disrespectful manner in which the CEO, assuming the airs of office without filling the seat, treated them.

Griffiths, of course, did not create the political wave that was about to hit SARFU in full force. He was merely another piece of driftwood collected along the way to be used as fodder in the process. So was a man named Brian van Rooyen, who became a willing tool of the political establishment once his effort to unseat me by open election as president of the GLRU failed miserably.

In October 1996, Van Rooyen tried to accomplish what Van Coller had failed to do six years earlier. Relying heavily on rumours and speculative reports, Van Rooyen complained that as the representative of a GLRU member club, he was not privy to the finances. Once again, the spectre was raised of a trust run by me like a family business. Representing a coloured club, Eldoronians, Van Rooyen also charged that not enough was done to promote the development of rugby among 'non-whites'.

I thus took the trouble of inviting Van Rooyen to go through our finances and thought that this would enable him to evaluate the fabricated claims for himself. But it was clear that he had already made up his mind and was not about to be deterred by the facts. It could not have been that he did not understand the financial statements, I thought. After all, he held a day job as an accountant. There simply had to be another explanation.

At an extraordinary meeting of the GLRU at the end of October 1996, Van Rooyen received only three out of 55 votes. After the election, somewhat over-wrought by the abuse heaped upon me and my family during the preceding weeks, I made comments which, in retrospect, might have been not only undiplomatic but unbecoming to say the least, and which I deeply regret today. I was quoted by *The Citizen* as calling Van Rooyen 'a fool' and 'too stupid' to ask intelligent questions about the union's financial affairs. Van Rooyen had actually been given 20 minutes during an executive committee meeting to work through the management accounts of the union but seemed at a loss at what to do with the material. But then diplomacy was never my strongest suit and, in this instance, having been subjected to a barrage of lies and half-truths, out of the question.

'You're gone now – and thank God you're gone,' I bristled, staring down Van Rooyen. 'You may be in politics but you're out of rugby and we can do without you.'

My statement to *The Citizen* proved to be somewhat off-beam, but then words spoken in anger often are. Van Rooyen was still in politics, but he was definitely not out of rugby either.

Waiting in the wings to make it all happen were the ANC government and its handmaiden, the National Sports Council. Van Rooyen was merely acting as a convenient Trojan horse in an attempt to unseat me from within. Now his defeat would be challenged with all the might the political establishment could muster.

Early in February 1997, GLRU manager Johan Prinsloo received a call from someone who identified himself as Van Rooyen's colleague at the firm of Labatt. He indicated that he had something of great importance to discuss. I asked Prinsloo to find out what it was all about. The mystery man suggested a meeting at a prearranged venue to present us with what he claimed to be incriminating documentation. When Prinsloo arrived at the restaurant, accompanied by a colleague to help identify the mole, they found a rather anxious 'informer' sipping tea in the corner.

He had with him a dossier and correspondence from the office computers, he claimed, containing clear proof of a conspiracy against me by Van Rooyen and others.

'But before I can hand these over,' he told Prinsloo, 'I will need R40,000 in cash. This is necessary to take care of my family once they find out I am the one who passed this stuff along. There are powerful men behind Van Rooyen.'

According to Prinsloo, the man appeared quite nervous.

'What do you mean by "powerful men"?' Prinsloo asked.

'What would you say if I mentioned the name Rupert to you?'

Prinsloo began to wonder. But the informant seemed like a truthful man. When he reported back to me, Prinsloo said that he had no doubt about the existence of such a dossier but that it was up to me to decide whether I wanted to pay for it. Although I was quite interested to know what this dossier contained, I was not willing to pay R40,000 or, for that matter, a solitary cent. Still, I found it prudent to call my lawyer, Fanie Cilliers, for an opinion. Prinsloo accompanied me to Cilliers.

'Is there anything embarrassing you might have done in SARFU or the Transvaal union?' Cilliers asked.

'No,' I said. 'Nothing.'

'Then send him to hell,' Cilliers advised.

I thus conveyed, through Prinsloo, my decision not to pay the ransom. There was enough work to take my mind off this odd episode, but from time to time I would for an instant revisit the event and wonder what Van Rooyen might have been up to.

During the evening of 14 February, while I was trying to catch up with work at my Ellis Park office, I received a call from my son Lucien from our fruit farm in the Cape. He sounded alarmed.

'Dad, did you see it on television?' he asked.

'No, son, I've been working.'

'Well, they had Tshwete announcing that he has received a document from Van Rooyen that warrants a full government inquiry into rugby.'

After our conversation, I immediately called the Sport Minister Steve Tshwete: 'Steve, what the hell is this all about? You could have told me first instead of going on television with an announcement about an inquiry.'

'No, Louis,' Tshwete countered, 'I must have been misinterpreted. All this stuff from Van Rooyen is just nonsense.'

Perhaps Lucien did misinterpret Tshwete's words? I called him back.

'No, Dad, I'm quite sure,' he insisted. 'Minister Tshwete left no doubt. You can watch the tape.'

Lucien was right. The press confirmed Steve Tshwete's announcement, as did members of my staff who had seen his appearance on television. Not only had he announced the commission, but also who would sit on the commission – a former judge, Mervyn King, corporate lawyer Michael Katz and an advocate by the name of Gilbert Marcus. To this day, I am at a loss to understand why Tshwete insisted that he had been misinterpreted. Surely he must have known that the facts would speak for themselves the very next day. I also took comfort in the fact that Tshwete did not have the power to appoint a commission. Only the State President had those powers.

When I encountered Tshwete a few days later after we emerged from a brief meeting with his director-general of sport, Mthobi Tyamzashe, he was still trying the soft-soap approach. I had called on Tyamzashe, accompanied by former rugby star Chris Dirks, who now assisted me at the Golden Lions Rugby Union, to demand a copy of the Van Rooyen dossier. I also handed him an auditor's report touching on all the aspects being mooted in the press. He flipped through the pages and looked up smiling.

'But this answers everything!' he said.

Still, I insisted, it is my constitutional right to know what these charges are. Tyamzashe thus promised to make it available. As we waited for an elevator, Tshwete stepped out and greeted me with a broad smile.

'Why don't you join me for tea?' he suggested.

He talked about the old days and how the two of us had helped each other along the way. He took great pride in his role as mediator to unify rugby and for having come to my assistance when everyone else had tried to crucify me over my playing of *Die Stem* at Ellis Park. He reminisced about the World Cup and how much it had meant for the country. Finally, we got to the matter of the pending inquiry.

'Louis, you can have the Van Rooyen dossier,' Tshwete said. 'Our copy was given to Mervyn King, but I will have it back in a day or two and send you a copy. It does not add up to much. It's just a lot of press clippings. Van Rooyen is out of his mind.'

We parted in a good spirit. Three days later I called Tyamzashe again to find out why the Van Rooyen dossier had still not been forwarded.

'Sorry, Louis,' he said, 'Van Rooyen had us sign a confidentiality clause stipulating that unless we proceeded with the commission of inquiry, we were not allowed to release the dossier.'

I was becoming impatient. In the meantime, the media were having a field day with leaks from either Van Rooyen or one of his accomplices in the government. The *Sunday Times* went to town with some of these wild accusations in a series of articles that were so libellous that I had no other choice but to file a

The International Rugby Board in 1995.

Above: Organising the World Cup in 1995 with Rian Oberholzer and Craig Jameson.
photo: Sunday Times.

Right: With Edward Griffiths, who was at that time, in 1995, CEO of SARFU.
photo: Sunday Times.

Speaking in 1995 when Nelson Mandela was made Honorary Patron of South African Rugby.

With Nelson Mandela shortly after the Springbok victory in the 1995 World Cup final.

photo: Wessel Oosthuizen.

case against them. The senior counsel I happened to brief was none other than Wim Trengove, who would later be the lead advocate for the state against SARFU – and me, of course.

There would be my final effort to get this dossier from Tshwete and his staff before I turned the matter over to my lawyers.

At our next meeting, convened at his request, SARFU found Tshwete a changed man. As Hennie Erasmus, one of our executive members, and Rian Oberholzer filed into his office, Van Rooyen was slipping out with a tape recorder in his hand. No small talk from Tshwete as he glowered at them from behind his thick glasses to announce that he was appointing a 'task team' to investigate SARFU's affairs.

Erasmus and Oberholzer objected to the inclusion of Ramsamy of the National Olympic Committee of South Africa, as it was unheard of to have one sporting body investigate another. Tshwete, however, remained firm. The battle lines had finally been drawn.

Only afterwards would we be able to piece together the odd sequence of events that led to this uncomfortable encounter. Van Rooyen must have been in Tshwete's office to play a recording that would shortly afterwards be aired by SABC, courtesy of Edward Griffiths, who had since joined the government-owned network. The tape concerned a conversation between Springbok coach André Markgraaff, who had replaced Christie, and one of his former players in Griqualand West, during which he made unfortunate remarks about black South Africans – using the dreaded K-word.

This was just what was needed to support the government's contention that rugby should be brought under political control and cleansed from all racist Afrikaners. What André Markgraaff said in a careless conversation was assumed to reflect the view of SARFU and me as its president. It was also charged in the press that I had known about the tape for some time and had decided not to take any action.

Markgraaff did contact me during December 1996 to ask whether I could put him in touch with a good lawyer. He sounded distraught as he told me about an incriminating tape recording. Just before the test against France, he said, someone had told him that there was a tape recording of a conversation where he used derogatory language about black people. The tape, he was told, might be sold to the news media. Despite the stress, he managed to score wins against both France and England before returning to South Africa and a well-deserved rest at his vacation cottage in the Cape. But the problem had obviously not gone away.

I had put him in touch with Fanie Cilliers and left it to them to sort the problem out on a lawyer-client basis. The first time I heard the full extent of Markgraaff's remarks in a conversation with his provincial rugby captain André Bester, who carried a hidden tape recorder with him, was when it was played on

SABC. In fact, my office had to purchase a transcript from the television network. Interestingly, the same people who had condemned me for having had certain crucial conversations in my office taped were now in full praise of Bester for having performed a yeoman service for his country. Markgraaff, furthermore, had not spared me either and, I would find out, had some caustic comments to make about me on the tape too.

The final meeting at Steve Tshwete's office on 21 February 1997 was a heated encounter between the two of us, with those in attendance mostly silent observers. Accompanying me were SARFU deputy president, Mluleki George, Johan Claassen, the former Springbok captain and a member of our executive, Hennie Erasmus, another executive committee member and Rian Oberholzer. Tshwete had Tyamzashe and a few other people at his side. I would only later learn that this meeting was also taped.

'I want to place on record right now and this is the last time we are going to do it,' I said, 'that we want the Van Rooyen document under Section 23 of the Constitution. The Constitution provides for me to defend myself and I will defend myself.'

Tell me what the allegations are, I challenged, and it will be answered right now. I had brought with me a briefcase bulging with contracts, SARFU minutes and other documents in anticipation of this opportunity. Tshwete declined because, he argued, he did not have his experts around. So what was this meeting all about? Why had we gone to the trouble of getting together?

Afterwards, it was announced that SARFU would be given the opportunity to answer Van Rooyen's allegations and that the Minister of Sport would appoint a task team, under the leadership of Director-General Tyamzashe, to probe our affairs. The three other members were to be the ones originally named to form the 'commission' – King, Katz, Marcus and Malindi, who had been added later.

Discerning outsiders must have been struck by the odd statement in this release that SARFU would apply to the courts for access to the Van Rooyen dossier. How could we be offered the opportunity to answer the allegations if we did not even know what they were? But logic is always the first victim when blind zeal makes its appearance. Markgraaff's huge mistake began to look like a minor matter in the midst of the swelling anti-white and anti-Afrikaner emotions with-in Tshwete's ranks.

In an appearance before Justice Roux at the Pretoria Supreme Court, we argued our case for the release of the Van Rooyen dossier so we could gain some insight into his allegations. The learned judge not only found in our favour but ordered the government to hand over the document without delay that very night.

He also posed the question: 'What kind of animal is this task team? There is no provision in our law for such a body.'

But his question remained unanswered and his instruction unheeded. It took

290

four days for us to be able to collect the document from Katz's – not King's – office. The excuse was that it had been lost and then miraculously found. I was there to take personal possession of the file. When I asked the lawyer Errol Knowles, who handed the file to me, how long he had been sitting on it, he replied: 'Several days.' We could, of course, have gone back to court, charging contempt, but decided to simply move on.

There was not much in the Van Rooyen dossier with which we were not already familiar. It consisted largely of press reports – many of them reproduced, it seemed, with the help of others in a cut-and-paste job – and it was easy to see why Tshwete had originally dismissed the document as useless. Revealing, however, were the communications between Van Rooyen and people in government evidently bent on driving me out at all cost. They obviously realised that, as in the past, when I resisted the Botha and De Klerk governments, I was not about to hand over the sport of rugby to this government either. A letter of encouragement by ANC cabinet minister Kader Asmal, written shortly after I thwarted Van Rooyen's feeble attempt to oust me from the Golden Lions Rugby Union, reflected the general attitude:

'Dear Mr Van Rooyen, I have watched the Louis Luyt spectacle with a sense of growing alarm, and I wish you to know of my warm support for what you have been trying to do. The juggernaut response by Luyt to your challenge and the juvenile way he attacked you suggest that - despite his apparent power – he is losing his grip.

'Luyt is rooted in an era in which it was expected of people like him to do execrable things for the established order – such as fronting for the government's *Citizen* newspaper – and of which he should be thoroughly ashamed. Yet he struts around the national rugby stage as if it is his private domain. He is having a grievously divisive effect on our public life, and your stunningly bold attempt to check him earns my warmest admiration and respect.

'My hope is that the new moves to call him to account will be successful; and, meanwhile, may I warmly commend you for your courage and commitment to the new order that we are trying, despite the Luyts of our world, to establish in South Africa.'

The letter was signed, 'Warm regards, Yours sincerely, Prof Kader Asmal MP'.

But among the other letters included in this 400-page dossier was an equally revealing one dated 11 July 1997, in which Brian van Rooyen begged American black activist, the Reverend Jesse Jackson, to intervene on his behalf to have Nike call off negotiations with SARFU. It became clear later that Nike was also growing tired of Jackson's continuous interference.

When Mthobi Tyamzashe arrived at my office with Michael Katz, Gilbert Marcus and a young black lawyer, Gcina Malindi, I told him I had had a chance to work through the dossier and found nothing of any substance. Attorney Alick

Costa, Hennie Erasmus and Rian Oberholzer sat in as we reviewed matters in a relaxed fashion over tea. Katz, who served as a director on our board when we listed Ellis Park, assured me that there would be no witch-hunt. It was purely a question of verifying the facts, he said. I was quite amenable to this approach and undertook to instruct all SARFU's member unions to be cooperative. That very evening, Katz called me to invite me over to have a look at his law library. I declined, but was nevertheless satisfied that we had reached a good understanding and managed to focus on facts instead of playing politics.

The same Katz would later, however, bellow that we at EPS were defrauding the SARS in VAT payments on RWC ticket sales. He succeeded in having EPS heavily penalised, but had the pants beaten off him in a unanimous judgment of the High Court of Appeals that must have left him red in the face. Katz, who is undoubtedly brilliant at company law, believes – mistakenly, in my opinion – that he is the best in any area of law. He is, however, something of a legal chameleon, serving – with the same fervour – FW de Klerk's National Party government as he now does the ANC government.

One of many of documents handed over by us to Katz and company was a written report from an independent auditing firm that addressed the bulk of the original charges regarding so-called nepotism and family involvement in Ellis Park that had now resurfaced in Van Rooyen's dossier. It was identical to the one given to Tyamzashe:

'[From:] Coopers & Lybrand, Johannesburg, 10 January 1997.

'[To:] The President, Transvaal Rugby Union, Doornfontein.

'[Re:] Ellis Park Stadium (Pty) Ltd.

'We confirm the following information in respect of Ellis Park Stadium (Pty) Ltd for the year ended 31 December 1996:

'Rental agreement Touch Down Restaurant: Ellis Park Stadium (Pty) Ltd is letting the premises, namely The Touch Down Restaurant to Ranko Sekota for 9 years and 11 months until 31 October 2004. The terms of this rental agreement is based on an option granted in the rental agreement to Ranko Sekota with the commissioning of the then new rugby stadium in 1984. The rental amounts to R8,588 (excluding VAT) per month for the first year and escalates by 7.5% per year.

'Stadium Sports (Pty) Ltd: Stadium Sports (Pty) Ltd is a 100%-owned subsidiary of Ellis Park Stadium (Pty) Ltd.

'Commissions – suite results: No commission is paid by Ellis Park Stadium (Pty) Ltd in respect of suite rental agreements.

'Liquor sales: Ellis Park Stadium (Pty) Ltd supplies liquor to Ellis Park suite holders and spectators.

'Tax deductions: Based on audit findings, Transvaal Rugby Union and Ellis Park Stadium (Pty) Ltd met the legal requirements regarding the deduction of employees' tax (PAYE) on payments to players.'

The letter was signed, 'Yours faithfully, Coopers & Lybrand'. Then, out of the blue, at the instruction of Mervyn King, Deloitte & Touche demanded detailed management accounts from us dating back to 1989, as well as a string of other apparently unrelated information. There was the clear inference of dishonesty on our part. The witch-hunt was on. I instructed our lawyers to inform Tyamzashe that we were withholding all cooperation until we received full particulars of all the accusations against us. On 30 July 1997, I instructed our member unions to cease all cooperation with the so-called task force.

On 6 August, Tyamzashe issued a press statement, announcing that President Mandela had 'happily responded' to Sport Minister Tshwete's indication that he might apply for the appointment of a judicial commission of inquiry. According to this release, Mandela had told Tshwete that 'a commission is yours if, in your best judgment, it is opportune'.

As it turned out, the people around Mandela had become rather careless in their zeal to go for SARFU's jugular. Under law, only the president could appoint a commission after he had applied his mind to the matter properly. Later, both Mandela and Tshwete denied under oath that this conversation had ever taken place and left Tyamzashe to sweat it out on his own.

With the help of attorney Errol Knowles of Edward Nathan & Friedland, Tshwete prepared a dossier of his own, incorporating not only the Van Rooyen papers but accusations levelled by the task team and their appointed auditors, Deloitte & Touche. It was heavy on political invective and virtually void on facts. I was held out to be the personification of everything that was wrong with rugby – 'an archetypal worst of old-style South Africans, brash and arrogant, proud of his lack of concern for the fellow citizens'. Conveniently omitted was any reference to my role in talks with the ANC, reforms and the unification of black and white interests in rugby. I had now become a roadblock to the ultimate take-over of rugby by the new government and had to be removed.

It had become abundantly clear that neither Tshwete nor those who advised him had any real interest in rugby or the facts. 'Even should a Commission of Enquiry determine that no irregularities are found,' Knowles wrote, 'there is an overwhelming public perception that has become abundantly clear to the Ministerial Task Team members collectively, and through their individual exposure to members of the public, that the administration of rugby is defective, dictatorial and, perhaps, even corrupt.' This biased and trumped-up report by Knowles was signed by King, Katz, Marcus and Malindi.

But all this blood in the water had attracted the sharks. The press was steadily ripping away at my image and reputation. In August 1997 the Natal Rugby Union, coincidentally known as the Sharks, took SARFU and me, personally, to court over the restructuring of the teams playing in the new Super-12 competition. The Sharks' CEO, Brian van Zyl, actually accused Rian Oberholzer and me of nepotism and improper conduct in the allocation of contracts. At the centre of this allegation was the suggestion by the Tshwete task team that my son Louis had improperly benefited from a contract with Nike. In reality, Natal was party to SARFU's annual general meeting on 5 October 1996, where the following resolution, extracted from the minutes of the executive committee meeting, was adopted: '10.16 Sponsorship Commission: It was resolved that a commission of 10% be paid to Mr L Luyt (Junior) in respect of all sponsorships obtained for SARFU by him. He was further mandated to negotiate the proposed United States Dollar sponsorships on SARFU's behalf.'

This same minute was passed and ratified by the full SARFU executive before the AGM, with Messrs Parkinson and Van Zyl present, adopted it unanimously. In fact, the same minutes contain an item confirming that it was agreed that President Nelson Mandela be reaffirmed as Honorary Patron of the South African Rugby Football Union. But that was then. Everything had taken a drastic turn for the worse since. The battle for control of South African rugby had begun in earnest.

On 22 September, President Mandela announced the appointment of a commission of enquiry under the chairmanship of Acting Judge Jules Browde, an old friend of his from Wits University. I chose to respond to the challenge in the weekly television rugby programme, *Boots and All*, led by former Springbok Naas Botha and Darren Scott.

'I'm fighting for the principle and for the rights of SARFU, the Gauteng Lions and everybody else involved,' I said. 'I don't believe that Steve Tshwete should have the right to tell me to hop, jump or sit.'

SARFU's executive agreed. Out of 22 members, only four voted against my suggestion that we challenge the validity of this commission of enquiry in court. Opposed were Keith Parkinson of Natal, Ronnie Masson of Western Province, Mluleki George of Border and Silas Nkanunu of Eastern Province. Masson later told me that if he had known the full extent of our case – as was explained by Mike Maritz when I invited him to address the full executive – he would have voted in favour. But that was typical of Masson.

As staunch ANC elites both George and Nkanunu had little choice but to oppose, even though they complained privately about being 'taken for criminals' by their government. So, on 20 October 1997, we filed our opposition to the appointment of the Browde Commission in a brief before the Supreme Court in Pretoria. Instead of our regular attorney, Alick Costa at the firm of Werksmans, and advocate Willem van der Linde, who were originally assigned the case, but were excused – they were clearly afraid of jeopardising their future with the government – advocate Mike Maritz appeared on our behalf.

Maritz, suggested to me by my law professor friend Dawie Botha, proved to be the man best suited for the onerous task of representing SARFU, the GLRU, the Mpumalanga Rugby Union, Blue Bulls Rugby Union – at the insistence of Hentie Serfontein – and myself as joint applicants in the case against Nelson Mandela, the President of South Africa, the Minister of Sport and the Director-General of Sport and Recreation.

By this time both Parkinson and George had signalled their intention to challenge me for the presidency at the upcoming election. I gathered that they, like the general public, were overly impressed by press reports and government pronouncements putting me in the past tense.

Billed as a major shoot-out, SARFU's annual general meeting at Newlands on 4 November 1997 turned out to be as much of a damp squib as Van Rooyen's fanciful dossier. In a secret ballot, 33 executives voted for me while Parkinson and George split the remainder at seven each.

'The public may want Luyt out,' reported the *Cape Times* the next day. '[But] those connected with rugby (and they were of varying colours and cultural back-grounds) do not share the public's enthusiasm for a Luyt send-off.'

The following paragraphs from the *Cape Times* aptly captured the spirit of the meeting:

'"I expected a full house," said Luyt immediately after the announcement of the vote. "No, I knew there would be two votes against me." His rugby audience offered the necessary reply. They applauded his re-election and his humour. It was fascinating to watch.

'Parkinson and George, understandably, were not leading the chorus, "For he's a jolly good fellow". George, by virtue of his "all-or-nothing" campaign for presidency, will play no further part on the national executive. Parkinson, his effort to dispose of Luyt always lacking conviction, has no such excuse.

'"Thank you for your time. It has been thoroughly enjoyable working with you," Luyt said to George. "And Keith (Parkinson), there will be another oppor-tunity for you in two years' time."

'Natal president Parkinson warned that he would be an "even bigger pain in the neck" as one of the 28 union representatives. It was light-hearted banter, the type synonymous with that of a champion who has just whipped his pretenders – and in keeping with an opponent powerless to stop the blows.'

Radio interviewers converged on me afterwards. The print media also wanted in. The bad guy had turned good, if only temporarily in the eyes of sceptics.

As part of the proceedings, the new Super-12 arrangement was approved and the right of my office to conclude sponsorships endorsed. This meant defeat for both Natal, who had challenged us in court, and Free State, who had objected to its inclusion as part of a grouping with the Golden Lions, Northern Free State and Griqualand West.

But, despite the light banter and seemingly relaxed atmosphere, it was also necessary for me to raise the matter that rested heavily on everyone's mind: 'SARFU – and I personally – have the utmost respect and admiration for President Nelson Mandela and we're truly sorry that he was called on to approve the commission of inquiry. But he is the country's chief executive and that's part of the job description.'

I added: 'Nonetheless, it is by majority vote that the executive decided to resist the appointment of the commission in court. It was not my decision alone.' The AGM unanimously endorsed our decision to contest the case.

While the two legal teams were going through the paces and the posturing that usually precedes actual court proceedings, there was still the chance to reach a compromise. Realising that there was no way in which Tshwete, Tyamzashe and the National Sports Council were about to give up their campaign to control rugby I directed my final appeal to Mandela.

The occasion was an hour-and-a-half-long visit with the president at his invitation in his Houghton home on 6 December 1997 – although the invitation was denied by President Mandela in court, but then later changed when I produced the facts.

The pretext of the meeting was the nine tickets he needed for his grandchildren to attend the soccer test against Brazil at Ellis Park the next day. But he, as did I, understood that the time had come for a face-to-face meeting, away from the forces that were sweeping us along towards a confrontation that neither of us desired. Even though I gently reminded him of the fact that the Springboks rugby test against Scotland was just about to be telecast in the hope that we might enjoy it together, the screen remained blank. We did, however, get to talk about the old days before we got around to the dilemma now facing us.

'They are scared of you, Louis,' he said.

'Why, Mr President, why?' I asked.

'I don't know, Louis, but they are scared of you.'

'Mr President,' I said, 'we can certainly resolve any problem as far as rugby goes without the expense and humiliation of a commission of inquiry.'

'If you had only talked to me before I signed the proclamation, we could have done that,' he said.

I could, of course, have informed him that Steve Tshwete had recently told me at Johannesburg International – while we were waiting to welcome the victorious Springboks' on their return from London – that he would approach the president to withdraw the commission as it would not serve South Africa's best interests. But it was too late now. Mandela had already made up his mind.

Tshwete had given that undertaking the day before the ANC party congress at Mafikeng started. Not unlike the National Party congresses of old, this one turned out to be a platform from which to please the extremists. Any hint of such a compromise would have been summarily dismissed as treason and cost both

Tshwete and Mandela dearly.

I left Mandela's home that afternoon with a heavy heart. My hopes of reaching a settlement had been finally crushed. The man whom I respected and liked was about to become my adversary in court. While I put on a bold face in public, promising to take the case where it led, even if it meant facing the president in open court, I kept hoping that our differences might be settled beforehand.

But it was not to be. On 26 February, the case opened in courtroom 6E of the Supreme Court in Pretoria, known as the divorce court. Our proceedings carried all the trappings of an acrimonious final separation between former partners. Tshwete, who sat two chairs removed from me in the courtroom, hardly acknowledged my presence. And two of the country's foremost legal minds, Wim Trengove, appearing for the government, and Mike Maritz, acting on our behalf, certainly provided great theatre as they cross-questioned each others' witnesses. While this might have been a source of great enjoyment for the standing-room-only gallery and journalists from around the world, it gave me no pleasure whatsoever.

Ask anyone whether he felt fulfilled after facing up to cross-examination by the likes of either a Trengove or Maritz, and he would be lying if he answered in the affirmative. I certainly felt as if I had gone into overtime in a hard-fought skirmish with Trengrove, who I have always respected as an incisive legal mind.

'Dr Luyt,' he started, 'you have a Doctor's degree in law, don't you?'

I knew exactly where he was leading. He was going to test my legal knowledge. And I was not going to be fool enough to leave myself open and give him the opportunity to make me look stupid.

Although I had successfully completed my doctoral exams at Pretoria University and was currently working on my LLD, I said, 'No, I'm busy with it'. That was the truth. I had successfully sat for the Doctoral exams on 5 October 1988 and fulfilled the prerequisite for a Doctorandus or Drs Juris equivalent at the University of Pretoria. A thesis was the only further requirement for my LLD degree, and I had, in fact, already finished half of it by that point.

I never doubted the correctness of our case. We stood on solid ground. The new rulers had most certainly over-reached in their eagerness to force rugby into their political mould. Our basic argument was that the legal requirements for the appointment of a commission as stipulated by the Commissions Act had not been satisfied. The Act clearly states that the matters to be investigated had to be 'of public interest' – not what is interesting to the public. This, we contended, did not apply to 'private autonomous associations such as SARFU and its constituent unions, and in any event not to its internal management'. These were all non-governmental, non-statutory bodies, which received not a single dime of state or taxpayer money. Relying merely on the Van Rooyen dossier, Mandela had clear-ly not properly considered the matter before he appointed his commission of inquiry.

Following me to the witness stand were Rian Oberholzer and Hennie Erasmus for SARFU, and for the respondents Tyamzashe, task team members Michael Katz, Gilbert Marcus and Gcina Malindi, and Tshwete. Curiously, the very task team that had been held up as a paragon of good governance and corporate responsibility repeatedly failed to meet our requests for minutes or documentation. When asked about the specifics of a particular meeting, Katz told the court that minutes had not been kept. King was conspicuous in his absence, while Marcus contradicted the chameleon's evidence.

Mike Maritz questioned Tyamzashe about his press statement in which he reportedly stated that Mandela had 'happily responded' to Steve Tshwete that 'a commission is yours if, in your best judgment, it is opportune'. The South African Press Association had it wrong, the Director-General of Sport explained. So where was the original? Once again, we were faced with the familiar response: Lost. Not available.

During the lunch break, Rian Oberholzer received an anonymous call from someone identifying himself only as a journalist who could not sit by listening to lies. He asked us for a fax number and within minutes we had the original press release in our hands. There was no identifying source number. When confronted with this document at the resumption of the proceedings, Tyamzashe put up a performance that will remain a classic long after every other detail of the case is forgotten.

No longer able to cover up, Tyamzashe now admitted that he did lie, not once, but three times. But, he added, these lies were simply told to scare SARFU into cooperating with the task team by threatening them with the possibility of a commission of inquiry. Explaining why he had lied under oath, Tyamzashe distinguished between 'honest' and 'dishonest' lies. His statements had been an example of an 'honest lie'. He also told the court that he saw 'nothing wrong in lying to protect the President'.

The following encounter ensued between Maritz and a flustered Tyamzashe:

Maritz: You always knew that you falsely attributed these words to the President, or rather that is your story?

Tyamzashe: I acknowledge that I attributed words to the President.

Maritz: Yes, now we don't accept that, because I'm going to argue that it is not true. I am going to argue to his lordship that you did not falsely attribute words to the President; you are lying under oath here to save the President. You have become the fall guy in this case, that is what I'm going to argue. You can comment on that.

Tyamzashe: Certainly, I'm not lying.

Maritz: Yes?

Tyamzashe: And I do not know if I am the fall guy.

Maritz: It is not even an honest lie, you say.

The court and some observers – including media that had been waging a vitriolic campaign against me – might have been shocked by this blatant admission of perjury on the part of a top government official. But Sports Minister Steve Tshwete told Parliament that he fully accepted and condoned this 'honest lie' by his deputy. He knew Mr Tyamzashe intimately, he said, and this lie had been an 'isolated incident' in 'unique circumstances' and 'under extremely trying conditions'. Instead of losing his job and being charged for perjury, Tyamzashe won thus praise and a raise.

In his own testimony, Tshwete dismissed comments attributed to him by several newspapers as false. Under oath, he even denied having had an interview with the journalists concerned – a denial that he later retracted. He also accused one of the journalists of being guilty of a 'blatant lie' (as, of course, opposed to an 'honest lie') in reporting comments attributed to him.

In the midst of all this 'honest' lying and dubious denying, it should have been obvious to everyone why presiding Justice William de Villiers found it necessary to call President Mandela to the witness stand. Here was the central figure and a man who everybody trusted being made to look dishonest and devious through the actions and words of his underlings. It was thus essential that he be afforded the opportunity to speak for himself. So Mandela was subpoenaed by Justice De Villiers to make an appearance on 9 March, but was unable to appear because of 'affairs of state'. In the meantime, Trengove asked that the order be revoked. The judge dismissed the application, and a new date was set: 19 March 1998.

All that had happened during the previous year flashed through my mind as Nelson Mandela stepped up to the witness stand. Preferring to take the word 'stand' to its literal extreme, he refused a seat and stood up for the duration of his testimony. Observers in the business of myth-building described this as a gesture of respect for the court. I believe, however, that he did so to demonstrate his authority over the man seated on the bench. Mandela's refusal to use the customary 'Lordship' in addressing Mr Justice De Villiers and referring to him simply as 'Judge' supports this contention.

'Then there is Dr Luyt,' President Mandela said during the opening of a long and, at times, acrimonious sparring match with Mike Maritz. 'Dr Luyt, we were collaborators, we were partners. It was in the course of our trying to normalise rugby as a national sport that I came to earn high regard for him. I still have high regard for him. There are of course very serious allegations, which have been made, but my approach to him is determined by my experience when I worked closely with him, and I will not give credence to the allegations that are being made. I hope that – subject to what the judge will decide in this case – I hope that commission will have the opportunity to sit down, to probe these allegations, and if that commission decides that there is no substance in these allegations, I will be one of the happiest men in the country because that will then free rugby from the paralysing atmosphere, environment, in which it has been plunged today. I will be very happy. But at the same time, Judge, if that commission decides that there is substance to the allegations, then I cannot allow personal relationships, however strong they are, to override the national interest.'

This was vintage Mandela. The man who had earned a special place in the hearts and history of his time for being instrumental in steering South Africa from the edge of the abyss into peaceful change was now applying his skills towards trying to repair the damage done by his underlings. But this time there would be no miracle. The time was long past for an amicable outcome or settlement. Politics had taken the front seat and Mandela and I were mere passengers speeding towards the cliff. 'Honest lies' provided the fuel.

It gave me absolutely no satisfaction to watch Maritz punching a few telling holes in Mandela's testimony. In one desperate, final effort to spare him this humiliation, I suggested during an aside at a tea break that he might still be in a position to settle the matter with a statement from the stand. In fact, the first offer came from Mandela himself when he said, 'Louis, you and I can resolve this matter within an hour.' I offered to 'give him what he wanted' and I meant every word. But, just as he had when I saw him in his Houghton home, he once again decided that it was 'politically, not opportune'.

Mandela's description of me as a 'pitiless dictator' will stay with me for the rest of my life. This was, short of the insults I had had to endure as a poor boy in the Karoo, the most hurtful experience of my life. Here was the man I admired most, dismissing me as heartless and cruel. But I also understood that these words were spoken by an already irate man in the heat of cross-examination by a brilliant advocate doing his level best to score points on my behalf.

One thing will, however, remain a mystery to me: Why did Mandela not simply withdraw the first commission, and appoint a new one – one without any of the loopholes that could be challenged in a court of law? This way, he would have been spared an appearance in court. In fact, even Judge Kriegler of the Constitutional Court would make the same observation.

The issue was, however, never raised again – not when Mandela welcomed me to Parliament a year later or during several encounters since. While our relationship never quite returned to where it was before we were both caught up in this unfortunate maelstrom, our mutual respect survived. So did personal concern for each other's wellbeing as I discovered when I received a call from Madiba after an emergency triple bypass operation in a Durban hospital in October 2001.

On the day of Mandela's appearance in the witness stand, Mluleki George distanced himself and his Border Rugby Union from SARFU's action. Since his defeat in a bid to unseat me, he had assumed the presidency of the ANC-controlled National Sports Council (NSC) bent on hijacking South African rugby. The NSC signalled its intent to prevent future tests, the Super-12 competition and the scheduled visits of Ireland, Wales and England unless the entire executive of SARFU resigned along with me.

It was much harder for me to swallow growing opposition from within my own ranks in SARFU. The executive that was previously solidly in support of our court challenge now began to waver. They were beginning to run scared as media pressures mounted.

The media accused me of having ordered Mandela to appear before court and when this was debunked, the objectivity of Justice William de Villiers who issued the order was brought into question. An allegation that he was my VIP guest during the 1995 World Cup made it to the front pages, while the correction explaining that the guest was actually *Rapport* editor Izak de Villiers was lost in the inside pages.

In the midst of all this rancour, some black members of SARFU's executive were the only ones, apart from me, who still openly defended our position. Silas Nkanunu was reported in the *Cape Times* on 23 March as saying that, while 'he appreciated the outrage and anger at President Nelson Mandela's forced court appearance', it should be noted that 'Luyt did not make the call'.

'Understandably, as SARFU president, Luyt is the central figure in the court case against the government,' Nkanunu explained, 'so he is bound to get the majority of the flak. But we must put emotion aside here. He did not call President Mandela to appear in court. The judge did it. Take issue with the judge. He made the decision. It is not a Mandela-versus-Luyt issue.'

Tobie Titus, who explained, 'The decision to go to court, by SARFU, was a democratic decision', joined Nkanunu. 'For people to now threaten rugby with boycotts and isolation is not the answer,' he said.

A SABC phone-in poll showed that out of 30,000 callers, 54 per cent felt I should remain as SARFU president. But the media was hard at work to whittle away at this support with half-truths, innuendo, mis-statements and 'honest' lies. And the strain was showing on my fair-weather friends at SARFU.

On 17 April 1998, Justice De Villiers rendered his verdict. He set aside President Mandela's decision to appoint a commission of inquiry. No reasons were given as, explained the judge, he was still in the process of writing his full judgment. The threatening throng of demonstrators draped in ANC colours in front of the courthouse seemed almost insignificant in comparison with what was to follow.

All the way back to Johannesburg, Adri and I were mostly silent, immersed in our own thoughts and holding hands as we often do when in need of each other's strength. While we were grateful that principle had won the day, we realised that this was bound to trigger yet another, even more severe onslaught from those who respected law only when it favours them. President Mandela simply gave notice that he would appeal. His followers, however, dismissed De Villiers and the court out of hand as remnants of the older apartheid regime, not worthy to be obeyed or respected.

'Look at the car next to us,' Adri suddenly said.

It was a black gentleman in a Toyota and he was smiling and giving us the thumbs up as he passed.

'At least one person on our side,' I quipped.

Those were prophetic words indeed, given the haste with which not only former friends and close associates at SARFU, but also my son-in-law, who I had ushered into rugby administration, jumped ship in the weeks that were to follow. In a rather strange way, Rian Oberholzer finally put an end to all the accusations of nepotism that had been levelled against me when he chose to cross over to the other side.

There was never any doubt in my mind about his potential and I was genuinely proud of his handling of certain arrangements during the World Cup. If I were equally attentive to his political leanings, his sudden switch in May 1998 might have come as a less of a shock. But I daresay that we were not the first and will not be the last family to be divided by crises. Historians tell us that the renowned Boer General Christiaan de Wet had a sibling who sided with the British enemy. But I had lost a son in the process – Rian was like my own son, and close family members often said as much.

I thus found myself in the midst of a firestorm. So did SARFU and Justice De Villiers, referred to by supposedly responsible members of government as the 'apartheid judge'. The National Sports Council demanded that the whole SARFU executive tender its resignation, while the ANC's alliance partner, Cosatu, threatened 'rolling mass action' and the picketing of international matches unless the NSC's demands were met. Following the lead of M-Net's Russell MacMillan, three other major sponsors – Vodacom, The Rupert Group and Bankfin - joined the lynch mob.

As before, whenever it waged war against rugby, the National Sports Council once again threatened to take away the Springbok emblem on which we had agreed after the conclusion of the World Cup. The new design, cobbled together in my office on a computer depicted the antelope jumping outwards over the national flower. Cricket and other sports had simply caved in and adopted only the protea as their new emblem. The Democratic Party, supposedly in favour of locking the state out of undue interference in private matters, limply opposed the witch-hunt against SARFU while at the same time taking swipes at me. Neither the New National Party nor the Freedom Front came out in my defence. Everyone was running for cover and I found myself standing alone, trying –

against all odds – to uphold a principle.

The Gauteng president of the National Sports Council, Bill Jardine, dismissed the court ruling as 'a petty victory' and vowed to continue the war against rugby. SARFU, he said, had until 7 May to decide whether to get rid of me and fall into step with the NSC and the government's demands, or face a boycott of international tours and the scrapping of the Springbok emblem. But, Jardine told an interviewer, SARFU will 'probably tell South Africa to go to hell'. He was way too generous in his assessment of the resolve on our side.

On 7 May 1998, when I arrived at the Ellis Park Stadium for a special crisis meeting called at the request of some members of the SARFU executive, I encountered a group of desperate souls, ready to jettison just about anything in order to stay afloat. It soon became evident that they believed the storm might subside if only they could rid themselves of the Jonah, a stubborn president insisting on sticking to principle.

Chris Heunis of South Western Districts, who was a seconded member of the executive at the time, stood up and started reading a motion of no confidence in me. In what was obviously a stressful exercise for someone rather inexperienced in the role, Heunis stumbled along. He cut a rather pathetic figure.

'I refuse to resign,' I said as I stood up, looking for someone I could address eye to eye. 'I represented you and won the case on your behalf. You unanimously mandated and urged me to go ahead. Now you are cowering in victory. I first need to see through the appeal against the decision before I can walk away.'

Next, Judge Piet Combrink – who served with Keith Parkinson on the Natal Rugby Board – rose to suggest that, despite our victory, we withdraw our action and apologise to Mandela.

'Piet,' I exclaimed, 'I'm surprised at what you're saying. I can't believe this, coming from a judge. In any event, if you or anyone else want to apologise, go right ahead and do so. I will not, because I would be insulting Justice De Villiers.'

Over my objection and the opposition of both the North West and Northern Free State, it was thus resolved that SARFU express its regret and apologise for any part it had in Justice De Villiers' subpoena of the president. It was also decided that a SARFU delegation, headed by Ronnie Masson and consisting of Hennie Erasmus, Keith Parkinson and Rian Oberholzer, would start negotiations with the NSC and the government over the appointment of an independent commission of inquiry. The latter turned out to be a moot point as the whole concept of an inquiry was dropped once SARFU capitulated to the government. It simply proved what I had maintained all along – and Tyamzashe had confirmed during his hapless appearance in court – namely, that the commission was merely a means to scare SARFU into surrendering.

When I asked for a show of hands in favour of my resignation, half of those present raised their hands, including the black members of the executive who had until then sided with me. As recently as 9 April, Silas Nkanunu had told newspapers that it was not I who had been the problem and expressed support for our right to challenge the government in court. In fact, now the black members – Nkanunu, Arthob Petersen, openly crying, Tobie Titus and Jackie Abrahams – stood up and marched out in protest against my decision to stay on in my post. They were under much greater pressure than the rest of this sad bunch. They walked straight across to the athletic stadium, where the NSC had its offices, and issued a joint press statement. Jungle justice had finally prevailed.

My son-in-law, Rian Oberholzer, also had no second thoughts on turning against me. Some days, I really want to believe he would rather not have crossed paths with me but, then again, he would probably have not been involved in rugby and may well have remained hidden away in some Foreign Affairs office, where he was previously employed.

I gave Rian a lot of credit for the section of the Rugby World Cup he had run under my close supervision and even asked Rotary International, who gave me a certificate of special recognition for my role in the tournament, to substitute my name for his. Today that is one of the certificates proudly adorning the wall of his office.

It was late afternoon when I returned to my office to call home and finish up a few pending matters. Piet Olivier and Dolf van Huyssteen of Northern Transvaal, Hennie Erasmus and a few fellows from Western Transvaal came around for a chat and a drink.

'Louis,' Piet said as he lifted his glass in a gesture of support, 'one thing you must know: You still have friends across the Jukskei River.'

The very next day Olivier was reported in the press as saying that he and his union were disassociating themselves from me, conveniently forgetting that his rugby union, at their insistence, was joined as co-defendants in the case. While travelling by bus with our team to Witbank, where we were scheduled to play against the South Eastern Transvaal Pumas, I received a call on my cell phone from the Falcons president, Rautie Rautenbach, to reassure me that he stood *bankvas* (one hundred per cent) behind me. On our arrival at Witbank, I would learn that that same morning Rautenbach had made a statement distancing himself from me. He later told me that his team sponsor MTN had threatened to withdraw their sponsorship unless he made a stand against me. The next year, however, Rautenbach lost the sponsorhsip deal anyway – even after I was no longer part of the establishment.

That weekend I had ample time to think things over. Adri and I spent many hours discussing the options. It was hard for me to declare defeat and hand over rugby to government control. But I had no other option. Only a fool would rush into battle with a troop of *hensoppers* behind him. It saddened me that all these grown men, who were rushing headlong into surrender, could seriously believe that they were doing what was best for the game of rugby.

Finance Week, which found itself much further from the scene than these frightened SARFU executives, had no trouble figuring out that the 'government is planning statutory controls over all sporting bodies of the sort once envisaged for non-governmental organisations'. 'It would represent control over sport activities,' the magazine pointed out, 'over who runs sporting federations, over whom is selected to play which sports and over sport sponsorships and finances. It would encompass state intervention into that part of the private sector even more Draconian than that carried out by apartheid-era governments.'

On Monday, 10 May 1998, I sent my letter of resignation to Rian Oberholzer to pass along to the SARFU executive. Eleven days later, they sent a delegation to Groote Schuur to formally apologise to Mandela. (Later I was told that Mandela had asked them to 'look after [Louis] as [he has] done so much for the sport'.) Before the end of the month, Silas Nkanunu became the first black president of SARFU and Rian Oberholzer was reconfirmed in his post as CEO. Mluleki George rejoined the executive as one of the NSC's point men on SARFU's board. In effect, the Minister of Sport had thus become rugby's boss.

The day after my resignation, I granted an interview to *Die Volksblad,* the Bloemfontein newspaper that first brought my name to the public's attention almost 50 years previously as a rugby player and budding salesman. I must have given the reporter his time's worth as his report was reprinted in several other journals around the country. Under the headline, 'Whites are spineless', I was reported as having described the whites as *slapgat* – unfortunately, the English tanslation as 'spineless' in other reports failed to capture the essence of the original Afrikaans term I had used.

'I can't put it any other way,' I was quoted as saying. 'There is simply no marrow left in their bones. The white person no longer believes he can protect that which is precious to him. I am no racist. Each nation has something it would like to preserve. What do we still want to protect? Nothing. That is when people turn against you – when they should stand up. That is the worst of all. The SARFU executive had allowed itself to be blackmailed and had in the process seriously jeopardised its control over rugby.'

'I'm not bitter,' I added, somewhat disingenuously, 'but I really thought there were more people with backbone. Their positions were, however, too important for them. There was pressure from the big sponsors. That is why they were for me one moment and against me the next.'

'I will never lie down,' I vowed. 'No man is my master. I bow only to God.'

'Certainly Dr Luyt is no Dale Carnegie school graduate,' wrote *The Citizen* a few days later, but 'we find it despicable that a minister and his director-general can openly admit to and condone lying for the purpose of bringing down Dr Luyt, and this raises scarcely a murmur. As for Dr Luyt, his fate was sealed a long time ago as he became surrounded by people whose opinions and loyalty were not based on principle but could be swayed by pressure. Now they have found new force to buckle under, new purse strings to clutch. We doubt whether what's left of the executive will have the guts to prevent the National Sports Council from ruining rugby.'

On 7 August 1998, almost four months after he announced his decision, Justice William de Villiers released his detailed judgment. It soon became apparent why it took him so long. Obviously aware that his decision would be taken on appeal, De Villiers went into great detail in explaining and motivating every decision and comment. The 1159-page document was the work of a jurist who turned a blind eye to political considerations and relied solely on a strict interpretation of the law.

Without fear or favour, he called the facts as he found them. He found both Tshwete and Tyamzashe to be lying and questioned the credibility of the evidence given by Mandela. 'That may be due to lack of veracity, or unreliability, or a combination of these factors,' De Villiers wrote in regard to Mandela's testimony. 'The President's overall performance on the witness stand was less than satisfactory. His overall demeanour is, to my mind, subject to material criticism.' He 'flatly refused to answer a number of questions' and 'to some extent the court was used as a podium for political rhetoric'.

These were brave words indeed from a man on the bench who must have known the consequences. In contrast to the *hensoppers* on my executive, De Villiers remained true to his profession and his calling instead of seeking the easy way out in order to preserve his position and ensure his future. The firestorm that ensued reached such ferocity that Judge President Frikkie Eloff felt obliged to caution that even high officials might run the risk of contempt of court charges. Leading the attack on the courts was Tshwete who would later, ironically, switch over from the national sport portfolio to the post of Minister of Law and Order.

But Steve Tshwete had not the slightest regard for his lies in Parliament or the judge's decision and, on 10 May 1998, he released a 'Press Statement on the Resignation of Dr Louis Luyt' issued by the the Ministry of Sport and Recreation:

'Louis Luyt's departure from the centre-stage of South African rugby is a breath of fresh air for many rugby loving people here and abroad. His autocratic behaviour and outright arrogance as he presided over the fortunes of one of the country's most treasured assets was a painful embarrassment for rugby in particular and sport in general.

'He shall be remembered more by the consistent manner in which he resisted all efforts to take rugby across the threshold into the new era and the way in which he alienated this sport from the majority of our people. Under his autocratic leadership, rugby deteriorated to a point where it had become a divisive instrument in the hands of a man who "will not bow to any man".

'There is a great deal of work for the new administration. The pieces are scattered all over the place. They must be put together speedily in order to restore lost confidences and loyalties, including the morale of the players at all levels.

'Development must not just be talked about. It must be seen to be done in a visible way that marks a break with the past autocratic one-man show. Once again, the courage of the executive members and the unions that terminated one of the saddest chapters in the history of rugby must be commended.'

What, I thought as I read this, had happened to the wide range of issues contained in the Terms of Reference of the Commission of Inquiry decreed by Mandela. Similarly, the impertinent demand for financial statements as far back as 1989 by Katz and his task team? It had all been an attempt to remove me because I was made out to be a racist. Nothing more, nothing less.

But strangely, in Parliament Tshwete and I became very close friends. In fact, Tshwete was the first person to send me a congratulatory note after my maiden speech in the House. Similarly, Kader Asmal, whose intellect I greatly respect, was the first person to congratulate me on my appointment to the Judicial Service Commission. So, it had been the race card after all and the judge had seen right through it. After all, even under oath, Tshwete denied any racial relevance when he was cross-examined by Mike Maritz.

The *Sunday Times*, in an editorial on 23 August 1998 opening with the headline, 'Nothing but lies, damned lies, from the government', had the following to say, after having gone into specific lies by state officials:

'The SARFU judgment shows the effect of such a tangle of deception: mistrust, suspicion and the undermining of the quality of public life. During his evidence to the commission (Court), President Nelson Mandela said that the situation in regard to Sarfu had reached "something in the nature of a nationwide crisis of confidence".

'We believe a nationwide crisis in confidence is indeed looming – but it no longer relates to SARFU. It is now a crisis over the willingness or ability of officials to tell the truth.'

After initially appealing to the Supreme Court of Appeals, the State Attorney, on behalf of President Mandela and the others, now decided to go directly to the Constitutional Court. We knew that the deck was stacked against us. Here was a court appointed by Mandela himself, consisting largely of people who were heavily involved in the Struggle, now being asked to rule over the findings of a man branded publicly as an 'apartheid judge' – someone who had the temerity not only to find in favour of Luyt and a bunch of 'racists', but to cast aspersions on the veracity of Mandela. Our odds of winning or getting a fair hearing were about as good as Tony Leon being elected president of South Africa. None to none.

The Blue Bulls Rugby Union, which had insisted on joining SARFU in the initial action, now bowed out, citing lack of funds. But, with the help of Dawie Botha, we pressed ahead, knowing that our goal posts had not merely been shifted – they had been removed. Even though we did not expect the president of the Constitutional Court, Arthur Chaskalson, to be particularly enamoured with our questioning of his fitness to preside over the case, the depth of his resentment when he dismissed our application in May 1999 still came as somewhat of a shock. But, then, these were hardly normal times.

In our brief, we pointed out that Chaskalson had had a long-standing and close lawyer-client relationship with Mandela since the sixties when he served on his defence team during the Rivonia Trial. They had become close and Chaskalson had served as the ANC's constitutional advisor during the negotiations leading up to Mandela's election as president.

On 9 May 1999, the *Sunday Times*, in an article under the headline 'Chaskalson no stranger to bitter recusal bids' reminded its readers that 12 years previously, appearing in a high-profile political case, Chaskalson had been on the other side of the courtroom, applying for Judge Kees van Dijkhorst and an assessor to recuse themselves because of 'political' bias. The recusal application was acrimonious and the judge made scathing comments about the defence team, accusing them of acting unprofessionally and improperly. Now the same charges would be levelled against us from the bench.

Chaskalson was also no stranger to me. In the seventies, he had been part of the team appearing for Gazocean in a civil suit brought against the French company by Triomf. I could certainly concur with former Justice Van Schalkwyk's description of Chaskalson in his book, *One Miracle is Not Enough*, as 'undoubtedly a fine jurist' who 'may have the ability to put aside his political inclinations when called upon to decide social issues' while recognising that 'the perception remains that the Constitutional Court under the leadership of its president is an ANC or ANC-sympathetic institution'.

Apart from Chaskalson, we also registered our objection against four other members of the Constitutional Court, three of whom were active members of the ANC hierarchy: Justice Langa, a founding member of the Release Mandela Committee in Natal, advisor during the transitional talks and a regular guest at Groote Schuur; Justice Albie Sachs, a prominent member of the liberation movement who had been very seriously injured through the actions of the previous government, a close confidant of former ANC president Oliver Tambo, and who had served on of the national executive of the ANC; and Justice J Jacoob, who had been involved as a defendant in several political trials in the past.

The fourth was Justice Johan Kriegler, son of an Afrikaner soldier of the old order, who had ingratiated himself with the new order, and headed up the Independent Election Commission (IEC) before his elevation to the bench of the Constitutional Court. Even though I had been a friend of this sharp advocate, who handled one or two cases on my behalf, I could not say for certain that he was ever a member of the ANC. Still, it was not difficult to see where his sympathies might lie. Not only had there been a serious fall-out between Kriegler and my attorney, Dawie Botha, but relations between the two of us had soured as well.

Half-way through the case, I received a frantic call from Dawie Botha. Kriegler and Goldstone were trying their damnedest to embarrass Maritz. There was no reasoning behind it all. Would I be prepared to end their mandate? Kriegler and Goldstone were hitting Maritz with everything they could lay their hands on.

I was saddened by the prospect of going into the last phase of this drawn-out legal battle without Maritz and the rest of my legal team, but reluctantly agreed to release Maritz. To my absolute surprise, I was accused in the press of running scared of the state. Nothing could, of course, have been further from the truth! But bullying judges seem to have a free run and, in court, would – in Kriegler's case, certainly – forget the standards of civility reserved for a senior advocate who, like him, was an official of the court.

The dismissal of our recusal application and the finding in favour of Mandela and others as appellants was about as surprising as hearing that the All Blacks had beaten Japan. We had had no real chance. The only issue that was ever in at least some doubt – however slight that might have been towards the end – was whether the Constitutional Court would go as far as awarding punitive costs against us as well. Fortunately, it refrained from the absurdity of damages but awarded costs to the state. As it turned out, however, that also came as no surprise as someone on the court fed the scoop to Phillip de Bruyn of *Beeld* before the decision was released.

Looking back at these events, the Latin quote *Quis custudiet ipsos custodes* comes to mind. Who will guard the guards themselves? As we entered the new millennium and the government continues to march relentlessly towards greater control of every facet of our lives, this question is even more pertinent. The losers in this sad episode were not only rugby, but also our courts. It was a sad time indeed.

But in 1999 I did not have too much time in which to brood over the past. Not yet. By the time the Constitutional Court ruled, I was already in Cape Town, representing my own political party, the Federal Alliance – and I was still involved in Transvaal rugby.

*Politics ought to be the part-time profession of
every citizen who would protect the rights and
privileges of free people and who would preserve
what is good and fruitful in our national heritage.*

Dwight D Eisenhower,
US President 1953–1961
English clergyman, 1834–1892

Chapter 15

THE SPORT OF POLITICS

Politics had long been a part-time profession. Throughout my years in business, I have never hesitated to speak up whenever I saw the need for change. My open defiance of an all-powerful National Party in the eighties, when they interfered in the private sector, and my widely publicised insistence that the time had come to free Mandela and restructure the government, caused me considerable personal grief and financial hardship. When I responded to Doc Craven's call to open talks with the ANC in an effort to break through the iron curtain the world had put up around rugby, I was branded a traitor. As a part-time politician, I facilitated the formation of the Democratic Party. Ironically, the same people who resented my insistence on dialogue with our black opposition would call me a racist when I stood up for our rights against the ANC government's interference in rugby.

In October 1998 I was no longer a part-time politician. I had crossed over from the politics of sport into the sport of politics with the formation of the Federal Alliance that would participate in the June 1999 general election. The transition was not without a good measure of anguish and soul-searching. My break from sport was, however, not complete. As chairman of Ellis Park Stadium, I still ran South Africa's strongest regional rugby entity and thus found myself still very much embroiled in the politics of sport.

My formal entry into the political arena happened without much enthusiasm from Adri, my children and some of my closest friends, who all felt that trying to halt the growing interference of the new government in our private pursuits was tantamount to trying to sweep the ocean back with a broom. Like the former government, their argument was that the ANC could – and would – damn well do as it pleases despite all the yapping and yelping of the little lapdogs in opposition. It had nothing to fear from a divided and disorganised array of smaller parties.

Soon after my ousting as president of the South African Rugby Football Union in a coup orchestrated by the ANC with the collaboration of certain persons within my own ranks, it became apparent that there were still a substantial number of people willing to fight for their individual rights. My widely publicised hard-hitting interview with *Die Volksblad* and a speech in similar vein before an overflow audience at a *Finance Week* business breakfast in Johannesburg on 7 May 1998 – in which I described white South Africans as 'spineless' and insisted that we stand strong on principle – unleashed a veritable flood of faxes, letters and phone calls of support. This led to growing speculation in the press that I might start a new political party to provide a home for those who felt that none of the existing splinter parties was making any headway in protecting their rights and ensuring their future.

Instead of reinventing the wheel, I believed that the solution was to unite the splinter groups into one cohesive opposition – a truly multiracial alliance that would attract support from a broad section of the population. By then it had become apparent that the ANC, despite all the protestations to the contrary, was heading towards dominance at any cost. With Mandela's announced departure from politics and Mbeki's thinly veiled threats, it had become clear that the honeymoon was over. Having had a taste of how even a moderate Nelson Mandela could be manipulated by zealous underlings into railroading rugby, I truly feared what a less tolerant Mbeki might sanction. Looking back today, it turned out to be a valid concern. It has gone way beyond merely black over white. It has become a tribal matter, with the Zulu and other language groups complaining about the ruling Xhosa Nostra's preference for their own in high posts and positions of privilege.

In a way, the Xhosa people are simply following the footpath left by the Afrikaners when they took over the country in 1948. They turned the civil service into a haven for Afrikaners and gave preference to their own in handing out government favours. They interfered in every facet of society. The likes of Malan and Verwoerd prohibited our sportsmen from mixing on the field with international teams that included even one person of colour. They pushed the ideology of racial purity as mercilessly as the ANC thrusts ahead today with its black empowerment and transformation at all costs. It took us quite a while to come to our senses – only to find ourselves facing a repeat of the past.

The ANC's determination to enforce black quotas on rugby and other sport is as lamentable as was the National Party's ban on mixed sport. It is a clear denial of one of the basic tenets of a free society: The right to free association and to compete on a basis of merit. Rugby was being turned into another arm of the bulging state apparatchik. In business, too, the new rulers' ham-handed enforcement of black empowerment made the National Party government's blatant political meddling look relatively mild.

Why, I asked my wife and myself, should I sit back and let the ANC do exactly what I so despised in the National Party? Adri, in her own calm way, posed the simple question: 'You are willing to lead, but are they really willing to follow?' As always, she had a very valid point. In my bruising battle in defence of rugby, I eventually found myself, for all intents and purposes, alone as the spineless rolled over and played dead. But, then, hope springs eternal and I felt that there might well still be some spunk left in the country. Even if there were only a few thousand, I owed it to them to make the case for a true democracy and respect for the rights of minorities.

There is no denial that my decision to enter politics was, in part, motivated by a desire to hit back at the politicos who had driven me out of rugby. I owed it to myself to put up the good fight even though the odds of succeeding looked rather miniscule. It was simply not in my nature to read the gossip in the Sunday papers and clip coupons while the country around me slid further into the abyss. I would rather storm the windmills in quixotic fashion than sit sedately at home.

As I set out to meet with opposition leaders in 1998 to try to convince them to put together their respective molehills and make a mountain, I was reminded of a similar episode almost 10 years earlier. In the wake of a brutal attack by the Botha government on Doc Craven and me after we had met with an ANC delegation in Harare, I decided to mount a counter-attack with the help of the three small opposition parties. Ironically, the man who had led the ANC delegation that met with us in Harare happened to be Thabo Mbeki and the one who had led the attack for 'talking with terrorists' was President PW Botha's deputy, FW de Klerk. Now, 10 years later, the man I wished to oppose more effectively by uniting splinters into a beam was none other than Mbeki, Mandela's heir apparent. FW de Klerk, who succeeded Botha, had already retired after talking to 'the terrorists', but allowing them to do most of the talking.

In 1988, finally fed up with the abuse heaped upon Craven and me for our sincere efforts to develop a dialogue and break the deadlock, I had picked up the phone and called Zach de Beer, leader of the Progressive Federal Party (PFP), to start the process of 'opposition building'.

'Zach,' I asked, 'if there was the opportunity for the three opposition parties to get together, would you be interested?'

The answer came quick and firm in his sonorous Oxford accent.

'Sure.'

And, yes, he would attend a meeting at my home at Saxonwold should the leaders of the other two parties – Dennis Worrall's National Democratic Movement (NDM) and Wynand Malan's Independent Party (IP) – agree to join. Both these parties were, in essence, one-man shows with still largely unrealised hopes of growth. Worrall, the academic, was full of ideas but rather short on organisation. Wynand Malan had already left the ranks of the National Party, partly with my encouragement, because of deep-seated differences with its leadership, to set up his own opposition of one.

Worrall's response was enthusiastic. Malan's was cautiously in the affirmative. Even though I knew him better than the others, he sounded distant and somewhat suspicious. Nevertheless, we all agreed to meet at my house on 18 August and I extended formal invitations.

I was soaking up the sun at my home in Ballito when three unexpected visitors turned up at the front gate. It was a delegation from the IP and PFP. Advocate Dawid de Villiers – or Lang (Long) Dawid, as his peers affectionately knew him – represented Malan's IP, while Rodger Burrows and Mike Tarr spoke on behalf of the PFP. De Villiers had made his name in the sixties as lead counsel in an impressive win for South Africa in the South West Africa (Namibia) dispute before the World Court in The Hague. I was not familiar with Burrows at all, but gathered that he represented his party's leadership.

As we dispensed with formalities and settled down on the main balcony overlooking the sea stirring our tea, De Villiers presented his case. The IP insisted that Willem de Klerk (brother of FW de Klerk) be the facilitator and that the meeting take place at another venue. Burrows had no problem with my Johannesburg home as a venue but raised strenuous objections against De Klerk having any part of the discussions.

While I shared Burrows' reservations about Willem de Klerk, I was perplexed by De Villiers' objection to my house as a venue. So I asked him outright and he was equally forthcoming with his answer:

'We regard this as an effort by you to grab control of the three parties.'

I could hardly believe my ears.

'I'm afraid it is my house or I am out,' I announced. 'While I share Rodger's reticence about Willem de Klerk, I am willing to give him a chance. But remember, we will never know what transpires between him and his brother. Or will we?'

In the next few days, further phone calls and personal exchanges between the parties finally led to acceptance of both the venue and the facilitator. But the distrust and gamesmanship refused to be erased. On the assigned morning, representatives from the three parties sat in their cars outside my property, waiting to see who would get out first – no one wanted to make the first move. They all bottlenecked at the side entrance at exactly nine in the morning and proceeded to the conference facility where Adri and my assistant Susan Kruger had made the necessary preparations. Mindful of the sensitivities that had surfaced during the run-up to the event, they took great care in ensuring that all the seating was exactly the same. A different pencil, notepad, glass or cup might well have been misconstrued as favouritism and derail the event. The parties were seated at three sides of the big table, with two seats reserved for De Klerk and me at the fourth.

I invited everyone to take their refreshments to their respective seats and called the meeting to order. All three leaders of the parties were present but PFP heavyweights such as Helen Suzman and Harry Schwarz were conspicuously absent. De Beer obviously still had some work waiting for him within his own ranks before there could be talk about an amalgamation of parties. Still, no one could ignore the significance of the moment – least of all the members of the press who were already taking up positions outside the gates.

But I was not merely trying to make history or headlines. My intent was clear: We had to find a way to unify against a dictatorial government that had led us all into an impasse and, in the words of Botha's predecessor, John Vorster, an alternative too ghastly to contemplate. We needed a new government.

'Welcome, ladies and gentlemen,' I said as I stood up and the chatter around the table subsided. 'I am indeed pleased that we could muster the courage to take this, in my book, giant step towards the creation of an opposition that can govern this country. I hope you all realise that no one can leave this property without some kind of agreement. In coming here, each and everyone of you have already admitted that you cannot make it on your own.'

I handed over to De Klerk and sat down. The discussions started. When it was my turn to make a statement, I proposed that we draw up a list of areas of agreement, set them aside and concentrate on disagreements on which compromise was needed. It soon became clear that the disagreements were more a matter of form than substance. On everybody's mind, I knew, was the question of leadership. But it remained an unspoken concern at this point, as we all realised that it might well kill the talks at this early stage.

At nine that night, 12 hours after we had started, we were ready to meet with the members of the press who had caused a traffic jam along Jan Smuts Avenue all day. Drinks were served. Willem de Klerk stepped up to the cameras and announced that enough common ground existed for further meetings between the parties. A date had already been set for the next meeting. A press release was handed out, confirming that 'the three parties would endeavour urgently to bring about the formation of a new political party... to promote the broad principle of a multiracial multiparty democratic order.'

Naturally, we received ample publicity both in the newspapers and on television. There was serious speculation that a new united opposition party might well draw support from an estimated undecided 25 per cent of the electorate. The government, however, remained silent. Botha and FW de Klerk were either unimpressed or determined not to give us any public recognition. Either way, I was certain, they knew much more than what they gleaned from the media, courtesy of Willem de Klerk.

On a Saturday in December 1988, at Zach de Beer's insistence, we held our second meeting at the Cape Town home of textile manufacturer Aaron Searle. As we got down to business, I could not help but think that this was an unlikely venue for the proverbial political discussions in smoke-filled rooms behind closed doors. Aaron's wife, the late Adele, had pasted large 'No smoking' signs all over the place.

It was here that the dreaded issue of leadership reared its ugly head for the first time. The press conference that followed lacked the fervour of the first and it showed in the reports that followed. We still had no name for the beast, but by the looks of it, *blouwildebees* (blue wildbeest or, more literally, 'blue wild beast') might have sufficed.

I was not surprised when Searle told us that his home would not be available for the next meeting and Zach de Beer asked me to host it. Still, the process continued to move along. The gathering at my house was well attended, but Suzman and Schwarz, who had also not attended the Cape Town parley, were again absent. We did what is usually done when seemingly insurmountable problems arise. We appointed committees. One to find a suitable name for the party. Another to resolve the leadership issue. Yet another to look after the financial affairs. I was asked to head the latter, but declined.

One Saturday, while supervising arrangements for a rugby game at Ellis Park, I received a call from Zach de Beer. He urgently needed me to brief the full PFP Congress at the Protea Gardens Hotel on our plans to establish a new party. On the way over, I hurriedly scribbled a few notes on the back of an envelope. It remained in my pocket, however, as I decided in the end that ad-libbing might be the best approach.

Zach met me at the front door and accompanied me to a seat next to the chairman. There were close to 200 members present, many of them staunch Bailey Trust types – the very sort of individuals who had indignantly rejected our appeal when De Villiers Graaff asked them to sell their shares in the *Rand Daily Mail* to us.

Here I was, trying to sell them on a new, yet to be named party! I cleared my throat and took a deep breath. The words flowed easily as they usually do when spoken in sincerity. The PFP and other splinter parties had had enough time to prove themselves to the voters and they had all failed to attract the disenchanted but still uncommitted, I argued. It is time to push self-interest to the backburner and put the country's interest first. But if the PFP believed that this was simply a matter of taking over the other two smaller opposition parties, it would be a grave mistake. There had to be a change in both direction and policy.

'Mrs Suzman,' I observed as I turned to where she was sitting in the front row, 'you look bored.'

'Oh no, my dear,' she responded in her quick-witted fashion, 'I have not said a thing all day.'

'That, Madam, is what worries me most.'

Laughter broke out. Even the stern-faced in the audience cracked a smile and I managed to conclude in a more relaxed atmosphere. Afterwards, De Beer thanked me profusely for helping to break down resistance within his own party. Significantly, at the next meeting held at my home, both Colin Eglin and Harry Schwarz, the man with the razor-sharp mind, joined in.

The time had come, I felt as we once again settled down in discussion, to stop nibbling at the edges and to bite right to the core. I turned to Willem de Klerk.

'We have been going on for quite a few meetings,' I said, 'and you have acted as the facilitator. May I ask you a straightforward question? Are you one of us?'

He shuffled his papers and rearranged his glasses.

'I have not yet made up my mind.'

'So what have you been doing here all this time?' I asked. 'We certainly cannot afford to have people in this room who cannot walk the walk.'

Silence.

We then moved on to the issue of leadership. The PFP argued that, as the strongest party, it should select the leader. Predictably, both Worrall's and Malan's supporters voiced their opposition. Then there was talk about shared assets and I asked the parties to declare their financial positions. Worrall announced that his Democratic Party was solvent but without a penny in the bank. Surprisingly, considering the signs of affluence I had noticed in the audience at the Protea Gardens, the Progressive Federal Party claimed to have a mere R10,000 in the bank. Wynand Malan confessed to being in the red to the amount of R80,000.

'Well, I'll pick up the tab for you,' I said to Malan. 'That makes everyone equal.'

This largesse did not, however, prevent Malan from wanting to jump ship only a few days later. One Sunday morning, I climbed into my car and drove to his house. He was at church so I waited. And when he returned, I wasted no time.

'Wynand,' I said, 'we have to know whether you are in. It is time to make your final decision, right now.'

'Louis,' he replied, 'I might leave politics altogether.'

'Then do it,' I said, 'but make up your mind please!'

He turned up at the next meeting at my home where the question of leadership was to be finalised. The assigned committee had already decided on the Democratic Party as an appropriate name and had designed a logo. Now the leadership committee put forward the brilliant idea of having a troika to head the party. I saw this three-headed monster as a cop-out, but it did seem to be the only way to keep all three parties happy.

'Ladies and gentlemen,' I said, 'Do you know why President PW Botha and his supporters are governing this country?'

There was dead silence. Adri looked particularly uncomfortable, realising no doubt what I was about to say.

'Well, let me give you the answer. It is because he has opposition like you.' They just stared at me as if struck by lightning, but did not say a word.

At the official launch of the Democratic Party at the Teachers Education College in Johannesburg, I was seated alongside the troika together with Willem de Klerk who, now apparently entirely committed, made an impassioned plea for new directions and policies to save the country from what was almost certain disaster. Eventually, I believe, it was this same argument that swayed his more conservative brother FW de Klerk to scrap apartheid when he succeeded Botha as president. Willem de Klerk and the three leaders extended a special word of thanks to me for bringing it all about. At my own request, I was not called upon to deliver a speech.

I was, however, asked – and agreed – to serve on the executive together with the troika and their adjudants, including Harry Schwarz, Tony Leon, Dawid de Villiers, Jan Momberg and a few other notables. Our first meeting was held at the Johannesburger Hotel.

Compromise had once again been taken to the extreme as the organisers tried to prevent friction between the three members of the troika. A young outsider, Professor Marinus Wiechers, was asked to chair the meeting. But there would be little compromise or tolerance once the politicos got going on who might qualify as members of the Democratic Party. To my utmost surprise, Harry Schwarz argued strongly that a certain Jan van Eck and Charles Radcliffe be blackballed because of their 'leftist' leanings.

Even though I did not know Van Eck or Radcliffe personally, I felt that anyone who accepted our manifesto should be free to join. I found myself pitted against a lathe of lawyers, the likes of whom were ready to shave me down to size. Dawid de Villiers, Wynand Malan and the rest all voiced their vehement support of Schwarz in his argument against Van Eck and Radcliffe.

At lunch, I was seated alongside Tony Leon, who was then a rising star in Johannesburg city politics.

'Tony,' I asked, 'why did you not help me in my defence of Van Eck and Radcliffe? After all, you're an expert in constitutional law, aren't you?'

'Louis,' he replied, 'you don't expect me to go up against these big guns? I am, after all, only a junior around here.'

Not long afterwards, 'the junior' would deservedly become the senior of them all. But before then much else was left dangling.

Shortly after the Johannesburger Hotel conference, I received a call from Hermien van der Merwe of *The Star* in Johannesburg. According to her own survey, she said, it was clear that undecided voters were not at all impressed with the idea of a troika or a triumvirate. They wanted a single leader.

'Would you accept that position if it was offered?'

'It was not offered,' I replied, 'and I haven't even given it a thought.'

Despite the denial, the mere fact that *The Star* had contacted me to enquire about my willingness to serve as leader if called upon to do so, lit a red light in some quarters. Soon Zach de Beer was on the telephone.

'Louis, I see you are also making a run for the leadership.'

'Zach,' I tried to reassure him, 'if you are referring to what Van der Merwe wrote, I will tell you exactly how I responded to her. I said I haven't even given it a thought.'

'But, Louis,' he said, 'I was hoping for your support.'

I, however, remained noncommittal. The troika went to parliament together, trying as best they could to keep this three-headed monster heading in one direction and speaking with one voice. During the winter break, I received a call from Zach de Beer. I was in Ballito, and he was in nearby La Lucia, staying with Harry Oppenheimer, and wanted to come over for a chat. He turned up in a windbreaker, casual slacks and tennis shoes. As we settled down over a cold beer on the terrace, he once again raised the question of my support for his leadership.

'Zach,' I explained, 'you're all fighting over the question of leadership. In my view, this is something that will evolve over time. The real leader will not be picked. He will emerge.'

After he left, I sat down and took serious stock of the situation. Over the previous few months, I had spent considerable amounts of my money and endless hours in order to form this new party. I had tried to focus on the ultimate goal, namely, winning the hearts and souls of the undecided electorate and eventually ousting the Nationalists. The three leaders had, in the meanwhile, been almost entirely preoccupied with the battle over who should be in charge. The time had come, I told Adri, to bow out. She seemed relieved. I wrote a letter to all three members of the troika, resigning from the executive and wishing them well. Zach de Beer responded by letter, accusing me of never having been 'one of us' – whatever that meant. Wynand Malan called me long afterwards to tell me how sorry he had been about my decision. Only Dennis Worrall wrote me a very decent letter to thank me for my contribution.

In the September 1989 election, I voted in favour of the Democratic Party. So did many other disenchanted former National Party supporters. The Democratic Party grew from 21 to 33 seats, while the Conservative Party – founded by Connie Mulder after he had been ousted in the wake of the so-called Information Scandal – leapt from 22 to 39 seats. FW de Klerk, who had ousted PW Botha as leader, was left with only 93 out of a total of 123 seats in Parliament. Being the consummate politician, De Klerk claimed that the votes for the more liberal Democratic Party were, in effect, votes for the National Party, and therefore 70 per cent of white voters had expressed themselves in favour of the reforms he proposed! To add credence to this claim, he went overboard in the next few months by giving away, at bargain basement prices, almost everything to the very same 'ANC terrorists' he had lambasted me for having met with in London, Frankfurt and Harare.

In the April 1994 election that followed this 'new dispensation', the African National Congress clobbered the rest by capturing 252 out of 400 seats in the National Assembly, elected on a proportional basis. The National Party came in second, with 82, and Chief Mangosuthu Buthelezi's Zulu-dominated Inkatha Freedom Party (IFP) third, with 43 seats. The Democratic Party captured a mere seven seats, four behind the right-wing Afrikaner-dominated Freedom Front and slightly ahead of the Pan African Congress' five. Tony Leon was now in charge of the Democratic Party, having followed in the footsteps of Zach de Beer, who – in the end – saw his wish realised when he had replaced the troika as the party's sole leader.

With ample justification, Leon could claim that in the run-up to the election, the National Party had stolen the DP's clothes while they were out swimming. The impression that the National Party had now assumed the role as the voice of the minority and therefore made the DP redundant was, however, incorrect. With FW de Klerk serving as Vice President, one step behind Vice President Thabo Mbeki, and the National Party being part of an alliance of sorts with the ANC and the IFP, this was hardly the case. Whether he liked it or not, De Klerk was compelled to take his cue from the newly installed President Nelson Mandela, with whom, it later turned out, he shared a rotten relationship.

As the 1999 election approached, several changes had taken place. To the surprise of no one, the National Party and De Klerk became history as he bowed out two years into the 'new dispensation' to make room for a young, rather soft-natured man, Marthinus van Schalkwyk, as leader of a reconstructed New National Party. A highly decorated general in our ill-fated war on the Angolan border, Constand Viljoen, was still wooing the conservative Afrikaner, while Roelf Meyer who had presided with De Klerk over the dismantling of apartheid and the liquidation of all political assets, jumped ship to form the United Democratic Movement (UDM) together with a former ANC firebrand, Bantu Holomisa. Chief Mangosuthu Buthelezi's Inkatha Freedom Party (IFP) maintained an uneasy alliance with the ANC in exchange for a few cabinet posts. The Democratic Party, in the meanwhile, was desperately trying to get its clothes back and reasserting itself as the voice of the oppressed white minority.

In May 1998, Hanlie Retief visited with me on behalf of *Rapport*, barely two weeks after I had been forced to resign as president of SARFU. Still nursing the scars after my lone battle against the ANC's highjacking of rugby and deeply disappointed by the desertion of some of my most trusted adjudants, including my own son-in-law, I did not hold back. I declared myself in favour of a new party that would be willing and able to fight against the ANC's Stalinist tactics. I could not help but notice that none of the existing ones had had the guts to oppose the ANC's assault on SARFU even though several newspapers had spoken out strongly, despite their apparent dislike of me personally. This was not a personal matter. It was a matter of principle. The time had come, I told Hanlie, for the opposition parties to unite and stop their bickering. No, I said, I would not be willing to become a leader of right-wing dissidents, despite wild talk of me as the modern-day Lion of the North.

In the ensuing weeks, I made the rounds to find out whether there were grounds for closer cooperation between the opposition parties. Once again, it became clear that self-interest reigned supreme. Tony Leon of the Democratic Party visited me in secret at my home. The discussion was cordial, but inconclusive and when news of the meeting leaked out, Leon insisted that we had agreed to confidentiality. But, ironically, *The Star* reported that the leader of the DP 'was not impressed with Luyt's proposal'. Leon also rejected the New National Party's proposal of a council of opposition parties in which all would have equal status, regardless of size. 'We don't want to be part of a rescue operation for a failing political party,' he was quoted as saying. I, in the meanwhile, can solemnly swear that I had never – ever – spoken to anyone about Leon's visit.

Marthinus van Schalkwyk, who had the unenviable task of presiding over the sad remains of the once omnipotent National Party, visited me too – at the Vineyard Hotel in Newlands, Cape Town. He was accompanied by, among others, Johan Killian, the Gauteng leader of the NNP, André Fourie, Sam de Beer and Daryl Swanepoel.

Even though Van Schalkwyk seemed confident that he had it within him to put Humpty Dumpty back together again, Killian had little taste for this reconstruction task and showed real interest in the prospect of a fresh start. But, as before, I was wrong in my assessment of the man and today Killian is a furious supporter of an alliance with the ANC.

Van Schalkwyk asked that our deliberations at that meeting in Cape Town remain confidential and I agreed. But the next morning, Cape Town's Afrikaans daily, *Die Burger*, carried the full story and Van Schalkwyk wasted no time in accusing me of being the 'leak'. When his former PRO, Jan Bosman, joined the Federal Alliance I learned the truth. Immediately after his return to his office, Van Schalkwyk instructed Daryl Swanepoel and Jan Bosman to engineer the so-called 'leak'. Certainly, a man to be 'trusted' In the same way, voters had trusted him during the 2001 local elections and were summarily 'sold out' to the ANC.

My discussions with Constand Viljoen of the Freedom Front and Ferdie Hartzenberg of the Conservative Party were friendly, but equally futile. These men on the right were not about to move towards the middle to join up with the likes of Leon. As a result, I was left with the choice of forming my own party or walking away into retirement, simply watching the ANC trample over individual

With vice-president Silas Nkanunu in 1997 after the Annual General Meeting when Muleki George and Keith Parkinson were defeated.

Campaigning for the Federal Alliance in Alexandra in 1999.

Left: After my retirement from the Golden Lions Rugby Union in 1998.
photo: Wessel Oosthuizen.

Below: With Steve Tshwete and Deputy President Thabo Mbeki at the Bafana Bafana match against Brazil in 1997.

and minority rights while criminals run amok in the streets and suburbs, poverty spreads and educational standards erode. There was no way in which I could let that happen without at least putting up a good fight, I thought. I owed it to my fellow South Africans and myself. So I disregarded advice from good friends and my own family, turned a blind eye to acerbic accounts in the press and established the Federal Alliance.

The announcement was made during a speech at the Midrand Chamber of Business conference, where I had been invited to be the guest speaker. Predictably, my formal entry into politics was manna to the media and fodder for Fedler and other cartoonists. I seemed to have introduced a little life into what seemed destined to be a pretty dull election with the only issue to be settled the ANC's determination to receive a two-thirds majority that would enable it to ride roughshod over the constitution.

'Luyt's style is very much to take on establishment figures grown complacent by years of doing business in the same old way,' wrote *The Star* on 5 October 1998. 'So his venture into politics is not unexpected and should be seen as the continuation of his one-man attempt to stop the ANC government in its tracks.' With 'considerable financial and other resources,' the newspaper argued, I was likely to run an election campaign 'that will be the envy of many opponents, hobbled by their staidness and their conventional ways of doing things.' But our politics, it concluded, 'does not need another Great White Hope – after all, we have the Democratic Party's Tony Leon, the Freedom Front's Constand Viljoen and the National Party's Marthinus van Schalkwyk.'

Considering the criticism heaped upon me by these opposition leaders for moving onto their turf, *The Star's* conclusion was not without foundation. Still, I did not see my role as that of simply another aspiring Great White Hope. It was my intention to try to unite an opposition against the flagrant excesses of a new government that showed all the signs of becoming what they and others detested so much in the previous regime. I wanted to put some backbone into a splintered opposition who, it seemed, had no will to fight. The leadership question was not my greatest concern.

'For a person who has had preliminary discussions with a range of politicians and other leaders,' observed *The Citizen* on 2 October 1998, 'Louis Luyt has drawn an extraordinarily negative reaction to the proposed launch of a Federal Alliance. Whether that is because some see him as a potential threat in an overcrowded opposition market, or because they don't like what he stands for, is difficult to determine. However, it is not accurate to write him off, as the DP's Douglas Gibson has done, as a bull-in-a-china-shop rugby boss who knows nothing about politics. Dr Luyt was instrumental in the formation of the DP, and had talks with the ANC when most of the establishment considered that treason. Even his court case against the government this year was heavily political.'

'Dr Luyt is no amateur in politics,' the newspaper continued, 'nor in organisation or administration. But what does he have to offer? A firm belief in law and order, and calling for the death penalty, are not novel ideas. Nor is his emphasis on health, education, and the need for community involvement, although all these themes have merit. Where he differs from many espousing similar ideas is in his image as a strong person who will stand up to anyone. Against this must be balanced the negative way he is perceived by some as an anachronistic champion of white Afrikaner resistance. In fact he preaches non-racialism consistent with his 1980s approaches to the ANC, but that is a message he has yet to convey successfully. We shall not be supporting Dr Luyt's Federal Alliance, or any other party, in next year's elections, but we do think the entry of a forceful, if domineering, character will liven up a political environment where there are too many wimps.'

Quick to join the chorus of critics was Willem de Klerk with whom my relationship had soured considerably since the years when I had afforded him free office space and secretarial staff after he had been ousted as editor of *Die Transvaler*. 'Dr Louis Luyt and his Federal Alliance will not cause even a quiver in the political barometer,' De Klerk told *Beeld*. He dismissed my entry into politics as 'political silliness' aimed at 'self-aggrandisement' and born out of a 'crushed ego'. But then I had not expected much else from this man whom I had come to accept as little more than a fair-weather friend when, as editor of *Rapport*, he refused to hold back on a blatant and untrue libellous story about me and Piet Uys in his newspaper. He seemed to have forgotten that the Democratic Party, which had been born out of the very same 'crushed ego' in 1989, had propelled him – and, eventually, his brother – into new political thought and action.

Even though I never became a consummate politician, I had, through years in the politics of business and sport, learned how to stay focused despite the jeers from the sidelines. Kraai van Niekerk, a former cabinet minister in the National Party government, joined the ranks and we received verbal support from several disillusioned members in the opposition. Nelia Pluddeman and General Kobus Bosman defected from the NNP to join the FA. So did Jan Vermeulen of Alberton, but he later defected to the ANC. Today, he is history. Sakkie Blanche also came over to the FA. Some sitting members were, however, careful not to walk over, as it would have meant giving up their seats and their livelihood. But several smaller extra-parliamentarian black parties joined forces with the FA.

Campaigning came with some difficulty. Being shown off around the country like a prize bull never really appealed to me. I was much more comfortable in private conversations. Drawing applause from large audiences, however, did have an invigorating effect and spurred me to continue. At the football field in Nelspruit, a crowd twice the size that had attended a meeting addressed by FW de Klerk when he was still leader of the NP, turned up to cheer me on. I went to

Soweto, where I was also warmly welcomed. At a speech before the residents of Stellenbosch University's Wilgenhof, I drew a standing ovation, to the surprise of Morné du Plessis whose son had come to listen and who happened to be a former resident of this illustrious, historical institution with a reputation for scepticism and cynicism.

In the final weeks of the run-up to the election, the *New York Times* observed, 'In a field of professional politicians, Louis Luyt stands out'. Its three-column report on 20 May 1999, under the headline 'New Party – The man of the house is... a man', compared me and my slogan 'We Mean Business' with American magnate Ross Perot who had shaken up presidential politics with his business-oriented approach. 'Luyt (pronounced "late") entered the race for a parliamentary seat only seven months ago,' wrote the newspaper, 'but he was already a household name – not always uttered in admiration – and doesn't shirk from spending money.'

Noting that the pollsters were giving me a mere 1 per cent of the national vote, the *New York Times* reporter took the trouble in trying to find out why there was such a buzz around my campaign. 'He's a strong leader,' Ria van Wyk, a retired teacher, told him. 'A go-get-'em type,' said Henry de Korte, a college student. 'Someone who could pull the country together,' said DP Badenhorst, a retired farmer.

Finding that at least 20 per cent of my audiences was black, the *Times* man approached a few of them to find out why they would come to listen to someone who had been made out as a right-wing racist. A black Klerksdorp resident, a 40-year-old storekeeper who declined to give his name, told the reporter that he feared being attacked and came because he had read the FA manifesto. 'My friends are disillusioned with the ANC, and most like Louis Luyt,' he told the reporter.

'Africans – African men, especially – like a man who is big and strong, who has authority,' explained Nomavenda Mathiane, a black reporter who had watched my campaign in black townships such as Soweto and Alexandra. 'They might not vote for Luyt, but they respect him.'

When he got around to interviewing me, the *New York Times* reporter raised the question of money. 'There had been reports,' he said, 'that you have so far spent R2 million of your own money.' I shook my head and smiled. 'I can't tell you how much I have put in altogether, but I will only admit that I spent R3 million last week alone.'

Despite all the letters, faxes and calls of encouragement, the old adage 'Talk is cheap' continued to apply. Any new political movement finds itself way back at the trough when it comes to corporate campaign largesse. Companies, understandably, prefer to stick with the status quo instead of taking chances on anything new. Individual contributions were too small to make even a dent in the bills. I thus had no alternative, but to dig deep into my own pocket. Mine turned out to be the most expensive votes ever in South African political history.

Encouraging initial results showing 'impressive gains' by the Federal Alliance soon made way for less optimistic reports and an eventual tally of some 80,000 votes or a mere 0.7 per cent of the total electorate – entitling us to two seats in the National Assembly and one in the Gauteng Legislature. There had been reporting of some gross irregularities at the polls, but I declined to pursue the matter. It was evident that the New National Party's and the Democratic Party's persistent propaganda against splitting votes to vote for a new party also had a severe impact. Kraai van Niekerk and I thus proceeded to Cape Town to represent the newly found Federal Alliance, mindful of the fact that Helen Suzman, as the lone representative of the Progressive Federal Party, had once managed to be quite a thorn in the side of the then all-powerful National Party. Kobus Bosman took up a seat in the Gauteng Legislature.

In a way, I could also take at least some satisfaction from seeing the Democratic Party, whose formation I had engineered in 1989, finally defeat the New National Party for the position of main opposition by 38 seats against 28. The IFP came second with 34. We were ninth in ranking among opposition parties, but I remained determined to make our presence felt by building consensus on issues of importance. I refused to give up on the idea of uniting the opposition and was quite willing to step aside – as I had in 1989 – once this was accomplished. Now, more than ever, such an alliance was needed as the ANC had captured 266 seats and was joined by a sole member of the Indian-inspired Minority Front to attain its absolute two thirds majority. While no one could stop the government from changing the constitution, a united opposition could hopefully serve as some deterrent.

When I stepped forward to be sworn in as a Member of Parliament and leader of the Federal Alliance, the irony of it all hardly escaped me. In front of me stood Arthur Chaskalson, the presiding judge at the Constitutional Court with whom I had been engaged in battle on the issue of Mandela's appeal. In the front benches now stood former President Mandela as I took the oath. When I completed the ritual and stepped forward, I was greeted by him with a slight smile. Next, President Mbeki grasped my hand in both of his. I had joined the club. I was no longer the outsider. But I would soon find out that professional politics is not something you simply step into. It is a slow growth process – one much too slow for my liking.

We rented a comfortable but not extravagant house in Westbrook Mews not far from Mbeki's official residence. It did not take great accounting skills to determine that the money I had spent on the election was only a beginning. My monthly outflow was many times the salary I drew as a parliamentarian. As an old hand in the game of parliamentary procedure, Kraai van Niekerk steered me around on a series of courtesy calls and inter-party parleys.

In the meantime, I was chiselling away at the text for my maiden speech during the induction debate following President Mbeki's State of the Nation address. There was no doubt great anticipation on the part of both friend and foe, all of whom wanted to see me come out swinging. I decided to stick to the tradition that dictates restraint on the part of newcomers when they make their maiden speeches in parliament. An attack on the government would simply have played into the hands of my detractors who wished to label me as a loose cannon.

I started off recalling my encounters with Thabo Mbeki in the days of his exile and summed him up as a very able adversary. Citing a few lines from Rudyard Kipling's famous poem 'If', I wished him strength in his new role as president. I then proceeded with a few comments about the economy. It included a plea for greater productivity and true incentives to spur development in rural areas. Agriculture, I argued, needed protection against subsidised foreign products. I urged the government to turn an estimated R15 billion in blocked rand accounts into government bonds. This would prevent a massive outflow of capital once these rands unblocked. *Finansies & Tegniek* welcomed this as one of the best proposals heard in Parliament for many years, and economists such as Jac Laubscher of Gensec praised it as an excellent way to deal with blocked rands. Four years later, the Minister of Finance, Trevor Manuel, would hint that this very same proposition might well be the answer, but without any reference to its original promoter.

The National Assembly itself is, of course, not the place where politics is practised. Crucial decisions and policy directions are the purview of numerous committees whose work goes mostly unnoticed. It is only when something sensational occurs that the media bother to report on their activities. Such was the case when the ANC voted in Parliament for my appointment over Douglas Gibson of the Democratic Party on the Judicial Service Commission (JSC), which, among other tasks, oversees the appointment of judges. The constitution requires that the National Assembly select three members from opposition ranks to sit on the JSC.

Visibly shaken by this snub, Gibson made a last-ditch effort to have the decision overturned, only to be rebuffed again. At a public meeting in Johannesburg, DP leader Tony Leon depicted me as a *werf bobbejaan* (tame baboon) for the ANC. I wasted no time in dismissing this attack as the rantings of a 'toothless Chihuahua', a joker masquerading as a politician. This unparliamentary behaviour outside the Assembly was great for the media but not so great for the opposition. Leon called me to say he was sorry and followed up with a letter of apology. We thus buried the hatchet. My best contribution was, however, in the Public Accounts Committee where I found myself frequently leading cross-examination under the able chairmanship of Gavin Woods.

Through it all, I tried not to lose sight of my original goal – to bring about unity between the splintered opposition parties and strengthen their stand against the ruling ANC, now able by mere voting strength to reshape the country and its constitution at will. I had no personal aspirations to be the leader. Politics, I knew, would never be my profession. But both Marthinus van Schalkwyk of the NNP and Tony Leon on behalf of the DP continued to distrust my motives as they were apparently unable to accept the fact that anyone could see a life beyond politics. In sheer exasperation, I described Van Schalkwyk, who I considered as a well-intended but rather naive politician, as *kortbroek* (short pants) – an implication that he was still too wet behind the ears to be wearing the long-legged trousers reserved for adults. The nickname stuck. Eventually, he and some of his colleagues walked over to the ANC in exchange for token positions in government.

In June 2000, the breakthrough came when an alliance was formed between the DP, the NNP and the FA under the banner of the Democratic Alliance. We put up a strong slate of candidates in Gauteng and made considerable headway in local politics. Tony Leon received my full endorsement as leader of the DA. 'The formation of the DA is proof that parties can set aside small differences and concentrate on the most important issue, namely the establishment of a strong and united opposition,' I told the press.

Shortly afterwards, I told the DA caucus that I would be resigning from my post to make room for 'younger blood'. I did so in late August 2000, at the end of the parliamentary session. When Parliament reassembled in October 2000, Douglas Gibson was proposed as one of the three opposition members on the Justice Service Commission, only to be defeated once again when the ANC threw its weight behind advocate Mighty Madasa of the African Christian Democratic Party (ACDP). This time, Tony Leon knew better than to describe the black appointee as a 'tame baboon', as that, no doubt, would have left him open to the charge of racism. It is entertaining to have whites call whites bad names, but when whites call blacks names, it is a serious matter – in fact, it could land you in criminal court. Of course, as I discovered long ago, the same standard did not apply when blacks threw derogatory descriptions at whites.

My final exit from the politics of sport was nevertheless not quite as smooth and uneventful as my retirement from the sport of politics, and my resignation as the chairman of Ellis Park Stadium followed in the wake of considerable intrigue and betrayal.

During my brief spell in Parliament, I received a visit from representatives of several smaller provincial unions who urged me to make myself available as a candidate for presidency of SARFU in the following election. They argued that since my departure no one had been looking after their interests. I was not

THE SPORT OF POLITICS

surprised, as the remnants of my staff that rolled over into the ANC-approved SARFU were more intent on placating the politicos in order to preserve their posts than the real job on hand. That included my son-in-law, Rian Oberholzer, who had been rewarded for his cooperation with the continued position of CEO under the new president, Silas Nkanunu.

While I sympathised with the plight of this delegation, I could not easily forget how their colleagues had run for shelter and left me exposed in the fight against the ANC's take-over of rugby. Still, I bounced the idea off Ngconde Balfour, who, as Minister of Sport, was now the *de facto* boss of rugby and all other sports. What, I wondered aloud, would be the response if my name came up for election? He did not reject the idea out of hand, but he did express one concern. What, he asked, would Rian Oberholzer have to say? I had to admit that he would probably not like it at all. It might upset his own future plans. Later, Balfour signalled via Jan Momberg and Kraai van Niekerk that it might not be a good idea, as the government preferred to see the South African Rugby Football Union continue under a black president. At the time, Balfour and I had developed a cordial relationship despite our deep-seated differences over the role of government in sport.

Not much came of the idea of me re-entering national rugby. In any event, it soon became a moot point when the fertiliser hit the fan at Ellis Park.

It had become customary for several of the smaller unions to meet with me and members of my executive at the Ellis Park Stadium to ask advice and solicit support before issues were raised at SARFU. The Golden Lions Rugby Union continued as the foremost regional force in South African rugby and, as chairman of the Ellis Park Trust, I was still in charge. The Golden Lions Rugby Union was very much under control of the Ellis Park Trust as it paid the players' salaries and handled all the finances.

It troubled me that SARFU always seemed to know within minutes whatever was said at these closed meetings between me and the unions. My suspicion was confirmed when Parkinson of Natal cautioned me to be careful as Rian Oberholzer appeared to be fully briefed on all our confidential discussions immediately after it happened. As I had no way in which I could confront my son-in-law and squeeze out the name of his informant, other means had to be found to plug the leak.

I told Willie Kruger, the financial director of Ellis Park, that through the process of elimination, I had concluded that Johan Prinsloo, CEO of the Golden Lions, could be the only one. And there was only one way we might know for sure. We needed the services of private investigators, who could come up with solid evidence. So Willie called in the head of a security firm that had done some work for us in the past.

Johan Prinsloo was a sparsely educated man whom I had hired from Ster Kinekor, the movie distribution house where he was a manager at one of the theatres and whom I carefully tried to hone into what, I believed, one who could become a good manager. A manager who would be able to learn and not be afraid to ask questions when he did not understand the complexities of general management.

Yes, they would be able to catch the culprit or culprits, the investigators told Willie Kruger. They had done similar work for South African Airways when their CEO, Coleman Andrews, wanted to catch staff pilfering and executing other misdemeanours. Their investigations had led to the dismissal of more than 90 people. I told them to do whatever it took, as I could no longer live with the knowledge that there was an informant and a traitor in our midst. Perhaps even more than one. So it was that, through this simple instruction, I gave the necessary authorisation for something that turned out to be almost illegal.

The investigators placed a tap on Johan Prinsloo's telephone and, although I never felt that it was necessary, afterwards even taped coach Laurie Mains' calls. Within a matter of days, the security people came back to tell me that one of the main culprits was Gert Augustyn, my deputy president at Ellis Park. I protested in disbelief. This man, I explained, had been with me for 14 years. I considered him a good friend and a loyal associate. The security guys shook their heads, almost sympathetically.

'Please read the transcripts, listen to the tape and make your own conclusions, Dr Luyt,' they said and left a stack of paper and a cassette with an extract of a conversation between Augustyn and Prinsloo on my desk.

I felt sick as I read through the highlighted verbatim exchanges, proving beyond a shadow of a doubt Augustyn's complicity with Prinsloo and Hennie le Roux in staging a revolt against me. With a heavy heart, I pushed the intercom button and asked my secretary Susan Kruger to arrange for Augustyn to come and see me. But I did so only after I had made sure that the office recording device, installed to record small executive committee meetings in my office, was in operation when he walked in.

At first, Gert Augustyn vehemently denied any complicity in this revolt. He would never do such a thing, he assured me.

'But Gert,' I said, 'you can listen to the tape if you want to. It's right here. All I can say is that I am deeply hurt. I would have trusted you with my life.'

His face turned white.

'Well, fire me then!'

'Oh, that I will indeed do,' I assured him.

Next, I spoke with Jomo King. He felt that there was not much he could do about Augustyn, who served both as an Ellis Park director and an 'A' Trustee of Ellis Park.

'No, but I could,' I told Jomo. 'I could also fire Prinsloo as a 'B' Trustee of Ellis Park, but it is your job to fire him as CEO of the Golden Lions.'

He agreed on this course of action and left.

In separate meetings with several other trustees of Ellis Park – Erna Bekker, Professor Henry Vorster, Avril Malan, Mickey Gerber and Hugh Bladen – all concurred that there was only one course of action. Both Augustyn and Prinsloo had to go. Gerber echoed my own sentiments when he agreed that they should be fired.

Then, to my utmost surprise, King called on me to tell me he had had a talk with Prinsloo and now felt that there were two sides to the story. The weakness of the man astounded me.

'Doc,' he protested, 'I must also listen to my CEO.'

'Jomo,' I replied, hardly able to hide my contempt for what seemed to be an shameless effort to shirk away from an unpleasant but necessary task, 'I do not understand what you're saying. Someone is either duplicitous or he is not. He cannot be both.'

King, however, had made up his mind. He was not about to take any action, he insisted. He seemed and, in fact, acted like a frightened child.

'Well, if you don't do it,' I told him, 'I will simply have to take legal action to have Prinsloo removed as a 'B' Trustee.'

When I sought legal counsel, I was told that I was right but that there was only one way to have Prinsloo removed as a trustee of the Trust: through a court ruling. Unfortunately, they informed me, for fear of a non joinder, all the other 'B' Trustees – Johan Gouws, Hugh Bladen and Jomo King – had to be joined. I had less compassion for Gouws with whom I enjoyed a cordial but relatively cold relationship after I failed to support his effort to beat Jomo King for the presidency of the Golden Lions Rugby Union. Gouws, like King, had promised to do something about Prinsloo but never acted. Later, the truth about Gouws and Prinsloo would surface.But the fact that Hugh Bladen, a good friend, had to be joined left a bitter taste in my mouth.

I tried to explain as best I could to King and Bladen that, as 'B' Trustees, we were merely fulfilling a requirement in law when we joined them in the action to be able to rid ourselves of a traitor in our midst. But I am not sure that they ever fully understood or accepted my assurances. It later turned out that King was unworthy of my concern for him in this matter.

At this stage, Prinsloo, Gouws and Augustyn, assisted by Laurie Mains' South African-born wife, Annemarie, had gone to work on the press to portray me as the felon who prowled on innocents and listened in on their private conversations through 'illegal' wiretaps. Even though both Gouws and King returned to my office for another discussion where they agreed to force Prinsloo into resigning, I would later discover that Gouws actually encouraged Prinsloo to stay on while

King stood idly by. I filed this evidence as part of the court particulars. To this day, I have never bothered to listen to any of the tapes except read the excerpts that were made available to the Supreme Court. In fact, one of the individuals who did listen to the tapes had advised me not to listen to them. 'They will make you sick,' he said – and I believe him.

The police, together with a senior Telkom employee, turned up at my offices at Ellis Park to search for the equipment used to tap the telephone conversations. I informed them that there was no such equipment in my possession and, in any event, their entry onto my premises without a search warrant was illegal. I summarily laid criminal charges against them at Jeppe Police station.

The gloves were off and the media were enjoying every moment. Even though there was wild speculation about 'criminal' proceedings against me, I rested assured in the knowledge that in at least three other cases the courts had ruled in favour of the right to protect one's interests through wire-tapping. And, to boot, in the most recent case filed in the Witwatersrand Division of the Supreme Court, Mr Justice Heher had done exactly that in an action brought against Protea Technologies when they used secret recordings to trap dishonest members of their own staff.

At the same time, I had severe criminal charges pending against a high-ranking official at Telkom and a top policeman for their intrusion onto my premises without a search warrant.

Avril Malan was still expressing full support for my actions even though it would later emerge that he had already filed court papers in support of Prinsloo. Eventually, however, the case would be withdrawn as both Prinsloo and Augustyn resigned their posts as Trustees and left. But, in terms of its Trust Deed, the Golden Lions Rugby Trust was obliged to pay the legal costs of Prinsloo as a former trustee. This step was interpreted by the press as a defeat for me. Nothing, in fact, could be further from the truth.

I was particularly perturbed by the observation of Pieter Conradie, a well-known lawyer who had interpreted this payment of Prinsloo's costs as a sure sign that I had had a very weak case, or worse still – no case at all.

If he had only gone to the trouble of calling his former colleague, Vorster, who was personally familiar and involved with the case, he would have known that we had had no choice in the matter by reason of the dictates of the Golden Lions Rugby Trust Deed of which Vorster was the author. To my utter surprise, Marinus Wiechers also stepped into the same trap, but that was understandable – he was a constitutional lawyer.

Unsettling, though, was the fact that none of the trustees even bothered to set the record straight – even though they were all quite familiar with the facts and party to the unanimous press statement released after this debacle. Perhaps they thought the press release was sufficient – although the newspapers went ahead with their erroneous reporting.

The events of that evening were duly recorded in the minutes. I refused to have Prinsloo sit in on a trust meeting and Vorster, who was an acting judge at the time, asked Prinsloo to accompany him outside. Vorster returned and asked the 'B' Trustees to join him outside. When he rejoined the meeting, Vorster announced that Prinsloo had resigned on condition that the case against him be withdrawn and his costs paid.

Erna Bekker, an 'A' trustee present during the discussions with Prinsloo, also confirmed his resignation. My assistant, Susan Kruger, also came in to report that Prinsloo had asked her to tell us that he was not coming back to the meeting as he had resigned. He had gone home.

I had no problem agreeing, especially as the very reason for the court case had been to have Johan Prinsloo removed. Furthermore, in terms of The Golden Lions Rugby Trust Deed, we had no other option than to pay a trustee's court costs. The trustees asked me to convey this development to attorney Alick Costa, who in turn called the judge at home to brief him accordingly. Incidentally, Vorster afterwards told me that he had heard, on what he believed to be good authority, that the presiding judge, Mr Justice Schwartzman, would have allowed the tapes as evidence.

My own opinion was that Mr Justice Schwartzman would have, in following the strict precedence *stare decisis* legal principle, been bound by Mr Justice Heher's judgment in the Protea Technologies case, and be compelled to follow this judgment. A decision handed down by the former Chief Justice, Mr Justice Corbett – in the *Sage* v *Financial Mail* case in the Appellate Division in 1994 – strengthened my belief that justice would prevail here.

But, with the threat of a court action out of the way Prinsloo, now openly supported by Gouws, suddenly changed his tune and with gay abandon insisted that he had never resigned.

I had one more trump card to play. According to the Articles of Association of Ellis Park (Pty) Ltd, it had had the authority to either enlarge or reduce the number of directors at will. It was not bound by Section 220 of the Companies Act that places restrictions on the removal of directors.

I thus canvassed Avril Malan, Hugh Bladen, Willie Kruger, Erna Bekker, Vorster, King and Mickey Gerber and received the necessary proxy vote to call an urgent special general meeting of the company. On a Friday afternoon, both Gert Augustyn and Johan Prinsloo were left out of a new, slightly smaller board.

In a rather odd way, I later learned about moves to have this decision overturned. After I had left the Ellis Park Stadium, I had an interesting telephone conversation with Cecil van Breda, the in-house lawyer at the firm of PriceWaterhouseCoopers. He blurted it out that he was busy with an opinion for the Golden Lions Rugby Union on the 'unlawful dismissal' of Prinsloo and

Augustyn from the Ellis Park board.

He was talking to the wrong man. I was the one who had had them removed.

'Cecil,' I said, 'are you going the section 220 of the Companies Act route? If that is what you're doing, you're barking up the wrong tree. Look at the Articles of Association of Ellis Park (Pty) Ltd and the answer is found in Clause 12 (3). I have now assisted you in earning your fee the fast way.'

He later admitted that I was correct.

During the rugby test against the All Blacks at Ellis Park the following day, my attorney, Alick Costa, remarked that he had overheard a somewhat strange conversation at the bar.

'Don't hold me to it because I might be mistaken,' he said, 'But I swear I overheard Avril Malan wishing Johan Prinsloo good luck and strength.'

I was tempted to dismiss this as a simple case of misinterpretation as Malan was one of my strongest supporters in the ongoing battle against Prinsloo and his cohorts. Only the evening before, he had used words like *verdoemend* (damning) to describe the evidence against Prinsloo and Augustyn at a dinner in honour of Frik du Preez.

But on Monday I would discover that Costa was far from mistaken when Malan called to tell me he had changed his mind.

'Sorry, Avril,' I replied, not even trying to hide my contempt for him, 'it's too late. You simply have to stick with our original decision.'

Only later would I discover Malan's name in numerous affidavits and phone calls on behalf of Prinsloo and Augustyn. For someone who had so often thanked me for providing him with a life-saving new opportunity after Gencor had 'retrenched' him, Malan's actions and deception were hard to fathom.

It was evident that someone had got to him. That someone, I suspected, was Johan Gouws, who had obviously convinced him to join the laager against me. After all, Gouws was vice president in charge of development in the GLRU executive and Malan reported to him during his tenure as manager of the development department before I, like Gencor, also found it necessary to put him on premature retirement.

My suspicion was soon confirmed when Gouws turned up at my office insisting that we call a full meeting of all the trustees. He argued that neither Augustyn nor Prinsloo had resigned in writing and that only the trustees themselves could settle the matter. The meeting was called for on 19 September 2000.

After a heated debate, Gouws resigned verbally with great fanfare and bravado. When he stood up to leave the room, he threatened that he would use the clubs against me.

'Go ahead – and then we can discuss your back-stabbing and conniving as well! I challenged this, to me, rather unsavoury character.

Prinsloo, who should have not, in fact, even have been present at this meeting since he had 'resigned' on 11 September, looked spitefully at me and suddenly unusually brave, hissed like a snake coming out of hibernation as he was leaving: 'After 10 years of loyalty (sic) and you do this to me. I'll see you in court!'

On 19 September 2000, the Golden Lions Rugby Sports Trust issued the following press release:

'Professor Johan Gouws of the Golden Lions Rugby Union tendered his resignation as a Trustee at a meeting of the Trust held on 19th September 2000, which resignation was accepted. In relation to the resignation of Mr Johan Prinsloo as a Trustee, the Trustees noted with regret the press reports in that regard and confirmed their unanimous acceptance of the correctness of what Professor Vorster had conveyed to them at the meeting held on 11th September 2000.

'In terms of the agreement reached between the Trustees and Dr Luyt, the legal proceedings against Mr Prinsloo were withdrawn and in terms of the provisions of the Trust Deed, all legal costs are payable by the Trust.'

How Gouws planned to use the clubs against me I don't really know. Less than a year later, he was ousted as deputy president and fought his ousting on a technical point and was then reinstated. He argued and claimed, rather irrationally, that the same clubs that voted him out a few weeks earlier now wanted him back. That was, incidentally, the same argument he had used to be reinstated as a 'B' Trustee after his verbal resignation on 19 September 2000.

Later, it would emerge that Gouws, Laurie Mains, Hennie Le Roux and my confidant, Corrie Pypers, had been conspiring against me. In the process, Hannes Strydom, Deon Boshoff, James Dalton, Janus Labuscagne and Hennie le Roux signed a document on behalf of the players asking me to resign. Eventually, Dalton could not live with this duplicity any longer and came to me to spill the beans – which I recorded – only to be ostracised by the rest. In the end, then, it became a vendetta not only against me but my son Louis, as well.

What we had done to deserve this I will never know, but there must have been some powerful motivation considering the diverse personalities who teamed together in the effort – strong enough to have Mains join with Gouws, whom he had once dismissed as a 'political animal' and whom he had banned from the Lions change rooms while regularly inviting me to join them.

Ironically, it had been Louis Jr who insisted that we hire Laurie Mains in the first place. 'Dad,' he said at the time, 'Laurie Mains is the best coach in the world and he is available. He is in Queensland, Australia and, if you want to win the Currie Cup, get him.'

I had contacted my friend John Spicer in Otago to ask for Mains' phone number. Then I flew Laurie and his wife out to South Africa for an interview, and introduced him to Jomo King, who was about to take over from me as president, and Augustyn, then my deputy. Mains, however, insisted on being employed by the Ellis Park Company and I readily agreed. I liked Laurie Mains immensely. I had known him since 1976 and we got on very well.

Mains lived up to all expectations and won the Currie Cup in his first season with the Lions. After the huge 64–0 defeat of the Cats in the Super-12 at the hands of Australia's Brumbies (ACT), he resigned but later withdrew it. Mains took it very personally – understandably so, because he had always set very high standards of excellence for his teams.

But he also made enemies along the road to victory. Rassie Erasmus and Chester Williams once came to see me about his attitude. Johan Botes of Free State, who arranged the meeting, told me over the phone that Rassie 'refuses to play for a pig'. We also had to mend relations with our main sponsor, Mr Price, because of Mains' continuous meddling. I personally had to go and see the likeable Allister McArthur, the Mr Price boss, to keep relations orderly. Sponsors do not come easily these days.

To this day, despite his shortcomings and his action against me, I still consider Mains as the best coach around. I now, however, understand the reasons why the New Zealand Ruby Union had not wanted to reappoint him as their national coach. In fact, I only recently learned that Mains lost his job coaching The Highlanders, his home turf's team, because of disenchantment with his ways. That came as no surprise.

Hennie le Roux was one of the players I had brought in from Eastern Province. He had been instrumental in Transvaal's revival. Unfortunately, he also lived up to the description used by Nick Mallett and Alan Solomons and echoed by André Markgraaff and Dick Muir: An insidious personality. He turned out to be a true *prima donna*, who could always be found right in the middle of a mutiny or gossip against management.

The words attributed to Julius Caesar by Wlliam Shakespeare – '*Et tu, Brute*' – spring to mind whenever I think of the role Corrie Pypers played in the revolt that led to my final exit from Transvaal rugby. Here was someone I had treated and trusted like my own son, who had turned up on the day of the long knives with the dagger drawn. The same applies to Hannes Strydom.

In September, at a meeting very much reminiscent of my last stand at SARFU, I informed the members of the board that I had decided to step down as chairman of both the company and the trust in December 2000 and to relinquish my life membership.

Murmurs rippled around the table. Hugh Bladen and Mickey Gerber insisted I reconsider. They implored me to at least hold onto my life membership. But I had had enough. I wanted to make a clean break from the bickering and backbiting that had been going on behind and around me while I tried to build this once failing and bankrupt union into the best in the country.

'No,' I said, 'I've made up my mind. I want no further part of either Ellis Park or the Golden Lions.'

I stood firm and broke all ties with Golden Lions Rugby and Ellis Park Stadium in December 2000. Ellis Park paid me back the R5 million I had loaned the company so that they had no need to touch the offshore investment it held.

When I left Ellis Park and the Lions, they had R67 million in offshore investments. Unfortunately, my ambitious relocation plan had not been implemented. It had called for the sale of the existing stadium to the national soccer body, the South African Football Association, for R110 million. The money would have come from two sponsors. We would then have built a state-of-the-art stadium on a 100-hectare site, with ample parking, near the airport at Kempton Park. Tenders were out and ABSA, Investec and Brait Bank had already made commitments to underwrite the project – Brait on the condition that I manage the undertaking until the entire amount was paid back. In the case of Brait, this was a particularly strange request especially as its chairman was none other than Mervyn King of 'task team' fame.

In the end, the whole soccer deal fell through without as much as a letter of explanation from SAFA, although we had received a firm offer from them through George Rautenbach of Megapro and had already drafted the relevant contracts. Soccer's governing body simply walked away and we were obliged to remain in Doornfontein where parking and traffic congestion had become a major problem.

A delegation led by Johan Gouws was rebuffed by ABSA who refused to extend a mere R15 million loan with the R67 million as collateral. First National Bank eventually agreed to extend credit to them.

Some months after my departure from Ellis Park, I received a call from Wally Walters, who had run into Jannie le Roux at a bash in Johannesburg.

'You know what he asked?' Wally reported. 'He wanted to know how you felt having been forced out of Ellis Park.'

'Much better than he felt,' I replied. 'You can tell him that I, at least, left Ellis Park with money in the bank instead of millions in debt.'

From the way things are going now, the next man to leave Ellis Park might well repeat Le Roux's feat. Only time will tell.

One press photograph that circulated far and wide was one of me cutting a lonely figure as I took 'a last stroll' across the turf at Ellis Park. It shows me frowning as if I carried a heavy weight on my shoulders. That picture, of course, could have been taken at any time during my tenure at Ellis Park.

While the triumphant moments will remain indelible, I can hardly forget the tough struggle and many agonising sagas that led to Ellis Park's eventual revival and financial success. Along the way, I obviously made one enemy too many and, sadly, quite a few of my supposed supporters and allies bought into the story that, with me out of the picture, happy days and free spending would return.

Adri and I decided to sell Solitaire, our home in Johannesburg, to a Catholic order that turned it into an upliftment centre. We then moved to our dream house in Ballito, determined to settle into a leisurely lifestyle. I was 68 years old and Adri, of course, much younger, at least in appearance and attitude. But I would soon discover that 'retirement' was not a word that belonged in my vocabulary.

Even though I moved to the Natal coast with the full intent to leave the past behind and fully enjoy the company of my children and grandchildren and a few remaining friends, controversy soon followed us down there. In a way, I was only too happy to invite this old companion back into my life as the walks on the beach, cocktails on the balcony, wading in the pool and dining out with friends began to look and feel too much like retirement.

EPILOGUE

It came without much warning at all. Even though I had experienced some discomfort and lack of sleep in the preceding weeks, I simply dismissed it as heartburn. Relaxing with a friend visiting from overseas over vintage South African wine at my home in Ballito, I thought, had something to with it. So I cut back on the wine. One day, he and Adri suggested I see a cardiologist. I dismissed their advice as alarmist.

But a few days after my friend left, it happened. My 'heartburn' suddenly turned into severe chest pains. I was rushed to hospital and underwent triple-bypass surgery. Strangely, one of my last thoughts before the anaesthesia took effect was a letter from Reverend Arnold Stofile I had come across in my search for documents as I cobbled this book together.

'You must agree that I am a bad guy,' wrote Stofile in June 1995 in his capacity as Chief Whip for the ruling ANC. 'I have taken so long before thanking you for assisting Buntu Siwisa with his fees at Natal University. Well, I am doing that now. Dr Luyt, if St Peter closes the doors of heavens on you, please let me know, for I think that he would be wrong to do so.'

The operation was a success and I did not have occasion to call on Reverend Stofile's assistance. But I can imagine him putting up quite a fight when needed. Through the years, first as a member of SARFU's board, then as Chief Whip and ultimately as Premier of the Eastern Cape, I had come to respect and sometimes resent his spunk. On at least one occasion, I threatened him with libel action when he flailed into a bitter personal attack on me for allowing *Die Stem* to be played at Ellis Park. Later, when he asked me to sponsor a promising black student, I happily complied as I have done in many other instances for promising white and black indigent students. I did so not for publicity or gratitude but for the pure personal satisfaction of seeing needy talent rise to the top.

When SARFU appointed a disciplinary panel to pontificate over the rugby future of Brian van Rooyen, the judge of the Supreme Court of Appeal, Lex Mpati, was appointed as chairman. I called the honourable judge and gently asked him to recuse himself.

'Why?' he asked in his usual, exceptionally courteous manner.

'Because judge,' I said, 'I happened to have paid for your daughter's university studies. What are they going to say when that comes out?' Judge Mpati had indeed forgotten, but quick as a flash he replied: 'You know, it never even crossed my mind. Of course I'm out!' And true to the jurist that he is, he immediately informed SARFU that he had a serious conflict of interest.

Shortly after I was transferred home from St Augustine's Hospital, a call came through from someone who identified herself as President Mandela's assistant.

Still smarting from a rather embarrassing episode some years previously when a radio personality impersonated Mandela and involved me in a drawn-out telephone conversation on the air over transformation in rugby, I must have appeared extremely dubious to Zelda le Grange. Next, the real Nelson Mandela came on line.

'Hi, Louis,' he said in his familiar charming tone. 'I am sorry this call is so late but I was on an overseas trip and only just returned. How are you doing?'

There was warmth in his voice. It was like old times, when we pulled together to lift South African rugby out of the morass to the top of the mountain. I will forever be grateful for his inspirational role without which we could never have beaten the all-round magnificent All Black team in the 1995 World Cup final.

I also did not forget that, after a dinner held in honour of Queen Elizabeth at the residence of President Mbeki, Mandela allowed the president and the royal entourage to proceed ahead of him and then followed. I was seated a few rows from the aisle when, by sheer coincidence, he saw me and wormed his way past cabinet ministers and other dignitaries to shake my hand.

'How are you?' he bellowed, smiling from ear to ear. 'Quite well, thank you, Mr President,' I said. I wanted to add 'and a hell of a lot poorer', but refrained – this was not the time and place to remind him of the court case and the costs that it had involved. Alec Irwin, Minister of Trade and Industry, who was standing next to me laughed out loud when I told him of my unspoken jest. 'You should have said it, the old man would have liked it,' he said and we both laughed.

Despite all the animosity that might have been engendered by the battle between SARFU and the government, my admiration and respect for this remarkable man remain undiminished. I have, in fact, always maintained that he is right up there with Jan Christiaan Smuts, who has been a favourite of mine since my boyhood. Quite fittingly, one of Smuts' followers into Parliament would turn out to be the man who put me on the road to business success. When every staunch Afrikaner Nationalist entrepreneur from Rupert to Hurter and Wassenaar shut their ears to my plea for loan capital, United Party MP and banker *par excellence* Frans Cronjé had come to my rescue. Without his able assistance and sage advice, all my grandiose dreams of building my own business empire would have come to naught.

'So, what has changed since you got a new lease on life?' asked a friend as we strolled along the beach.

'Not much,' I replied. 'Everything's still basically the same. Controversy seems to be my constant companion.'

At that stage, I had already agreed to chair the Northern Transvaal ex-players trust and to serve on the union's board over strong objections from family and remaining friends. My insistence on drastic changes to stop the bleeding of the

Blue Bulls met with resistance. I also found myself embroiled in a heated public debate with Sports Minister Ngconde Balfour after the appearance of a little book called *Crisis in Rugby* in which Johan Volschenk quoted from interviews with, among others, Jannie Engelbrecht, Frik du Preez and me.

'Where, in the past, rugby bosses ran rugby in South Africa without much ado, they now have visions and missions,' I was quoted as saying. 'One would think that SARFU's Vision 2003 would be to win the World Cup again in 2003, but this is not even mentioned in the six pages of the document. The only detailed aim that the common rugby guy will find in the rather heavily worded document is that, in line with the ethos of a non-racial democracy, 60 per cent of the staff at SARFU and 40 per cent of the management must be black by the year 2003.'

Enraged by my stand against affirmative action and my questioning of President Thabo Mbeki's contention that South Africa needs to lose for a while for the sake of black advancement, Balfour once more lost his cool and went on a name-calling spree. As always, the spectrum of racism was raised.

'Rest in peace, dinosaur,' he screamed out to the whole world – forgetting that the black president of SARFU, Silus Nkanunu, was already 71 years old. 'Rest in pieces' would have most probably better described Balfour's wish at the time. But, never slow to retaliate, my response was so severe that the honourable minister has, so far, quite wisely decided to call a unilateral truce.

But I had finally decided to leave rugby administration. My decision was made easy for me when I saw the hapless way in which that magnificent union was managed. Only one person on the executive made it to provincial level. The same people who came in revolt – and justifiably so – against apartheid's job reservation and insistence on keeping sport white now seem hell-bent on setting their own quotas on a basis of colour. Imagine for one moment the disruption and uproar that would ensue if the United States government decided that henceforth its largely black basketball and football teams should be changed in line with its vast white majority! It would transform dream teams into night-marish losers. More importantly, it would make a mockery of merit.

I have no doubt that the talent among black and brown South Africans will rise to the top, as it has already done in the case of Errol Tobias, Chester Williams, Breyton Paulse, Deon Kayser, Lawrence Sephaka, the brilliant Gcobani Bobo and others. Errol Tobias' performance at Ellis Park when he became the first coloured player to play for the Springboks, prompted Dick Greenwood, the English coach at the time, to exclaim: 'He is not coloured – he is pure gold!' I heartily agree.

And there are many more nuggets of gold among black South Africans ready to rise to the top in their own time. However, to push black players prematurely from the minor leagues into Springbok teams merely to satisfy quotas promulgated by government is not only racism in reverse but an insult to current and future black stars, as well as one sure way of destroying rugby. Nowadays, provincial teams, strapped for money, are being offered a ransom of R25,000 for the scalp of every white coach replaced by a black one and R18,000 for that of every white director. SARFU, with the full complicity of my own former son-in-law, who still serves as CEO at the ANC's pleasure, seems hell-bent on raising the spectrum of racism on any given occasion to help speed up affirmative action at all cost.

Recently, Brian van Rooyen found my unlisted number and made an appointment to see me at my home in Ballito. 'Spend the night,' I urged him and he readily accepted. I was pleased to be able to sit down with this likeable man and many things became clear to me as we talked late into the night.

Only then did I realise how many snakes I carried in my bosom through the years. The double-talk and lies to which both he and I were subjected saddened me. Van Rooyen and I had had an excellent relationship before he decided to oppose me. He had problems with the development department and Prinsloo, the Golden Lions CEO. Then Prinsloo, entirely out of the blue, advised me that Van Rooyen was bowing out of rugby, citing his workload at Labat, the company he headed. I now believe Van Rooyen and matters are now much clearer.

Van Rooyen looked me straight in the eyes when he confided that he had told the task team he could find nothing improper or wrong at the Golden Lions Rugby Union. More disconcerting to him was the fact that the union's executive was trying to sideline him. He decided to fight them and managed to upstage the conniving Ferreira as well as Sampie Pienaar and Mac Hendriks, the other coloured vice president on the Golden Lions executive, to become deputy president following the death of Gouws. He is by far the most experienced and best qualified as a former player among their ranks, and I have a feeling that King might well be the next to be ousted.

What a pity we could not have had this talk before his infamous 'Dossier' in 1997. But then he had been, in effect, nothing more than a pawn in a power play that was bound to happen – with or without his cooperation. Van Rooyen complained to me about the running of the Golden Lions, but there is no need for a revolt. The ANC has already won the battle and is about to win the war.

I was, however, shocked to hear that Rian Oberholzer had actually orchestrated Van Rooyen's full reinstatement into rugby through Eastern Province, because Oberholzer had also been targeted by Van Rooyen when he accused me of nepotism. But that was before Oberholzer had opted for a mass betrayal of me and switched sides.

I dare anyone to point to any instance where I stood in the way of black advancement in sport. In contrast to my critics, I have been chipping away at racism in sport since the seventies, starting with golf and continuing through athletics to rugby and other pursuits. Lee Elder, the first black golfer to play in

South African tournaments, came here through my invitation as the sponsor of the PGA back in 1974. I also helped fund Sydney Maree and other athletes on overseas stints. I sent coloured player Peter Lamb to the US. In the process, I stuck my neck out and turned the other cheek to the cheap shots and insults hurled by the very people who now pretend to be colour-blind. Transvaal, under my leadership, became one of the first provincial rugby unions to include a black player, Owen Nkumane, in its ranks – and Owen, it needs to be said, became a Springbok on merit. I forced clubs to integrate so that every player would have an equal opportunity. Doc Craven and I were ostracised because we dared to talk to 'black terrorists' in an effort to find a way out of the impasse of the eighties.

Nick Mallett, in a book produced in collaboration with Rob van der Valk, claimed that I 'inserted a clause' in his contract when he was appointed the Springbok coach, insisting that the team be chosen on merit. This was done, Mallett and Van der Valk claimed, because I 'feared a whole wave of black players or English-speakers would be immediately selected by this liberal, loose cannon', whom I had 'grudgingly' appointed as coach.

It was not the first time, and will certainly not be the last, where facts were twisted to make me fit the scarecrow image created by my detractors. Once again, the facts simply refuse to fit the story.

Van der Valk, in his wisdom, details at length how Mallett stood up to me. It is true that I did not want to see Mallett when André Markgraaff called me to ask for an interview with Mallett. I was not keen. I simply did not know the man and he did not know me. But that did not deter him from writing a vitriolic article about me in *SA Sports Illustrated*. And that was the first thing I confronted him with when he and Markgraaff did eventually come to see me.

'I did not write the headlines. The sub did it,' he justified rather feebly. 'But if it gave offence, I apologise,' he said, rather subdued.

'Why was I not considered for the coaching position when André resigned?' he queried.

'Very simple,' I replied. 'I discussed you with André and he thought you would be too volatile. It's as simple as that.'

Mallett immediately turned to Markgraaff and accused him of being jealous of him and things almost turned ugly. I intervened.

'I have come here to ask you for the coaching job, Dr Luyt,' he said. 'Can we put the past behind us?'

'Let's. But you still have to impress the coloured members of the executive to accept you. The guys from Boland in particular think you are a racist.'

There was no contract. Furthermore, it was Mallett who came from Boland to SARFU with serious charges of racism dangling over his head. Mallett's job interview with the SARFU board under my chairmanship was duly recorded and transcribed, as all these proceedings were and still are.

A question put by Tobie Titus about Mallett's *SA Sports Illustrated* article – headed 'Stuff affirmative action' – elicited a long-winded, albeit somewhat incoherent explanation. Mallett ultimately concluded by saying that selection should be on merit, which is exactly what I wanted to hear. I followed up with a few questions and the following exchange took place:

Luyt: If you had to pick – because the coach, as you know, really picks the side – do you believe in that?

Mallett: Yes.

Luyt: He gets advice from the selectors, but he really is the guy that picks the side.

Mallett : I think it is very important.

Luyt: Okay. Now, to address what Tobie Titus asked you, on your horizon do you see coloured players going on tour?

Mallett : Ja, definitely. I think in a group of 36 players, I think we can talk about the size, but I was thinking about the tour. As an end-of-season tour, there is a possibility with a group of that size to show your willingness to promote these players. I think there are players. I think Breyton Paulse is one of them. McNeil Hendriks, Dale Stanton and Jeffrey Stevens, if he had not injured his shoulder, but he is in the process. There are other guys from...

Luyt: Thank you, Nick.

So, here I was, trying to make sure that we do not appoint a racist as a coach only to be portrayed later by Mallett himself as the one who had tried his level best to prevent 'a liberal' from running amok with the appointment of 'black players or English speakers'. It was also the first time I had ever been accused of being an Anglophobe on top of my purported hatred for black people! Mallett's collaboration with Van der Valk on the book is, unfortunately, not an isolated occurrence. Fairly recently, Mallett was quoted in a British newspaper as saying that I had said that the world needed us more than we needed the world. What utter rubbish! Why would I have risked everything to get South Africa back into world sport if that had been my point of departure?

In my contention, Mallett – together with Rian Oberholzer – was the sole reason we did not win the Rugby World Cup for the second time in succession in 1999: their infatuation with the wonderfully gifted but severely injured Bobby Skinstad meant that they selected him at the expense of the most successful and best Springbok captain ever, Gary Teichmann.

In several other so-called tell-it-all books by coaches, players and peripheral figures the authors chose to remain thin on facts and light on logic in an effort to change history. In reading these fancy fabrications, I remind myself of Doc Craven's advice when we were both in the firing line in the early eighties for having the temerity to talk with Thabo Mbeki and other ANC exiles. 'Take it from whence it comes,' he would say. In the end, sadly, our own long close relationship would itself be soured by malicious gossip. I had been merely trying to help when I went to see an ageing and weakened Doc and suggested that we lighten his burden by making his position an honorary one and leave the day-to-day affairs of SARFU to an executive chairman. I had made this suggestion in good faith as someone who viewed Doc Craven as an elder statesman and friend who needed to be protected from the rigours of the time.

At the next SARFU board meeting, however, it was apparent that the rumour mill had gone full circle and that Craven believed this to be a ploy on my part to oust him so that I could take over the reins despite my repeated assurances that I was not interested in the position of president. I had always believed – and openly stated – that Fritz Eloff should be the natural successor to Craven.

At the following board meeting, Doc Craven greeted me without the usual warmth and informality, but I will always remember with pain the cold hand-shake of our final encounter. This was the last time we exchanged words. Shortly afterwards, Doc suffered a heart attack and died. To this day, I am bothered by the sudden and abrupt farewell of a man I was privileged to know as a friend and mentor. I have to believe that there will be the opportunity to set the record straight in the afterlife.

'So, do you believe in heaven?' is the question that we seem to ask more often of each other as we cross the threshold between middle age and maturity and spend more time considering our own mortality.

In the Karoo towns in which I grew up, religion was not a simple matter of choice. With the exception of a few Jews and Catholics in the community, everyone flocked to the high steeple of the Dutch Reformed Church on Sundays. Everyone, that is, who happened to be white. Colour had its privileges in faith. So did wealth. I clearly remember the day when my family, as newcomers to the church in Britstown, filed into a pew reserved for the rich and was ordered to move to the back. As I have said before, this embarrassing experience was not without its benefit, however. It certainly helped strengthen my resolve to escape the pain of poverty.

Church services and Sunday school took up the entire day and play was out of the question. As kids, we came to consider Sundays as a sombre ending to the week and an appropriate precursor to black Monday when the school week started. But as we moved closer to Saturdays, our spirits lifted. That was a day of sport, celebration and fun.

Even though I felt no compassion for religion as the Dutch Reformed Church practised it, I was certainly never without faith. Much more meaningful to me than these segregated services were home gatherings after dinner, which the servants would attend and join us, the children, squatting on the floor. There was an intimacy entirely lacking in church where a *predikant* (reverend) delivered his hell-and-damnation message from a towering pulpit.

Still, as parents, Adri and I followed the proven formula for character-building in our children and steered them to church on Sundays. Even though I found myself in a position not only to buy a pew, but a whole church, I had no desire to see our names on bronze plates on reserved seats. I continued to feel as though I was merely going through the motions and the rituals until one day my life would turn around as the result of a tragedy.

Ian Anderson was like a son in my house. This young man turned out to be a brilliant rugby referee – the rare kind who is almost invisible on the field while retaining full control of the game. I still fondly remember his visits on Sundays when we would chat about rugby laws and a range of other issues. At an early stage in his short career, Ian was invited to handle an international game at Twickenham, but I felt that he was not quite ready and sent Freek Burger instead. That was a huge mistake. He, however, got his chance and excelled, and proved to me that Burger was not even in the same league. Ian's life was cut short in a fatal car accident, and Adri and I attended the funeral service conducted by Dr Allan Maker at the Presbyterian Church in Parkview, Johannesburg. In fact, we were so impressed with the piety and presence of this Princeton graduate that we decided to switch churches.

An old Irish proverb perhaps best summarises life: Twenty years a child, twenty years running wild, twenty years a mature man – and after that, praying. It takes a while, but we all come to the realisation that we are not as powerful or as independent as we might once have thought. These days, I am given to a lot of prayer for my family, my friends and my country – sometimes even my enemies, although it remains hard to do so. I am sure that they have a tough time, too, when it comes to including me in their prayers – if at all.

'What do you seek in a friendship?' asked an interviewer fairly recently. 'What are the most important character traits you seek in a person?'

'Loyalty and principle,' I replied, without any hesitation.

Throughout my life, I have never sought fair-weather friends – the kind who pass along a few favours. Friendships built on such a premise never last. True friendship develops when the chemistry is right and two people really care about each other's wellbeing. There is a loyalty that remains intact despite occasional and sometimes severe differences. It has been my privilege to have a few true friends – with Adri obviously topping the list. John Norton and his wife Margie, Dawie Botha and his wife Jean Marie are such people. So are Izak and Rina de Villiers, Fanie and Melanie Cilliers, Fanie and Lydia Vermaak and Willie and Jantjie Kruger. The two inimitable secretaries – Louise Bernard and Susan Kruger – I have had over the last 34 years remain very special to me. So do Frik du Preez, Kevin de Klerk, Wally Walters, Piet Uys, Ray Mordt, Olaff de Meyer and Kobus Wiese. It has, however, also been my bad fortune to pick up a few 'friends' who stayed for the ride while the going was good and aborted when greener pastures beckoned.

Nothing and no one is more despicable than the person who considers 'principle' a mere mantle for the moment, ready to be dropped when it suited the occasion. I have far greater respect for those who cling to their principles and beliefs, wrong as they might be in my view, than the ones who sway back and forth like seaweed caught in the tide.

Have I at times made bad decisions or taken the wrong course of action? Definitely. Even though I was raised in the Calvinist faith, I do not wholly subscribe to the doctrine of predestination. God has given us a free will and, as fallible humans, we tend to screw up at times – both in our personal relationships and in our professional life. The test of our faith, I believe, is how we deal with these mistakes.

I have had no problem in accepting apologies from those who approached me to 'set things right' while there was still time. My problem has been to seek reconciliation with those whom I might have treated too harshly in the past. I have been falsely accused of many things, but I can honestly say that obstinacy and obduracy are not among them. I do indeed have a good measure of both, especially when it comes to matters of principle and loyalty.

When I said, in an unguarded moment, that I knew sports writer Dan Retief, and that I did not trust him and did not like him, I was false. Retief's credentials are as solid as one could ask for, and I do like and trust him. He is still king among sports writers.

In business, I lived to regret my ill-advised partnership with Anton Rupert and my ill-considered and rather stupid involvement with the government's covert actions in the seventies. At times, I still wonder what might have happened if I had taken Nedbank to court instead of accepting a watered-down settlement. My fears that Nedbank might not have had the money to compensate me even if I won the case proved to have been unfounded as the Reserve Bank eventually came to its aid to the tune of hundreds of millions US dollars – which also put paid to the constant rumours that Nedbank's woes were caused by its exposure to Triomf. Triomf only borrowed $59 million. Today, Nedbank is the largest bank in South Africa and, as such, is highly respected.

Still, money is no longer an issue. I have had the good fortune to retire with sufficient funds to live comfortably and to ensure that my family will not be in need. In the eighties, I derived a certain satisfaction from being listed by a leading publication as the third richest man in South Africa. Much more meaningful to me was the honour bestowed on me by the *Sunday Times 'Business Times'* when, at the age of 36, it selected me as one of the top five Businessmen of the Year. To this day, I can remember every detail of that surprise call from editor Steve Mulholland, a journalist and publisher whom I consider the brightest and best in his field. It is a pity that no place can be found for him in the cabinet, either as Minister of Finance or of Trade and Industry. He would excel at either.

By far the greatest intellectual I ever encountered was the Afrikaans poet Dirk Opperman. Just one session with him was sufficient to bring me to that conclusion. The occasion was the annual awards dinner for the Louis Luyt Literary Prize, arranged by Tafelberg Publishers. Here was a great man whose works gave us but a small glimpse into the vastness of his vision and thought process. I had agreed to sponsor this yearly literary award to encourage both aspiring writers in the same way as my donations did deserving students. Opperman's intellect was far superior to that of any other person I have ever met.

I also came to meet and visit with former State President PW Botha and marvelled at his political insight and, of course, refusal to negotiate around principle and loyalty. Together with his charming wife, Barbara, Adri and I witnessed another side to this much-maligned man. And although I never agreed with his political viewpoint, I honestly wished I had known him better – and a lot earlier. It is safe to say that FW de Klerk took all the credit for something started by his predecessor without blinking an eyelid. Botha would never have allowed distractions during the difficult times of the negotiations with the ANC. He would have been absolutely focused.

It is disconcerting for me that SARFU has reverted to a practice of employing people who criticise it. This was certainly true of Harry Viljoen, no stranger to soliciting the goodwill of newspaper reporters, who appointed his most severe critic, Mark Keohane, to the position of communications manager. With Viljoen gone, SARFU was left to deal with the whims of this rather sinister man. Then, on the eve of the 2003 World Cup, the most significant event for any player, it was Keohane, leaking accusations of racism and deceit to the media, who dragged South African rugby even closer to the abyss and into its worst crisis ever.

How is it possible that Geo Cronjé did not understand, or was not made aware of, the sensitivities of racial issues? And instead of condemning Oberholzer's bungling of this matter, he got the thumbs up from his rubber-stamping board – all of whom, in my opinion, should have tendered their resignations immediately.

Throughout my business career, I have always tried to heed the advice of an ancient philosopher against the danger of being owned by money instead of owning it. Extreme poverty in my youth inspired me to rise out of that miserable condition. At the same time, the cold-hearted attitude of the rich neighbours of my youth – and even, I must admit, within my own extended family – made me determined to share what I could. What is the use of money if it is merely gathered for its own sake?

Today, as a septuagenarian with time on his hands, I continue to thoroughly enjoy the company of my seven grandchildren. Corlia and Rian – now separated – live in Cape Town and have two teenagers, Lourens and Iana, while Lucien and

Vanessa, who farm near Porterville, have Timothy Louis and the twins, Seth and Matthew. Adri has a daughter, Jessica, and Louis Jnr and Lynnette, a son Louis Ethan, who recently won the 'Baby of the Year' award – and a car to go with it. Grandparents tend to spoil and Adri and I are no exception.

My wife and I were severely shaken when we learned that Oberholzer had decided to end his marriage to my daughter, Corlia. Although this came as no real surprise to us, we had always hoped that this marriage would survive despite the odds pitted against it. Adri and I were always extremely wary that we did nothing to upset the marriage given the strained relationship between Rian Oberholzer and me. We understood that, as a wife, Corlia had to support her husband for the sake of her children and continued harmony at home. Perhaps the identification with me as a father-in-law became too much in the end. Hopefully, some day, we will know.

Adri and I have now exchanged our spacious quarters at Ballito for a more intimate, smaller house on the property. My dream home has been transformed into a luxury niche hotel, Ballito Manor, managed by Louis Jnr and his wife, Lynette. I remain tuned in to what is happening in politics, business and sport through regular contacts with and visits from former associates and opponents. Not only do I owe this to myself, but to my children and grandchildren. Let it never be said that I gave up on any issue where my contribution could have made some difference. I would be negligent if I did not exercise my rights as a citizen of this country, which has all the ingredients to be great but too often comes up short as a result of a lack of true leadership.

As I sit and think of what is of the past and ponder the future, I cannot but feel with some sense of pride that I left rugby with an inimitable record – 78 per cent test wins - but sad when, where there was once a proud South African rugby side, I see the rugby abyss widening and us disappearing therein. Even a note from that great Australian Leo Williams – 'I hope your health is good. I would have thought you would have had a call from SARFU by now. Nothing has gone right there since you left' – does little to console my spirit about our game of rugby.

A standard blood analysis to check my liver, kidneys, pancreas, cholesterol levels and prostate gland showed, to our great alarm, the possible presence of cancer of the prostate. This organ was swiftly removed and, once more, God again smiled on me. There was no malignancy. I was given yet another chance to enjoy life.

I cannot help but smile when I think of the answer I gave PG du Plessis in a television interview in 1976, when he asked me, 'What type of a loser are you?', and I responded, 'I lose with a smile, but I hate the winner'.

INDEX